CANADIAN IMMIGRATION AND SOUTH ASIAN IMMIGRANTS

CANADIAN IMMIGRATION AND SOUTH ASIAN IMMIGRANTS

The story of South Asian immigrants who are
an important piece of the Canadian mosaic,
bringing diversity, which is the driving force
of creativity and innovation to build
a strong and prosperous Canada

ABDUR RAHIM

Copyright © 2014 by Abdur Rahim.

Library of Congress Control Number:		2014914669
ISBN:	Hardcover	978-1-4990-5873-4
	Softcover	978-1-4990-5874-1
	eBook	978-1-4990-5872-7

All rights reserved. No part of this book may be reproduced or transmitted in any form or by any means, electronic or mechanical, including photocopying, recording, or by any information storage and retrieval system, without permission in writing from the copyright owner.

Any people depicted in stock imagery provided by Thinkstock are models, and such images are being used for illustrative purposes only. Certain stock imagery © Thinkstock.

This book was printed in the United States of America.

Rev. date: 09/15/2014

To order additional copies of this book, contact:
Xlibris LLC
1-888-795-4274
www.Xlibris.com
Orders@Xlibris.com
541199

All human beings are basically the same, whether Easterners or Westerners, Southerners or Northerners, rich or poor, educated or uneducated, from this religion or that religion, believers or nonbelievers—as human beings, we are all fundamentally the same. Emotionally, mentally, physically, we are the same. Physically, maybe there are a few differences in the shape of our noses, the colour of our hair or skin, and so on, but these are minor; basically we are the same. And we have the potential to transform our own mind and attitudes.

—**Dalai Lama**

A molecular biologist from John Hopkins asserts that each one of us has around 6.7 billion relatives.

—**Roberts Dorothy**

A nation's culture resides in the hearts of its people.

—**Mahatma Gandhi**

Difficulties in your life do not come to destroy you, but to help you realize your hidden potential and power. Let difficulties know that you are difficult.

—**Dr. A. P. J. Abdul Kalam (ex-president of India)**

Confidence and hard work is the best medicine to kill the disease called failure. It will make you a successful person.

—**Anonymous**

At the beginning, Earth was a single vast land and water with no boundary lines or demarcation marks whatsoever. Man drew lines on the Earth; made country maps of various shapes; imposed rules, regulations, and orders; controlled, managed, and governed with power; restricted people's movement to cross-country borders for ruler's benefit. Thus immigration laws were being created.

—**Abdur Rahim**

DEDICATED

To my parents who gave me the love of life.

To my wife, daughters, son-in-law and grandchildren
Who gave me the joy of life.

To all people who taught me the purpose of life and love.

Contents

Foreword 13
Acknowledgment 15

PART ONE

1. Introduction 23
2. Canadian Immigration and Immigrants 33

    2.1. The beginning 33
    2.2. Late twentieth century 37
    2.3. Role of immigration 39
    2.4. Immigration policy overview 41

        2.4.1. Early immigration policy 41
        2.4.2. Immigration policy during and after First World War 42
        2.4.3. Immigration policy following Second World War 43
        2.4.4. Canadian immigration policy during 1970–2002 44
        2.4.5. Canada's new policy: "Canada Experience Class" 47
        2.4.6. A Review of Canada's immigration system in 2012 49
        2.4.7. Myths about Canadian immigration 51

3. Visible Minority Immigrants in Canada 55

    3.1. An overview 55
    3.2. Visible minorities in the Federal Parliament 58
    3.3. Visible minorities in the public service of Canada 60
    3.4. Social inclusion and visible minorities..................................... 64
    3.5. Visible minorities in the Canadian labour market.................. 67
    3.6. Job market: Challenges face the visible minorities 72
    3.7. Understanding foreign credentials... 74
    3.8. Visible minority and Canadian media 77
    3.9. Elimination of racial discrimination... 81

4. South Asian Immigrants 84

   4.1. South Asian diaspora 85
   4.2. The early South Asian immigrants.. 86

      4.2.1. The *Komagata Maru* incident..87
      4.2.2. Continuous Journey Regulation......................................91
      4.2.3. Government of Canada apologized 92
      4.2.4. Lifting of barriers..93

   4.3. South Asian population in Canada in 2011 94
   4.4. The skilled South Asian diaspora.. 96
   4.5. South Asian arts and music.. 98
   4.6. Societal norm, religiosity, and language................................ 100
   4.7. Challenges of aging.. 106
   4.8 South Asians in Canadian politics 110

      4.8.1. South Asians in Fortieth Parliament................................112
      4.8.2. South Asians in the Forty-First Parliament of Canada....112
      4.8.3. South Asian senators in the Forty-First
             Parliament of Canada...112

   4.9. South Asian heritage month 114

5. Second-Generation South Asian Canadians 118

   5.1. Key cultural values... 119
   5.2. Ethnic identity formation... 120
   5.3. Parenting stress.. 121
   5.4. Parents and children relationships....................................... 122
   5.5. Generation gap and bicultural conflicts................................ 124
   5.6. Mixed marriage 128

PART TWO

6. Experiences and Challenges Faced by
   the South Asian Immigrants 135
7. What Children of South Asian Origin Think?
   Opinions about the Key Issues...143
8. Discussion...190

9. Conclusion 221
10. References 227
11. Annex 1: Stories of South Asian Immigrants 244
12. Annex 2: South Asian Marriage 304
13. Annex 3: Glossary of Prominent Immigrants
    of South Asian Origin 319
14. Annex 4: Canada's Best Diversity Employers 352
15. Annex 5: Glossary of Terms 360
16. Annex 6: Recommended Reading 373
17. End Notes 382

Index 391

Foreword

The "Canadian Immigration and South Asian Immigrants" is an important book, and the first of its kind, that provides a comprehensive background on South-Asian Canadian history. It is a great reference guide to the understanding both the immigrant experience of South Asians in Canada, as well as our remarkable history in this country.

From the Kamagatu Maru to the painful settlement process and thriving in Canada through seemingly insurmountable challenges, this book catalogues the important history of the struggle of the South-Asian immigrants in Canada. It also demonstrates how South-Asian Canadians are a law abiding citizenry, respectful of all cultures and traditions, and who seek acceptance and respect in return.

It brings me joy to know that Abdur Rahim, who is a Canadian of Bangladeshi origin, has taken the initiative to write this book, as there are not many books about the South Asian experience in Canada. By reading his thoughts on Canadian immigration and the immigration process, we open our minds to the greater conversation of the South Asians' struggles in Canada.

I am very much impressed by his thoughts about Canada, especially when he discusses diversity as an essential component of the Canadian nation building experience, and the integral role that South Asians played in that building process. Rahim has put particular emphasis on the second generation Canadians of South Asian origin focusing on issues such as, identity, bicultural collide, career, and economic, social and cultural integration. I believe that their success stories will inspire all second generation Canadians to aspire to personal success, and to build a better Canada. The book offers valuable insights to all second generation Canadians.

I encourage you to read the book, and share it with others, to help continue this conversation as we work to facilitate the progress of South Asians in Canada.

MOBINA S.B. JAFFER, Q.C
Senate of Canada from British Columbia

Acknowledgment

This book would not have been possible without the support and encouragement of many individuals. First, I would like to thank my ex-colleague Ellen Jarjour, a senior human resources advisor at Natural Resources Canada, for her sincere effort in firsthand editing of some sections of the manuscript. She had been very critical about Canadian immigration history and accuracy of the information in the public domain. She was the first person who offered her precise feedback to keep manuscript moving along. I am honoured by her sincere support as and when asked for. I also thank Samina Ali, ex-director at Natural Resources Canada, who always inspired me to continue my research and finish writing the manuscript.

I am deeply grateful to my sincere friend Dr. Shaukat Hassan, a senior policy advisor at the Canadian International Development Agency (CIDA) and who recently returned from Afghanistan after serving as the country director of USAID's Anticorruption Program, for his strong support, encouragement, professional wisdom, and critical review of the manuscript without which I could not have brought the manuscript to its final form. His help in editing, chapter structuring, organisation of ideas, and in other technicalities including content analysis have greatly enriched the quality of the book. I am truly indebted to him for his contributions.

I am thankful to my longtime friend Mustafa Choudhury—currently retired from the federal government of Canada and worked a number of years in Canadian Immigration and Citizenship—who read some of the chapters and offered his feedback on the relevancy and flow of the theme. He always encouraged me to continue working on the book.

My heartiest thanks go to Dr. Maksudar Rahman who had been on the journey of writing the manuscript with me from the very beginning. I would also like to thank some of my ex-colleagues who encouraged me at different times and inquired about the progress of the book, which helped to speed up my work. They are Suzie Gollain, Joanne Paquin, L'Ecuyer Marie France, Tasneen Kawsar, and Dr. Mark Hammer. I feel privileged and thankful to Dr. Joseph Stewart Oake of the Ottawa Hospital and Stephanie Richenhaller of Royal Bank of Canada, who expressed their warm appreciation and encouragement for writing this book.

My sincere thanks extend to copyeditors and the staff at Xlibris Publishers whose professional and dedicated services, undoubtedly, raised the book to a high standard in terms of quality, value, and worldwide marketing. Ms. Didi Rodrigues, Kathy Santos, Marie Giles and Lorie Adams of Xlibris deserve special thanks for their proper advice for the improvement of the book from publishing point of view.

My special thanks to the Honourable Canadian Senator, Mobina S.B Jaffer, Q.C for graciously writing the foreword for the book.

Last but not the least, I would like to thank the second-generation Canadians of South Asian origin who participated in an opinion survey and shared their thoughts and views on a number of issues and challenges they faced in their daily lives in Canada. Their ceaseless efforts continue to strengthen Canadian diversity and multiculturalism. I want to acknowledge all the immigrants of South Asian origin who generously shared their stories online, which not only encourage but also show path of success to ethnic minorities and second-generation Canadians of South Asian origin in particular. My special thanks to Pradip Rodrigues, editor of *CanIndia News*, and Asma Amanat of *South Asian Generation Next* magazine for their support and cooperation in gaining permission to use stories of South Asian Canadians posted in their websites. I am deeply indebted to them and the magazines.

Canada

Spread over the Northern Horizon the vast land, high mountains
Enormous water resort and solid rock of icebergs stays in Mother's womb
Laying on the semi circular edge the whole beautified objects with open eyes
And there smiles the sky, sun kisses all over her celestial body.
Four seasons over the horizon bring colorful seasonal beauties
Transform them into an art gallery of creator's self drawn art
Exhibits under the open sky; behold the purity in the north.

In Tagore's[1] word, "What a celestial beauty endured, Oh dearest mother you bloomed out . . ."
Yet, very little in expression, no words in my treasure to describe your beauty
Yet, my mind not filled in full.

The mother I describe is not Tagore's "Bongo-Mata"[2] but the mother of all nations
The mother of the Natives, the Whites, the Blacks, the Christians, the Muslims
The Jews, the Buddhist, the Sikhs, the Hindus and for all others . . .
From the east coast of the Atlantic to the shore of the Pacific
Embedding 35 million human off springs on the vast graceful
Land and water the Mother Canada proudly stands on the edge of earth.

Aboriginals, the only humans lived peacefully in solitude
Far from now at the very beginning
In the open field under stars and moon
They cared, loved, and preserved the land and water with artful work.

One fine morning a new human race appeared on the land
The European invaders put their strong foot prints on the graceful land.
Thousands of Aboriginals; children, old, men and women
Mercilessly killed by the European Whites for no reason
Motive of Whites was to conquer the land and settle.
Two humans by color, race and nature from two edge of Earth
Side by side they lived in non-equilibrium arrangements.
The Whites with supremacy in muscle and tactical power

---

1 A world-famous poet, writer, philosopher, and a Nobel Laureate lived in Calcutta, India.
2 Mother—poet Tagore expressed/defined Bangladesh as Mother.

Established the rule of the land but Aboriginals; the true owner of the land
Being the subject of torture, suppression, oppression of the Whites
Grew the deepest frustration and agony, aches and miseries
In Aboriginals' hearts and minds.

Everything changes in the course of evolution through time's scale
The ingredient of nature, the lives of all levels including the human
The old orders change yielding place to new; codes of life and color of civilization
Fragrance of greens and flowers grow in the minds of new generation
The consciousness of their forefathers' guilt paves the path to establish the truth.
The sons of the Whites renew the promises of the past
On disputed lands to return to Aboriginals.

On the new era, civilization is safeguarded, independence gets freedom
Citizens contribute labour and lives, money and resources
From the battlefield in foreign soil return to homeland the bodies calm, cold and dead.
So many tales heroes' story to unfold of blood and tears
They have built a nation with true democracy
And political justice and fairness practices prevail
Introduces Zero Tolerance in the coexistence thus equality
Is established among races, colors, religions and nations
New ways and means in the social, economic and political structures
For optimal distribution of wealth and power being created
Builds up corrupt free rules under the umbrella called social welfare
Where the capitalistic form of state grows
Universal health care system and medical benefits, best in the world
Social safety net prevails, guaranty unemployment benefits to unemployed
And has been old age security pension for senior citizens
For students, high quality education with no or little cost

People bring love in ruthless world; build new life in broken hearts
Defeat for the thugs but good people wins
Feared Humaun Azad;[3] everything would go disdained
Under the notorious people's grip
Perhaps in some part of the world but not here in Canada;
The belief has grown in me very strong.
Everything is rescued from being gone into the hands of thugs
Here bad turns into good, ugliness to beauty
Had Humaun Azad been alive today would have been happy to hear this.

---

3   A professor and renowned writer of Bangladesh origin

Brevity, honesty, and strong personality the people possess
In crucial juncture of the present time
They stand bold and confident with towering head in world forums
Topped among nations the best place to live in
In all goodness of social, economic, political measures
United Nations Organization proclaimed.

Holding a Canadian passport travel from Tetulia[4] to Victoria
To any part of the World
There is free access with no obstruction what so ever
Oh! You are a Canadian, Welcome . . .
Reception a Canadian gets at any destination port of entry.

Thirty years I have traveled places on earth
And singled out the one "Canada"
I behold her and imprinted her beauties into my inward eyes.
Enticed me the attributes, the power of giving
The power of tolerance, the power of understanding
The power of harmonious relationship
Every day of my life here I gathered
Golden seeds from her treasures bit by bit
The pearls from her sea, the diamonds from her mines
And from people, the friends, safe heaven, life's precious gift
And that the deepest love grows in my heart
And that I loudly pronounce, Canada, you are beautiful.

I'm one piece of the Canadian mosaic—the diversity
Where we all don't look alike but live, think and work together
Being a South Asian, Bangladeshi—born I am a proud Canadian.

—Abdur Rahim

---

4   Northernmost district of Bangladesh (specifically mentioned to signify the Earth's horizontal surface from one part to any other part that one can travel)

Part One

All human populations are in some sense immigrants.
—Neal Ascherson

While history is marked by the hybridity of human societies and the desire for movement, the reality of most migration today reveals the unequal relations between rich and poor, between North and South, between East and West, between Whiteness and the Others.
—Hasha Walia

1

Introduction

The idea of writing something about Canada took root in my mind a year or so after I arrived in Canada thirty years ago. I was a postgraduate student at McGill University, Montreal, in the Province of Quebec. Being a student and an ethnic minority in a city like Montreal, which comprised multiethnic population, I had the privilege of coming across students and the general public from various backgrounds and ethnic groups. I was very interested to learn about the experiences and challenges faced by ethnic minorities, particularly about their struggle to thrive in Canada. The idea of writing, however, remained dormant and never received priority due to my own struggle to settle in Canada and succeed in building a decent family life. As I approached retirement from government service, my long-cherished desire to write a book was rekindled, and I embarked on writing this book.

During all these years in Canada, I learned one very distinct thing about Canada—namely, that Canada is a country of opportunity; this, all immigrants can take for granted. Canada is an open, democratic society where every citizen has equal rights, privileges, and opportunities, and can pursue and achieve desired goals provided that he or she is smart, hardworking, and strategic. It is not an easy task to achieve success. Although it is tough and very competitive, those who arrived in Canada are hardworking and tough too. One can divide ethnic minorities into two broad groups. While some are generally struggling to achieve their dreams, others are doing extremely well. The smart thing to do may be is to follow the footsteps of those who become successful. Learn from them, avoid their mistakes, but emulate their practices that led to success. We also know that there is subtle and systemic discrimination in the job market, which makes ethnic minorities most vulnerable. However, instead of lamenting about it, one must find ways and means to get out of the situation and thrive. We have to keep in mind that our achievements depend on how much we can adapt, adopt, learn, and apply.

The second-generation of immigrants is a demographic cohort that includes both children born in Canada to immigrant parents and those (often referred to as the 1.5 generation) who immigrated to Canada as children. According to Statistics Canada, of the second-generation aged fifteen years and older, 14 percent people are of visible minority status. This particular age cohort of second-generation visible minorities is relatively young and has joined or is making its way into the labour force. Also, this second generation is the key link between their parents' culture and a new way of living that is thought of as Canadian. They are the agents of sociocultural change. The second-generation children of visible minorities groups, whether born in Canada or abroad, often face intense challenges due to differences between their cultural background and the culture of the community into which they are trying to integrate. Added to this are the normal growing pains of youth, making for awkward and complicated situations. Their everyday experience in Canada involves subtle racism and other forms of discrimination, which adversely affect their integration into Canada's social and economic mainstream. Pluralism in a society can operate well only when all members of that society (including immigrants and their children) participate in and identify with the host society. Social scientists have argued,

> *Based on certain measures of civic participation, recent arrivals and their children are engaging reasonably well with Canadian society, However, on other measures, such as a sense of belonging to Canada and trust in others, there is a gap between immigrants and the rest of the population, and this gap seems to remain for the second generation despite their progress over time on other measures such as income.*[1]

The discussions on various topics and themes in this book are informed by the work of social scientists, academicians, and researchers who addressed the myths associated with the second generation. Their transition from youth to adulthood, educational attainment, entry into the labour force, career development, and finally the formation of their own family and households reveal what makes the second generation distinctive and demanding. Addressing these issues and concerns generate greater awareness, inquisitiveness, and meaningful discussions not only among the people of the South Asian communities but also among the Canadian public in general.

Many South Asian Canadians are successful in Canada, while many others are not; there are multiple reasons for that. Systemic discrimination in the labour market or industry is only one such reason; other reasons might include the lack of effort or adopting unsuccessful approaches. Those who succeeded have a story to tell, as well as a powerful message to send: "Don't give up!" Many such examples are presented in this book.

The objective of this book is to capture the experiences of the first-generation South Asian immigrants and share them, both successes and failures, with their children's generation. There are important lessons to be learned here, and one hopes that these lessons will assist the newer generations to fare better. It will not only benefit them but also help to build a more prosperous and equitable Canada. While the intended audience for this book is the second generation of South Asians, one hopes that it will have a far greater reach as well.

This book is divided into several sections. It opens with a discussion on migration, followed by a brief overview of the history of immigration to Canada that began long before Europeans set foot on this second-largest country in the world. The narrative then moves on to the book's primary focus—that is, South Asian immigration, which is divided into multiple subsections that address particular topics of interest.

Immigration perspective

The people who move from one country to another are called "migrants" and become "immigrants" when they settle in the destination country. This process of migration and the immigrants have led us to think, know, and understand the diversity of people around the world. Throughout history, people migrated from place to place for survival, or to survive better. The right to travel or migrate in search of a better life has not been a universal right but a privilege. Several variables are involved in the process of migratory movement. For example, intensification of state regulation on migration, remapping of geopolitical space based on national boundaries, and introduction of passport and visas have significantly impacted on migrant movements. The International Organization for Migration (IOM) states that there are more than two hundred million migrants around the world today.[2] Europe hosted the largest number of immigrants, with seventy million people in 2005. North America, with over forty-five million immigrants, stands second, followed by Asian countries, which hosted nearly twenty-five million immigrants. Most of today's migrant workers come from Asia.[3]

Australia, Canada, and the United States traditionally receive the most immigrants. Over the past half century, the volume of immigration has grown in those countries, and its composition has shifted away from Europe (the historically dominant source), towards Asia, Africa, and Latin America. The European countries for centuries had been sending out migrants but were suddenly transformed into immigrant-receiving countries. The trend was prominent just after 1945; virtually all countries in Western Europe began to attract significant numbers of workers from abroad. Although the migrants were initially drawn mainly from southern Europe, by the late 1960s, they mostly came from developing countries in Africa, Asia, the Caribbean, and the Middle East (Douglas S. Massey et al. 1993). By the mid-twentieth century, countries in Southern Europe, such as Italy, Spain, and Portugal, which only a decade before had been sending migrants to wealthier countries in the north, began to import workers from Africa, Asia, and the Middle East. At the same time, Japan and in recent years South Korea and Malaysia, with its economic development and high standard of living, began receiving immigrants from poorer countries in Asia to meet its labour demands.

The recent boom in immigration has made citizens, officials, demographers, and social scientists revisit the popular concepts, theories, and assumptions on international migration. There is no single coherent theory of international migration. Rather, there is a fragmented set of theories, often segmented by disciplinary boundaries; and the major research on migration involves areas such as sociology, demography, economics, geography, psychology, and political science (Brettel C. and Hollifiel J. F. 2000). The oldest theory on migration dates from 1885 when Ernest Ravenstein formulated the laws of migration (Ravenstein 1885, 1889). He argued that migration is closely connected with "push and pull" factors. Since then a variety of explanations were proposed to explain how international migration takes place. The most common explanation is that migration is a unidirectional or bidirectional movement (i.e., emigration, immigration, or return migration) caused by isolated factors, such as economic or political ones. This consensus reflects Ravenstein's push-pull model, where pull and push factors initiating migration are present in the source as well as in the receiving country or region (Lee 1966).

The review of literature suggests that the most important theories of international migration are the neoclassical economics theory, the new economics of migration theory, dual or segmented labour market theory, world system theory, and the social capital theory. They are briefly described below:

Neoclassical Economics Macrotheory is probably the best-known explanation of international migration. It stems from the theoretical model explaining internal labour migration in the face of economic development. The key assumptions[4] are

- o   The international labour movement is caused by the differences in wages between a sending country and a receiving country.
- o   The elimination of wage differentials will end international migration of workers, and migration will not take place in the absence of such differentials.
- o   International labour movement is influenced by labour market mechanisms. It means that other kinds of markets (insurance market, capital market) do not have an important effect on the international flow of workers.
- o   The international labour migration can be controlled by government regulation of labour markets in both sending and receiving countries.

Neoclassical Economics Microtheory corresponds to the macroeconomic model of individual choice. The key assumptions[5] are

- o   Rational individuals migrate because a cost-benefit calculation leads them to expect a positive net return (usually monetary) from movement.
- o   Migrants estimate net returns in each future period by taking the observed earnings and multiplying them by probability of obtaining a job in the destination country to obtain expected earnings from the destination country.
- o   The policies that affect expected earnings in sending and receiving countries can influence the size of migration flows.

The New Economics of Migration is a theoretical model that has arisen in response to the neoclassical theory (Stark and Boom 1985). The key assumptions[6] are

- Families, households, and other culturally defined units of production and consumption are those that count in the analysis for migration research (not individuals).
- A wage differential is not a necessary condition for making a decision about migration to other country; households may have strong incentives to diversify risks through movement even in the absence of wage differentials.
- International migration does not necessarily stop when differences in wages disappear across national boundaries. Incentives for migration may continue to exist if other markets within sending countries are absent or imperfect.
- Governments can influence migration rates not only through policies that influence labour markets but also through those that shape insurance markets, capital markets, and futures markets. Government insurance programs, particularly unemployment insurance, can significantly affect the incentives for international movement.

Dual or Segmented Labour Market theory links immigration to importance of institutional requirements of modern industrial economies. According to Michael Piore (1979), the main cause of international migration is a structural demand within advanced economies for both highly skilled and lower-skilled workers. Immigration is not caused by push factors in sending countries but by pull factors in receiving countries (ibid.). The key assumptions[7] are

- International labour migration is largely demand based and starts with recruitment by employers in developed societies or by governments acting on their behalf.
- Because the demand for workers from other countries is structurally built into the needs of the economy and is expressed through recruitment practice rather than wage offers, differences in international wages are neither a necessary nor a sufficient condition for arising and existing migration of labour workers.
- Governments are unlikely to influence international migration through policies that produce small changes in wages or employment rates; immigrants fill a demand for labour that is

structurally built into modern, postindustrial economies, and influencing this demand requires major changes in economic organisation.

The Worlds System theory argues that migration is a natural consequence of economic globalization and market penetration across geographic boundaries (Wallerstein 1974). This theory also assumes that world society focuses on cultural globalization where people increasingly share cultural values globally, and thus see economic imbalances and in turn migrate as a consequence (Hoffmann-Nowotny 1989).

Social Capital theory is a theoretical model that explains international migration through the concept of migrant networks. According to this approach, interpersonal networks connect migrants, former migrants, and nonmigrants in the countries of origin and destination. This is in fact a theory of cumulative causation, meaning migration sustains itself by creating more migration (Massey 1990). The Social Capital theory also assumes that international migration expands until network connections are wide enough that all people who wish to migrate to that country can do so without difficulties; however, controlling migration becomes very difficult as migrants' network are created outside the country and occurs irrespective of policies pursued.

It is believed that every country is the product of multiple overlapping generations of immigrants (Stalker 2001). Previous literature, however, suggests that the very early large-scale migrant movement is likely to have occurred in Asia (Lee Hanson 1961). There are discussions about the movement of people/migrants during the historical period of globalization. Held et al. (1999) mentioned about four periods such as "pre-modern" period, which covers a very long period around nine to eleven thousand years age ending in 1500; the "early modern era," which covers the period circa 1500–1850; followed by the "modern era," which covers 1850–1945; and the "contemporary period," which starts from 1945 and is ongoing. What we note from this historical categorization of migrant movements is that it provides us a framework of understanding of the differences between the various forms and types of migration. Aligned with this categorization, Stalker describes migrants into five categories:

1. *Settlers:* migrants who intend to live permanently in a new country
2. *Contract workers:* admitted to other countries under the condition that their stay is of a temporary nature
3. *Professionals:* employees of transnational corporations; work permits are issued to immigrant professionals

4. *Undocumented workers:* smuggled into a country or they overstay their tourist or student visa
5. *Refugees and asylum seekers:* claim asylum because they would not qualify for admission as migrant workers

Apart from these categories, we need to know who the migrants are. A common definition of the term "migrant" could be "a person who comes to a country where he/she was not born but settles there on a temporary or permanent basis." The *Collins Dictionary of Sociology* defines migration as "the movement of people from one country to another, who declare an intention to reside in the latter." Thus, we may say that "emigrants" refers to people who move out of the country, and "immigrants" refers to those who move into a country. It is also important to know that the general public perception of the migrant is far more complex than it is thought and portrayed in the definition. If migrants are defined as people who were born outside the country in which they reside, then why are the children, grandchildren, and great-grandchildren of migrants (who were born in the country where their ancestors settled, but not outside the country) in Australia and Germany referred to as second/third/fourth-generation "migrants"? (Rose Baaba Folson, article in the book *Calculated Kindness* 2004).

Canada perspective

The name "Canada" originated from Huron-Iroquoian word "Kanata," meaning "village," referring to Stadacona, a settlement on the site of present-day Quebec City. Canada is a relatively new nation and most importantly is an immigrant country. It is a vast country capable of absorbing millions of the world's population. Canada is the second-largest country in the world in land area, after Russia. It has the longest border with water of any country in the world. The country stretches from the Atlantic Ocean in the east to the Pacific Ocean in the west with the Arctic in the north, and Canada's territorial claim extends to the North Pole. This country is indeed the only habitable country of its size that is underpopulated and underdeveloped as far as its vast land, water areas, and natural resources are concerned. It serves as a meeting ground for the people of various cultures, races, and ethnic groups from almost every part of the world.

The native North American Indians were the first and original inhabitants who occupied the whole country. They formed themselves into tribes, and each of the tribes claimed a portion of the country's land for settling and hunting purposes. Historically, the native people had more or less uncontested dominion over their tribal territories and the people within their respective tribes. They had governed, made laws, waged wars, and had their own political, social, cultural, educational, and economic, and property systems. They had political sovereignty explicitly attached to their title to tribal lands. After the European arrival, the colonial powers gradually took political control over the land and the native people, and the colonial legal systems accepted the territorial boundaries that tribes once established but imposed European's own concept of native rights (Sampath Mehta 1973). The first Europeans to settle in Canada were the French and the English and are still referred to today as "the two founding peoples of Canada."

Looking at the twentieth-century migratory movement, we see the impact of the shift from colonial rule to neoimperialist governments and their administrations. But the anticolonial rebellions throughout the colonies compelled a change in the administration of colonies (Dua 2000b). Two parallel ideas of modernity prevailed in the colonial relationships in the mid-nineteenth century; civilization versus barbarity, and progress versus tradition (ibid.). In this relationship, colonial dominance was justified as the "white man's burden" to rescue the "darker" parts of the world from barbarism and primitiveness (ibid.). Therefore, imperialism continued the colonial practice in a "backward" country like India.[8] This type of colonial rule can be seen in the immigration policies and in the public perceptions of immigrants in Canada. The story of Canadian immigration is not only an orderly growth of population but also a catalyst to national development, a mirror of Canadian societal and cultural values, often economically self-serving and racially biased (Harold Troper 2012).

In the last decades of the twentieth century, there have been changes in the politics and immigration policies in Canada with the changing roles of Canada's socioeconomic and cultural development needs. Canada's immigration is characterized by open, nondiscriminatory admission practices. These practices along with the impact of globalization have contributed to huge changes in the composition of permanent and temporary migration of people in Canada. The most apparent outcome is the dramatic increase of multiethnic visible minority population among Canada's population. Statistics Canada reveals that Canada is now the home of about 6.3 million visible minorities (2011 National Household Survey).

South Asian

Over the years, the South Asian population (which is now the largest group among the visible minorities in Canada) has evolved from a small homogenous community to a uniquely diversified population of different origins, ethnicities, religions, and languages. At the beginning of the twentieth century, between 1905 and 1908, about five thousand South Asians, who were mostly male Punjabi Sikhs, entered Canada. But subsequently the number of South Asians increased rapidly, reaching 917,100 in 2001 and 1,262,865 in 2006. According to 2011 National Household Survey (NHS), the South Asians in Canada exceeded slightly over 1.5 million, a growth rate of 24 percent from 1,262,865 individuals according to the 2006 census.

Second-generation Canadians of visible minority families represent a group of young Canadians facing unique challenges. They experience racism, discrimination, bicultural conflicts, peer versus family pressure, intermarriage problems, and so on. The challenges they face are primarily of two kinds: (a) those within the family between generations and (b) those derived from cultural practices that pit "otherness" against Canadian mainstream norms and practices. For the second-generation South Asians, dealing with intergenerational conflicts as well as racism faced within the dominant society are facts of life. It is worth mentioning, however, that some literature suggests that second-generation visible minority youths experience less racism compared to the experiences of their parents (Reitz and Somerville 2004; Reitz and Banerji 2007). They also suggest opposite view, and that is, the second generation may experience more racism than their parents because their linguistic fluency, educational attainment, and high expectations of the rights of citizenship pose a threat to the dominant group (ibid.). Furthermore, the area where the members of the second generation face difficulties most is the entry-level job market. Being the largest visible minority group, second-generation South Asians are no exception. Whether racial discrimination is felt by an individual or by a group, there is a consensus that it is a significant issue in Canada. This calls for changes in public policy and more research on racism in general and an examination of labour market discrimination and its causes in particular.

You look at the history... the aboriginal people welcomed the first settlers here with open arms, fed us and took care of us... that continues today; we welcome people from all nations to come in and share.

—Peter Stoffer

2

Canadian Immigration and Immigrants

2.1. The beginning

Aboriginal people lived in what is now "Canada" long before any Europeans landed on its shore. Archaeologists believe that North American aboriginals originated in Asia and came over the land bridge connecting Siberia and North America during the Ice Age. Aboriginals first lived in Canada anywhere from ten thousand to thirteen thousand years ago, as scientists believe, although the precise time of arrival of the ancestors is not known.

When did Europeans first reach North America? This question has preoccupied historians for many years. Although evidence is scanty, some speculations are abounds. However, there are two facts that we know happened. First, more than one thousand years ago, Vikings from Norway set out on a series of daring voyages to explore the east coast of North America, who would become the first Europeans. In stages they established settlements in the Shetland Islands, Faroe Islands, Iceland, Greenland, and finally Newfoundland and Labrador. Second, John Cabot sailed from Bristol to North America in 1497. Beyond these facts, there are arguments that Portuguese voyagers sailed to Newfoundland in the 1470s—indeed that Joäo Corte Real was the actual "discoverer" of America.[9]

Western European began to visit the Grand Banks during the summer months on a regular basis shortly after 1497. During 1534–1536, Jacques

Cartier, a French sailor, made two voyages, with the hope that he could establish an inland presence in the region. Few years later, he returned for a third time to the region and established a small settlement near where Québec City stands today. During the seventeenth and eighteenth centuries, there were number of different settlements that were established on the Newfoundland coast, mainly by the English and French. While the area of initial settlement in Canada belong to France, the British came along and founded the Hudson's Bay Company and get involved into competition with the French trade. The situations become worsen when British and French settlers entered into clash against each other, resulting in seven years of war in Europe. In 1759 the British defeated the French and the Treaty of Paris was signed; the deal was that Canada belonged to Britain. However, the French and British continued their dispute in the nineteenth century, and eventually the British North American Act was made to establish Canada into a country what it is today. In course of time, the Canadian Pacific Railway was built and united the vast country together. All provinces were part of the government by 1912 except Newfoundland, which eventually joined in 1949.[10]

During WW I, Canadian immigration policy and administration was aligned to economic necessity and allowed the southern and eastern Europeans to enter Canada, but others such as Blacks, Chinese, Indians, and Japanese were not welcome. Moreover, the head taxes, landing taxes, bilateral restriction agreements, and travel restrictions were imposed on them. Consequently, these restrictions in fact prohibited the immigration of all Asians. Canadian authorities also did not allow for the settlement of female Asian immigrants with the anticipation that this would encourage Asian men to settle permanently in Canada. Great Depression of the 1930s reduced immigration significantly. Like the rest of the world, Canadians were preoccupied with the economy in the 1930s, which was reflected in the immigration policies. Around March 1931, all nonfarmer immigrants were banned other than Britons or Americans. As a result, immigrants' numbers plummeted from 1,166,000 in the decade 1921–1931 to only 140,000 between 1931 and 1941, since Canada did not fully recognize the fact that the economic and social condition in Europe was severely bad. As such, no special measures were taken to permit the entry of refugees from Europe. As a result, thousands of desperate refugees from Europe were prevented from entering Canada during the 1930s. Many of them were Jews who fled persecution at the hands of the Nazis. Thousands of Jews refugees who managed to escape the Nazi oppression and torture sought refuge in Canada, but their appeals were rejected. Ironically, those who remained in Canada were subjected to an increasing xenophobia.[11]

Following the end of World War II in 1945, Canadian immigration regulations remained unchanged for some time. However, due to postwar economic boom, growing job market, and an increasing demand for labour, Canada gradually reopened its doors to Europeans for immigration. Initially, Canada encouraged the "traditionally preferred immigrants"—namely, from the United Kingdom and Western Europe. Subsequently, when immigrants from other European countries were permitted to enter Canada later, immigration from Eastern Europe was stopped due to the Cold War. At the same time, the Soviet Union and its allies sealed off the borders to the west. Nonetheless, large numbers of immigrants entered Canada from southern Europe, particularly from Italy, Greece, and Portugal. It is worth noting that the postwar Canadian immigration was not focussed on agricultural or rural-based resource industries like in the past. In contrary, Canada emerged as an industrial power after World War II and many postwar immigrants filled jobs in the new urban-based manufacturing and construction sectors. As expected, the skilled and educated immigrants had better opportunity in the job market due to this new policy.

It is obvious that the immigrants who fought along with other Canadians in the war made sacrifices in the postwar era for a common cause. Therefore, they demanded same status like other Canadians rather than being treated as a second-class status in the country. Also, those immigrants rejected the sanction imposed on them as part of ethnic and racial discrimination and demanded human rights reform. This demand was supported by many like-minded Canadians. They put pressure on governments to legislate against discrimination on the basis of race, religion, colour, and origin in the areas of employment, accommodation, and education. As pressure mounted, Canadian immigration underwent changes. As a result, Canadian governments, both federal and provincial, slowly responded to the pressure for human rights reform. Consequently, the government initiated proactive approach to eliminate racial, religious, or ethnic barriers to Canadian immigration.

The breakthrough between old and new immigration system in Canada took place in the 1960s. Consequently, racial discrimination in immigration was omitted from Canadian immigration legislation and regulations, and the Canadian government adopted a nondiscriminatory immigration policy. Under the new policy, admission was based on personal attributes rather than the applicant's place of birth. This policy opened Canada's doors to many prospective immigrants who were previously rejected as undesirable. In 1971, for the first time in Canadian history, the majority of the immigrants entering into Canada were of non-European ancestry, which has been continuing ever since. As a result, Canada has become a multicultural society as well as multiracial society. However, it does not mean that anyone who wishes to enter Canada can do so without difficulty. While restrictions on the basis of race or national origin are no longer a barrier, strict criteria to determine the desired candidates for entering into Canada are still in place.

During the 1960s and 1970s Canada responded to the conditions of refugees from various countries and admitted many refugees. For example, Canada accepted Hungarian refugees who were displaced after the Hungarian uprising of 1967. Similarly, Canada also accepted Czechoslovakian refugees after the crushing of political reform in Czechoslovakia by the Soviet Union in 1973. The government of Canada also made special allowance for refugees driven by political upheavals in Uganda, Chile, and other third-world countries. Importantly, Canada admitted the refugees from those countries beyond its normal immigration regulations and procedures. Moreover, government of Canada enacted a new Immigration Act in 1978, under which its commitment to the resettlement of refugees from oppression was established. It is, however, important to note that normally, refugees would not be admitted to Canada as an exception to immigration regulations. But the admission of refugees, who have had a well-founded fear of prosecution in the country of origin, would be considered as an integral part to immigration law. By critically reviewing these measures, one could argue that refugee admission remains controversial.

There are two different routes by which refugees have arrived in Canada. First, with the cooperation with other countries and international refugee agencies. Canadian immigration officials travel overseas to interview and pick refugees from among those who have found temporary sanctuary outside their country of citizenship, often in a neighbouring country. This process has generally worked well. For example, the first major refugee resettlement program under this new legislation was during the early 1980s, when Canada welcome to Southeast Asian refugees, and particularly those from Vietnam, often referred to as the "boat people." Many of the boat people were selected from among those who escaped Vietnam in tiny boats and eventually found themselves confined to refugee camps in Thailand or Hong Kong awaiting permanent homes.

The second route is one that refugees chose by themselves to come to Canada. Canada has to deal with persons who are not chosen abroad by immigration officials but who somehow make their way to Canada and declare themselves to be refugees upon entering Canadian borders and ports. For example, persons claimed refugee status in Canada after disembarking from flights between Eastern Europe and Cuba, which landed to refuel in Gander, Newfoundland. These men, women, and children had escaped the horror of war and persecution in Central America, Africa, the Middle East, the Indian subcontinent, and China and sought sanctuary in Canada. Once they are in Canada, each candidate claimed to be a refugee with a legitimate fear of persecution in his or her homeland. We know that political torture and murder, ethnic cleansing, and riots are very common in various regions in the world. Therefore, people who are the victims escape from their country and seek refuge to other countries including Canada. But there are fake refugees as well who also seek refuge to Canada. Therefore, it became the responsibility of Canadian officials to determine if each individual claimant was truly a refugee or not. To do this, Canada devised an inland refugee determination process designed to justify and judge each claim at a time. If it is determined that the claimant is a legitimate refugee, he/she is granted the right to stay in Canada as an immigrant. If not, the claimant may be deported to the country of origin or to a third country of choice.

2.2. Late twentieth century

As the refugee volume grew steadily in Canada during 1980s, the refugee status determination process becomes a difficult job to process applicants in normal speed. Therefore, it was a concern that many of the refugee claimants were not really legitimate refugees but were individuals looking for a detour to overcome the Canadian immigration regulations. Some Canadians complained about the fact that many fake refugees abused the Canadian immigration and refugee system. Others argued that government was not doing any good for Canada when they permitted individuals to claim refugee status from within Canada. The concern was that the government was not following the proper procedure to pick and choose from the pool of refugees abroad. The main point raised was that Canada should select refugees, not the other way around.

The refugee issue become more serious in Canada in the late 1980s when two cargo ships illegally stranded on Canada's east coast and unloaded their cargoes of Sikhs and Tamils who claimed refugee status in Canada. There were overreacted fears that Canada was about to be flooded with refugees. Eventually, Canadian Parliament and immigration authorities thought about tightening up the refugee regulations and procedures. As a result, there has been a streamlining of the refugee determination process. Consequently, Canadian authorities started working closely with other countries and transportation companies to make it more difficult for individuals to reach Canada and claim refugee status. At the same time, many liberal-minded Canadians thought that some legitimate and genuine refugees would be denied Canadian sanctuary by these changes.

During the late 1980s and early 1990s, new avenues opened up for immigrants to enter into Canada. The new avenues in fact were for those with employable skills or significant financial resources. Many foreigners with capital took the advantage of the program and invested in Canadian enterprises, and others started businesses that created new employment in Canada. As a result, the number of entrepreneurial or business immigrants rose dramatically in the 1990s. A significant number of those entrepreneurial-class immigrants who took advantage of the program were a significant number came from Hong Kong. As expected, many sought a safe harbour for themselves, their families, and their assets in advance of the Chinese takeover of Hong Kong in 1997. Majority of them settled in Vancouver and Toronto. Interestingly, most of these entrepreneurial-class immigrants did not speak English or French (the two official languages of Canada). In the late 1990s, the annual inflow of immigrants to Canada plummeted. Many argued that an economic slowdown in Asia in the late 1990s impacted that inflow and reduced the number of immigrants. It was also argued that due to this economic slowdown, Canada failed to meet annual immigration target of 220,000 immigrants, which is 1 percent of its population.

As the international and national economic conditions changed rapidly in the late 1990s, economists, social scientists, and policy makers began debating about Canadian immigration. Many argued that Canada needs to increase the immigrant population. The key point in the argument was the low birth rate and higher longevity among Canadian population. Given this population scenario, more immigrants were needed in order to make Canadian economy more vibrant and dynamic. Many others challenged this proposition. Their concern was that with more and more jobs requiring a highly skilled workforce, immigrants were no longer necessary, as they were of low-skilled or unskilled people. Others feared that immigrants would not create any viable wealth in the Canada's economy rather would take only low-paying jobs or would be dependent upon Canadian social welfare system.

In general, Canadians are supportive of immigration in spite of the skepticism. In the mid-1990s the federal government commissioned a panel to review Canadian immigration legislation and policy. Panel's principal recommendation was that the government should initiate public consultations to examine the immigration policy thoroughly, with particular emphasis on (1) the alignment of policy with Canada's changing economic and social reality, (2) accepting of highly educated immigrants who have economic flexibility needed to succeed in a constantly changing Canadian job market, and (3) commitment to refugee resettlement.

2.3. Role of immigration

As Canada's sociocultural, demographic, and labour market conditions have changed substantially since the late twentieth century, Canada's approach to immigration faced challenges. Such shift and the challenges demand examination of the appropriateness and effectiveness of Canada's policies on immigrants and foreign workers. Immigrants provide manpower to help develop Canada's vast national resources, cultivate agricultural land, and build a strong manufacturing base. At the same time, they brought energy, skills, experience, and new ideas to this country. From a sociological perspective, they brought new cultures and ethnicities that helped to mould the perspective of fairness, openness, opportunity, respect, and sharing among the people of different races, colours, languages, and origins. This led to the growth of multiculturalism and diversity and to the growth of Canada's vibrant cities like Toronto, Vancouver, Montreal, Ottawa, and Calgary, which are now among the most ethnically and culturally diverse cities in the world. As we know, diversity in its many forms has been the cornerstone of Canada's multiculturalism policy, which is considered a distinct social goal of Canada as a nation (Siemiatycki 2005).

One of the significant roles of immigration was to contribute to Canada's population growth (Health and Welfare Canada 1989; Guillemette and Robson 2006). It is a well-accepted fact that Canada's population and the workforce are aging rapidly. This is the result of the aging population of post-WW II "baby boomers," the below replacement level birth rates, and higher levels of life expectancy. This has reached a point where immigration will account for the major share of Canada's labour force growth. Nonetheless, the eldest members of the baby boomers will approach retirement age by 2018. As a result, the huge exodus of retirees will lead to significant skills shortages in Canada's labour market, a situation where immigrant population can and will fill the labour demand and rescue the labour market from shrinking. Immigrants contribute labour market skills, fill labour market gaps, increase productivity, and help maintain economic growth by increasing aggregate expenditure (Conference Board of Canada 2009, 2010). Immigration also contributes to tax revenues for a lengthy period because immigrants usually migrate at an early age of their working lives, thus offering fiscal benefits to government funds or reserves (M. Beach, Alan G. Green, and C. Worswick 2011). Apart from economic roles, immigration also has noneconomic roles to play. It contributes to family welfare by facilitating family unification. Noneconomic roles also include a humanitarian component. For example, each year Canada brings significant number of refugees who face persecution in their country of origin; thus, Canada fulfills its humanitarian refugee commitments.

What about the long-term and short-term economic benefit of immigration? One would argue that a larger population and economy is likely to increase the talent pool, size of the domestic human resources, and internal energy, strength, and ability of Canada. This, in turn, would increase the country's economic and social strength and power (Studin 2010). A large population is required to develop Canada's vast land and grow its agricultural sector. In the 1950s, the immigrant population helped to develop the primary and manufacturing sectors (M. Beach, Alan G. Green, and C. Worswick 2011). A large labour force is likely to increase the potential for innovation and can make technological advancement (Simon 1989). Business class immigrants can generate investment and capital and can increase international networks and trades. Increased immigration generates a larger economy, which provides greater opportunities for economies of scale (ibid.).

Another long-term benefit of immigration is the increase of living standards or the gross domestic product (GDP) per capita of Canadians (Drummond and Fong 2010). This economic indicator would likely to attract human capital and skills, which would generate growth in the knowledge-based economy. This was one of the objectives of Canadian immigration policy in the 1960s and 1990s (M. Beach, Alan G. Green, and C. Worswick 2011). Regional economic growth is an area where immigration can play an important role. Beach et al. argue that different regions have different labour forces with specialized skill sets. Various programs involving provincial and municipal stakeholders as well as federal immigration funding agreements were sought to address local needs. The issues have been discussed and proposals have been made to move immigrants away from Toronto, Vancouver, and Montreal to smaller urban centres and lower-income regions aimed at raising their economic growth rates thereby narrowing regional income differences (Green 2003). Although such initiatives may not be very successful initially, because immigrants generally move to regions and cities where jobs are available, but persistent policy, effective program implementation, and sustainable program funding would give positive results.

In terms of short-term goals or economic benefits of immigration, literatures reveal limited insights on the issue. Immigration is likely to generate dynamism in the labour market in the sense that there is an increased flexibility to the immigrant workforce who tends to be more mobile compared to the Canadian-born workforce, at least in their initial years in Canada. They typically move towards economic booming areas where labour demand is very pronounced. This helps mitigate workforce demand and provides scale of adjustment as economic development occurs (ibid.). It is also thought that, since recent immigrants are more likely to change jobs than nonimmigrants, they demonstrate greater occupational mobility than their nonimmigrant counterpart. Such patterns suggest that immigrants are likely to respond to economic shock more flexibly than the Canadian-born workforce (Green 1999). As immigrants are a flexible workforce, they help fill the immediate occupational gaps and specific skills shortages. For example, immigrant workers will fill the labour gap during seasonal peaks for certain jobs, and others will take low-paying jobs that Canadian-born workers will not do. It is important to note that this job flexibility of the immigrant worker is an effective alternative tool on the part of the employers to reduce the bottlenecks in the production processes and outputs relatively quickly and cost effectively (M. Beach, Alan G. Green, and C. Worswick 2011). One of the objectives of Canada's 1970s immigration policy was based on this perspective. The key theme of the policy was that during good economic times, increased immigrants must be admitted in Canada, and during poor economic times, when unemployment rate is very high and there are a huge number of underutilized domestic workers in the labour market, the number of immigrants should be reduced. This role of immigration continued until early 1990s (ibid.).

2.4. Immigration policy overview

> *Our hopes are high. Our faith in people is great. Our courage is strong. And our dreams for this beautiful country will never die.*
> —Pierre Elliot Trudeau

2.4.1. Early immigration policy[12]

After the 1867 Confederation, the government realized that a large number of immigrants would be beneficial for Canadian economic in order for strengthening national demand for domestic goods and stimulating the country's manufacturing sector. Moreover, it was thought that settling immigrants to the largely uninhabited lands would secure national sovereignty, especially in the west. Subsequently, in 1869, the federal government passed the first *Immigration Act* and established the basic framework of Canadian immigration policy. The act emphasized an "open door" policy to allow more immigrants to enter Canada. The open-door policy had very few restrictions on who could immigrate to Canada. But the act, however, had some barriers on persons with disabilities, the ill, and the poor. Also, if an individual posed a threat to public safety due to disease or illness, she/he was required to buy a $300 bond upon entering Canada. Moreover, those who were blind, deaf, insane, or infirmed were recorded by the captain of the ship that transports them. However, some discriminatory elements were not removed from the policy. For example, it was necessary that the ship's captain pay a sum of money for those who were destitute or poor immigrants.[13]

In order to promote Canada as a destination of immigrants, the federal government opened immigration offices in Great Britain, continental Europe, and the United States. The other objective of opening these offices was to facilitate the immigration process. Moreover, an act known as *Dominion Land Act* of 1872 was enacted in order to attract immigrant settlers to the western Canada, under which free land was provided to male immigrants. By examining the Immigration Act carefully, we see that the "open door" policy was highly discriminatory. Under this policy, the federal government's intention was to attract farmers and labourers, whereas urban workers, artisans, and tradesmen were purposefully discouraged. Discrimination was also noticed in the policy, as it emphasized more on immigrants of Caucasian ethnicity, preferably of European or American nationality. Nonetheless, one of the discriminatory act that was implemented by the government was the *Chinese Head Tax and Exclusion Act 1885*. One may argue that this was one of the most blatant forms of discrimination in the history of Canada. The fact was that thousands of Chinese workers were brought in Canada during early 1880s to help the work of Canadian Pacific Railway (CPR). Moreover, the federal government was harsher on each Chinese immigrant by imposing a large tax on each of them, and they were denied Canadian citizenship. However, after thirty-two years of imposition, the restrictions on Chinese immigrants were finally removed in 1947.

2.4.2. Immigration policy during and after First World War[14]

During the First World War, Canada imposed greater restrictive action to prevent easy and free flow of immigrants into Canada, and as such, the government suspended or cancelled all immigration from enemy countries. Residents from those countries who were living in Canada after the WW I were considered as enemy under the *War Measures Act* of 1914. Under this act, these residents were required to register with the government and they were not allowed to join any associations or movements in Canada. Many were even kept in prison camps or deported from Canada. Subsequently, an act known as the *Wartime Elections Act* was introduced in 1917, which seceded the voting right for those from enemy countries.[15]

These policies continued after the war. One may argue that there were reasons behind these tighter policies. For example, as mentioned earlier, the open-door policy was viewed as a strategy to help economic growth in Canada. But after the WW I, there were political and economic challenges Canada faced, such as the rise of communism, organised labour movements, and the Great Depression. Therefore, government introduced an exclusionary immigration policy with the anticipation that the new policy would help in bringing good results for Canada in two ways: (1) social control and harmony, and (2) protect Canadian workers from losing their jobs to cheap foreign labours. Under the exclusionary immigration policy, people of certain ideological or ethnic backgrounds were the victims of the policy. A more discriminatory *Immigration Act* was introduced in 1919, which empowered the government to exclude specific groups from being immigrated to Canada. For example, the section 38 of the act prohibited entry of Doukhobors, Hutterites, and Mennonites due to their particular religious affiliation and practices. As the rise of Russian communism was a concern, section 41 of the act allowed the government to deport antigovernment activists living in Canada.

2.4.3. Immigration policy following Second World War[16]

The Second World War had changed the whole world. After the devastation of war, reconstruction work began in the countries vastly affected. There were demands of all kinds of resources, including human resources, and thus economic growth accelerated. Like other developed countries, Canada had experienced significant economic growth, and that Canadian workers would lose jobs to cheap foreign labour was no more a concern. At the same time, the Canadians started to think positive about the welfare state and multiculturalism. They become more tolerant accepting different ethnic groups, and refrained from racial and religious discrimination attitude. After the WW II, Canadian policy makers considered immigration as a viable tool for economic growth. As a result, the government of Canada removed the ban on *Chinese Head Tax and Exclusion Act* in 1947, and the Senate Standing Committee on Immigration and Labour introduced many reports on immigration policy in 1951, including the recommendation to reestablish open-door immigration policy.

Given those nondiscriminatory policy changes, some discriminatory practices still continued as seen in a new *Immigration Act* that was passed in 1952. The act established "preferred classes" of immigrants, which included British subjects and citizens of France, the United States, and only those Asian immigrants who wished to reunite with immediate relatives in Canada. Moreover, in pursuant of the act, the government of Canada acquired the power to exclude or limit immigration, according to their preferences, of certain groups.

In the 1960s, several key changes were made in the immigration policy. A major change took place in 1962, when the government introduced regulations that eliminated racial discrimination. Under this policy, potential immigrants would not be denied entry to Canada based on their colour, race, or nationality. Subsequently, the government introduced a *white paper* on immigration in 1966, which recognized immigration as a key factor for population and economic growth. Yet there was string attached to it. The white paper recommended only those who are highly skilled but not the unskilled people. One may argue that this was impartial. For example, there were no quotas or no restrictions on the number of people who could immigrate to Canada. The only eligibility criterion for candidates is the pass mark in a points system based on a number of skill sets. They are (1) whether the prospective immigrants have the knowledge of English or French (Canada's two official languages), (2) whether they had arranged employment in Canada, (3) whether they had a relative or family member in Canada, (4) whether they had proper education or training, and (5) whether they were immigrating to an area of Canada with high employment.[17]

Another group of immigrants is the refugee. The term "refugee" is commonly used to refer to a particular class of immigrants, specifically those who are forced to leave their home country due to war, political persecution, social violence, or natural disaster. Canada signed the United Nations Convention on the Status of Refugees in 1969. It is worth noting that previously Canada admitted refugees on a case-by-case basis and did not formally recognize refugees as a class of immigrants until 1969. But it took several years for the government to institute formal procedures for determining claims to convention refugee status, which was finally implemented in 1978, when amendments to the *Immigration Act* were introduced.

2.4.4. Canadian immigration policy during 1970–2002[18]

In the early 1970s, the government of Canada thought immigration as a priority issue and committed to look immigration into a broader perspective and to review it thoroughly. As a result, a study was commissioned by the government to collect background information related to the immigration policy issues and to identify new policy options. To make the study more authentic, reliable, and valid, provinces and stakeholders were invited to participate and submit their briefings. After the study was completed, a *green paper* on immigration was prepared in 1975. The green paper recommended one key issue—that Canadians should welcome ethnic diversity and emphasized for the continued importance of immigration as a strategic tool to be used to meet Canada's labour market needs. It was also recommended in the green paper that initiative should be taken in order to attract new immigrants who want to settle in more remote and less populated areas. These indeed were very realistic and timely approach. Eventually, a Special Joint Senate House of Commons Committee was created for two key reasons: (a) organise public hearings on immigration policy and (b) provide recommendations on new legislation.

The government of Canada subsequently introduced a new *Immigration Act* in 1976, which emphasized several reforms and developed the basic framework for Canada's contemporary immigration policy. In this new act, the importance of planning and provincial consultation on immigration was a key element. The act also strongly emphasized the fact that the government must set targets for the number of immigrants to be admitted each year as well as to consult with the provinces regarding their immigration issues. Above all, one of the most important elements in the act was the introduction of new categories for immigrants. They are as follows:

- *Independent class/Economic class*: individuals applying for landed-immigrant status on their own initiative
- *Humanitarian class*: (a) refugees (as defined under the United Nations Convention on Refugees) and (b) other persecuted and displaced persons not covered under the UN Convention
- *Family class*: including the immediate family, parents, and grandparents of individuals already living in Canada
- *Assisted relatives class*: distant relatives who were sponsored by a family member in Canada and who met some of the selection criteria of the independent class

Under the new classifications, the points system only applied to the independent or economic class and assisted relatives class. So what is noticed in the system is that humanitarian or family classes were not within the points system. One more category called business class, which is not listed here, was included by amending the *Immigration Act* in 1980s. Under this category, individuals were required to bring certain amount of financial capital to start a business or invest in Canada. Statistics show that business class category of immigration has been used extensively by the people of Chinese origin. Between 1983 and 1996, approximately seven hundred thousand Chinese, mainly from Hong Kong, immigrated to Canada, bringing billions in investment funds. We also observed that the nature of Canadian immigration has changed significantly as a result of immigration policy reforms in the 1960s, '70s, and '80s. Between 1900 and 1965, Europe was the primary source of immigrants to Canada. Afterwards, large volume of immigrants came from Asia. Other countries from where significant numbers of immigrants came to Canada were Africa, the Middle East, and South and Central America.

One important issue related to immigration and refugee needs to be addressed. We are aware that after the September 11, 2001, terrorist attacks in the United States, the security matter has become a serious issue in the United States and in Canada. The government of Canada introduced the *Immigration and Refugee Protection Act,* which is an act of the Parliament of Canada, which replaced the Immigration Act 1976 as the primary federal legislation regulating immigration to Canada. The *Immigration and Refugee Protection Act* came into force on June 28, 2002. Although this legislation retained much of the previous legislation's framework, the eligibility status for refugees was tightened. However, it extended family entitlements to same-sex and common-law relationships and enabled the couples under such relationships to bring their partners to Canada.

Government gained new powers to deal with terrorism under this legislation, particularly after the September 11, 2001, terrorist attacks in the United States, which included arrest, detain, and deport landed immigrants under the suspicion that they could be security threat to Canada. As a security, in order to protect from terrorist attacks, Canada and United States made a joint Safe Third Country Agreement in 2002. One could argue that this agreement could have implications for refugees and asylum seekers. Under this agreement, refugees were not permitted to make refugee claims to the country of initial entry, which was not the case previously. Before the September 11, 2001, event, refugees seeking immigration to Canada could enter the United States on a travel visa and subsequently could claim refugee status at the United States border. The main purpose of this legislation was to prevent refugee claimants and asylum seekers to enter Canada through United States. So it has negative implications for many genuine refugees and asylum seekers who could manage to enter United States but would not be able to seek asylum in Canada.

However, the *Immigration and Refugee Protection Act* has positive implications because it emphasized the importance of immigration aimed at improving Canadian society and economy and to create a culturally diverse nation. The act provided guarantees that the policies would be consistent with the *Canadian Charter of Rights and Freedoms* and the *Universal Declaration of Human Rights*.

2.4.5. Canada's new policy: "Canada Experience Class"

One of the most recent major breakthroughs in Canadian immigration system is the introduction of Canadian Experience Class (CEC) within the Independent or Economic Class in 2008. Under the new CEC, people who are temporary foreign workers and international students with Canadian work experience can apply for permanent residency. This means that the CEC is a good tool for those who want to become permanent residents of Canada (except the fact that they intend to live outside the province of Quebec, which has its own selection system) and who are currently or were previously temporary residents of Canada. The key criterion to become eligible to apply for permanent residency status for the temporary foreign workers is obviously the Canadian experience. For international students, the applicants must be from Canadian postsecondary institutions that have been enrolled for at least for two years full time and have had at least one year of full-time skilled work experience in Canada after graduation. In both cases, occupational categories like managerial, professional, technical, and skilled trades, as defined by the Canadian National Occupational Classification (CNOC), qualify for permanent resident status. Certainly, applicants must have an authorization permit to work in Canada and a work visa under the high-skilled temporary foreign worker (TFW) program.

There is a basic difference between the concept of "skilled worker" under CEC and Skilled Worker Program (SWP). Skilled worker under CEC is one who has actually received a particular skilled occupation in Canada and worked for a certain period of time in Canada by holding that occupation. On the contrary, applicants in the SWP are examined using a points system that focuses on certain criteria such as education, language, ability, skill sct, age, etc. As we see, the CEC evaluates "skill" retrospectively, whereas the SWP looks "skill" prospectively. It is interesting to note that technical occupations and skilled trades are accepted in the CEC but not in the SWP. Workers who would not qualify by the points system in the SWP would be admitted through CEC. Precisely, the key objective of both programs is to select immigrants who would have strong potential for success in the future labour market (Sweetman and Casey 2010).

The immigration system also includes new programs in partnership with, or exclusively by, the provinces. These programs generally ensures the participation by the provincial governments and employers in the selection of immigrants, increase the use of temporary foreign workers, enhance the opportunity for certain types of temporary foreign workers to become permanent residents, and give the federal government more authority to control the flow of immigrants of particular types with respect to particular occupations. Although the federal government has taken the lead role in terms of immigration selection throughout the Canada's history, for many years the province of Quebec has had its own skilled worker program and is largely responsible for selecting its own immigrants.[19] More recently other provinces are playing a role in immigrant selection, primarily through the Provincial Nominee Program (PNP). This program has two basic objectives: (1) to locate more immigrants in the regions and provinces outside of the three major cities, and (2) to meet the workforce needs of employers in those provinces, usually short-term labour market needs. Figure below summarizes the various routes to permanent and temporary residency in Canada (Ana M. Ferrer et al. 2012).

Routes to Permanent and Temporary Residency to Canada

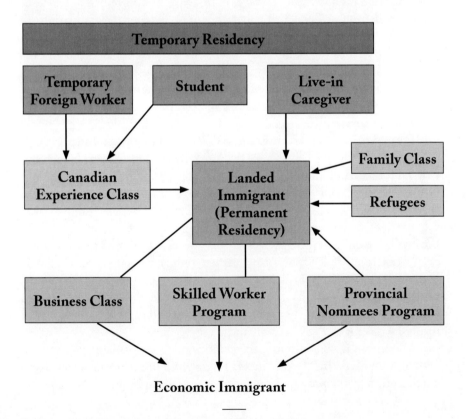

2.4.6. A Review of Canada's immigration system in 2012

In the year 2012, some important changes were made on many aspects of immigration system in Canada, such as economic class immigrants, refugee reform, temporary workers program, permanent residency, and citizenship.[20]

The economic class immigrants are brought under a program called Federal Skilled Worker Program (FSWP). This program is very important component of Canada's economic immigration in which immigrants are selected by points system. In 2012 some changes in the points system were made in the program, which are as follows:

- o points increased for the first official language spoken;
- o younger applicants get more points;
- o points decreased for work experience gained outside of Canada; and
- o credential assessment by a third party is a requirement at the time of application.

There are changes for skilled tradespersons who were not qualified under the FSWP criteria. In the case of tandpersons, applications are accepted only from individuals with occupations on a predetermined list. This system allows Canadian employers to choose potential candidates from a pool of prescreened workers and at the same time can remove unsuccessful applicants in no time from the long list of candidates.[21]

Prime Minister Stephen Harper introduced the *Protection Canada's Immigration System Act*, which is an amendment to the *Refugee Reform Act*. The purpose of this act is expedite the applications of refugee claimants from countries that do not have the history of refugee. It is expected that this process, which will take only forty-five days, will help to screen out the unfounded claims faster. In addition to measures to tighten human trafficking rules, the *Protection Canada's Immigration System Act* makes mandatory the provision of biometric data for all temporary resident visa applicants, which will help to minimize fraudulent applications.[22]

The most substantive changes were made in Bill C-31, an act to amend the Immigration and Refugee Protection. The Canadian Council for Refugees is seriously concerned that the changes to the law will create a two-tier system of refugee protection in Canada. It makes refugee protection in Canada dangerously vulnerable to political whims, rather than ensuring a fair and independent decision about who is a refugee. It also includes costly measures to detain refugee claimants. Bill C-31 received Royal Assent on June 28, 2012. Most of its provisions relating to the refugee determination system were implemented in December 2012.[23] The council expressed some concerns about the changes, which are as follows:

- Hasty timelines deny refugees a fair chance to prove their claims.
- Some claimants will have fewer rights because they come from a "designated country of origin."
- Some claimants will face mandatory detention, fewer rights in the refugee determination system, and a long-term bar on permanent status because they are "designated" as "irregular arrivals" by the minister of Public Safety.
- One-year bar on access to Preremoval Risk Assessment (PRRA) for refused claimants.
- One-year bar on applications for humanitarian and compassionate consideration.

For more information about the changes to the refugee system, see http://ccrweb.ca/en/refugee-reform.

It is now easier for employers to bring temporary foreign workers (TFWs) to Canada. Human Resources and Skills Development Canada (HRSDC) initiated an Accelerated Labour Market Opinion (A-LMO) process to approve employers seeking to hire a TFW. The HRSDC also changed the rules on pay for foreign workers. Employers are allowed to pay TFWs who are in the high-skilled position 15 percent less than the prevailing wage, and 5 percent less than the prevailing wage to those TFWs who are in the lower-skilled positions.

The government is going to table new rules for international students. The rules will allow educational institutions to host international students and also to permit international students to work part time off campus. The purpose of these changes is to attract international students who are likely to be the potential permanent immigrants at some point. The government also indicated the preference for two-step immigration—that is, temporary residency first followed by permanent residency. This two-step process would likely ease requirements of the Canadian Experience Class (CEC). In this process, TFWs in high-skilled jobs will require twelve months of in-Canada work experience, instead of twenty-four months as required in the earlier system, to apply for permanent residence through the CEC.[24]

In an effort to minimize fraud and support legitimate applications in the family sponsorship, the government has introduced two new rules.[25] They are as follows:

- Individuals who became permanent residents in Canada through the spousal sponsorship program must maintain their permanent residency for five years before they can in turn sponsor a spouse.
- For couples who have been living together for two years or less and have no children together, the sponsored individual will receive provisional permanent residency for two years. If the sponsored individual wants to remove the provisional status, the couple must prove that they have lived in a legitimate relationship in Canada.

The Bill C-43, *Faster Removal of Foreign Criminals Act*, provides the Citizenship and Immigration minister with power to deny people from coming into Canada. The bill would allow the minister to deny temporary resident status to foreign nationals based on public policy considerations. The bill would make it easier for the government to deport an immigrant with permanent resident status who has been sentenced to six months or more for a crime. There would be no right to appeal. The Canadian Bar Association (CBA) commented that while the association welcomes an amendment that would allow more temporary entrants to Canada, the majority of the proposed changes to Bill C-43 are unnecessary and unjustified.[26]

Sponsorship of parents and grandparents is currently suspended, and no new applications have been accepted since November 2011. However, beginning in December 2011, parents and grandparents of Canadian citizens and permanent residents may apply for a new "super" visitor visa. This visa allows parents and grandparents to stay in Canada for up to two years at a time and can be renewed for a period of up to ten years. Only parents and grandparents and their spouses are eligible to receive this visa. In addition to standard temporary resident visa application materials, they must purchase medical insurance for the duration of their stay in Canada.[27] For more information about the changes to Canadian immigration in 2012, see the site www.cic.gc.ca.

2.4.7. Myths about Canadian immigration

In my thirty years of experience in Canada, I have come across many Canadians from all walks of life. I have talked with them and shared opinions on various issues and concerns that Canadians value most. As an immigrant, I have always been interested to know about immigrants and immigration matters. Among many other issues, I have noticed that there are anti-immigration sentiments among Canadians. These sentiments have grown from several myths about immigration. But the reality may be different than the myth. It is true that people from all over the world have migrated to Canada to improve their lives not just to survive. In order to improve the quality of life, they have to work hard and excel their best ability and power to succeed.

Canada is built up by immigrants for many generations and that it becomes a country of immigrants. Economists and demographers believe that Canada's population and economic growth sustainability is dependent upon immigration given Canada's negative birth rate. Although one may argue that immigration leads to increased unemployment, but it is not true. The matter of fact is that the increased automation in the workplace is the key factor for people's job loss. Whereas, a larger population base and a larger workforce result in more and more goods and service that are being provided and consumed. Therefore, additional workforce in the labour market creates more jobs, which in turn results in economic growth. Majority of the immigrants are highly skilled and educated, and they are almost twice more likely to have university degrees than their white Canadian counterparts. Yet immigrants earn less and have higher rates of unemployment, and their qualifications and experience are not recognized or are underutilized by the Canadian employers. Yet there are myths about immigration. Below are some of the perceived generalized myths about Canadian immigration:

- Immigrants are a burden on the economy, and a net tax loss for the government.
- Immigrants take jobs from Canadians.
- Immigrants are a drain on social services.
- Immigrants are not integrating and threaten Canadian values. Their level of education is low, and many cannot speak English or French.
- Canada receives more than its share of refugees.
- Canada has an open-door immigration policy.
- New immigrants don't contribute much these days and are different lot from previous waves of immigrants.
- Canada can get rid of immigration by raising the retirement age and increasing birth rate.
- Multiculturalism has failed, and immigrants don't assimilate into the Canadian mainstream culture.

- Increased immigration leads to an increase in crime.
- Refugee claimants pose threats to Canada's security.
- Canada does more than its share to assist refugees and asylum seekers when compared to other countries.
- Canada needs large numbers of immigrants because it will face massive shortages of skilled labour in the coming decades.
- We need immigrants to do the jobs Canadians won't do.
- With an aging population and lower fertility rates, Canada needs high levels of immigration to provide the workers and tax base required to support social services for retirees.
- High levels of immigration are required to ensure Canada's prosperity.
- Canada is sparsely populated and can support a much larger population.
- We need a large immigrant stream to delay the effects of an aging population.
- Canada's population will collapse immediately without high immigration.

These are only a few of the perceived myths, but there are much more. Regardless of what the opponents of immigration advocates, the reality is that immigration is a positive force on Canada's growth and prosperity; the economic benefits outweigh the costs. While every policy on immigration may not be perfect, Canada has made efforts to improve conditions in which new immigrants can flourish and has been recognized internationally as a leader in immigration front. From my experience in living, working, and learning in Canada, I am convinced that Canada is doing relatively good on the immigration front among the immigrant receiving countries in the world. But the level of success must continue. We, therefore, need foreign talent, especially the specific skills set in different sectors and industries, in order to sustain the country's demographic and economic growth. Canada needs immigration just as much as skilled immigrants need Canada as their new home.

International Migration Outlook 2013 report reveals that the employment rate for Canadian immigrants in 2012 was the third highest in the OECD countries. This suggests that immigrants are integrating well into the labour force (Clément Gigna 2013). The report also reveals that more than 50 percent of Canadian immigrants are highly educated, which places Canada at the top among the OECD countries. Moreover, a significant number of the almost one hundred thousand foreign students visiting Canada each year who decide to stay after getting a degree from one of Canada's world-class universities like McGill University, University of Toronto, University of British Columbia, University of Ottawa, Queens University, etc. Other categories of immigrants have also been looking for opportunities to come to Canada because of the job prospects, the multiculturalism, and the citizenship that Canada offers.

For more detailed information and the reality against the myths, one can see the following sites:

http://canadiandesi.com/read.php
www.immigrationreform.ca/english/view
http://www.theglobeandmail.com/report-on-business/economy/economy-lab/for-canada-immigration-is-a-key-to-prosperity/article
https://ccrweb.ca/documents/FFacts.htm
http://www.sustainablesociety.com/population/immigration-myths

In a world darkened by ethnic conflicts that tear nations apart, Canada stands as a model of how people of different cultures can live and work together in peace, prosperity, and mutual respect.
—Bill Clinton

3

Visible Minority Immigrants in Canada

3.1. An overview

Canada's population composition is ethnically heterogeneous, as its citizens have come from many countries of origin and cultural backgrounds. The one way to depict cultural diversity in Canada is to describe in terms of its population size those who do not belong to the two charter groups (i.e., *Bilingualism and Biculturalism)*. This group of population refers to Canadians neither British nor French origin, and can be identified as "Third Force." This way of defining diversity was adopted by the Royal Commission of Canada in 1960s. While recognizing the charter status of the British and French, the Royal Commission of Canada also acknowledged the contributions of other noncharter groups.

Historically, Canada relied upon Western Europe, Great Britain in particular, as the major supplier of immigrants. After the end of the World War II, Canada maintained its policy of favouring immigrants from United States, United Kingdom, and other European countries. In the 1960s there were major changes in the immigration policy, which placed emphasis on education and occupational skills as key criteria for selecting immigrants. As mentioned in the previous section, changes in immigration regulations in 1967 resulted in the adoption of a universal points system in assessing prospective immigrants, irrespective of country of origin or racial background. Those regulations reflected Canada's attempt to compete for skilled labourer across the world (Li 1992). Evidence suggests that between

1954 and 1967, Canada lost 60,230 people to the United States. They were in the professional, technical, managerial, and entrepreneurial occupations. During the same period of time, Canada received only 33,119 people in these occupations from the United States (ibid.).

Since 1970s, the visible minority[28] population in Canada has been on the rise. The term "visible minorities" received official recognition in 1984 as Commissioner Rosalie S. Abella identified this group as one of the four designated employment equity group in the Royal Commission report. The Employment Equity Act of 1986 as such had included "persons who are, because of their colour or race, in the visible minority in Canada" as one of the designated groups. The other three groups are women, aboriginal people, and people with disabilities. In pursuant of the act, federal employers including crown corporations required to take special measures to improve visible minorities' employment opportunities (Statistics Canada 1986).

The visible minority population has grown steadily over the period. In 1981 there were slightly more than one million visible minorities who represented 4.7 percent of Canada's total population; by 1991, they climbed to 2.5 million (9.4 percent); by 1996, it was 3.4 million (11.2 percent); and by 2001, their numbers had reached to almost 4 million (13.4 percent of the total population. Between 2001 and 2006, the visible minority population (slightly more than 5 million; or 16.2 percent of the population) increased at a faster pace than the total population; its growth rate was 27.2 percent, which is five times faster than the increase for the population of Canada as whole, which was 5.4 percent only (Stat Can 2006 Census). In 2011 visible minority population increased to 6.3 million, or 19.1 percent of the population, according to 2011 National Household Survey (NHS). Between 2006 and 2011, the visible minority population increased by 23.5 percent—almost four times faster growth rate than the increase for the population of Canada as a whole, which is 5.9 percent only (NHS, 2011).

The growth of the visible minority population was largely due to increasing number of recent immigrants who were from non-European countries. In 1981 55.5 percent of the new immigrants who arrived in Canada in the late 1970s belonged to visible minority group. In 1991, 71.2 percent recent immigrants belong to this group, and the proportion reached to 72.9 percent in 2001. Recent immigrants who arrived between 2001 and 2006, 75 percent of them were members of visible minority group. This figure increased to 78 percent between 2006 and 2011. Canada's projected visible minority population would likely to be accounted for roughly one-fifth of the country's total population by 2017 (Stat Can 2005). According to the scenarios developed for the projections, the visible minority population would continue to be strengthened by sustained immigration, higher fertility, and younger age structure. The 2011 NHS data showed that the median age of this population was 33.4 years, compared with 40.1 for the rest of the population. Under the low- and high-growth scenarios of these projections, Canada could have between 11.4 million and 14.4 million persons belonging to a visible minority group by 2031, more than double the 6.3 million reported in 2011. The rest of the population, in contrast, is projected to increase by less than 12 percent.

Of the 6.3 million visible minorities in 2011, 31 percent were born in Canada, 65 percent were born outside Canada, and a small proportion (4 percent) was nonpermanent residents in Canada. These proportions vary from one group visible minorities to another. For example, of about 87,300 Japanese, 55,000 (63 percent) individuals were born in Canada, the largest such numbers. This is because Japanese had a long history in Canada and had no major immigration influx in recent times. Among two largest visible minorities, 31 percent of South Asians and 27 percent of Chinese were born in Canada. Although both groups have a long history in Canada, their immigration patterns in recent decades has kept the proportion of those were born in Canada relatively low. In other words, the proportion of foreign born among South Asian and Chinese is high. According to NHS data, a total of 1,567,400 individuals identified themselves as South Asian, the largest group. The top-three source countries are India, Pakistan, and Sri Lanka. A small proportion (1.5 percent) of South Asian was Canadian-born with both parents born in Canada. Among 1.3 million Chinese immigrants (coming from China, Hong Kong, and Taiwan), only 2.8 percent were third generation or more.

While Asia including the Middle East is to be the major source regions for visible minority immigrants, there has been a decline in the proportion of inflows from Asia. The share fell from 60 percent in 2006 to 56.9 percent in 2011. Of the total immigrants arrived (close to 1.2 million) between 2006 and 2011, more than one-third came from the Philippines (13.1 percent), China (10.5 percent), and India (10.4 percent). The Philippines recorded the largest increase of any country between intercensal periods—75,000 arrived between 2001 and 2005, which doubled to 150,000 between 2006 and 2011. As a result, its rate of increase also doubled for 7.6 percent to its current rate of 13.1 percent. In contrast, the immigrants arriving from China and India (the major source of countries in previous censuses) declined from 270,000 combined (27 percent) to 240,000 combined (21 percent) during the same period (Observation, TD Economics May 2013).

Canada is becoming more and more a multilingual society, one-fifth of Canadians whose mother tongue is neither English nor French, who collectively speak more than two hundred languages. Of the 6.8 million immigrants, a majority (97 percent) reported one mother tongue, and only 3 percent reported multiple mother tongues. Of the immigrant population who reported single mother tongue, about 1.6 million, or 23.8 percent, reported that their mother tongue was English. Another 3.4 percent reported French as their mother tongue. The remaining 72.8 percent of the immigrant population reported a mother tongue other than English or French. Chinese languages (Chinese, Cantonese, Mandarin, and other Chinese languages) are most common mother tongues among the immigrants whose mother tongue is not English or French. A total of about 852,700 people reported these languages in the NHS, 2011. The Chinese languages are followed by Tagalog (a language of the Philippines), reported by 320,100 people; Spanish, reported by 306,700; and Punjabi, reported by 305,400 people. Others are, among top ten, Arabic, Italian, German, Portuguese, Persian (Farsi), and Polish. It is important to note that a majority (74.5 percent) of Canada's foreign-born population are able to communicate and conduct conversation in more than one language, compared to 36.6 percent of the total population who can do the same. It is also the fact that immigrants who can speak more than one language have knowledge of English or French beside a nonofficial language. For example, among all immigrants, 61 percent are able to speak English or French and one or more nonofficial language(s), and 10 percent speak English and French and one or more nonofficial language(s).

Visible minority population comprised of mixed unions are on the rise. The 2006 census indicates that there were 289,400 mixed unions involving visible minority persons with a nonvisible minority person or a person from different visible minority group. This was an increase of 33 percent from 2001 census; whereas only 6 percent increase for all couples between 2001 and 2006 censuses. Japanese had the highest proportion (almost 75 percent) of mixed unions involving one Japanese person, followed by mixed unions involving one Latin American person (47 percent), and mixed unions involving one person from blacks (41 percent). South Asians and Chinese, on the other hand, had the least proportions of mixed unions (about 13 percent couples had mixed unions involving South Asian visible minorities and slightly higher than 17 percent couples had mixed unions involving Chinese visible minorities).

3.2. Visible minorities in the Federal Parliament

The first visible minority MP elected to Parliament was Douglas Jung in 1957. He was born in Canada, but his parents migrated from China.

He was elected by conservative party ticket from Vancouver Centre riding and served for two years. In 1968 Lincoln Alexander was the Canada's first black MP, followed by Pierre De Bané—a Palestinian-born Arab. For several years, visible minorities as MP grew slowly but increased in their numbers in the five elections since 1993. In that year's election, thirteen visible minorities were elected to Parliament, which grew to nineteen in 1997 and fell to seventeen in 2000 and grew again to twenty-two in 2004 (Jerome H. Black and Bruce M. Hicks 2006).

In the recent election in 2006, the number of visible minorities MPs increased to twenty-four; among them eleven MPs were of South Asian origin, five MPs were of Chinese origin, four MPs were of black origin, three MPs were of Arabs origin, and one was of Japanese origin. Importantly, though, is that while more visible minorities than ever before become MPs, they still represent a lower proportion of the legislature (only 7.8 percent) than their representation in the population, which was 13.4 percent. In the 2008 election, there was no improvement in the number of seats in the House of Commons by the visible minorities. In fact, it declined from twenty-four visible minorities MPs in 2006 election to twenty-one in 2008. On the other hand, the proportion of visible minorities in the Canadian population increased from 16.2 percent to 17.3 percent between 2006 and 2008. These suggest that in the last five elections, visible minorities were worse off in terms of their representation in the Canada's House of Commons.

From the strong support for multiculturalism in Canada, it was the expectation that Canada's Parliament should represent the ethnic diversity. Apart from Francophones and Anglophones, which require substantive representation in the political institutions, there should have representation of the "third element" that makes up the other portion of Canada's multicultural society. In fact, the Royal Commission on Bilingualism and Biculturalism incorporated this third element and formed the basis for the multicultural policy framework, which was delivered by ex-prime minister Pierre Trudeau in 1971.

Although a greater number than ever before of visible minority candidates ran for the office in 2008, fewer were eventually elected. There are reasons for that. Karen Bird discussed this issue and suggested that the most significant barrier is the incumbency factor. Political parties are reluctant to replace incumbents or unwilling to subject the incumbents to nomination challenge. As a result, the less the seats change hands, the less the opportunity for newcomers, visible minorities, in particular, for nomination. It is believed that with the parties' changing behaviour and policy suite (including creation of ethnic outreach committees, ethnically targeted campaign, and growing number of visible minority candidates), the parties can gain much by nominating and running visible minority candidates, especially in the ridings where the minorities constitute a large segment of the population.

Previous research suggests that there is no ethnic group in Canada that exhibits homogeneity of voting preferences as demonstrated by African Americans in the United States and by Franco-Arabs in France (Karen Bird 2007). With a few exceptions, Canada's ethnic ridings are multiethnic. For example, in the highly ethnic riding of Scarborough-Rouge River, visible minorities comprised of almost 85 percent of the population, and yet it includes several large ethnic communities, such as Chinese (34 percent), South Asian (23 percent), and blacks (13 percent). Although very little is known about the political participation and voting patterns of ethnoculture, ethnoracial, and immigrant communities in Canada, some research on political behaviours of particular ethnic groups revealed interesting findings. South Asians, than any other ethnic groups, are more politically engaged and influential. It is also the fact that South Asians have somewhat achieved the levels of political representation proportional to their presence in the general population. On the other hand, Chinese ethnic group relatively has low levels of political representation compared to their presence in the general population in Canada.

3.3. Visible minorities in the public service of Canada[29]

*Equality in employment will not happen unless
we make it happen.*
—Justice Rosalie Abella

The above remark made by Justice Rosalie Abella in her landmark 1984 report, "Equality in Employment," is a reminder that employment equity is everybody's business and that a concerted effort is necessary to ensure that all Canadians have equitable access to employment opportunities in the public service of Canada. The Federal Public Service is the largest employer in the country and, as such, committed to be representative of the country's changing demographics and evolving workplace norms in an effort to create a workplace that is reflective of the Canada's diversified population. Moreover, ensuring representation of Canadian public in the federal public service is a significant and crucial step towards strengthening public institutions and improving the quality of the public service as a whole. One of the federal government's first initiatives to promote employment equity was the implementation of the first *Employment Equity Act* in 1986. However, the 1986 Act applied only to federally regulated companies that have one hundred employees or more (primarily companies in the banking, transportation, and communications sectors), requiring these employers to eliminate workplace barriers and implement employment equity plans in relation to four specific target groups such as women, aboriginal people, persons with disabilities, and members of visible minorities.

In 1996 a new and substantially revised *Employment Equity Act* came into force, which extended the applicability of the employment equity regime to the federal public service as a whole. The current act maintains its focus on the same four target groups, known as "designated groups" as the former act, and requires that their employment status be monitored within the federal public service and the federally regulated private sectors. Under the act, the federal public administration is required to promote and achieve representation numbers for designated groups that are equivalent to workforce availability numbers for these four groups in Canadian society as a whole. If the representation numbers in the federal public service for these groups are lower than their workforce availability number, federal government departments and agencies are required to implement policies and practices to increase representation levels to close the "representation gap" (the difference between the workforce availability numbers for these groups and their actual representation levels within the federal public service).

About four years after the enforcement of the current act, the federal government implemented a new policy initiative titled "Embracing Change[30] in the Federal Public Service." This initiative was implemented in recognition of the fact that the government had not yet reached the employment equity objectives and goals required by the act. Specifically, "Embracing Change" involved the implementation of strategies to increase the representation of visible minorities in the federal public service. Through this initiative, the government set two recruitment benchmarks:

- by 2003, one in five people hired to positions in the federal public service should be members of visible minority groups; and
- by 2005, one in five employees appointed to executive positions should be members of visible minority groups.

The plan also dealt with issues such as promotion and the career development of visible minorities, and measures for developing a more inclusive and supportive culture for visible minorities in the federal workplace. In an attempt to monitor the progress of these legislative and policy initiatives and inspired by concern about the low levels of representation of visible minorities in the federal public service, the members of the Standing Senate Committee on Human Rights ("the committee") began examining issues of alleged discrimination in the hiring and promotion practices of the federal public service in November 2004. At the same time, they reviewed the extent to which targets to achieve employment equity for minority groups were being met. While progress was clearly being made in this area, the committee nevertheless undertook to investigate the extent to which the federal public service has managed to overcome impediments to hiring women, aboriginal people, persons with disabilities, and visible minorities to determine what the consequences of the employment equity framework have been and to provide recommendations for how to move forward in the future.

The results of the first stage of the committee's study were tabled in the Senate in February 2007, in a report titled "Employment Equity in the Federal Public Service—Not There Yet." The committee learned that the public service has reached some of its goals for hiring women, aboriginal people, and persons with disabilities. These groups are now represented within the federal public service at a rate that is higher than their workforce availability. However, the public service had still not yet met its goals for hiring visible minorities, who continue to be represented at less than their workforce availability. In 2010 the Standing Senate Committee on Human Rights conducted a study "Reflecting the Changing Face of Canada: Employment Equity in the Federal Public Service." The committee charted the progress that has been made by the federal government in meeting the key objective of the *Employment Equity Act*. Based on the workforce availability numbers from the 2006 census, the committee found that while the federal public service appeared to be meeting this key objective for women, aboriginal people (ABO), and persons with disabilities (PWD), it still was not doing so for visible minorities (VM). Based on the new numbers available for the core public service in 2008–2009,

- women are represented at a rate of 54.7 percent (their workforce availability rate based on the 2006 census is 52.3 percent);
- aboriginal people are represented at a rate of 4.5 percent (their workforce availability rate based on the 2006 census is 3.0%);
- persons with disabilities are represented at a rate of 5.9 percent (their workforce availability rate based on the 2006 Participation and Limitation Activity Survey [PALS] is 4.0%); and
- visible minorities are represented at a rate of 9.8 percent (their workforce availability rate based on the 2006 census is 12.4 percent).

However, the most recent data available from the Treasury Board Secretariat, based on workforce availability estimates, using 2006 census data, found similar results; some increases in the representation levels of all four designated employment equity groups within the public service since 2006. It is important to note that representation rates for women, ABO, and PWD remained the same for some time but exceeded their workforce availability (WFA); whereas the representation of visible minorities (VM) remained below their WFA (see table below).

Representation of EE Groups in the Federal Public Service, 2006 to 2010, with Estimated Workforce Availability Based on the 2006 Census

EE Group	2005–06 (%)	2006–07 (%)	2007–08 (%)	2008–09 (%)	2009–10 (%)	WFA (%)
Women	54.0	54.5	54.9	55.1	55.1	52.8
ABO	3.8	3.9	4.0	4.2	4.2	3.8
PWD	5.5	5.5	5.7	5.6	5.6	4.0
VM	9.6	9.8	10.3	11.1	11.6	13.0

Source: Office of the Chief Human Resources Officer, Treasury Board Secretariat.

It is to be noted that these numbers may not tell the entire story or present as accurate a picture as one might wish. There are weaknesses in the methodology for calculating recruitment rates.[31] It is also important to discuss the employment equity (EE) in the light of federal government's decisions on the elimination of the mandatory long-form census. Instead, government has introduced National Household Survey in 2011 aimed at gathering data on immigrant population and ethnic makeup of Canada. Ivan Fellegi, a former chief statistician who led the agency between 1985 and 2008, says the long-form census is still a better representation of the Canadian population than the National Household Survey. Others believe that due to the lack of data because of the cancellation of the mandatory long-form census, the government's employment equity reports still refer to 2006 census data on the employment equity groups.

Due to the constantly changing nature of Canadian labour force, the use of 2006 census data to estimate workforce availability (WFA) for EE groups and the government's EE report for 2012 is not a true representation of the situation. The government must use rigorous statistical estimation techniques to determine the accurate percentages of EE groups in the Canadian labour force. The results achieved during the past years in terms of representation of EE groups in the federal public service likely to affect severely by the recent government workforce adjustment. It is to be noted, however, that the latest Public Service Commission (PSC) figures show that some EE groups (PWD and VM) are severely affected by job cuts. For example, federal employees who identify themselves as VM account for a large proportion of employees who are currently on the list managed by the PSC. The current workforce adjustment directive does not require the employer to maintain the representation of EE groups. This is not helping the EE groups who are affected, and thus increases their vulnerability and could lead to a significant decrease in their rate of representation in the federal public service.[32]

The Senate Committee stated that employment equity in the federal public service remains a serious issue and that the public service must work to build a culture of respect and diversity before real employment equity goals can be achieved. This is just not about bringing more visible minorities in the public service; it is about creating a better workplace with a culture of diversity and a better representation of Canada's diversity. The committee further commented that the goal of the task force on the participation of visible minorities in the federal public service was to transform the public service into an institution that better reflects Canada's diversified population and establish as a role model of Canada's mosaic.

3.4. Social inclusion and visible minorities

Social inclusion is about the fact that all people are able to participate as valued, respected, and contributing member of the society. It incorporates multiple dimensions of well-being, which is achieved when all people have the opportunity and resources necessary to participate fully in economic, social, and cultural activities. The fact is when poverty divides us, social inclusion can unite us. Whenever too many people fall too far behind the rest, the true meaning of our whole society is likely to undermine and value diminishes. Inclusion demands goals and policies that avoid separating the people. Inclusion calls on us to strive for a nation in which everyone lives with purpose, dignity, and satisfaction. Inclusion describes what Robert Kennedy called our desired "bond of common fate." It is about closing physical, social, and economic distances separating people, rather than only eliminating barriers between *us* and *them*.

Canada is a country of immigrants where newcomers and visible minorities make up more than half of the population in its big cities. Given the diversity of population, the role of immigrants including visible minorities plays a critical role in the notion of social inclusion. Moreover, at the very root of social inclusion, there remains a powerful metaphor to address the immigrants' settlement challenges facing Canada today. It is the foremost demand of the immigrants' (visible minorities in particular) that they are included in the mainstream societal norm. They want to be full and equal participants in the economic, social, political, and cultural stream of their new country by dismantling the barriers in all these dimensions of life.

To talk about social inclusion, it is essential to address Canada's multiculturalism policy. Michael Dewing (Social Affairs Division, Library of Parliament) referred to multiculturalism as the presence and persistence of diverse racial and ethnic minorities who define themselves as different and who wish to keep their ethnic identity. Ideologically, multiculturalism is based on a set of ideas built in Canada's cultural diversity, and thus it is built in within the management of diversity at the policy level through federal and provincial initiatives. Multiculturalism policies in Canada are rooted within their historical origins.[33] In fact, Canadian multiculturalism evolved through political process among two "founding nations" (English and French) and the immigrants of European origin, but without the political participation of visible minority immigrants who arrived during the past two decades (Ratna Omidvar and Ted Rechmond 2003). Furthermore, Winter (2001) pointed out that multiculturalism and the antiracist policies are not adequately designed to resolve a number of broad issues, such as demands for Quebec independence, aboriginal claims to land and autonomy, or antiracist mobilization by visible minorities that includes both immigrants and Canadian-born.

In reality, social change does not happen overnight. There was time when aboriginal people on reserves had no right to vote, nonwhite immigrants were unwelcome, there were quotas to limit the number of Jews at Canadian universities, women were barred from business clubs, homosexuality was a criminal offence, and so on (Andrew Parkin and Mattew Mendelsohn 2003). We know that change has always been a gradual process, but it is obvious. Today, young Canadians are comfortable with diversity, craving for equality and prepared for further change. There is almost no evidence of any looming backlash against immigrants and visible minority groups. At the same time, multiculturalism is welcome by most Canadians and is a source of pride for all immigrants or visible minorities (ibid.). Yet immigrants, visible minorities in particular, are more likely to feel the pain of discrimination and racism in Canada. In a sense, they are threatened with social exclusion. Census data suggest that recent immigrants are not doing well economically or progressing at the same pace as previous generations of immigrants did. While many factors are responsible for this, discrimination perhaps plays a role. Canada must continue to make progress in removing barriers to full participation of immigrants and minority groups in the social, economic, and political life; then and only than the promise of new Canada with diversity and multiculturalism would be fulfilled (ibid.).

Nevertheless, Canada's inclusive policies on citizenship acquisition may be recognized as one of the world's best. Those policies are very important factors for social inclusion. For example, newcomers are eligible to become Canadian citizens after three years of residence in Canada. It is also to be noted that the newcomers (which include immigrants, refugees, and refugee claimants) receive many rights, which have both legal and practical implications for social inclusion. However, the real possibilities for economic, social, and political inclusion of all newcomers are contradictory to the official promises of multiculturalism and antiracism. The contradictions have been discussed by Ratna Omidvar and Ted Richardson (2003) in "Social Inclusion and Canada's Official Multiculturalism."

The contradictions are also revealed in the Council of Europe study in which Canada was a candidate based on its history and experience of cultural diversity. The study report suggested both positive as well negative sides of Canada's cultural diversity. By any international standard, Canada has attained top position in terms of overall quality of life and becomes the model for other countries to follow. On the contrary, the report also pointed out that "diversity is seen in Canadian policy circles as one of fault-lines exposing cracks in the Canadian façade of social cohesion. For example, cultural diversity tends to intersect with economic and other types of polarization, thus jeopardizing Canada's reputation for leadership on these issues and challenging its image as a caring, open and compassionate society"(Greg Baeker 2002). As we know, social inclusion has not happened in all walks of life of the visible minorities Canada.

In terms of policy response to diversity, measures have been taken to acknowledge and support diversity. The report has noted that progress has been made, but the issues are not resolved yet. For example, aboriginal people, women, visible minorities, and the persons with disability reiterated the fact that serious shortcomings are required to be corrected in terms of cultural democracy as it is being practiced currently in Canada. Greg Baeker argued Canada's formal commitments to broaden the idea of diversity and equality through the Canadian Charter of Rights and Freedoms and other legislative and policy instruments. However, people representing various ethnoracial and visible minorities claim that these measures have failed because those legislative and policy instruments continue to function within the dominant framework of English- and French-speaking Canadians, and do not accept the salient issue of power imbalances. It suggests that Canada has a long road ahead in resolving contradictory diversity demands and that the understanding of diversity involves an ongoing negotiation of conflicting interests (ibid.).

3.5. Visible minorities in the Canadian labour market

We have discussed in earlier sections that after the 1980s, the source of Canada's immigration shifted from Europe to the third world, and the largest influx of the new immigrants were from Asia, the Middle East, Africa, and Latin America. Needless to mention that the immigrants from these parts of the world are of cultures, languages, and religions that are quite different from the majority of Canadians of European background, majority of them are classified as visible minorities. These immigrants were expected to face unique challenges competing in Canadian labour markets in order to perform equal or better than the mainstream competitors. In recognition of this situation and in support of these visible minorities, Canadian governments have introduced action programs called "employment equity" programs (Patrick Grady 2011).

According to Statistics Canada's projections, the labour force would become older and increasingly ethnoculturally diverse—almost one-fourth among the entire labour force would be aged fifty-five or over by 2021, and there would be higher proportions of foreign-born people including vast majority of visible minorities in the labour force. Projections also suggest that while the overall participation rate will likely decline, the diversity of the labour force will increase. This projected decline in the overall participation rate will largely be attributed to demographic phenomena, like aging of the baby boomers, increasing life expectancy, and lower fertility rate (i.e., rate below replacement level of two children per women).[34]

Numerous studies have shown that visible minorities experience racial discrimination in the labour market. They are more likely to be unemployed or underemployed and are more likely to have lower earnings than their white counterparts. The 2011 National Household Survey (NHS)[35] data released by Statistics Canada focused on labour outcomes by racial status show a grim picture of employment status of visible minority groups. The unemployment rate in 2011 was 9.9 percent for visible minority workers compared to 7.3 percent for white Canadian workers. This difference is even greater with gender differentials—the difference in unemployment rates between visible minorities and white Canadian workers is significantly greater for women (10.6 percent for visible minorities versus 6.7 percent for whites) than for men (9.3 percent for visible minorities versus 7.8 percent for whites). The data also reveal the uneven outcomes for various ethnic groups. For example, the unemployment rate is very high for Arab workers (14.2 percent), followed by black workers (12.9 percent), South Asian workers (10.2 percent), and Chinese workers (8.3 percent). A high level of education has not even narrowed the unemployment rate gap between visible minorities and white Canadians. In fact, the gap was greater for visible minorities and white Canadians (7.9 percent and 4.1 percent, respectively). Also the fact that unemployment rate is much higher for visible minority youths (aged twenty to twenty-four) than for white Canadian youths of same age (17.7 percent and 14.1 percent, respectively).

Although unexpected, but a reality in the Canada's labour market is the fact that there is a big difference in unemployment rate between visible minorities who were born in Canada and white Canadians—11.8 percent for visible minorities versus 7.4 percent for white Canadians. The gap, however, is somewhat smaller yet noticeable for younger age group (twenty to twenty-four) who were born and educated in Canada, and the white Canadians in the same age group who were also born and educated in Canada (17.2 percent and 14.1 percent, respectively). It is important to note that this difference in unemployment rates for those born and educated in Canada cannot be explained with reference to undervaluation of foreign credentials and work experience, which affects immigrants. One could argue that this difference may be due to overt discrimination in hiring and layoff decisions of employers, or to the fact that visible minority workers tend to be employed in more precarious jobs. Therefore, 2011 NHS data suggest that visible minority workers suffered most in terms of employment outcomes from the impact of economic recession of 2008–2009, when the overall unemployment rate in Canada averaged 7.8 percent.[36]

A study released by Canadian Race Relations Foundations (CRRF) shows that good jobs and promotions in the workplace continue to elude many visible minorities, as racial discrimination is present in the workplace and that diversity is generally seen at the bottom and middle level of the labour force pyramid. The report also reveals that despite the fact that visible minorities have higher levels of education than white Canadians counterpart, they have lower levels of employment and income. The report is based on the analysis of quantitative statistics and focus groups across Canada. The focus group participants have agreed the fact that employment success is dependent on the right skills and education, but also have strongly emphasized the existence of racial discrimination in the workplace. Based on the findings of the report, the CRRF's chief operating officer commented that employment equity alone is not the remedy to eliminate racial discrimination in the workplace, but it is also important to eliminate the barriers faced by visible minorities in accessing their desired professions and trades and put more effort into raising public awareness about the existence of systemic discrimination in the workplace.[37]

Previous studies (Picot 2008; Picot and Sweetman 2005; Picot and Hou 2008) taking data from Statistics Canada reveal that the recent immigrants have performed poorly in the labour market. This raises the question whether the social benefits offered by the Canadian welfare system is compatible with the economic benefits to Canada that are expected to generate from the open immigration policy of admitting highest level of new immigrants per capita (Patrick Grady 2011). However, the mass immigration policy can be defended by the fact that the children (who were born and educated in Canada) of the new immigrants are expected to do better in the Canadian labour market than their parents and other Canadians. Skuterud (2010) compared visible minority immigrants' labour market outcomes to their grandchildren and found evidence of intergenerational convergence, which suggest that the children outperform their immigrant parents, and the grandchildren outperform the children. Thus one might argue that in a few more generations ahead, labour market disparity between Canadian-born visible minorities and their white Canadian counterpart will eventually disappear. This is just an expectation, but we have to wait and see how many generations it takes to happen, if at all the argument holds.

In a speech given at the Canada Post Headquarter in Ottawa on May 14, 2009, the Honourable Donald H. Oliver, QC, Senator, the Senate of Canada, pointed out something on discrimination in the Canadian workplaces. He cited the largest survey ever conducted on visible minorities in Canadian workplaces (catalyst/Ryerson Study) and said, "Almost three-quarters of visible minorities working in Canadian organisations feel that 'whom you know' is more important than 'what you know.' Many of them further cite a 'lack of fairness in career advancement processes.'" At the same time he appreciated a number of federal departments who are the diversity leaders in terms of representation and career progression of the visible minorities. They are Statistics Canada, CSIS, CRA, and Health Canada. He further said that these federal departments and agencies clearly have strong executive support for diversity and that their executive teams can take great pride in their stunning results in increasing the representation of visible minorities at all levels. The senator quoted a comment from Martin Jacques, a professor at the London School of Economics, Asia Research

Centre, "Wishing racism was not true, denying it is true, will never change the reality. We can only understand and tackle racism if we are honest about it . . . And when it comes to race—more than any issue—honesty is in desperately short supply."[38]

In reality, what we see around us is that racism exists everywhere in the world. Visible minorities always find it difficult to survive in such kind of racist environment. They face a lot of problems whether related to getting jobs, salaries, and other social status, and that they always lack behind in those compared to white population. Opportunities don't come easily for them; they are born to fight for it. A study conducted by the Canadian Centre for Policy Alternatives and the Wellesley Institution suggested that minorities are obtaining their hard-earned share in Canada's economy. The study quoted Statistics Canada's data available in 2006, which suggest that visible minority earned approximately 81.4 cents for every dollar a white person had earned. A white person is blessed with better pay for the same kind of work done as compared to nonwhite. This brings about the earning disparities between visible minorities and their white counterpart, which further contribute in their standards of living. Moreover, the employment figures proved the fact that visible minorities are no way equal to the whites in Canada. It showed that unemployment rate among the visible minorities was around 8.6 percent as compared to white Canadians' unemployment rate of 6.2 percent. This difference stresses on the fact that whites are preferred more over the nonwhites, and it also could be the fact that nonwhites have difficult access to job opportunities available in the market, in spite of Statistics Canada's findings that visible minorities showed more interest and willingness to work rather than the whites.[39]

One of the cherished notions of Canadian multiculturalism is that the children of immigrants succeed economically like mainstream Canadians. As the new immigrants are mostly nonwhite, non-Caucasians, those immigrant children are more likely belong to a visible minority group and that the eldest are in their forties and have established themselves in the workforce. It is, however, evident that Canadian-born visible minorities and those who came to Canada as young children earn less than their similarly qualified white counterpart.

While part of it may be networks that are likely to lead to high-paying jobs, straightforward discrimination is a part of it. The children of visible minority immigrant parents go to university at much higher rates than the rest of the population. Yet their earnings compared with those of their Canadian-born white colleagues are less, and inequalities become apparent. A Canadian-born visible minority man earns about 18 percent less than a Canadian-born white man with similar education and experience, according to Simon Fraser University economist Krishna Pendakur. For women, the wage gap is 3 percent. We have a labour market where good jobs that pay good money are not equally accessible by white and visible minorities. This wage gap reflects odds with Canada's self-image of a society that is growing with diversity. Patrick Grady (2011), an author of a research paper on the relevant subject, described the performance of the second generation of recent immigrants as an issue of discrimination in the Canadian labour market and critical for Canada's future. "There seems to be a large visible minority discount being built in [to the market]. I think that's going to cause future social tension," Mr. Grady said. "You wouldn't expect to find that visible minority immigrants who have the same levels of education as Canadians from the same schools would suffer such a discount."

There are important differences between visible minority groups. A study by Waterloo economist Mikal Skuterud found a wage gap of 8 percent for Chinese Canadians whose parents were immigrants. For South Asians of the same generation, the gap was roughly 13 percent; and for blacks, it was about 19 percent. There are also differences across regions, according to a study by Professor Pendakur and his brother, sociologist Ravi Pendakur. Results in Montreal, where the gap for men is about 30 percent, are much worse than in Toronto, where it's fewer than 15 percent, and Vancouver, where it's less than 10 percent. In the public sector, where employment equity law applies, a StatsCan study found the wage gap for men was only 3 percent—about four times smaller than its findings for the private sector. These earning gaps will put pressure on government to make result-oriented action through its employment equity programs, without which the employment equity program will only just a low-priority policy within the bureaucratic agenda.

Professor Skuterud's research shows that while the earnings gap diminishes for specific groups with subsequent generations, it doesn't disappear. Professor Pendakur, as an economist, is reluctant to suggest government intervention in the labour market but said that extending employment equity laws to the private sector might be necessary. He cites a recent study done by economist Philip Oreopoulos, which found that job applicants with English-sounding names were 40 percent more likely to get an interview than those with identical résumés of an Indian or Chinese name. The magnitude of the differential seems to be increasing, rather than decreasing. It was suggested that we need to address this issue and take measure to eliminate such systemic bias and take a more active public role in the private sector.[40]

3.6. Job market: Challenges face the visible minorities

Employment challenges can result from various factors such as age, education qualifications, class and ethnicity, place of birth, gender, and so on. Many youth who recently migrated to Canada find that because of their ethnic identity, they have a significant negative effect on their labour market trajectory. Some studies show that lack of "Canadian" work experience is a critical barrier to employment for many immigrant youth, particularly those who are members of racialized groups. Immigrant youth are less likely to have worked during their secondary and postsecondary education than those youth born in Canada (Kilbride et al. 2004; Kunz 2003). Nearly 60 percent of Canadian-born youth between the ages of fifteen and nineteen have work experience prior to leaving high school, compared with only 25 percent of migrant youth (Statistics Canada 2007b).

The difficulty to enter in the job market is faced not only by the foreign born in particular but also by the visible minority youths in general (Pendakur 2005; Pendakur and Pendakur 1998; Tran 2004). Discrimination against ethnoracial minorities is also based on skin colour and by the name as well. Literatures suggest that signs of membership, particularly one's last name, are also important stigmas (Oreopoulos 2009; Silberman et al. 2007). For example, job applicants with English-sounding names are more likely to get an interview than those with identical resumes and an Indian or Chinese name. Professor Pendukar contended that we have labour market in which good jobs that pay good money are not equally accessible by white and visible minorities. These gaps exist despite the cherished notions of Canadian multiculturalism, which strongly promotes that the children of all immigrants are expected to succeed economically in such a way that makes them indistinguishable from other Canadians.

Family and friends networks are a significant source of information about employment opportunities. But coming from immigrant families is a challenge for the ethnic minority youths. They usually lack the networks of family and friends who are useful for finding jobs (Shields et al. 2010). Even when ethnic minority youths rely on their friendship networks, they are less likely to find good work because their social ties are small and less robust (Fang et al. 2010). Due to their smaller and less powerful networks, these youths are less likely to obtain desired career occupational jobs than their white-born counterpart (Perreira et al. 2007). Most visible minority youths find their first work in low-skilled, low-paying jobs in the service and retail sectors. Those jobs are temporary, to gain job experience and to earn money towards further education, or just for "getting by" (Sean Lauer et al. 2012). However, as they earn experience, develop technical skills, and enhance educational level, they are expected to get better jobs—better-paying and permanent jobs in future.

Unemployment and underemployment among the visible minority youths have been higher than in the general population in Canada. The reason is the fact that the new generation of visible minority youths face many challenges in entering the job market and securing a stable and well-paid job (Miu Chung, Sean Lauer, and Surita Jhangiani 2008). Previous studies (Cheung 2005; Palameta 2007) and the data presented earlier section suggest that visible minority youths (who were born in Canada or came to Canada when they were young and have gone through the Canadian education process) have lower income and tend to have less-desirable jobs than their counterpart in the general Canadian population.

Miu Chung et al. (2008) explored the job-seeking experiences of new generation of visible minority youths, including the impact of educational attainment (such as with and without university degree) and aspirations on searching and finding jobs. The results are not praiseworthy for the ethnic minorities. Youths without university education are more likely to change jobs somewhat regularly, and these changes of jobs are often lateral moves rather than to better jobs. It is also the fact that many of them work at the entry-level positions in the labour-intensive service sector jobs. Quite often these youths find jobs through walk-ins and cold calls on employers. Interestingly, many of youths find jobs with the coethnic employers because of their lack of experience to find jobs outside their ethnic enclave of employers. There are, however, drawbacks in working with the coethnic employers; they expect too much and do not pay fair wage to the coethnic employees. Another way of finding job is the personal contacts, which gives information about job openings or personal reference to an employer. Personal contacts also reduce the job-searching time, and as such, youths quite often use this contact from friends but not from family members. Interesting to note that very few youths seek help from employment service agencies to find jobs. Although these youths do not have university education, many of them feel the importance of having a university degree. At some point in their job-searching endeavour, many of them take courses in order to upgrade their skills and credentials, but may not necessarily be for the completion of a university degree.

Unlike minority youths without university degrees, the youths with a university degree are likely to look for jobs in the areas of their expertise, as they see value in their credentials. Yet these youths seek material support in their job search, such as preparing a professional resume, writing a cover letter, and interviewing practice—in a nut shell, how to navigate the job application process of their desired profession. Miu Chung et al. (2008) found that youths having university degrees look for long-term career jobs and that they spend more time and effort on job searching, which can be stressful and sometimes frustrating. Ultimately, however, a majority of them find jobs in their professional fields except those with degrees in liberal arts (ibid.).

There is abundant evidence that members of visible minorities and aboriginal people face barriers in gaining access to jobs for which they are qualified and that their talents, education, and abilities are too often underutilized, reported by John Samuel and Associates Inc. from a study done for Labour Program Human Resources and Social Development Canada. The author also believes that if the abilities and talents of all Canadians are to be fully engaged in creating a productive economy and a healthy society, then it is essential to ensure that the workplace is fair and inclusive for all Canadians (John Samuel 2006).[41]

In order to support young Canadians, there are several employment programs that are available for all citizens that ethnic minorities can take advantage of opportunities. For example, department of Human Resources and Skills Development Canada supports several employment programs to help Canadians including those facing barriers to employment. The government of Canada also provides funding to provinces and territories for skills and employment training programs through Labour Market Development Agreements. Moreover, there are specific programs for newcomers in Canada to help new immigrants to have services like job mentoring and counselling, preparing resumes and cover letter, preparing for a job interview, list of prospective employers, etc. One can go to various web pages of government departments to have access to information for those services and supports.

3.7. Understanding foreign credentials

It is obvious that the diversity of backgrounds, such as languages, education, and training among immigrants are different than those among Canadian-born citizens, which creates challenges for foreign credentials and qualifications recognition programs in Canada (Penny Becklumb and Sandra Elgersma 2008). It is important to note that foreign credentials and qualifications recognition is one of the reasons that may lead to employment barriers, particularly for the skilled immigrants. Canadian employers usually prefer to hire Canadian-born applicant over an immigrant for a number of reasons. For example, (1) employers may think that foreign credentials are of lower calibre than equivalent Canadian qualifications; (2) they only hire candidates with Canadian work experience, which new immigrants don't have; (3) immigrants lack official language proficiency; and (4) Canadian employers lack knowledge about the foreign education and experience of recent immigrants (ibid). All these suggest one thing—that discrimination between immigrant and Canadian-born candidates exist in the labour market.

The government of Canada initiated identification of issues related to credential recognition in 1980s, and some improvement was made in 1990s. Penny and Sandra have reviewed government initiatives related to foreign credentials in a paper published by the Library of Parliament in 2008. Some of the highlights are presented here:

- The Department of Human Resources and Social Development Canada (HRSDC) has instituted a *Foreign Credential Recognition Program*[42] aimed at improving foreign credential recognition processes for targeted occupations or sectors, both regulated and nonregulated. Funding is available for projects developed by different Canadian organisations, including regulatory bodies, educational institutions, businesses, professional groups, and sector councils. Federal funding is also available for projects developed by provinces and territories as well.
- The *Going to Canada Portal*[43] is a program that provides information about Canada for prospective immigrants so that they can make informed decisions before coming to Canada. Along with general information about Canada, it also provides information about working, labour market, employment categories and opportunities, wage rates, job duties, skill requirements, etc. As part of the *Going to Canada Portal,* a "Working in Canada Tool" has been created by the government. Immigrants and foreign workers are in a position to determine what their occupation is called in Canada, whether it is a regulated occupation or not; if regulated, what is the name and contact information of the regulator, and so on.
- The *Foreign Credentials Referral Office*[44] *(FCRO)* is the key federal initiative that helps foreign trained workers in getting the information they need to know how to have their foreign credentials recognized in Canada. The FCRO also helps finding labour market information, job search tips, and information about English and French translation services of their degree or diploma.

- There are provincial initiatives regarding foreign credentials recognition and related issues. Alberta has a loan program for accreditation expenses known as "Immigrant Access Fund." British Columbia has instituted "Skills Connect for Immigrants Program," which provides a range of employment-related services, including credential recognition. Ontario's "Bridge Training Program" provides training and orientation to newcomers to help find work in their field. The Ontario legislature has passed the *Fair Access to Regulated Professions Act 2006*.[45] The act requires Ontario regulators to have fair and open registration process—meaning clear assessment of academic credentials. Under this act, the government of Ontario has created an Office of the Fairness Commissioner.[46] Ontario also has established Global Experience Ontario (GEO)—an access and resource centre for foreign-trained individuals. The GEO centre provides information regarding the process for licensing and registration in Ontario, and refers people to regulatory bodies, community or employment agencies.

Apart from these approaches stated above, an alternative approach is being used in Canada. This basically is a way to choose those foreigners that have already had their credentials and qualifications recognized in Canada. As described in an earlier section, the federal government, in 2008, created a new system called Canadian Experience Class (CEC).[47] Under this program, foreigners who have either worked in Canada as a temporary worker or studied in Canada as a foreign student qualify for permanent resident status in Canada. At the provincial level, immigrants are also being admitted each year under a program called "Provincial Nominee Program" (PNP). So far nine provinces and one territory have PNP agreements with the federal government under which they select immigrants according to their own labour market needs by using their respective selection criteria.

We have mentioned earlier section that recent newcomers to Canada are not experiencing the employment level and economic success of previous generations of immigrants. While this issue is complex and many reasons for this exist, the failure of Canadian government and institutions to ensure fair recognition of the credentials and qualifications of the immigrants may be one of the potential explanations for this prevailing trend of economic downturn for the newcomers in Canada (Penny and Sandra 2008). Therefore, the foreign credentials recognition issue has increasingly gained importance. At the same time, there is an understanding that improving the processes and getting progressive and rewarding results on foreign credentials recognition is a formidable task. However, it is also vital to revisit the foreign credentials recognition issue and to overhaul the existing process.

3.8. Visible minority and Canadian media

Media plays a crucial role in the creation of social identities and is responsible for the ways that Canadian society is interpreted by its citizens. It is an important source of information by which the people gain knowledge about their country and the people. In journalism as well, objectivity, accuracy, and representation are among the most important journalistic values. Given that expectation we have, Canadian media and the journalists are not so fair and objective in functionality as we observe. What we observe is that the Canadian news media has consistently marginalized, underrepresented, and stereotyped visible minority groups. Previous research have demonstrated that Canadian media propagates certain negative traits about visible minorities into the headlines. Obviously, negative connotation of visible minorities is likely to teach them that they are threatening to the wider society. This is not a good thing for the minorities, as this portrayal is damaging to their psyche. Minelle Mahtani argues that "ethnic minorities in Canada do not see themselves mirrored in the media, and this perpetuates feelings of rejection, trivializes their contributions, and devalues their role as citizens in their nations" (Mahtani 2001).

Representations of visible minority groups are often inadequate or nonexistent. Even when they are portrayed, those portrayals are often stereotyped and demeaning. Given the fact that visible minorities have a strong presence in urban centres, yet visible minorities cultural mosaic is not reflected in the Canadian media, both in terms of on-screen presence and working behind the scenes and in the ways various groups are represented. For example, news reports often misrepresent or underrepresent visible minority content; Canadian TV shows have been criticized for failing to include enough visible minority characters. It is also the fact that an overwhelming majority of journalists do not identify as belonging to a visible minority group (Mahtani, M. 2001). In other words, visible minority journalists are not visible in the Canadian media based on proportional representation.

Studies have shown that distorted images of visible minorities are prevalent in news media. It appears that news reports are framed around cultural narratives that reflect a structured storytelling process, where certain groups are often positioned as "villains" and others are portrayed as "heroes." For example, white Canadians are often shown in news media to be heroic or morally upstanding when compared to a "villain" from a visible minority, particularly in stories about crime. One may argue that through this process of storytelling, the media reinforce ideas about who is trustworthy and untrustworthy, who is a "troublemaker," and who should be feared (Baht, V., Mihelj, S., and Pankov, M. 2009). In the context of Canadian mosaic, more ethnic minority faces are expected to appear in the Canadian media.

In Canada, news is often framed in a context that privileges the white majority by portraying majority members in a positive sense. Moreover, the news industry overwhelmingly tend to favour sources that are affiliated with government, which often results in only one side of a story being told, which is interpreted by white majority group members (Ungerleider, C. S. 1991). When visible minorities are portrayed in news media, they are frequently shown as deviants, social problems, or a threat to the so-called ideal Canadian way of life. These news representations also support cultural stereotypes. For example, images of Muslims or Arabs are being portrayed as terrorists, or women are being mistreated through female circumcision, forced marriage, and "honour killings." This shows the point that moral panic (such as public outcries about certain issues or about certain populations, usually generated by the media) has arisen as a result of negative portrayals of Asian and Middle Eastern minorities (Mahtani, M. 2001). In 2006 only less than 6 percent of CBC employees were visible minorities (*Conseil des Relations Interculturelles* 2009). However, there are some the reasons as to why visible minorities are so underrepresented in the newsroom. They are as follows:

- Some news agencies have stated that individuals from visible minority backgrounds tend not to choose occupations in journalism.
- Networking barriers often exist for minority populations.
- Hiring referrals are provided by producers, writers, and editors already working in the industry, who are usually white.
- There is a lack of official recognition in Canadian media for credentials and qualifications gained outside of Canada.
- There is a lack of employment and training for visible minorities due largely to biases in hiring. No Canadian news agencies report having programs that train visible minorities to take leadership roles (*Diversity Watch* 2004).
- There is reluctance on the part of visible minorities to apply for newsroom jobs due to fears of harassment by coworkers or affiliates

such as police (*Chronicle World. Teen-age Black Journalists Target UK Racism*, 2011).
• Many people also hesitate applying for newsroom jobs because they fear having their status as members of a visible minority becoming the defining aspect of who they are and why they are a journalists (Evans, D. 2005).

One may argue that the underrepresentation of visible minorities in Canadian media is indicative of media's ignorance about visible minorities. This is particularly a matter of disappointment in the context of Canada's multicultural principles, since they are being used as a governance framework for ethnic diversity in Canada (Mahtani, M. 2001). In this regard, it is worth noting that one of the multicultural policy objectives is the full involvement and equal participation of ethnic minorities in mainstream institutions.

The practice of negative media depiction of visible minorities is a long-past phenomenon. For example, anti-Chinese news and stories were published in the newspapers in late nineteenth century (Anderson 1987). In the contemporary times as well, news about visible minorities remain invisible from magazines and soap operas in Canada (Media Watch 1994). Study conducted by MacGregor reveals the fact that visible minority women were absent in the magazine *Maclean's* over a period of thirty years. Mahtani (2000) pointed out that interracial relationships in dramatic series are rare in Canadian media drama, and even if depicted, the relationship is portrayed problematic. The author further commented that the successful mixed-race relationship is completely absent given that there are more interracial relationships in reality at present than before in Canada. Evidences on ethnic minorities in terms of their representation in Canadian entertainment programs also reveal stunning facts on ethnic minorities. In eight dramatic series, only 4 percent of the female and 12 percent of the male characters were depicted from ethnic and racial backgrounds (Media Watch 1994). In six major Canadian newspapers, of the 895 news stories published, only 14 percent mention minorities (Miller and Prince 1994). This neglect and the very invisibility of visible minorities and their issues in Canadian media obviously shows that visible minorities feel a sense of "otherness" (Mahtani, M. 2001) and in some way "social exclusion" in Canada, as one can argue.

Not only ethnic minorities have been underrepresented but also they are misrepresented in the Canadian media and that portrayals of minorities are often stereotypical and demeaning. A study conducted by Charles Ungerleider found the difference between objective reporting and the distorted image of ethnic minorities is so prevalent in most news coverage in Canadian news media. In fact news reporting is storytelling of people, which means the news coverage projects people as heroes, villains, and victims. So by projecting ethnic minorities as villains, reporters consciously or unconsciously tell us the stories about who troublemakers are and who good people are. When these stories are repeated in the news, minorities become stereotyped. Minelle Mahtani has reviewed the major studies in the area of media and minority identity and summarized the findings. What she has found in her review is that Canadian studies on ethnic representation in the media have revealed the fact that media has been unable to effectively project the real picture of Canadian society in which ethnic diversity is accurately depicted. As such, the narrowly projected image of ethnic minorities has negative impact on their ability to be proud of their positive contribution to the Canadian society. This is a serious matter because it creates a divide between ethnic minorities and the white Canadians—a divide that makes visible minorities as "others" and the whites as the real "Canadians."

Looking into some specific issues, researchers have pointed out that in the media, ethnic minorities have been presented as threats, and they are portrayed as inscrutable and incompatible with the dominant culture. The depiction of Asian population in Canada has also been examined by previous research. For example, news reports consistently reported the Asian crime wave in Ottawa (Riley 1993). In the TV news documentaries, the Asians were portrayed as threat to national resources and that they are social problem facing Canadians (Dunn and Mahtani 2001). Reviewing a large number of articles, Greenberg (2000) found that several newspapers were very critical of the refugees where they were portrayed as disease-carrying people who posed threat to the Canadians both in terms of physical and economic well-being. Obviously, media coverage of Islam-related issues has changed dramatically since the September 11, 2001; not only did the news coverage increased significantly but also the way the Islam was depicted has changed as well. The "War on Terrorism" has been the powerful slogan for the rise of Islamophobia (fear or hatred of Islam) in the Western world including Canada. This Islamophobia was reflected negatively in the media about the Muslim populations; the most significant Islamic stereotype is the radicalized insurgency that leads to "jihad" or holy war against the West, which is exemplified by the media as violent act. For example, the character of Sayid Jarrah on ABC's show *Lost*.

3.9. Elimination of racial discrimination

> *I have fought against white domination, and I have fought against black domination. I have cherished the ideal of a democratic and free society in which all persons will live together in harmony with equal opportunities. It is an ideal which I hope to live for, and to see realised. But my Lord, if needs be, it is an ideal for which I am prepared to die.*
>
> —Nelson Mandela, defence statement during the Rivonia Trial 1964. Also repeated during the closing of his speech delivered in Cape Town on the day he was released from prison twenty-seven years later, on February 11, 1990.[48]

We have not forgotten the well-known event of Sharpeville tragedy or Sharpeville massacre, which captured worldwide attention. The event involved police firing and killing sixty-nine people at a peaceful demonstration against the apartheid "pass laws" in Sharpeville, South Africa, on March 21, 1960. After six years of that event, the International Day for the Elimination of Racial Discrimination was established as remembrance day of racial discrimination.

The UN General Assembly called on the international community to increase its efforts to eliminate all forms of racial discrimination when it proclaimed the day as a UN Day of observance in 1966. It also called on all world states and organisations to participate in a program of action to combat racism and racial discrimination in 1983. It held the World Conference against Racism and Racial Discrimination, Xenophobia, and Related Intolerance in 2001.

Racial and ethnic discrimination occur on a daily basis, hindering progress for millions of people around the world. Racism and intolerance can take various forms—from denying individuals the basic principles of equality to fuelling ethnic hatred that may lead to genocide—all of which can destroy lives and fracture communities. Since the Sharpeville massacre, substantial progress has been made in the struggle against racism. The apartheid system in South Africa has been dismantled. Racist laws and practices have been abolished in many countries, and an international framework for fighting racism, guided by the International Convention on the Elimination of Racial Discrimination, has been established. The Convention is now nearing universal ratification. Yet still, in all regions, too many individuals, communities and societies suffer from the injustice and stigma that racism brings.[49]

On March 21, 2013, the Honourable Jason Kenney, minister of Citizenship, Immigration, and Multiculturalism, issued the following statement on the International Day for the Elimination of Racial Discrimination:

> *The International Day for the Elimination of Racial Discrimination is an opportunity for Canadians to join with other freedom-loving people around the world in reaffirming our commitment to reject and eliminate all forms of racial discrimination. While we can be proud of our own country's successful pluralism, we need to ensure that all Canadian citizens reject extremism, do not import ancient enmities, and continue to embrace Canada's tradition of ordered liberty, which guarantees the equality of all citizens under the law. Through initiatives such as the Office of Religious Freedom, our Government will also continue to condemn acts of racial hatred around the world. These acts often accompany the targeting of religious communities. As Minister of Citizenship, Immigration and Multiculturalism, I encourage all Canadians to continue to uphold the fundamental values of our free, democratic and peacefully pluralist society and to reject all forms of unjust discrimination.*[50]

Canada Union of Public Employees (CUPE) released statement on the occasion of International Day for the Elimination of Racial Discrimination and has issued a reminder of the struggles and challenges that racialized workers and Aboriginal peoples have endured in Canada. The organization has emphasized the fact that Canada's labour force is made up of diverse groups of workers who experience discrimination and inequality in employment. For example, racialized workers earn 81 percent of what the rest of Canadians earn, and Aboriginal workers earn only 71 percent. These workers are concentrated in lower-paying and often precarious jobs. Despite this, the Haoper government seems determined to increase inequality and nurture an environment that predisposes workers to racist forms of discrimination and maltreatment. This is clearly noticeable in the Temporary Foreign Workers Program (TFWP). Temporary foreign workers are paid less than other workers and are denied basic human rights and rights of citizenship. They are frequently subjected to harassment, abuse, unsafe working conditions, and extreme exploitation. They tend to suffer in silence for fear of deportation. Furthermore, the government has increased resources for conservative priorities that perpetuate racial profiling and criminalization of racialized and Aboriginal communities.[51]

Racism still exits. People worldwide experience systemic racism and oppression, direct or indirect racism, which includes acts of violence, hate crimes, and harassment. Frank Dimant, CEO of B'nai Brith Canada, released a statement to mark International Day for the Elimination of Racial Discrimination as follows:

> *Today, as we mark the International Day for the Elimination of Racial Discrimination, a day that is supposed to celebrate an end to racial dissension, we are mindful of the ongoing atrocities being carried out against religious minorities. Recently, we have decried the violence against Christian communities in Pakistan and Nigeria. One year ago today, members of the Jewish community in France were burying those tragically murdered in the Toulouse. Women across communities are threatened with violence and intimidation on a daily basis. So today must be more a day of action than one of celebration. Too many around the world are depending on such a renewed commitment in counter racial discrimination and extremism. With institutions such as the newly established Office of Religious Freedoms created by the Canadian Government, Canadians can and must make a difference.[52]*

In the year 2013, the theme on racism was "Racism and Sports," chosen by the Office of the UN High Commissioner for Human Rights to highlight the problem of racism in sports, which remains a disturbing occurrence in many parts of the world, as well as to raise awareness of the role sports can play in combating racism and racial discrimination. Secretary-general of the United Nations Ban ki-moon has the following messages on the occasion of International Day for the Elimination of Racial Discrimination 2013: "We must join forces to end racism, and sport can help reach this goal. On this International Day, let us recommit to ending racial discrimination and realizing our vision of justice, equality and freedom from fear for all."[53]

No matter what our origin is—French, English, Irish, Italian, German, Spanish, Russian, Chinese, South Asian, or whatever, but most importantly we are proudly Canadian. At the same time we are tremendously proud of our cultures, heritages and achievements and we will continue to build upon our commitment to working together.

—The Author

4

South Asian Immigrants

By definition used by South Asian Association for Regional Cooperation (SAARC), South Asia comprises India, Pakistan, Bangladesh, Sri Lanka, Maldives, Nepal, Bhutan and Afghanistan. Most South Asians are immigrants or descendants from these countries, but immigrants from South Asian communities established during British colonial times also include those from East and South Africa, Guyana, Trinidad and Tobago, Fiji, and Mauritius, and others come from Britain, the United States, and Europe (Buchignani 2012; *Canadian Encyclopedia*). South Asian population comprises people from a diversity of ethnic backgrounds that include Bangladeshi, Bengali (West Bengal, India), East Indian,[54] Gujrati, Hindu, Ismaili, Kashmiri, Nepali, Pakistani, Punjabi, Sikh, Sinhalese, Sri Lankan, and Tamil ancestry. South Asians may have been born in Canada, on the Indian subcontinent, in the Caribbean, in Africa, in Great Britain, or elsewhere. Thus, the South Asian population could have been defined as visible minority, composed of two groups in terms of their birthplace; one group born in foreign countries and the other group born in Canada.

In terms of ancestral background, South Asian immigrants are very diverse, and many of them came from various parts of the Indian subcontinent. Since the mid-1800s, people from India migrated to Fiji, Mauritius, South Africa, and the Caribbean to work primarily in agriculture as indentured labourers. During the period between 1905 and 1908, some five thousand South Asians, predominantly Punjabi

Sikhs, entered British Columbia where they worked mainly in railroad construction and in the logging and lumber industries (Kelly Tran, Jennifer Kaddatz, and Paul Allard 2005). Historically, the South Asian immigrants in Canada remained very small in numbers during the early 1900s. By the mid-1900s (around 1960s and 1970s), the South Asian community evolved from a small homogenous group to relatively a large and diverse population in terms of birthplace origins, ethnicities, religious, and languages.

4.1. South Asian diaspora

The term "diaspora" refers to a dispersion of a people from their original homeland. It was originally used to refer to the dispersion of the Jews from Palestine, following the Babylonians' conquest of the Judean Kingdom in the sixth century BC. Until fairly recently, it was used to refer to Jews living outside of modern-day Israel. Now it is used more widely for all the movements of people away from their homelands. The South Asian uses this term to refer to people who originate from the following Asian countries: Afghanistan, Bangladesh, Bhutan, India, Maldives, Myanmar,[55] Pakistan, Nepal, and Sri Lanka.

The story of the South Asian Diaspora began after 1834, the year of abolition of slavery in the European colonies. The end of slavery created the need for new source of labour in various British colonies. Among the vast labour source in the British colonies, three-fourths of them were in India. Thousands of Indians were shipped as indentured labourers to the tea, coffee, rubber, and sugar plantations in Ceylon, Malaya, Mauritius, Fiji, Trinidad, Guyana, Jamaica, and British Honduras (Belize). Others were sent to Africa to work on the first African railroad, from the Kenyan coast to Lake Victoria. Sikhs went to Singapore and Hong Kong to be policemen, and Nepali Gurkhas and some Sikhs were recruited as soldiers (Haroon Siddiqui 2004). Majority of labourer came from north-central and northeastern parts of India, and a sizeable minority came from the Tamil and Telugu-speaking regions of the south.

4.2. The early South Asian immigrants

South Asian immigration to Canada began at the beginning of the twentieth century. That was the year of the coronation of Edward VII in 1902, which marked the first contact of South Asians in British Columbia, Canada (the then colony of British Empire). The tradition, in fact, was started with Queen Victoria's diamond jubilee celebration 1887, when representatives from across the British Empire came to London for the ceremony (Buchignani et al. 1985), including more than a thousand Indian troops that travelled to London via Canada (Rose Baaba Folson, edited, 2004). Although many Indians had already migrated to other British colonies as indentured labourers during the nineteenth century, the first South Asian (i.e., Indians) migrants to Canada arrived in British Columbia in and around 1903 (Buchignani et al. 1985). Interestingly, these Indian migrant workers had been living in BC without much notice due to a number of factors: (a) their numbers were low, (b) the strong anti-Chinese and anti-Japanese sentiment in BC, and (c) the fact that Indians were British subjects migrating from one British colony to another. Unlike other radicalized groups, Indians had a legal right due to British colonialism. Indian population as such increased and became more visible. These Indians were men, and the majority of them were Sikhs.

According to the government of Canada (at that time known as Dominion government), the numbers Indians arrived in Canada between 1904 and 1908 (Sampat Mehta 1973) are as follows:

Fiscal Year	Numbers
1904–05	45
1905–06	387
1906–07	2124
1907–08	2623

The negative sentiment of "colour" presence of South Asians developed among the white British Columbia population, which resulted in a ban of any further South Asians entering the country in early 1908. It is worth noting that this ban was not officially lifted until 1947. Literatures reveal that the Sikh men living through the 1930s depression passed hard time, yet they did not line up in the soup kitchen but helped each other within the community.

4.2.1. The *Komagata Maru* incident[56]

"If we are strong and have faith in life and its richness of surprises, and hold the rudder steadily in our hands, I am sure we will sail into quiet and pleasant water for our old age," said the famous British travel writer Freya Stark.

His words came true what happened with 376 passengers aboard the Japanese ship liner *Komagata Maru* in the journey from India to Vancouver when the unfortunate events took place at Burrard Inlet between May 23 and July 23, 1914. The journey of *Komagata Maru* engraved its name in the history of struggles for justice and freedom. The shocking history of *Komagata Maru* is as follows:

Komagata Maru was hired by Gurdit Sing, a Sikh entrepreneur, who traveled to bring 376 passengers (comprising 340 Sikhs, 24 Muslims, and 12 Hindus) from India to Canada. These migrants from British India[57] believed that, as British subjects, it was their right to settle anywhere in the British Empire given the fact that Britain had assured them of their equality in any county within the empire. However, the Canadian government did not allow any passengers to land, and the ship was forced to anchor half a mile off the Vancouver's shore. Unfortunately, the dramatic standoff lasted for two months, and the ship was sent back to India with no provisions from the Canadian government. When theses migrants returned to India, there was an armed standoff with British colonial government. It was so sad that twenty-six people died in that incident.

It is important to note that there was a strong prejudice against nonwhite residents in Vancouver in those days. As an example, an anti-Oriental riots occurred in 1907. In the same year, about nine hundred Sikhs arrived in Vancouver aboard the Canadian Pacific steamer *Monteagle*. Hearing this news, white Canadians reacted badly. Many white residents thought that the new arrivals must not be permitted to get off the ship. In fact, the *Komagata Maru* did not depart from India but from Hong Kong. The ship was scheduled to leave in March, but it did not because Gurdit Singh was arrested for selling tickets for an illegal voyage. He was later released on bail and given permission by the governor of Hong Kong to set sail, and the ship left Hong Kong on April 4 with 165 passengers. Other passengers boarded at Shanghai port. The ship departed from Yokohama on May 3 with additional 376 passengers, which arrived in Burrard Inlet, near Vancouver, on May 23, 1914. Later, Bhagwan Singh, Barkatullah, and Balwant Singh, who were the members of the Indian Nationalist revolutionary group, joined the ship en route.

When the *Komagata Maru* arrived in Canadian waters, it was not allowed to dock in the port because the premier of British Columbia, Richard McBride, gave a statement that the passengers would not be allowed to disembark. Meanwhile, a "Shore Committee" had been formed with Hussain Rahim and Sohan Lal Pathak. Protest meetings were held in Canada and the USA. At one such meeting, held in Dominion Hall, Vancouver, it was decided that if the passengers were not allowed to get off, Indo-Canadians should follow them back to India to start a rebellion.

The situation turned worst when Vancouver mayor Truman Baxter organised an anti-Asian rally where the prominent politician H. H. Stevens spoke in that rally and said that he had no ill feeling against people coming from Asia, but he reaffirmed that the national life of Canada would not permit any large degree of immigration from Asia. He believed in principle of a white country and a white British Columbia. His speech was applauded loudly by the crowed. Sadly, all the passengers were declared inadmissible by a board of inquiry.

Meanwhile, the Vancouver Maritime Museum picked up the story: "In the early morning hours of July 19, 1914, *Sea Lion*, with 35 immigration officers armed with rifles borrowed from the Seaforth Highlanders, and 125 Vancouver Police officers approached *Komagata Maru* to force the vessel from Vancouver harbour. The angry passengers resisted any effort to board anyone on their ship. But their effort was in vain. Manning the rail, an armed group shouted and threatened to board the tug. Moreover, *Sea Lion*'s captain brought her in close, grappled and then tied on to *Komagata Maru*. Battle started between passengers and police as one man with an axe chopped at *Sea Lion*'s line. Finally, as a gunman aboard the ship opened fire on the tug, the line was cut and the tug retreated."

Canadian government ordered the harbour tug, *Sea Lion*, to push the ship *Komagata Maru* out back to its homeward journey. Finally, the new Royal Canadian Navy was called in. On July 23, 1914, the *Komagata Maru* was turned around and forced to sail back to Asia because the ship had violated the exclusion laws as the authority claimed. In fact, the passengers did not have the required funds, and they had not sailed directly from India, which made it more difficult for entry because this was another entry requirement. However, only twenty-four of its passengers who already had resident status in Canada had been allowed to disembark. But more than three hundred others were sent back to India.

This incident raised tensions among members of Vancouver's Sikh community. Some did not like a local immigration official name William Hopkinson who once served in Calcutta Police Force. He spoke Hindi fluently. Hopkinson came to Vancouver in 1907 and was hired by the Canadian government as an immigration inspector and interpreter. He was also responsible to monitor the activities of East Indian extremists living in British Columbia and to develop a network of pro-British Sikh informants. Apparently, he disguised himself as a Sikh named Narain Singh and gathered information. He had been one of the men aboard the *Sea Lion*. Ironically, a man named Mewa Singh shot Hopkinson to death at the provincial courthouse in Vancouver. As a consequence, he was hanged for the murder. A community hall in the Ross Street Sikh Gurdwara is named for him.

The *Komagata Maru* story continued further. On September 26, 1914, the ship, with its passengers on board was on the sea for four months and reached Calcutta, capital of West Bengal, province of India. In Calcutta, a British gunboat stopped the ship and held the passengers as prisoners. Later they were taken to a place called Baj Baj, a Calcutta suburb, and told them that they would be sent to Punjab on a special train. But many of the passengers were reluctant to go to Punjab; rather they wanted to stay in Calcutta. The reason was that the passengers wanted to place the *Guru Granth Sahib*, which they brought with them on their journey in *Gurdwara* (Sikh place of worship) in Calcutta. But the British officials did not allow it and insisted the passengers to go to Punjab instead. When the passengers rebelled and marched toward Calcutta, they were forced back to Baj Baj. Passengers refused to go back. Eventually, a police officer attacked Gurdit Singh, who led the passengers to organise the protest, but another passenger stopped the officer. Then gunfire broke out as a result. Sadly, twenty passengers were killed, and another nine were wounded. This incident was known as the Baj Baj Riot. Gurdit Singh managed to escape and lived in hiding till 1922. However, Mahatma Gandhi urged Gurdit Singh to surrender to the authority; he did surrender. He was imprisoned for five years.

The story of *Komagata Maru* was written in the history book and rightfully honoured in India and Canada. In 1951 the government of the new Republic of India established its first monument at Baj Baj, Calcutta, to commemorate the massacre there. In 1989, in Vancouver, a plaque commemorating the seventy-fifth anniversary of the departure of the *Komagata Maru* was placed in the Sikh Gurdwara (temple) in Vancouver. A plaque commemorating the eightieth anniversary of the arrival of the *Komagata Maru* was placed in the Vancouver harbour in 1994.

The sensational story of *Komagata Maru* was remembered at all time by many. On May 23, 2006, ninety-two years to the day after the arrival of the ship, the *Vancouver Sun* published an article by the title: "Descendants of passengers aboard the ill-fated *Komagata Maru* want to open discussions with the federal government about a formal apology and possible compensation over Canada's racist immigration laws early this century."

4.2.2. Continuous Journey Regulation

Komagata Maru incident was so significant that in 1908, Canada introduced the "continuous journey" regulation to its Immigration Act. Under this new regulation, all immigrants were required to come to Canada by direct journey from their country of origin. About twenty-six thousand South Asians entered in Canada a year before this regulation was enforced, although only a few dozens managed to enter in Canada. The Canada court exercised the right to bar entry to the passengers and thus did not allow disembarking.

This is for the first time that a ship carrying immigrants was turned away from Canadian shores; that ship was *Komagata Maru*. Unlike *Komagata Maru* incident, when a ship with 347 European refugees arrived in Halifax in 1948, it was allowed to anchor with warm reception. Moreover, there was a special display at Pier 21, the national immigration museum in Halifax, dedicated to these Europeans' voyage and arrival (Kazimi 2011). The Continuous Journey Regulation did not mention about race or nationality, thus applicable to all immigrants, yet it was an open secret policy that the regulation applied only to people from British India. At that time, Canadian Pacific did run a very lucrative shipping line between Vancouver and Calcutta, but the Canadian government forced the company to stop this service. As a result, it was impossible to travel to Canada from India. One could argue that this was an under-the-table policy that Canada undertook to enforce a hidden "white Canada" policy. It is worth noting that when restrictions on Asian immigration were enacted, Canada accepted large volume of European immigrants. Statistics show that over four hundred thousand Europeans were accepted in the year1913 alone—a number that was unsurpassed at that day. What was learned is that the purpose of chartering the *Komagata Maru* by Gurdit Singh was to challenge the Continuous Journey Regulation and to open the shore for immigration from British India to Canada.[58]

4.2.3. Government of Canada apologized[59]

The government of Canada created the community historical recognition program to provide grant and contribution funding for community projects linked to wartime measures and immigration restrictions and a national historical recognition program to fund federal initiatives. The announcement was made on June 23, 2006, when Prime Minister Stephen Harper apologized in the House of Commons for the head tax against Chinese immigrants.

On August 6, 2006, Prime Minister Harper made a speech at the Ghadri Babiyan da Mela (Festival of the Gadhar Party) in Surrey, British Columbia, where he stated that the government of Canada acknowledged the *Komagata Maru* incident and announced the government's commitment to "undertake consultations with the Indo-Canadian community on how best to recognize this sad moment in Canada's history." On April 3, 2008, Ruby Dhalla, MP for Brampton–Springdale, tabled motion 469 (M-469) in the House of Commons, which read, "That, in the opinion of the House, the government should officially apologize to the Indo-Canadian community and to the individuals impacted in the 1914 *Komagata Maru* incident, in which passengers were prevented from landing in Canada."

On May 10, 2008, Jason Kenney, secretary of state (Multiculturalism and Canadian Identity), announced that the Indo-Canadian community would be able to apply for up to $2.5 million in grants and contributions funding to commemorate the *Komagata Maru* incident. Following further debate on May 15, 2008, Dhalla's motion was passed by the House of Commons. On May 23, 2008, the Legislative Assembly of British Columbia unanimously passed a resolution "that this Legislature apologizes for the events of May 23, 1914, when 376 passengers of the *Komagata Maru*, stationed off Vancouver harbour, were denied entry by Canada. The House deeply regrets that the passengers, who sought refuge in our country and our province, were turned away without benefit of the fair and impartial treatment befitting a society where people of all cultures are welcomed and accepted."

On August 3, 2008, Prime Minister Stephen Harper appeared at the Thirteenth Annual Ghadri Babiyan Da Mela (festival) in Surrey, British Columbia, to issue an apology for the *Komagata Maru* incident. He said, in response to the House of Commons motion calling for an apology by the government, "On behalf of the government of Canada, I am officially conveying as prime minister that apology." Some members of the Sikh community were unsatisfied with the apology, as they expected it to be made in Parliament. Secretary of State Jason Kenney said, "The apology has been given and it won't be repeated, thus settling the matter for the federal government." The apology was due since long, and the Canadians, Indo-Canadians in particular, expected it much earlier. Canadians appreciated government's apology for the historical *Komagata Maru* incident and marked as positive measure towards eliminating discrimination.

4.2.4. Lifting of barriers

Canada eventually had lifted its ban on Indian immigration in 1945; after one year, the United States did the same. Canada's immigration barriers were gradually dismantled during a very long period between 1947 and 1970. As a result, the Indian population in Canada increased from a few thousands to sixty-seven thousand in 1971 (Jain 1993). At the same time, some restrictions on the type of immigrants who could come to Canada were introduced, which were governed by the need for labour. In 1967 Canada permitted "in-land" sponsorship, and also a provision was made for visitors to apply for landed immigrant status while in Canada. The intrinsic idea of these attempts was mainly to attract European to come (Wood 1983). But the outcome was not as expected by Canadian government. In fact, more non-Europeans than Europeans took the advantage of the provision. The unexpected influx of non-Europeans created panic among white Canadians. As a result, the provision was withdrawn in 1973, and the regulations were further changed, which required prearranged employment for independent or nominated applicants in jobs. Interesting, in the process, the Canadian employer has to establish that no Canadians citizens was available for the job (ibid.). Subsequently, a second wave of demand for blue-collar sector jobs in the labour market becomes evident, leading to changes in Canada's immigration policy. Unfortunately, such policy change affected Indian immigrants because higher caste Indians were not willing to work in blue-collar jobs (Ghosh 1983).

Gender effect is another important factor among the South Asian immigrants because women, at that time, were considered mainly as "dependents" and were barred from applying for independent landed immigrant status. Literature suggests that South Asian women were seen as a threat to the white Canadians because it was commonly believed that South Asian men with women would grow families, which in turn would become communities, and that ethnic communities would likely to threaten the image of white country (Dua 2000). Since South Asian women were only spouse and daughters of men, not the productive labourers, which is in contrast with other nonwhite immigrants—for example, the Black

Caribbean women or Filipinas who were domestics, nurses, and nannies by profession—these women were considered as independent migrants and were not allowed to bring spouses or children. It was argued that South Asian women did not fit into Canada's nation-making project designed to meet the continued demand of immigrants aimed at meeting labour demand and populating its vast land.

4.3. South Asian population in Canada in 2011

According to the 2011 National Household Survey, South Asians in Canada now comprise the country's largest visible minority group, surpassing the Chinese population in Canada for the first time. About 1.6 million South Asians live in Canada, representing 4.8 percent of the total Canadian population, or 25 percent of the total visible minority population in Canada. South Asians are the largest and one of the fastest-growing visible minority groups in Canada. The number of South Asians in Canada almost doubled from 671,000 in 1996 to 1,262,865 in 2006 and 1,567,400 in 2011. The Chinese (the second-largest group) is comprised of slightly over 1.3 million, which is accounted for 21 percent of visible minority population. Whereas, the black population (third-largest group) is comprised of slightly below one million, which is made up of 15 percent of the visible minority population in 2011.

Not only does South Asian population have the largest share among visible minorities in Canada overall, but they also have the largest share in Toronto, Calgary, Edmonton, and Hamilton. The table below shows top-three visible minorities in selected metropolitan areas in 2011.

Visible Minority Population and Top-Three VM Groups; Selected Census Metropolitan Areas, Canada, 2011

Geographical Location	Total Population	Visible Minorities	Top-Three VM by Rank
Canada	32,852,325	6,264,755 (19.1%)	1. South Asian 2. Chinese 3. Black
Toronto	5,521,235	2,596,420 (47%)	1. South Asian 2. Chinese 3. Black

Montreal	3,752,475	762,325 (20.3%)	1. Black 2. Arab 3. Latin American
Vancouver	2,280,695	1,030,335 (45.2%)	1. Chinese 2. South Asian 3. Filipino
Ottawa-Gatineau	1,215,735	234,015 (19.2%)	1. Black 2. Arab 3. Chinese
Calgary	1,199,125	337,420 (28.1%)	**1. South Asian** 2. Chinese 3. Filipino
Edmonton	1,139,585	254,990 (22.4%)	**1. South Asian** 2. Chinese 3. Filipino
Winnipeg	714,635	140,770 (19.7%)	1. Filipino 2. South Asian 3. Black
Hamilton	708,175	101,600 (14.3%)	**1. South Asian** 2. Black 3. Chinese

Source: Statistics Canada, National Household Survey, 2011

In 2011, around 1,204,900 South Asians were in the Canadian workforce. This number represented one-quarter of the total visible minority workforce, or 4 percent of the total workforce in Canada. The largest majority of the South Asian workforce is concentrated in Ontario and British Columbia (82 percent), and almost 10 percent in Alberta, and only a little higher than 5 percent in Quebec. The National Capital Region (NCR) has a South Asian workforce population of slightly higher than 2 percent. The large majority of South Asians worked in one of Canada's thirty-three census metropolitan areas. Toronto and Vancouver accounted for 70 percent of South Asian workers.

Overall, among youths aged fifteen to twenty-four, South Asians had similar workforce representation compared to those for nonvisible minority Canadians (14 percent and 15 percent, respectively). However, South Asians has a higher representation than the nonvisible minority workforce not only in the twenty-five-to-forty-four age group (33 percent versus 30 percent) but also in the forty-five-to-sixty-four age group (22 percent versus 19 percent). In contrast, South Asians has a much lower representation than the nonvisible minority Canadians in the sixty-five-to-seventy-four age group (5 percent versus 10 percent). This age group of South Asian population is the first generation of immigrants who struggled very hard to settle in Canada, as they faced a lot of barriers, especially in the job market. One could argue that they retired from (among many others) work out of frustration of being discriminated in the job market and due to work fatigue as they grew older.

South Asians in Canada are more likely than the nonvisible minority population to have a university degree. In 2011, 25 percent of South Asians in Canada had either a degree at bachelor level or above compared to 18.6 percent of individuals in the nonvisible minority population had the similar degree. Proportionately, more South Asians have a certificate or diploma below bachelor level compared to nonvisible minorities in Canada (6 percent versus 4 percent). In contrast, South Asians who have no certificate, diploma, or degree are proportionately lower than the nonvisible minorities in Canada (14 percent versus 21 percent), which in fact goes favourably to South Asians' educational credibility.

4.4. The skilled South Asian diaspora

South Asian countries have been the sources of skilled, semiskilled, and low-skilled migrants to the world markets. India, Pakistan, Bangladesh, and Sri Lanka are the major suppliers of engineers, doctors, IT professionals, educators, scientists, and accountants to many countries of the world. These South Asian diasporas have been playing an important role in their source economies by contributing in ways such as long-term investments, technology, and knowledge transfer, influencing host country companies and investors to establish joint ventures and technology licensing arrangements, philanthropic contributions to communities in the home country, influencing public opinion about their home countries through the popular media, politics, and cultural channels, and so on (Rupa Chanda 2008). All these facilities and avenues provide platforms to promote trade, commerce, and investment between host and source countries. They also serve effective links in keeping overseas South Asians connected to their roots. The encouraging fact is that the governments in South Asian countries are now recognizing these avenues to flourish. Some governments have also taken targeted initiatives to institutionalise diaspora linkages and to utilise them more meaningfully and effectively (ibid.). The South Asian diaspora has been spread across numerous regions and countries around the world such as

- Persian Gulf countries like Saudi Arabia, Kuwait, and the United Arab Emirates
- African countries like Uganda, Kenya, Nigeria, and South Africa
- South East Asian Economies—predominantly Singapore and Malaysia
- Major industrialized economies—the United States, Canada, the United Kingdom, Australia, and New Zealand

It is important to note that many unskilled and some skilled migrant labours have headed towards the oil-rich Gulf countries in recent years, and the bulk of skilled migrants from South Asia have gone to the OECD countries, particularly the English-speaking industrialized countries of the United States, Canada, Australia, United Kingdom, and New Zealand.

In terms of macroeconomic impact, remittances constitute a significant contribution of their GDPs and foreign exchange earnings in South Asian countries. In absolute terms, India receives the largest amount of remittances in the world; estimated at US$27 billion in 2006–2007. Pakistan and Bangladesh received remittances of nearly US$5 billion each in 2006–2007. Remittances have grown twelvefold for India between 1991 and 2006, more than sixfold for Bangladesh and Sri Lanka, and over twofold in the case of Pakistan between 2002 and 2007. The table below shows the huge growth in remittances that have taken place since 1990 for all four South Asian countries.

Remittance inflows into South Asian Countries (millions of US dollars)

Year	India	Bangladesh	Pakistan	Sri Lanka
1990–1991	2068	764	NA	362
1995–1996	8507	1217	NA	675
2001–2002	15398	2501	2390	984
2002–2003	16387	3062	4237	1097
2003–2004	21608	3372	3871	1205
2004–2005	20525	3848	4168	1350
2005–2006	24102	4802	4600	1736
2006–2007	27195	4925	4988	2068

Source: RBI Handbook of Statistics on the Indian Economy, Foreign Exchange Policy Department; Bangladesh Bank; State Bank of Pakistan; Central Bank of Sri Lanka, Statistics-External Sector.

In all these four countries, remittances constituted more than 30 percent of total export earnings and financed at least 18 percent of these countries imports, and the remittances far exceeded foreign aid and foreign investment in these four countries (ibid.). Moreover, certain initiatives have been taken by the South Asian governments to provide institutional structure and support to enable the flow of remittances through the financial system. For example, the Ministry of Overseas Indian affairs has developed an electronic remittance gateway to make it easier for overseas Indians to remit money to India. Remitter cards have been introduced in Bangladesh to encourage overseas Bangladeshis to remit money to Bangladesh through the branches of nationalized banks and through exchange centres in Bangladesh. Also, investment promotion bodies have been set up in the Sylhet district of Bangladesh, which is home to many expatriates.

The Overseas Pakistani Investment Conference has enabled Pakistanis abroad to invest in Pakistan. Yet South Asian countries do not have very well-developed institutional infrastructures to handle their overseas population and to leverage their assets, expertise, and knowledge for the benefit of their home countries' economies. In contrast, China has much better and well-developed policies to encourage overseas Chinese to return to China as well as to leverage the assets and human capital. The Chinese government encourages overseas Chinese scholars and innovators to come to China on short-term visits under special programs. The government also uses its network of overseas centres and consulates to disseminate information about various opportunities in all sectors of the economy in China (ibid.).

4.5. South Asian arts and music

The Indian subcontinent has a rich tradition of cultural and ethical practices. It is also rich in ancient literature in multiple languages. Despite century-old political divisiveness, music, dance, ritual customs, modes of worship, and literary ideals are similar throughout the subcontinent. Neither political clashes nor shifting boundaries could negate this rich mosaic that is the Indian subcontinent.

South Asian arts and dances exhibit similarities in composition and characteristics. Sculpture also draws its inspiration from the arts. Also, for the rhythmic movements and exposition of emotion in dance, music is essential. Furthermore, knowledge of literature and rhetoric is equally essential, as it serves as the background for the flavour (*rasa*) to be expressed in music, dance, sculpture, or painting. The folk arts were closely linked with the elite arts. For example, tribal group dances shared common elements with classical art, dance, and music. Thus, all the arts are closely linked together. It is also a known fact that artists always enjoyed a high position in South Asian societies. Poets, musicians, and dancers were held in high esteem in the royal court.[60]

South Asia has always been subjected to strong foreign influences, which has affected people in all walks of life. For example, Indo-European people known as Aryans brought to the Indian subcontinent the hymns known as Vedas. Hinduism is believed to have its roots in Vedic hymns. A very rich body of secular literature was written first in Sanskrit and later in other languages such as Tamil, Kashmiri, Gujarati, and Bengali. Music and dance played a very important role in the religious and secular life of the South Asian people, and the Hindu religion played a key role in the dissemination of art and culture throughout Southeast Asia. The two Hindu epics, the *Ramayana* and the *Mahabharata*, were the principal conduit.[61]

Indian music was introduced in Canada by few musicians who visited Canada in 1930s. The first and the most prominent one was Uday Sankar. Other prominent ones were Rahul Sariputra and Swami Anand Veetarag. Later, dancers and musicians from India came to Montreal to perform at the India Pavilion at Expo 67. Gradually, more Indian artists came to Canada; among them were T. K. Murthy, Ali Akbar khan, Ashish Khan, Ustad Amjad Ali Khan, Ravi Shankar, Pranesh Khan, Sankaranarayanan, and the dancers Sujata and Asoka. During 1970s, Indian music earned more popularity through various performances in Canada's big cities. Eventually, Canadian universities started offering courses on Indian music—theory, vocal, and instrumental techniques.

It is worth noting that many Canadian musicians went to India to learn Indian music. Among them were Welford Russell, Rosette Renshaw, Harry Somers, Gilles Treblay, Teresa Stratas, Bailey and John Bird, Charles and George Sippi, and many others. Walter Kaufmann was the music director during 1938–46 for All India Radio in Bombay. He wrote several books on Indian music and related subject. As Indian community grew, Indian Canadians established several musical communities, organisations, and clubs, and organised musical events such as classical ragas, Shabd Kirtan, solo chanting of scriptural verses, Karnatic music, Bhajan, Gazals, folks, and many others. (For more information, see the site http://www.thecanadianencyclopedia.com/en/article/india-emc/.)

Many Indian music and dance schools were opened by local Indian Canadians and by artists who came to Canada from India and eventually settled in Canada. The Shastri Indo-Canadian Institute is one of the highly acclaimed institutions in Canada that promotes understanding between India and Canada through academic activities including research and exchanges. The institute's program of performing arts grants contributes to the development arts and music along with other major fields of study.

Indian dance plays a key role in the cultural heritage in the subcontinent. Indian dances such as folk dance, classical dance, and modern dance are very popular in Canada. Introduction of Indian dances in Canada began during 1960s and 1970s by prominent Indian dancers like Rina Singh (Katthak dancer) and Menaka Thakkar (Bharatanatyam/Odissi dancer). In course of time, Indian dance was acknowledged as classical art by the arts council of Canada and Canadian audience at large. As a result, several artists specialized in Odissi, Monipuri, Bharatanatyam, and Katthak dancers came to Canada and settled. Their works resulted creation of several dance companies in Canada such as Lata Pada's Sympradaya based in Mississauga and Manta Nakra's Kala Bharati in Montreal and many others. The remarkable contribution of Thakkar towards achieving Canada's recognition of Indian dance as an authentic and bona fide dance system is worth noting. His work on the contemporary expressions of traditional dance genres opened new avenue for blending of Indian traditional forms and the genre of new Indian dance into the Canadian mainstream. Based on his concept, Kala Nidhi Fine Arts (an organisation of his sister Sudha Thakkar) presented an international dance festival in 1993. (For more information, see the site http://www.thecanadianencyclopedia.com/en/article/india-classical-dance/.)

4.6. Societal norm, religiosity, and language

South Asian Canadians are of widely varying backgrounds, yet they have a very strong social, cultural, and community bond where they maintain an extended family ties, kinship, and community relations. South Asians, even those who were born in Canada, have close ties with their family living in their home country or the birthplace of their parents or grandparents. This family contact, however, seems to be weaker; drop from first generation to second generation. According to Ethnic Diversity Survey (EDS) 2002, the proportion of those keeping in touch with family members in their countries of origin dropped to 75 percent of second generation from 88 percent from the first generation.

As already mentioned, although South Asians come from different countries of origin and religious affiliations, they have a shared cultural value system that is characterized by a strong family bond (Assanand S., Dias M., Richardson E., and Waxler-Morrison 1990). Family is very important to South Asians. Unlike the individualistic values system in the Canadian host society, South Asian families emphasize interdependence among family members across the life span. The seniors usually live in predominantly family-oriented households; and the majority of them live with spouse or family members. Valuing their family networks, they also give great importance to their ethnocultural community attachment. For example, when many of the earliest South Asian immigrants faced economic hardship, social discrimination, and loneliness, they looked for South Asian community support. The community, in return, worked together and provided food, housing, jobs, financial help, and friendship ties (Buchignani et al. 1985).

It is quite likely that the younger generation is different than previous generations in terms of attitudes, lifestyles, and even values and perspective of life as a result of growing up in the Western world. For example, younger generations are expected to defer the authority to make major life decisions to older family members, believed to have the wisdom and experience to guide children's day-to-day affairs and life decisions. Evidence suggests, however, that although young adults acculturated into Canadian society may attempt to express individual interests and goals and often challenge parental authority, South Asian younger adults tend to practice and preserve South Asian parental cultural values and norms (Kwak and Berry 2001). Authors also found that South Asian parents and young adults maintain their cultural identity, value system, hierarchical family structure, and traditional customs after immigration. Mate selection and marriage seem to be the key factor in young adults retaining their culture of origin (ibid.).

Like linguistic traditions, South Asians keep strong attachment with their ethnic customs and traditions, such as food, outfit/clothing, holidays and celebrations, etc. Religion, another aspect of diversity, adds vibrancy to the South Asian cultural mosaic in Canada. The Indian subcontinent is the root of three major religions: Hinduism, Buddhism, and Sikhism. South Asia is also the home of a very large population of Muslim faith, predominantly in India, Pakistan, and Bangladesh. South Asia is also the home of a Christian population, although relatively small in proportion compared to other four religions. South Asians of different religious faith have settled in different parts of Canada. Religious affiliation and ethnic origins are closely associated; Punjabi ancestry is predominantly Sikh; Pakistani and Bangladeshi ethnic origins are mostly Muslim; and Indian, Sri Lankan, and Nepalese ethnic origins are predominantly Hindu. Despite the different religiosity of the South Asians, they all place a strong sense of importance to their respective religious affiliation. Importantly, the second generation also holds similar view.

South Asians demonstrate an active economic life in Canada. The era of South Asians' economic life began when early Sikh people arriving in BC were initially involved in the lumber industry. They are still in this industry not only as workers but also as lumber mill owners. With the wave of influx of new South Asians immigrants in Canada after 1960s onward, many skilled professionals of various ethnocultural backgrounds are now well established in their professions. In fact, South Asians have been widely distributed among various occupational groups in the 1970s with the arrival of an increasing number of blue-collar and white-collar workers (Buchignani 2012; *Canadian Encyclopedia*). It is worth noting that the many South Asians, expelled from Uganda and other African countries, came to Canada and established successful businesses. Interestingly, Canadian South Asian women, many of whom never worked outside the home when they were back in their country of origin, have become active participants in a variety of blue- and white-collar jobs in Canada. A large majority of South Asian working age women are now involved in paid work (ibid.).

South Asians who were born outside Canada strongly maintain their mother tongue. More striking is the fact that even Canadian-born South Asians with at least one foreign-born parent learn to speak a language other than English or French. Parents believe that transfer of language between parents and children is very important. On the other hand, English is the most prominent one when South Asians first learned a second language. Among the nonofficial languages reported as a mother tongue, the most common include Punjabi, Tamil, Urdu, Gujurati, Hindi, and Bengali. One South Asian language carries a significant milestone in the modern history of language movement in the world. This language is "Bangla" (in English it is known as Bengali). The brief history is as follows:

International Mother Language Day is an observance held annually on February 21 worldwide to promote awareness of linguistic and cultural diversity and multilingualism. It was first announced by UNESCO on November 17, 1999. Its observance was also formally recognized by the United Nations General Assembly in its resolution establishing 2008 as the International Year of Languages. *International Mother Language Day* originated as the international recognition of Language Movement Day, which had been commemorated in Bangladesh since 1952, when a number of students and general public were killed by the Pakistani police in the city of Dhaka during Bengali Language Movement protests.

On March 21, 1948, Mohammed Ali Jinnah, the governor-general of Pakistan, declared that Urdu would be the only official language for both West and East Pakistan. The people of East Pakistan (now Bangladesh), having the mother language Bangla, started to protest against this. On February 21, 1952, students in the present-day capital city of Dhaka called for a provincial strike. The government invoked a limited curfew to prevent this, and the protests were tamed down so as to not break the curfew. The Pakistani police fired on the students despite these peaceful protests, and a number of students were killed. Four of them were Abdus Salam, Rafiq Uddin Ahmed, Abul Barkat, and Abdul Jabbar.

(Shaheed Minar, or the Martyr's monument, located at Dhaka University Campus, Bangladesh, commemorates the sacrifice for Bengali Language. Source: 21st February International Mother Language Day: http://www.google.ca/searc?q=21st+february+international+mother+language+day)

How February 21 became *International Mother Language Day*[62]

The pioneer of the *International Mother Language Day* is Rafiqul Islam, who is remarkably polite with a penetrating vision. He was a Freedom Fighter in the battlefield against the Pak Army, and his younger brother was killed in combat. He now lives in Vancouver.

It began when Rafiq realized that some languages of the world are simply not there anymore. He felt that some beautiful plants of this colourful garden of different human languages did not suffer natural deaths; they were simply killed by criminals in different disguises. With the strength of peace, he started his lonely crusade against this monster, which would soon leave a permanent mark towards the progress of peace for mankind on this planet. And soon, he was not alone. Others joined struggle. Let us walk through the chronological dates of the developments.

1) January 9, 1998. Rafiq wrote a letter to Mr. Kofi Anan to take a stand to save all the languages of the world from the possibility of extinction and to declare an *International Mother Language Day*. Rafiq proposed the date as February 21 on the pretext of 1952 killing in Dhaka making the occasion of the Language Movement.
2) January 20, 1998. From the office of the secretary-general, the chief information officer Mr. Hasan Ferdous (a Bangladeshi and knowledgeable writer as well) advised Rafiq to propose the same from any member country of the UNO.
3) January 20, 1998. Rafiq established "A Group of Mother Language of the World" with Abdus Salam (another Bangladeshi), two English-, one Hindi-, one German-, one Cantonese-, and one Kachhi-speaking people. They again wrote to Mr. Anan, with a copy forwarded to Mr. David Fowler, the Canadian ambassador to the UNO. Rafiq and Salam continued communication with the Canadian government.
4) Mid 1999. Mr. Hasan Ferdous advised Rafiq and Salam to contact the director of Languages Division of UNESCO, Mr. Joseph Pod. Mr Joseph advised to contact Anna Maria of UNESCO. Anna Maria (who played a very strong role in the process and of whom we are grateful) advised them to formally place the request to five member countries, Canada, India, Hungary, Finland, and Bangladesh.
5) Education minister of Bangladesh, Mr. Sadek; Education secretary, Mr. Kazi Rakibuddin (who was also the director general for National Commission for UNESCO); Prof. Kofiluddin Ahmad, director for the National Commission to UNESCO; Moshiur Rahman, the

director of the PM's Secretariat; the Bangladeshi ambassador to France, Mr. Syed Moazzem Ali; counsellor for the same, Mr. Iktiar Chowdhury; senior advisor to the secretary-general of UNESCO, Mr. Tozammel Huque (Toni Huque) of USA; and many other people were involved and became active in the process. They worked tirelessly to convince twenty-nine countries to support the proposal. The rest of the Bangladeshis throughout the world were not aware of the drama that was unfolding. With Rafiq and Salam, the whole Bangladeshi-Vancouver kept their fingers crossed.

6) September 9, 1999, was the last day of submitting the proposal to UNESCO. But it did not arrive yet! The restless Rafiq and Salam passed sleepless nights, did not move from the telephones, and closely monitored their e-mails for any news. In Dhaka, the prime minister of Bangladesh, whose signature was required in the document, was in the Parliament on that day. Once her duties with Parliament would have ended, the deadline for proposal would pass. This meant that the proposal would not reach UNESCO in time and the dream would not be realized. The PM instructed to fax the proposal to UNESCO office in Paris, pending her signature. The fax reached hours before the dateline.

7) The prime minister faxed the signed proposal to the UNESCO office in Paris. The fax reached in the last hours before the deadline.

8) November 16, 1999. The proposal was not raised (lack of time?) in the scheduled UNESCO meeting.

9) November 17, 1999. The proposal was raised; supported by 188 countries including Pakistan; not opposed by a single country; *and passed as a decision.*

10) In 2000 UNESCO declared February 21 the International Mother Language Day. It is a commemoration of the sacrifices of Bengali people in their struggle to secure their mother tongue and an overall celebration of "linguistic tradition, cultural diversity, and multilingualism."

Millions of people of Bangladeshi origin across the globe and in Bangladesh shared the same feeling as Nafiza Islam of Toronto as expressed her feeling about Ekushey February vis-à-vis *International Mother Language Day* as follows:

> If one were to walk down a street in Bangladesh today, they would most certainly encounter flower wreaths and bouquets being placed at the Shahid Minar, a monument built in Dhaka to

honour those who lost their lives in the *Bhasha Andalon*, and the evergreen Ekushey February song. And sitting here in Toronto today the realization of the movement is still there. Bengalis around the world are blogging about *Ekushey February* through various means and even after 60 years, people have not forgotten.

21st February serves as a reminder that people do not always fight for oil resources, broken alliances, territorial transgressions, or the numerous other matters that take center-stage in world politics today but people also fight for the right of expression, for the right to speak their mind in their own language. International Mother Language Day is not only a celebration of the victory of the Bangla language but an appreciation of language itself. Whether we speak Bangla, Hindi, Urdu, English, French or any other language, the important thing is to honour the tradition of our mother language and understand its importance in our lives. So, let us remember and celebrate the 21st February not only because of the sacrifices that were made by Bangladeshi people, but because of the legacy that it has left to the world. *Ekushey February* is a tribute to the beauty of the 6912 languages throughout the world; a reminder in today's chaotic world that heritage is still very important.

Various multicultural groups in Canada celebrate International Mother Language Day. While Canada honours the languages and heritage that immigrants from all over the world bring to our cultural mosaic, the government of Canada has not yet officially recognized and do not celebrate the International Mother Language Day. The motion to recognize February 21 as International Mother Language Day called on the federal government by East York MP, Hon. Matthew Kellway, was rejected by the Parliament. Scarborough Southeast MP Don Harris, who seconded MP Matthew Kellway's motion, resented the Parliament's decision.

4.7. Challenges of aging

The first-generation South Asian in Canada are increasingly comprised of people who are beyond middle age or nearing old age, and these groups of people have been growing steadily. For example, in 2001, there were around 55, 000 (which is 6 percent of the all age groups) South Asians aged sixty-five and over, which increased to around 90,400 (which is 7 percent of all age groups) in 2006, and around 130,110 (which is 11 percent of all age groups) in 2011.

South Asians in Canada are very diverse, and they have different experiences of aging among various religions, cultures, and linguistic groups. One of the intriguing facts is that the more they grow older, the more they appear to be religious. This gives them more of spiritual bond and a sense of identity. Like other immigrants, South Asians demonstrate strong courage in facing challenges they encounter in Canada. However, some argued that they often lose sight of the physical fragility and dependency they incurred with aging. With this hard reality, the lifestyle of the aging people changes. For example, people often visit sick friends and relatives in homes and hospitals, and even attend funerals instead of celebrating births and marriages, which were very common events during presenior times (Desai 1990).

It is true that migrating to a new country is stressful for seniors who are no longer working and hope to live with their son or daughter during their retired life. But once they arrive, they have to adapt to another culture and learn the customs and traditions of a new place even with their own community. When these seniors come to the Canada, they have to rely on their children and grandchildren. As they are more dependent on their children, they face several barriers like language, cultural, and social differences. Many families want their parents or in-laws to be at home with them. South Asians do not believe in leaving their parents in old age or retirement homes where most seniors live. It is not uncommon to see many of the seniors, especially male, hanging out in malls and community centres. The female counterparts rarely hang out together in the malls; instead, they prefer to stay home.

Children and/or grandkids at home are either hooked up with their shows and computers or are busy chatting on various social networks with their friends. Getting nobody around to talk to, grandparents feel alienated at home. English is commonly used by children to answer their grandparents even though they understand their mother tongue. Missing homeland and lamenting at the erosion of social and cultural values, these seniors sometimes speak out to voice their frustration. In response, some South Asian adults (such as sons and daughters of the seniors) draw attention to the positive aspects of living together or having their loved ones at home. They believe that the seniors bind the family together and create an atmosphere of heritage culture. More importantly, children can learn the value of family and tradition when grandparents live under in the same home (ibid.).

Despite the impact of acculturation process, many traditions are alive within the South Asian communities. For example, extended family concept still remains central to South Asian Canadians and has significant influence on family values and customs. Parental authority in the family is very strong, which has significant influence on children's conduct and behaviour. Yet some traditions are gradually changing, yielding place to new under the influence of Canadian mainstream values and practices. While families are the main source of social support of the elderly, such support is likely to cause stress in the family. The day-to-day responsibilities for caring elderly relatives usually go to either wife or daughter or daughter-in-law. When someone, especially younger women, is required to provide such support, it is very hard for them to do so when they are working full time outside the home; as a result, they have to give up the job. But if they continue working and take the responsibilities of elderly care, they consistently undergo extreme fatigue and stress. It is particularly hard for adult working children to maintain elderly care responsibilities when they have children of their own.

Many South Asians immigrants bear in mind the expectations (which may be unrealistic as some can argue) about the lives they intend to lead after retirement and later years. While some live under the illusion that they will go back to the country of origin after retirement, others think that they will live with their children in the same household in Canada and that the children will take care of them at the old age in meeting their needs. Whether this idea is realistic or not, it depends on the individual and family within the culture and tradition they brought up. Thus, it would not be fair to make any generalization in this concern. But one thing is certain—that whether parents live with children in the same household or they live in a separate lodging, it is important to maintain close relationships with parents and independent adult children. However, traditionally, South Asians live within extended family units, with children, their spouses, siblings, parents, and grandparents all under one roof. It's a practice that exists still today among South Asians in Canada. It is also very common to hear that youngsters are moving away from the joint family structures. In an attempt to avoid family squabbles stemming from small differences that can easily boil down to more serious disagreements, those youngsters choose an independent living into their new lives. One may foresee that the nuclear family is taking over the extended family.[63]

But there are exceptions. Nina, twenty-seven, and Sam, thirty-three (married three years ago), left their downtown Toronto apartment to move into a duplex in the suburbs. Among the many reasons why young couples gravitate towards life in the suburbs was the prime motivation that Sam wanted his aging parents to live with him. For them, the support and care their aging parents need is often a primary consideration. They lived on their own for a few years and felt good about having established their relationship on their own terms and are comfortable enough to change around their living arrangement. "It's not an easy adjustment, but it's one that both Nina and I have given a lot of thought. We considered the alternatives, and truth be told there aren't many," says Sam.[64]

As mentioned earlier, there is always the cultural influence on the value placed on the family system by South Asians. But for many married couples, the reality of living with in-laws in an increasingly fast-paced world can create some very real issues. Emotional as well as economic issues come into play. Ali Hamid, thirty-five, convinced his mother (after Ali's father passed away) to move in with him and his wife in Ottawa. "We can rest easy at night without having to worry about her being all alone," says his wife, Sadia, thirty-five. Even though Sadia did not have much of a relationship with her in-laws before, she is happy with the decision to have her mother-in-law move in with them. Sadia values teamwork, empathy, and communication as the key ingredients in making their new family life work. Ali's mother appreciates her son and daughter-in-law's invitation to their home. Unlike Ali's mother situation, not all in-laws are as welcoming of the idea of moving into their children's home. Issues of control and independence are often linked to financial charge, and many feel that ownership of the home they live in gives them an upper hand, if not control, of their living arrangements. Alternately, a jointly purchased home or shared financial responsibility may level the playing field and allow parents and children to get through the challenges ahead.[65]

In South Asian cultures, sons are traditionally considered the primary breadwinners of a family, and it is acceptable for a son to look after his parents in their old age. However, the situation may be different in the daughter's case. Are parents comfortably living with their married daughter and son-in-law? Even today, there are parents who are still attached to traditional stigma and consider it a matter of pride not to take this kind of support from a married daughter. However, with more and more women gaining financial independence, they feel that they too have the right to support and care for their parents should the need arise. "I look forward to providing for my parents even after I get married. It shouldn't matter whether I am a girl or a boy; they're my parents . . . My future husband will have to understand that," said a twenty-two-year-old Sonia Ahmed.[66]

There is a fundamental difference in the transitions from living on one's own to living with in-laws. The most obvious reason, among others, is the fact that in-laws are not one's parents. No matter how close a person is to their in-laws, it is very rare to find the same candid relationship that one grows to expect from one's own parents. An in-law's love, though sincere and generous, can be conditional. Often issues arise within families because a spouse expects his or her in-laws to fit in the roles defined by their own parents, and vice versa. In such a case, it is important to understand that each family is unique with different ways of interacting. As aging population increases among South Asian immigrants in Canada, families simply cannot provide the needed help and services of the elderly. Thus, institutional and community-based support services are necessary to help aging people. These services and supports will help them to live independently in partnership with families and friends. South Asian seniors must be prepared for the challenges they are currently facing and will more seriously face tomorrow.

4.8 South Asians in Canadian politics

South Asians' political involvement began in the province of British Columbia (BC). Prior to the 1960s, they involved primarily in lobbying for elimination of the legal restrictions for South Asians, enacted by the BC Legislature and changing Canadian immigration laws. Afterward, they became involved on other political fronts, for example, lobbying for government support for community and cultural programs, and for greater access to immigration of South Asians. Although they held local level offices, they did not start to participate at the federal level not until the 1970s. After the 1980s, that participation became even more extensive.

The following is the list of South Asians involved in Canadian politics:

First South Asian Canadian candidate in Canada: Hardial Bains, Marxist-Leninist Party of Canada, Eglinton, 1972 federal election

First South Asian elected in Canada: Moe Sihota, BC New Democratic Party MLA, Esquimalt-Port Renfrew 1986–1991, Esquimalt-Metchosin, 1991–2001

First South Asian Provincial Premier: Ujjal Dosanjh, BC New Democratic Party, February 24, 2000 to June 5, 2001 (Punjabi)

First South Asian leaders of a major political party: Raj Pannu, Alberta New Democratic Party, February 2, 2000–2004 (MLA 1997–2008)

(Punjabi). Note: Hardial Bains was the first South Asian Canadian to lead a political party. He founded and led the Marxist-Leninist Party of Canada from 1970 to 1997.

First South Asian female MPs: Yasmin Ratansi, Don Valley East, Liberal MP 2004+ (Ismaili, Muslim), Nina Grewal, Fleetwood-Port Kells, Conservative MP 2004+ (India, Sikh), and Ruby Dhalla, Brampton-Springdale, Liberal MP 2004+ (India, Sikh) (Yasmin Ratansi is the first Muslim woman elected in Canada, and Nina Grewal and Ruby Dhalla are the first Punjabi women elected in Canada.)

First South Asian MLA elected in BC: Moe Sihota, BC New Democratic Party MLA, Esquimalt-Port Renfrew 1986–1991, Esquimalt-Metchosin, 1991–2001

First South Asian MLA elected in Manitoba: Gulzar Cheema, Manitoba Liberal MLA Kildonan, 1988–1990

First South Asian MPP elected in Ontario: Murad Velshi, Ontario Liberal MPP Don Mills, 1987–1990

First South Asian MLA elected in Nova Scotia: Leonard Preyra Nova Scotia NDP MLA Halifax Citadel, 2006–present

First South Asian School Board Trustee elected in Canada: Neethan Shan, York Region District School Board, 2006–present

South Asian Canadian senators:

- Mobina Jaffer - Liberal senator, 2001–present. South Asian presidents, vice presidents, and secretaries of political parties
- Sav Dhaliwal - former president of the BC NDP
- Raj Sharan - former president of the Newfoundland and Labrador Newfoundland and Labrador New Democratic Party
- Joseph Thevarkunnel - NDP candidate in 2000 federal election for Oak Ridges

First Tamil-Canadian candidate to run in Ontario:

- Chandran Mylvaganam, NDP candidate in 1993 by election in Don Mills

First Tamil-Canadian elected in Canada:

- Logan Kanapathi, elected councillor for Ward 7 in Markham, Ontario, in 2006
- Neethan Shan, elected York School Board Trustee for Markham Wards 7 and 8

First Tamil-Canadian and Tamil Female elected House of Commons:

- Rithika Sitsabaiesan, elected member of Parliament for Scarborough-Rouge River, Ontario, in 2011.

4.8.1. South Asians in Fortieth Parliament

In the October 14, 2008, elections for Canada's Fortieth Parliament, ten South Asians were elected in the 308-member parliament. Of these, nine Indo-Canadians elected as MPs by the general Canadian electorate were of Punjabi origin. Gurbax Malhi was the first turbaned Sikh to become an MP in Canada in 1993 and returned to parliament for the sixth time.

4.8.2. South Asians in the Forty-First Parliament of Canada[67]

Elections held on May 2, 2011, for Canada's Forty-First Parliament saw seven South Asians elected to the 308-member parliament. They are Deepak Obhrai, Devinder Shory, Tim Uppal, Nina Grewal, Jasbir Sandhu, Baljit Singh Gosal, and Rathika Sitsabaisan.

Deepak Obhrai, Devinder Shory, Tim Uppal, and Nina Grewal have been reelected for the Canada's Forty-First Parliament. A number of MPs elected for the Fortieth Parliament lost seats in the Forty-First Parliament. They are Navdeep Bains, Sukh Dhaliwal, Ujjal Dosanjh, Ruby Dhalla, Yasmin Ratansi, and Gurbax Malhi.

4.8.3. South Asian senators in the Forty-First Parliament of Canada

Currently there are three South Asians in the Forty-First Parliament of Canada. They are Salma Ataullahjan, Mobina Jaffer, and Asha Seth.

Salma Ataullahjan (born in 1952) immigrated to Canada from Pakistan thirty-one years ago. After settling in Toronto, she pursued a career in real estate, a profession in which she has worked for the last twenty-one years. Born into a family with a long-standing history of political activism, Ms. Ataullahjan has spent many years actively involved in the social and political affairs of her community.

A natural consensus builder, Ms. Ataullahjan has served many organisations including on the executive of the Pakistani Canadian Professionals and Academics; as founder and chairperson of the Parent Council of David Lewis Public School; as a member of the South Asian Regional Council; as a former president and current vice president of the Canadian Pashtun Cultural Association; and on the executive of the Toronto chapter of the Citizens Foundation, a charity organisation that builds not-for-profit schools in the poorest districts of Pakistan.

Mobina Jaffer (born in 1949 in Uganda) was educated in both England and Canada, earning her bachelor of laws degree (LLB) from London University in England. She has completed the Executive Development Program at Simon Fraser University in Burnaby, British Columbia. Since 1978, Mobina Jaffer has practiced law at the firm Dohm, Jaffer, and Jeraj.

Senator Jaffer also has a broad background in personal injury cases, civil litigation, and matrimonial law. She has been, since 1997, the vice chair of the Canadian membership committee for the Association of Trial Lawyers of America; since 1993, a member of the board of governors of the Trial Lawyers of British Columbia; and since 1994, working with the Immigration and Refugee Board on gender and race issues. In 1994–95, Mobina Jaffer served as a member of the Canadian Bar Association Multicultural Committee; from 1995 to 1999, was a member of the Peoples Law School Committee; and from 1992 to 1996, was a member of the Law Society of British Columbia Multicultural Committee.

She currently serves as the immediate past president of the YWCA of Canada and a member of the Aga Khan National Conciliation and Arbitration Board. A member of the board of directors of YWCA of Canada since 1995, Mobina Jaffer was the president between 1999 and 2001. Also, she has served as a member of the Beijing Organizing Committee from 1995 to 1996, a member of the board of Lions Gate Hospital in North Vancouver from 1995 to 1996, a member of the Canadian Panel on Violence Against Women from 1992 to 1994, a director of New Door Transition Home from 1991 to 1992, a member of the Hastings Institute from 1990 to 1994, a representative of the Duke of Edinburgh Award for North Vancouver from 1987 to 1999, founding president of Immigrant and Visible Minority Women of British Columbia and the Yukon from 1987 to 1990; and a director of the Big Sisters Organization from 1978 to 1980. Mobina Jaffer sought election to the House of Commons at federal general elections for the constituencies of North Vancouver (in 1993) and Burnaby-Douglas (1997). She served as the vice president (English) of the Liberal Party of Canada from 1994 to 1998. In 1998 Jaffer was elected as the president of the National Women's Liberal Commission.

Dr. Asha Seth (born in 1939) is an obstetrician and gynaecologist in family practice, Toronto, Ontario. Recognized as a pioneer and patient advocate in the medical field, Dr. Seth received the prestigious Council Award from the Ontario College of Physicians and Surgeons in 2010.

An active philanthropist, Dr. Seth is involved in a number of charities serving local and international communities. She founded the NIMDAC Foundation, which raised funds for organisations such as the Heart and Stroke Foundation, the Canadian Foundation for the Physically Disabled Persons, and the Canadian National Institute for the Blind. She is also national board director of CNIB and was also actively involved with St. Joseph's Health Centre Foundation, assisting with initiatives to help raise funds for the health centre's new patient care wing. Dr. Seth completed her bachelor of medicine, bachelor of surgery (MBBS) at the King Georges Medical College in India and completed her resident training in Obstetrics and Gynaecology at the Royal Berkshire Hospital in the United Kingdom. Upon arrival in Canada, she continued her training at St. Joseph's Health Centre and at the Hospital for Sick Children in Toronto.

All these South Asian Canadians are dignitaries, and they are the assets for the South Asian community in Canada. These elected officials can make valuable contributions not only to the South Asians but also to the ethnic minorities at large. Undoubtedly, South Asian MPs and MPPs are in a position to address many important South Asian vis-à-vis ethnic minorities' issues in the appropriate forum, including in the Parliament, and they have the power to influence. Let us hope that they would use their full power to do better for the community.

4.9. South Asian heritage month

The first South Asians first arrived in Canada in the year 1897, when soldiers from the Indian army passed through the country on their way back home from London, England, after attending the Diamond Jubilee of the reign of Queen Victoria. Some of these Indian soldiers later returned to live in Canada permanently. The first known Caribbean based South Asian was Dr. Kenneth Mahabir, a Trinidadian medical student who came to Halifax in 1908 and stayed on.

The events marking the coming of South Asians appeared not until 1980s. The events were pioneered by Indo-Caribbeans, descendants of the Indians who had first arrived in the West in Guyana in 1838 and in Trinidad in 1845, and who had made a second migration to Canada in large numbers since the 1960s. They are a community of more than two hundred thousand Indo-Caribbeans in Canada who seek to preserve their culture and heritage that is notably different from that of the other South Asians in Canada. But they acknowledge always that their destiny is to make closer ties with other South Asians in order to make a better life for them all.

In 1986 a Toronto-based group Ontario Society for Services to Indo-Caribbean Canadians (OSSICC) was formed primarily to celebrate the upcoming 150th anniversary of the arrival of Indians to Guyana in 1988. OSSICC continued to celebrate Indo-Caribbean Heritage Day until the year 2000, with interest coming mainly from Indo-Caribbeans. In 1997, the Indo Trinidad Canadian Association (ITCA) was formed and immediately started Indian Arrival Day celebrations that year. In that year too, community activist Asha Maharaj organised a display of Indian artifacts, the Trinidad and Tobago Association of Ottawa held its first celebration, and the Caribbean East Indian Cultural Organization headed by radio host Richard Aziz organised an Indian Arrival celebration in Toronto. By 1998 ITCA had decided to celebrate the event as Indian Arrival and Heritage Day and held a huge show at the Etobicoke Olympium. It was never an Indo-Caribbean for ITCA but always Indian, meaning all people with roots in the Indian subcontinent.

Indian Arrival and Heritage Month: Since 1997 ITCA and later the Council for Indian Arrival and Heritage Month had decided not to make this an Indo Caribbean event. They realized that Indo-Caribbeans were only about 10 percent of the "Indian" group in Toronto, and if they confined Indian Arrival to Indo-Caribbeans, it would remain forever a marginal event. By 1999 ITCA had moved to celebrate the month of May as Indian Arrival and Heritage Month.

By the year 2000 a council for Indian Arrival and Heritage Month was in place, composed of people from ITCA, OSSICC, the Guyanese group GEAC, the Hamilton group CICA, and several individuals. The group was marking the arrival of Indians in the West as 1838 when the first landed in Guyana, and 1897 as the year the first Indians (Punjabi Sikh actually) arrived in Canada. The catch line from the letterhead for the Council in 2000 was "Commemorating the 162nd anniversary of the arrival in the

Americas of the people and heritage of the Indian subcontinent." This included all the groups who are now satisfied to be called South Asians, such as Indians, Pakistanis, Sri Lankans, etc.

Even though the council tried to attract the support of the other groups, it was a hard sell, and they did not usually get a positive response. In the Caribbean, the word "Indian" includes everybody who came from what was then united, colonial India. In Canada it was different. When the word "Indian" was used, the assumption was that it referred to people who had come from India, if it wasn't confused with native Indians. Many of the Punjabi Sikhs did not relate well to India because of their political problems with that country and did not want to see themselves as Indians. The Pakistanis did not respond to the words "Indian Arrival and Heritage Month" or to "Indian Arrival events." The Sri Lankans also said they were not Indians and ignored Indian Arrival and Heritage Month. There were similar problems with people from Bangladesh and Nepal. The Indian Arrival celebration was going nowhere.

Becoming South Asian Heritage Month: When Indian Arrival and Heritage Month was launched at the Scarborough Civic Centre in 2001, the keynote speaker was Raminder Gill, at the time the South Asian member of the Ontario Parliament. Gill said he would introduce a bill in the legislature to legitimize the event, and he did so later that same year. Gill obtained multiparty support for the bill but was told the legislature would not accept Indian Arrival and Heritage Month because it would cause confusion with the Indian Act and other laws relating to native Indians. The name was changed to South Asian Heritage Month, and the bill received unanimous support and was signed into law in December 2001.

Since then, South Asian Heritage Month has grown dramatically. Dozens of celebrations take place each year, including events at the Ontario Parliament, the Gerard Street bazaar, numerous religious and community groups, and the media. It has been embraced enthusiastically by the Sri Lankans, Pakistanis, and most of the twenty-plus subgroups in the South Asian community. Efforts are being made to extend the celebration throughout Ontario and to other provinces and territories in Canada.

Act to proclaim May as South Asian Heritage Month and May 5 as South Asian Arrival Day

South Asian immigrants began arriving in Ontario at the start of the twentieth century. Working primarily in the sawmill industry, South Asian immigrants settled in various parts of the province. For South Asians, the month of May has been a time of celebration and commemoration of their arrival from the Indian subcontinent to the Americas beginning on May 5, 1838.

While most South Asians came to our country from India, many others came to Ontario from such places as Pakistan, Sri Lanka, Bangladesh, Uganda, Kenya, South Africa, Mauritius, Singapore, Malaysia, Fiji, the United Kingdom, Trinidad and Tobago, and Guyana. Today, South Asians make up a significant proportion of Ontario's population and are proud to draw upon their heritage and traditions, contributing to many aspects of culture, commerce, and public service. It is appropriate to recognize and pay tribute to the contributions South Asians have made and continue to make to the development and general welfare of Ontario. Her Majesty, with the advice and consent of the Legislative Assembly of the Province of Ontario, enacts as follows:

1. May 5 in each year is proclaimed as "South Asian Arrival Day."
2. The month of May in each year is proclaimed as "South Asian Heritage Month."
3. This act comes into force on the day it receives *Royal Assent*.
4. The short title of this act is the *South Asian Heritage Act 2001*.[68]

Since receiving proclamation in December 2001, South Asian Heritage Month has been celebrating the presence and heritage of people with roots in the South Asian countries. Often celebrations highlight South Asian history, arts, heritage, and culture, but it is also important to recognize the contributions of South Asian workers to Canada's economy and society, said Ontario Federation of Labour (OFL) president Sid Ryan. He also noted that South Asians represent one-quarter of the racialized workforce and 4 percent of the total workforce in Canada, making them the country's largest racialized group. Based on 2006 census report, most South Asian workers in Canada are well educated, yet they are underrepresented in managerial and skilled occupations and overrepresented in semiskilled and low-skilled occupations. Given their accomplishments are vital part of Canadian history, and their contributions are well recognized by Canadian industries and businesses many South Asian people in Canada have faced harassment and discrimination in the workplace and in society, commented by OFL executive vice president Irwin Nanda, the OFL's first executive officer of South Asian descent.[69]

> *It is the task of the rising generation of Canadians to create a new confidence and a new sense of cultural and civic duty in Canada. Unless we achieve some success on this front; and I believe we are beginning to do so; the very real attractions of the vigorous society to the South of us may attract too many of our people. Then the human resources and skills required to shape and direct a complex industrial economy will simply not be available to us in Canada.*
>
> —Mitchell Sharp

5

Second-Generation South Asian Canadians

According to Statistics Canada, the generational definitions are as follows: first generation is anyone not born in Canada, second generation is anyone born in Canada with at least one parent not born in Canada, and third generation is anyone with both parents born in Canada. Of the second generation aged fifteen years and older, 14 percent people reported visible minority status; South Asian is the second largest after Chinese, being the largest group. This particular age group of second generation visible minorities is relatively young and has joined or making their way into the labour force.

Statistics Canada has released its projections of the diversity of the Canadian population, for population grown between 2006 and 2031. By 2031 almost half (47 percent) of *all* second-generation Canadians (that's people who were born inside Canada, and at least one parent immigrated to Canada) would be visibly diverse. The estimations show how visibly *and* culturally diverse Canada would be in just twenty years from now. The important fact is that they are economically mobile and generally more culturally mobile than the general population, and certainly more economically and socially mobile than new immigrants.

According to Statistics Canada, this population is the most educated and very well integrated into Canadian society. As the *Globe and Mail* commented back in 2003, they are the drivers of "the New Canada." But there are pains and stress among the second-generation youths, as they are caught between two cultures. Second-generation coloured youths open up about bullying at school and cultural conflict at home. Like other second-generation visible minority youths, children of South Asians immigrants are in the same boat and are faced with similar challenges in their daily lives in Canada.

5.1. Key cultural values

In the concept of collectivism of the South Asian culture, the primary importance is emphasized on the welfare of the family, which usually includes grandparents, aunts, uncles, and cousins. Family members are expected to sacrifice their personal desires to ensure the well-being of their families in a situation when individual and family goals conflict (Almeida 1996; Ibrahim et al. 1997; Segal 1991). The importance of collectivism encourages familial interdependence throughout the lifespan of children. For example, they tend to remain emotionally dependent on their parents well into adulthood (Almeida 1996; Segal 1991). As a consequence, parents and grandparents always exert significant amounts of influence in all aspects of their life, with elders being respected and admired as wise guardians (Ibrahim et al. 1997; Segal 1991). Since South Asian parents often perceive their children's individualism as a loss of control, adolescent autonomy is not considered very desirable (Dosanjh and Ghuman 1998).

The differences in the values and ways of life make the cultural transition process challenging for second-generation South Asian youths, as they are exposed to the values and norms of the mainstream Canadian culture through their school experiences and media exposure (Baptiste 1993; Berry 2001). In order to align two cultures, Berry (2001, 2003) suggested that first- and second-generation immigrants must make two critical choices related to their cultural preferences: (1) how much of their heritage cultural beliefs and practices to retain, and (2) how much they wish to interact with and adopt the values and practices of the dominant Canadian culture. Berry outlines four possible outcomes to make these two decisions. They are (a) assimilation, complete adoption of the host culture's values and beliefs; (b) separation, full identification with the heritage culture and detachment from the dominant culture; (c) integration, selectively incorporating aspects of each culture; and (d) marginalization, rejection of both the heritage and dominant cultures (Berry 2001). However, South Asian parents and adolescents tend to adopt different acculturation preferences; with parents emphasizing separation and youth favouring integration (Segal 1991; Talbani and Hasanali 2000; Wakil, Siddique, and Wakil 1981). These differences in the cultural norms among South Asian parents and youth are likely to affect adolescents' achievement of a consolidated bicultural identity.

Family conflicts also arise in the situations when South Asian youths wish to pursue an unconventional career path that is perceived by parents as less important and of lower value, to begin dating, or to adopt behaviours typical of youth in the mainstream Canadian culture (Almeida 1996; Segal 1991). South Asian parents consider these behaviours as foreign to their culture; they interpret their child's adaptation to those values as a sign of "cultural corruption." As a consequence, the parents respond by applying increased pressure on their children to conform to their expectations (Sharma 2000; Wakil et al. 1981). South Asian youths are socialized since birth to believe that family loyalty and a sense of duty toward one's parents and relatives are very important, and as such, parents feel that it is their moral obligation to regulate their children's behaviour (Segal 1991). Parents quite often experience increased stress when their efforts to regulate their children's behaviour fail or backfire. They also consider their young children's attempts to assert their autonomy as arrogance (Kurian and Ghosh 1983; Wakil et al. 1981). Moreover, parents interpret their adolescents' preferences for the dominant Canadian culture as a sign of their own failure to effective parenting (Almeida 1996). The differences between the values of the "collectively" oriented South Asian culture and those of the more "individualistic" mainstream Canadian culture draw attention to the potential for family conflict in cultural identity formation among first- and second-generation South Asian immigrants (Aneesa Shariff 2009).

I put the cultural conflict as a challenge South Asian second-generation youths in Canada face, and urge them to use their wisdom and rational in Mahatma Gandhi's perspective about culture from the following phrase:

> *I do not wish to have my windows closed and my doors shut. I want winds from all cultures to blow freely about my house. But I refuse to be blown off my feet by any.*

5.2. Ethnic identity formation

To establish a consolidated bicultural identity for the second-generation South Asian youths involves conscious reflection about and resolution of their attitudes toward both their own cultural group and the majority group in Canada (Berry 2001; Phinney 2003). One may argue that ethnic identity is a dynamic and multifaceted concept, and it may be defined as one's sense of commitment to and a sense of being within one's ethnic group (Phinney 2003). Exposure to the dominant Canadian culture's values and beliefs is obviously making the ethnic identity development process more challenging for the ethnic minority adolescents like South Asian youths when parents and peers of this group of young people exert opposing cultural pressures (Phinney 2003).

Previous studies have demonstrated that the ethnic identity formation process can be particularly problematic for South Asian youths due to the fact that their parents quite often enforce and regulate on their children's life the traditional South Asian values and behaviours (Kurian and Ghosh 1983; Segal 1991; Talbani and Hasanali 2000; Wakil et al. 1981). These authors have found that South Asian adolescents behave and interact differently inside and outside of the home due to their parents' rejection of Canadian mainstream culture influences on their beliefs and behaviours. Trouble with the identity formation process is likely to arise when South Asian youths are forced to live within the heritage culture, particularly when they feel a stronger connection to the dominant Canadian culture. When South Asian youths are faced with these identity conflicts, they have reportedly been found to have delinquent behaviour, alienation from family, stress, and depression (Shams 2001; Talbani and Hasanali 2000; Wakil et al. 1981).

Another aspect of identity formation among South Asian adolescents is the gender differences. Girls are more likely to have higher levels of identity conflicts compared to boys, and have more family restrictions are placed on girls freedom because they are viewed as eventual mothers who will pass on cultural beliefs and practices to the next generation (Almeida 1996; Dion and Dion 2001). It is also the fact that South Asian gender role is characterised by differential parenting practices for sons and daughters, which put girls under more intense pressure from parents. As a result, girls are subject to stress, depression, and anxiety related to interruption in the ethnic identity development process (Dion and Dion 2001; Talbani and Hasanali 2000).

5.3. Parenting stress

As stated earlier, South Asian culture is collectivist in nature. Due this nature, the acculturation and identity development in the second generation South Asian youths have become central to family building and functioning (Almeida 1996; Farver, Narang, and Bhadha 2002; Segal 1991). As South

Asian adolescents are well exposed to the values, behaviours, customs, and practices of the dominant Canadian culture through their peers, school experiences, and social media, they often question their traditional South Asian beliefs and customs. It is very normal to do so in terms of identity formation during adolescence. However, South Asian parents may react to this exploration and emerging identity transformation as a sign that their children are being "corrupted" or gone astray by negative Western influences (Segal; Wakil et al. 1981).

According to Swearer (2001), "Parenting stress can be conceptualized broadly as tension experienced by a parent in various areas of parent-child interactions." More closely, looking from the immigrant perspective, when young children are being absorbed more in the cultural norms of the host country than their parents' heritage culture, the parents start to believe that they are losing control over their children, resulting to high level of parenting stress (Dosanjh and Ghuman 1998; Farver et al. 2002). South Asian parents evaluate their task of child rearing in terms of the degree to which they have been able to guide their children effectively so that the children can make right decisions in life (Almeida 1996). Obviously, when parents perceive their children's autonomy negatively, they interpret this as a failure in their parental duties. As a consequence, challenges parents face and undergo stress. They also react to their children's divergent cultural preferences with anger, and the feelings of guilt and shame on their part emphasize for increased level of monitoring of their children's activities and behaviours (Carolan, Bagherinia, Juhari, Himelright, and Mouton-Sanders 2000; Segal 1991).

5.4. Parents and children relationships

Quite often the relationships between parents and children are depicted as battleground, given the changing roles of South Asian immigrants while settling in Canada. Many immigrant parents feel that their parenting ability is under stress (Tyyska 2006). Economic situation, poverty, unemployment, underemployment, multiple job holding, and shifts in gender-based economic and domestic roles create conditions where parents cannot provide attention and care to the children they deserve (Tyyska 2008). As a result, the customary family roles between parents and children are likely to change. For example, when male in the family (i.e., husband and father) experience loss in their work status, it is likely that they experience the loss of their status as head of the household. It may also be the case that women (i.e., wife and mother) are compelled to seek gainful employment. In that situation, women get added status in the family (Ali and Kilbride 2004), which in turn creates tension that can contribute to an onset of family violence against women and children (Creese et al. 1999; Tyyska 2005).

Other changes in the intergenerational relationships in the families emerge from the children's cultural adaption of and alignment with the Canadian norms and practices as compared to their parents. Undoubtedly, children learn English and French languages much better and faster than their parents, which leads to intergenerational problems. Language gaps quite often create conflict in the parent-children communication and sharing of culture and identity (Anisef et al. 2001). Also the fact that many parents rely on their children as mediators or translators in dealings with matters related to schools, hospitals, social services, etc. (Ali and Kilbride 2004; Creese et al. 1999). As a consequence, children are likely to take new roles and responsibilities in the family, but parents want to retain the usual authority over the children, a situation that leads to tensions within the family (Creese et al. 1999).

We have discussed earlier on many other issues related to intergenerational gaps, such as desire to fit in their peers and the desire to meet their parents expectations, mixed marriages, and so on. It is, however, important to note that adolescent girls in many South Asian families have less freedom of movement and decision-making power than their brothers. Another salient feature in South Asian families is the parents' fear for their daughters and sons in two different perspectives; fear for daughters is related to dating (link to premarital sexuality), and fears for sons is related to drugs and violence (Anisef et al. 2001; Tyyska 2006). Although most of the South Asians are traditional in terms of their cultural heritage, there are many families, those living in Canada, that are somewhat moderate or nontraditional. Those who are traditional, family relationships are hierarchical in terms of both gender and age. Parents have distinct expectations from boys and girls. For example, young members in the family, particularly the young girls, have very little influence in the communication and decision-making process in the family. But for those who are nontraditional families, gender relations are less hierarchical, and thus young members are open to communicate and can involve in the decision-making process. Traditional families are subject to parental control over their children and expectation of obedience and family loyalty. There is a concept of trade-off between parents and children in the familial relationships—that is, parents usually provide financial support to children, and in return, children are expected to support parents during old age.

Gender division of work is another dimension of relationship among members of the family. Men are the breadwinners in many South Asian families, while women perform the bulk of daily domestic responsibilities. But there are families where women also work outside home and bring money in the family. In these families, women are overworked, as they perform the domestic works as well as participate in the labour market for gainful employment outside the home. This situation leads to the notion of double day of work for women. This cycle of double-day work continues through generations, as more and more girls are being involved in gainful employment outside the home. Thus, the customary system—wage-earner status that gives the male family members more say in the family—is likely to change among the second and third generations of South Asian immigrants. It seems that in many families, the demands of decent living that involve both male and female in the gainful employment and lack of any help in the family is the driving force towards changes in wage-earning and domestic work arrangements of the younger generations (Tyyska 2008).

5.5. Generation gap and bicultural conflicts

A great deal of research on visible minority immigrants including South Asians origins is available in both academic and nonacademic literatures, which address the problems of acculturation, such as language, job, educational credentials, the learning the cultural norms of Canadian mainstream society, systemic racism, and so on. But it is not right to assume that visible minority population is always immigrants. By assuming that the problems of racism are related to immigrants, then the presence of others who were born and brought up in Canada (i.e., children of immigrants), who also face challenges racism and exclusion, are ignored. When the first-generation South Asians face language, job, foreign credentials, and cultural exclusion, the second-generation youths struggle with the identity of national belonging in their day-to-day life.

Previous research explored the challenges second-generation South Asians face dealing with racism within the Canadian mainstream peer culture, which suggests that the context of difference between immigrants and the second-generation youth are different—the immigrants *arrive* in Canada within the difference, whereas their children *grew up* within the difference (Mythili Rajiva 2004). Basically, this means that second-generation children are less likely to face systemic barriers than their parents faced because younger generation finds easier time succeeding in the job market, building career, and integrating socially into the mainstream Canadian cultural norms and values. Given the fact that the immigrant parents face more barriers in the labour market and more unpleasant job experiences than their children grown up in Canada, the latter suffers from identity crisis and are open to self-doubt and confusion. As Rajiva pointed out, for the second-generation children, the biggest challenge is the growing up in the context of difference at a time of their lives when belonging is very important. This sense of belonging with peers is very crucial in their adolescence, as it allows them to build a sense of positive identity at this developmental period.

One of the key concerns for the second-generation children is the fact that they have the difficulties of being in between two cultural identities and experiences—that is, they are neither fully part of their parents' homeland culture nor completely part of the Canadian mainstream culture. Intergenerational tensions between immigrant parents and their children born in Canada have also been related to the racism and discrimination in the larger society experienced by the second-generation children. Although they were born and growing up in Canada, they are being seen as radically different in a broader national context, where the "Canadianness" is the popular reflection of "whiteness" (ibid.). The respective struggles of both parents and children for belonging in Canadian society constitute the difference between the two generations. Their struggles are different in terms of nature as well as the extent. The obvious fact is that immigrant parents experience more overt discrimination than their children born in Canada, but they have a stronger source of self-esteem (Bagley 1987; McAdoo et al. 1993). On the other hand, second-generation youths face greater challenge of developing a sense of negativity in terms of self-esteem and self-identity, as they are aware of the fact that they will be perceived, to a lesser or greater extent, as immigrants or foreigners by the white Canadians (Aujla 2000). The following interview responses from the second-generation youths provide examples of how they felt about racism they experienced during their adolescent years in Canada:

"I know people who were born here and somehow we always feel we are strangers because we're visible minorities, so at first sight people will always see you as coming from somewhere else. In many cases you still have to prove yourself" (in *Identity and Politics: Second Generation Ethnic Women in Canada;* Mithili Rajiva 1996).

"During my adolescent years, it hindered my development as an individual because everyone kept hounding me about the fact that I was different, that I looked different (not that I sounded different) and it led to feelings of inferiority; difference became something negative. It happened all the time when I was younger and as I was growing up" (in *Identity and Politics: Second Generation Ethnic Women in Canada;* Mithili Rajiva 1996).

"Just in terms of like feeling ashamed and I guess what you were saying, like about trying to blend in and not be seen as Indian, I remember when like sometimes at school, people would make comments about Indians, not to me, but about Indians, in front of me, and when I heard those things, it used to make me feel so awful inside, so awful. And like that incident with my mom when she was dressed in a Sari, like I was so, I don't know, I just didn't want to be associated with it. It's that whole thing that you talk about, being seen as different" (in *Racing through Adolescence: Becoming and Belonging in the Narratives of Second Generation South Asian Girls;* Mithili Rajiva 2004).

Second-generation South Asian Canadians quite often identify themselves with two different cultures, namely mother culture and Canadian culture. Mother culture is acquired from parents, relatives, and the ethnic community to which they belong. On the other hand, Canadian cultural norms are acquired through schools, media, social services, the neighbourhoods in which they live, and peers. Canadian cultural norms also acquired through either English or French language, while mother cultural norms may be acquired through a different language (Lalonde and Giguere 2008). Although diversity among the second-generation South Asian Canadians exists, they share some of bicultural features. Generally speaking, cultural conflicts are likely to be experienced at different levels. For example, at the group level, second-generation youths may experience discrimination because they have been perceived as not "fitting in" the Canadian culture on the basis of criteria such as skin colour, accent, or type of dress (ibid.). More precisely the authors stated as follows:

> A conflict between the two sets of cultural norms of the bicultural individual is more likely to be evidenced when the two cultural identities of bicultural individuals are simultaneously salient to the individual, when these identities evoke two sets of norms that are incompatible and when the individual feels some commitment to each set of norms.

Bicultural conflicts are likely to occur when Canadian norms and heritage norms are incompatible in terms of behavioural perspectives at various fronts in the social norms and customs, such as partner selection for marriage, sexuality, and identity. We will briefly discuss bicultural conflicts on these issues in the following paragraphs.

Within the heritage/mother cultural context, life partner preference and selection is usually done within homogeneous cultural group where the potential partner shares ethnic, religious, and linguistic characteristics. In Canadian culture, marriage is seen as the union of two individuals, and young adults are expected to find their partners without their parents' assistance. In contrast, in many Eastern cultures, including South Asian culture, marriage is seen as the alliance between two families, and in many cases, they may be arranged, preferably by parents. Although individual's selection of a marriage partner is desirable, obligations and duties may be more important than personal preferences. Young adults of heritage/mother culture are expected to respect their parents' desires and expectations regarding the choice of a spouse, and love may be better conceptualized important that may follow marriage rather than one that precedes it (Goodwin and Cramer 2000).

Given the fact that family is the primary important aspect of heritage/mother culture for the second-generation children of South Asian immigrants, the expectations of the family plays a role in their mate preferences. Lalonde et al. (2006) found similar results—second-generation South Asian adults internalize some of the norms of their heritage culture and that they have strong preference for traditional attributes in their partners (e.g., family reputation, parents' approval, etc.) compared with the preferences of their European Canadian peers. Chastity is an important attribute in a mate within the cultural context of sexuality. Lalonde and Giguere (2007) found a strong preference for chastity among the second-generation South Asians and Chinese adults in choosing a mate. With respect to premarital sex, both South Asians and Chinese Canadians disapproved premarital sexual intercourse, unlike their white Canadian peers, although this difference of disapproval is more pronounced among South Asians.

Another potential area of bicultural conflict is the identity conflicts. While white Canadian cultures have strong norms of autonomy and independence, the South Asian cultures, on the other hand, have strong norms of family connectedness and interdependence. Lalonde and Giguere (2007) have examined this conflict in two situations and found that (1) the transition from living in familial home (i.e., moving out of familial home) to other types living arrangements by the South Asian young adults is less common than their white Canadian counterpart, and (2) education and career choices of the South Asian youths usually pursue the kind of work that are valued and recognized by the family or heritage community (e.g., engineering, medicine, business, law, and high tech etc.), whereas the white Canadian youth are more open to select wide variety of field of study including fine arts, literature, theatre, filming making, journalism, etc.

5.6. Mixed marriage

The phenomenon of "mixed" marriage is the inevitable result wherever human beings come together to form a common society. In Canada this is exactly what has been happening in everyday life of ethnic and white Canadians, as we all know that the migration of diversified ethnic and cultural groups has been the story of Canadian life. Canada has shared the flavour and cultural diversity of many nations where South Asians have made special impact over half a century.

The mix of relationships between cultures begins from peer pressure outside home, when children start going to day care or school. They learn in their classroom and in the playground that they are one of many other children from a variety of ethnic and national backgrounds, in big Canadian cities in particular. In the schools, there grows in the minds of Oriental children including South Asian children a new sense of awareness of something that is white Anglo-Saxon and is called Canadian. This idea of "Canadianness" grows in the emerging interests of the ethnic children that are shared at home through the medium of television. Thus all the TV programs, such as baseball, football, the world of cartoons, and other programs that are watched by the children, are cultural seeds that germinate in the fertile minds of children of ethnic background, which serve to produce a Canadian identity (Jacqueline A. Gibbons 1990).

In schools, the children learn new games and find new friends who come from a variety of ethnic backgrounds, and there are new relations between girls and boys as they explore the new world of other young people. They learn about friendship as well as conflicts, animosities, hostilities, and biases. Jacqueline argued that the ethnic children may find themselves involved in the complicated circumstances and entangled within the ethnic enclaves, where antagonism is also a sign of vulnerability. The author further stated that these schisms can be along the lines of class, gender, religion, and ethnicity. They either constitute the fabric of new alliances or of greater schisms and splits. They may deeply be involved in a difficult situation in the intergroup conflicts, as well as making cultural and ethnic alignments. This can either create animosity or can be the fabric of new liberal values. The new relationships, based on liberal values and ideas, can create the possibility of interethnic marriage.

When the second-generation youths go to universities and colleges, they continue to move in an increasingly differentiated and heterogeneous world that is almost always defined as "Canadian." Romances come and go, and crucially, the sense of identity is merged with the mainstream that is called Canadian. Therefore, ethnic identity may become less important for these young adults. It is worth noting that for the South Asian boys and girls, there are different means and ways as alternatives to the dating and mating of mainstream North American society. Sometimes parents arrange marriages for their sons and daughters according to traditional family networks or practices. A spouse can be found through personal contact or through advertisements in community newspapers, either at home or in Canada. The decision may be left entirely to the parents, or it may be shared by the son or daughter concerned. When the young adults accept this practice, it is very much the way that maintains religious, ethnic, and educational values. In contrast, many others want to adhere to the customs of their new country by meeting their partners in life and marriage through the networks and friendship patterns of Canadian society (ibid.).

South Asia is the home of most of the universal religions of the world. The South Asians who have come to Canada have brought religions and cultural and social practices that are deeply influenced by their religious identity. The second-generation children of South Asian immigrants inherit this legacy. Their parents practise Hinduism, Buddhism, Islam, Christianity, Sikhism, or Jainism, and they attend temples, mosques, *gurdwaras*, or churches. Religion plays a key role in the mixed marriage, and the potential of it depends on the degree of religious orthodoxy in the household. Given the importance of religion in the family, the children are raised with particular rules and prohibitions, and they participate in the rituals, prayers, and practices of the particular religious orthodoxy. Many second-generation children may choose to adhere to that particular religious orthodoxy, or they may react against it. These responses are determined by the tastes and values developed by the second-generation children in the course of their life. These religious beliefs may be the power to shape marriage for the next generation, and the particular intimacy of religion and cultural identity creates special challenges for the South Asian family involved in the experience of "mixed" marriage (ibid.).

Another aspect of mixed marriage is the heterogeneous friendships of a different ethnicity or religion. This amount to an immense challenge parents face in everything they have lived for and in everything they have believed in. As Jacqueline states, "Liberal words are belied by conservative admonitions; fears are expressed and threats made in family discussions." When the daughter or son expresses to parents the fact that he/she is going to marry an individual outside of ethnic origin, the initial parental response is very much predictable and protective. The initial response is that the marriage outside of the own ethnic community can be a problem and that there are too many unknowns. There is also the large extent of fear of divorce, which is very much common in mainstream Canadian society unlike South Asian cultural practice. Parents express their concern, not only about the future of their children but also about the offspring of the children and pose question to the fact that the offspring will belong to neither one culture and religion nor the other. This is a valid question indeed, as they are very real in the most practical sense of fears and anticipations.

Arranged marriages are quite common in South Asian cultures, and they are seen as fulfilling the needs of the family rather than the individuals. In such arrangements, future partners are introduced to each other after families are carefully screened for factors such as reputation, socioeconomic status, and the education of the future partners in order to ensure successful matching between the two families. Therefore, family approval of a future spouse is important and necessary, and the children of South Asian parents are not encouraged to follow their own decisions like the children in the mainstream Canadian parents. Moreover, partners would not only be expected to have same social status but would also be expected to share a common cultural and religious background. Parents usually introduce prospective couples to each other and leave it to them to make their own decisions to make a relationship that may lead to marriage. Interesting to note that parents are often find "auntie-network" (an effective network whereby aunties pass on information about eligible young people through a string of contacts) very useful for matchmaking of young adults.

But is there any guarantee that a marriage will be perfect and reasonable if it is arranged by parents or family? In today's modern world, it is just not possible to predict. For example, those who look back to home (such as India, Pakistan, Bangladesh, Sri Lanka, etc.) for a partner, it can create culture shock for the emigrant partner. Also, an arranged marriage may be unacceptable to the second-generation youths, especially to the educated youths. Based on some schools of thought, one may argue that mixed couples are especially conscious of the importance of success (as they choose their spouse by themselves and that they are committed to prove to their parents that they can make the mix marriage successful) and thus will try and work very hard to achieve marital longevity and success at any cost.

While we know that as the second-generation of South Asians gradually become more and more integrated, intermarriages are natural phenomena, but it is not easy as it sounds. There are challenges in intermarriage, and they are dependent upon the differences in the background characteristics of couples such as education, cultural orientation, mind-set, tolerance power, and most importantly the religious attachment. Research suggests that interfaith marriages have a higher divorce rate, although differences in religion may not be the only reason for marriage failure. For example, South Asian societies in the Western world by and large still remain skeptical and less supportive of intercultural and interfaith marriages. South Asians, because of their strong knit family system, generally are more demanding than Western system of family life. In interfaith marriages, in particular, couples have to deal with many pressures such as maintaining religious decorum for fear of being labelled traitors of their respective faiths and as betrayer of familial and societal norms.

Moreover, the question of whether one of the couples would convert the religion or each would follow their own faiths would come into play. Conversions seem to be an effective solution to the problem that likely to arise after the birth of children, but it is not so in reality. The spouse who converted under certain pressure may develop feeling of betrayal for the original faith, and trouble with newly adopted faith tends to create psychological problems and tension in the conjugal life. Another challenge faces the couples—whose religion the children would follow. When the couples are unable to reconcile their religious differences, these can cause friction in the family and affect the emotional and psychological well-being of the children. Sometimes couples compromise to a point that children will be brought up with the teachings of both religions and allowing them to decide for themselves once they are old enough to make that decision. Generally, it is observed that some religion overpowers the other. For example, in Islamic faith, it is strongly imposed that children must be raised in Islamic traditions and believes. Within the Indian community, interfaith marriages are more common between members of Hinduism, Shikism, and Jainism than between Hindus and Christians or Muslims. Originating from the religious differences, intermarriages between Hindus, Shiks, and Jains tend to have fewer problems than between Muslim and Hindu, or Christian and Hindu, or Muslim and Christian couple.[70]

The 2006 census results suggest that the visible minority having the least number of mixed marriages were South Asian persons, with only 13 percent marrying non-South Asian spouse; followed by Chinese, being one of the lowest proportions of mixed unions outside their ethnic group (17 percent). Research based on sample survey of South Asian and European Canadians revealed that the traditional normative expectations regarding dating among South Asian Canadians are much stronger than among the European Canadians (Ayes K. Uskul et al. 2010). The authors commented that South Asians are more likely to support endogamy and oppose intergroup relationships, which have the potential to jeopardize heritage cultural continuity (ibid.). The study further suggests that stronger traditional normative expectations regarding intergroup dating are more among older generation compared to the younger generation of South Asians. While more than 40 percent of couples married in the Catholic Church in Canada were of mixed religions, the proportion of Muslims seeking interfaith marriage remains very low in Canada.[71]

After more than thirty years of living in Canada, I have witnessed that ethnic intermarriage among South Asians has become a statistical reality. Obviously, one challenge some first-generation South Asian families face is the ethnic or religious "otherness" as their children become educated and move forward in socially, occupationally, and to some extent economically varied cultural milieus in Canada (ibid.). Despite parents' continued efforts to restore and maintain heritage cultural ties, the second-generation South Asian Canadian youths have crossed many of the barriers and have made much headway towards occupational and educational success. When many South Asian parents may see intercultural mixed marriage as a good step, others may think otherwise. No matter these marriages are made within a particular religious doctrine and cultural norms or not, they are the unions of two young loved persons of opposite sex. Of course, those young people who choose such mixed marriages are paving the path to a multicultural adventure and blending that is both bold and brave, who have overcome many social, cultural, and religious barriers in their marriage decisions and have brought change in the tradition of marriage.

Like many social scientists, demographers, and researchers, I share the view that intermarriage is not only a strong indicator of integration but also an indicator of the progress of multiculturalism in an ethnically diverse society like Canada. It is a process of building on shared aspirations and values, and mutual respect and tolerance, which positively contributes to the advancement of social inclusion, integration, and multiculturalism, which promotes and advocates respect and tolerance of all cultures. Intermarriage also strengthens Canadian identity in that the children of intermarriages (with their bicultural or multicultural identities) become Canadians by their parents' definition as indicated when asked to identify their ethnic origin in the population census. This is particularly the case when one parent is white Canadian or one parent is ethnic minority, either Canadian-born or overseas-born. These intermarriage outcomes contribute to social integration of ethnic groups. Further discussion about marriages, both South Asian and intermarriage have been included in the annex 1.

Part Two

6

Experiences and Challenges Faced by the South Asian Immigrants

There were thousands of immigrants of South Asian origin that came to Canada. But immigration to Canada was not always easy for many of them. It was more so when they arrived and struggled to settle and thrive in a new country they called home. Each person had a story to tell about their challenges, struggles, successes, and emotions that make up the experiences of representative group of South Asian immigrants. While statistics can provide a broader view of immigrants, they do not give an in-depth and personalized experience that they want to share. It is the individual stories of South Asian immigrants that enable us to know and understand what they experienced in their struggle to settle and thrive in Canada.

A good number of stories of Canada's immigrants of South Asian origin who came to Canada as a kid, teen, or young adults were reviewed. Each of them shared, in their own words, the experiences and challenges faced in Canada. Their strategies of success and their inspirations and advices might be the footstep for new immigrants of ethnic origin in general, and for South Asian immigrants including the second-generation youths, in particular, who wants to get results from their own struggle. It is important that the readers know each of those stories. While those stories cannot be reproduced in this book, the readers can explore websites where those stores are posted, such as canadianimmigrant.ca, sagennext.com, and canindia.com. The lessons one can learn from the stories of successful people of South Asian origin have been highlighted in the following paragraphs. These are the experiences, challenges, and most importantly the hard work of the Canadians of South Asian origin who prospered, thrived, and achieved the desired goal.

The review of their stories points to recurring elements, starting from racism and discrimination to the assumption of assimilation, integration, and social inclusion that come into play in the struggle to prosper. A common element is that racism exists in Canada, but South Asian children are capable of reframing the Canadian narrative in their own ways to establish their rights and sense of identity and Canadianness. Most importantly, the new generation youth must work hard to achieve it because multiculturalism in Canada is incomplete, and labour market discrimination is overlooked by the overwhelming majority of white Canadians.

Statements from South Asian immigrants' children suggest that they are committed to their goal. They claim to have phenomenal drive that powers them onto great heights—the early difficulty that they face can fuel ambition that makes them achieve their goal much more than the average person. They emphasized that there are barriers faced by ethnic minorities when it comes to hiring practices, yet one should not give up but try hard and give the best of their ability to overcome the barriers.

Soma Choudhury, a corporate lawyer, attributes her success to hard work. Her tips for immigrants who want to become successful lawyers are simple—work hard, work hard, work hard. You are going to face barriers, but you can't get sidetracked by it. She further said that networking is very important; talking to people is helpful. "Be upfront about the fact that you are an immigrant and that gives you adaptability," she said. Her final word of wisdom is "Don't give up."[72] The same idea resonates among many other South Asian Canadians. For example, Sandy Sidhu, an aspiring artist, believes hard work and having faith in oneself are the key to success. She played in the military science fiction television series *Stargate Universe*. She also believes that both fate and hard work go together. Deesha,[73] a rising Canadian South Asian music talent, has captured audience across Canada and across the globe by her dedication, hard work, and love for music. Summy Uppal,[74] a successful banker, advised South Asians to be passionate about their career. As the economy increasingly becomes competitive, the new generations will face greater challenges in terms of career development, he believes. Quasim Ali, a law student in the Canadian and American Dual JD program at the University of Windsor and University of Detroit, advised young lawyers or students who wish to pursue law to demonstrate their presence, as 90 percent work in the legal profession is how one markets oneself. One should try to make a difference in one's locality and get the best references to show the law schools that one is more than just books.[75]

Although there are racism and discrimination in Canada, South Asians do believe that Canada is a country of opportunity. Newcomers should be receptive, be positive, take right attitude, and be patient with dreams. Afghan writer and community worker Ariana Yaftani[76] advised immigrants to be open to new way of thinking and viewing work through a different lens. Pakistani-born journalist Natasha Fatah supports a bicultural lifestyle by retaining her own cultural and religious roots while integrating into the Canadian society and workplace culture. She believes that it is important for immigrants to integrate into Canada's mainstream society because Canada is definitely their new home.[77] Dr. Deepali Kumar, a physician-scientist at University of Alberta, echoes a similar view. She thinks that in addition to maintaining heritage culture, it is also important to put ourselves out there and be part of the Canadian mainstream culture.[78] Steve Gupta, president and CEO of Easton's Group of Hotels, believes that opportunity brings luck, and if someone doesn't grab the window of opportunity, it's going to knock on someone else's door. His own experience is that when an opportunity came his way, he accepted it with passion, drive, and willingness to put in a lot of hard work. The harder he worked, the luckier he was.[79] Toronto entrepreneur Haroon Mirza is a self-made millionaire at the age of twenty-nine. He and his two business partners credit hard work and timely advice for their success. They made millions of dollars by selling the company to Intel but continue to be a chip maker. They believe that any new immigrants to Canada can accomplish many things if they set sights on them.[80]

Tazeen Qayyum, a reputed miniature painter, is a very successful practicing professional artist who established herself within the South Asian contemporary arts community. She achieved considerable success during her fifteen years of hard work in Canada. She said that Canada has strong support system and opportunities for the arts that one can take advantage of. Her advice to fellow South Asians is that one should always focus and concentrate on the continuous improvement of the quality of the work, and success will come naturally.[81] Avish Sood is a young marketing and sports professional whose career choice, dedication, goal, strategy, and hard work made him a successful person. But his achievement was not without challenges. One of the biggest challenges, as he mentioned, on the road to success is the *distraction* in life. Specifically, he said that it is easy to postpone work and get involved with the wrong people; it is therefore imperative that one should not deviate from one's end goal.[82]

Reza Satchu is an entrepreneur, the creator of University of Toronto's most highly rated undergraduate course, Economics of Entrepreneurship. He is also the founding chair, cochair, and cofounder of the Next 36. Prof. Reza Satchu came across various paths of success in his long career. His advice is that when people fail, they don't try again—this is wrong. But trying and failing is much better than not trying at all; at least one can learn something if one fails. Among other advice from him are that one needs to work on one's weaknesses, and put oneself in a situation where one is forced to get better at them, get access to leaders and mentors, stay relevant, and don't believe in fate at all.[83] Another successful person is Murali Murthy. He is the author of the best-selling *The ACE Principle*. He is a creative director and advertising strategist who was holding senior position at various agencies across United States and Canada. He classified immigrants into two groups—successful and unsuccessful. The successful immigrants understand Canada and at the same time understand what it takes to thrive, succeed, and achieve the desired goal. His main strategy of success is to follow the path of successful immigrants, learn from them, and excel.[84]

Take the example of Malhotra, who immigrated to Canada thirty-three years ago and now known as the "Angle of the North." She is a physician and has been working on women's health issues, especially among the First Nations of Northern Saskatchewan. Malhotra was awarded the Saskatchewan Order of Merit in 2001, the Order of Canada in 2006, and in 2008, was proclaimed Citizen of the Year in Prince Albert, the city where she got her start in Canada. Her hard work paid off. It is true that immigrant doctors face many challenges, and we all know the fact that to become a doctor in Canada, especially for the immigrant doctors, is extremely difficult. Yet Malhothra offers the key advice to those who want to become a doctor in Canada—study hard.[85]

A Bangladeshi immigrant who holds a PhD degree in medical science got a job in the health-care field at the Canadian Mental Health Association (CMHA) without having a Canadian license. His name is Rayhan Hossain. He got the internship through the Bridge Training Program for Internationally Trained Psychologists and Allied Mental Health Professionals. People get frustrated and discouraged by failure, but he advised them not to be discouraged, rather to find out the mistakes of failure, to listen to the successful people.[86] Another Bangladesh-born immigrant Dr. Ashish Paul has an amazing success in Regian. He is known as the "best doctor in Regina"—title given by the readers of Regina's local newspaper. The award has no monetary value, but it's definitely an honour, Dr. Paul believes. He and his wife, Dr. Shefali Dutta (also a medical doctor), spent eight years in Namibia and South Africa and practiced medicine. However, Dr. Paul has to pass Canadian medical exams to continue practicing in Canada. He passed some exams but still need more exams to pass. He is committed to complete all the required exams. His wife is also taking exams and determined to complete all the exams to get license to practice in Canada. Again this is the story of hard work, dedication, and commitment to achieve a goal.[87]

Mina Mawani, president and CEO of Canadian Women's Foundation for the last twenty-two years, sent a strong message to women and girls that newcomers face struggles, but they must have confidence in themselves that have to use valuable assets like friends and families, and that they should always have a positive disposition. She also believes that learning from other women's expertise and experience help face many challenges.[88] Afghan-born Dr. Walter Heidary faced many challenges, but his dedication and hard work brought him success. His best advice to new immigrants is to work hard, work hard, and work hard. He further added that opportunities in Canada are abundant, and one has to pursue in the right way. If one has the potential, drive, and firm determination, he/she can definitely achieve the desired goal.[89]

Tahmeena Bokhari is a college professor and a social worker who came to Canada with her parents when she was a child. She advised South Asians to keep their roots in addition to prospering and progressing among other Canadians. Although it is hard to compete with white immigrants, South Asians youths can succeed eventually. She pointed out that according to Canadian immigration history, it takes about three generations for ethnic immigrants to be at par with the white counterpart. This is true in the case of education, career, and even for full participation in civic society and enjoying a quality of life within the Canadian norm. As a final note, she emphasized that South Asian youths must understand, know, and love themselves; only then the strength can come from within, which in turn leads energy to work hard and make success.[90] We learn a good lesson from her experience and dedicated work—that is, one can struggle to thrive in Canada and keep the ethnic roots at the same time. It may take longer time for some than others.

Adarsha Metha is a renewable energy advocate. With an undergraduate degree in applied math and computer science and a master's degree in applied maths, she focussed on environmental fluid dynamics. The benefits of renewable energy may be multipronged, yet very few South Asians understand it; although there are so many things that South Asians can do to help with our environment, she said. One may argue that first generation of South Asians are unaware of the concept of renewable energy.

However, the second generation of South Asians can be proactive and can do something because they know it from Canadian education curriculum. Adarsha encourages young women to pursue opportunities in this area. She worked hard and put herself into career building while maintaining family responsibilities at the same time. She attributes her success story by admitting the fact that it is the hard work, commitment to career, and striving for good results. Later, she became the chair of the board of directors of the Canadian Wind Energy Association in 2009.[91] Her success story suggests that sometimes a good mentor, a motivator, is an extremely important factor to lead to success.

Entrepreneur and lawyer Meleni David provides excellent legal services to her clients and their families who experience personal injuries. Sri Lankan-born Meleni is a recipient of the Top 25 Canadian Immigrants of 2012 Award and the National Ethnic Press and Media Council of Canada Award from the lieutenant governor. She openly speaks about her challenges and the road to success. She agrees to the fact that the industry is male dominated, but she doesn't want to believe that this trend will continue for long. She works hard to succeed in this field and not only encourages but also trains and grooms other female lawyers to be successful. Her advice to new immigrant women is that they should believe in themselves and believe in their power. Women have a duty to raise their children to their best ability, but that does not mean that their lives end there. They should have a purpose of their own life, and they should pursue it with the help and support from their families in order to fulfill career dreams.[92]

Baldev Padam views Canada in a more realistic way and believes that Canadians can learn from South Asian immigrants through the Canadian mosaic. In recent decades, immigrants from Asian countries settled in Canada who brought their diverse cultures and social norms. Because of its ethnic and cultural diversity, Canada becomes a model country in the world and may be called as the other United Nations of our world. Yet there are gaps between Western and Eastern cultural and normative lifestyles that exist in Canada. Eastern people are more likely to live in ghettoes, whereas Westerners are not prepared yet to come closer to them. We, however, observe the changes among the young generation of Canadians. Baldev has brought up the saying from of Rudyard Kipling's famous lines, "Oh East is east, and West is west and never the twain shall meet." Baldev said that it may not hold good for long. He believes, "younger White Canadians slowly, but surely are getting closer to lilting bouncy Bollywood music and folk dance, like Bhangra, and have developed taste for Indian foods like samosas and Tandoori chicken and other cuisine." South Asian youths are doing well in schools and universities. The South Asian youths and their white counterparts are socializing and mixing freely at university level without any prejudice, which is obviously a good sign; or the fact that South Asian arts and culture are being accepted widely in North America, which is likely to narrow down the gap between two cultures in the long run. Given the fact that none would like to say goodbye to one's culture, yet people of all colours, shades, and races, including the first nation, together could make Canadian mosaic.[93]

One can read the amazing story of Sudarshan Gautam, a Nepal-born Calgary resident whose both arms are amputated. He drives a car and does mountaineering. He is tough, and difficulties know he is difficult. He uses his feet to eat, write, and perform daily activities of life. He also published a book on Bill Clinton in Nepalese. According to him, "Disability is not an inability, but a great challenge." He also runs an auto-detailing business and famous in Calgary. His next aim is to establish a Guinness Book world record of scaling the Everest without arms. He has planned a cross-country drive across Canada where he will try to meet every possible politician and spread the message that disability is not an inability at all. What we learn from Gautam's life is that determination and hard work count for success and that a person's disability can't stop him to succeed in life.[94] Indian-born Mathur became the first South Asian to reach the semifinals of the televised singing contest. Entering into Canadian Idol is a challenging work and an adventure, she said. Her success was the result of hard work and family support. She also credits her success to Canadians because of her network with key people. Not only was her talent recognized by many people whom she met, but they also helped her. She believes that newcomers must be adaptable and can follow this path. However, she mentioned that the biggest challenge for the newcomers in Canada is to get the right opportunity. One way of getting opportunity is volunteering, which can be a first step to overcome this problem, she emphasized, because she did the same. It helped her to build contacts with key people.[95]

South Asian MPs and MPPs addressed a number of important issues and provided advice that can be very useful to second-generation Canadians of South Asian origin. Some emphasised the importance of proper education, struggle, and hard work as the key to success. Others said that South Asian Canadians are vibrant, energetic, determined, and talented people who can nurture the qualities necessary to achieve success in their areas of interest including politics. They recommended that members of the South Asian community should get involved beyond their ethnocultural organisations and reach out to the broader community-based organisations. They should take ownership of the community to bring change; this is how belonging and social inclusion takes into effect. Some also mentioned the weaknesses of the South Asians that need to be overcome such as "leg pulling" and fighting within the community.[96]

There is a view that South Asian politicians holding offices do not always deliver results for the South Asian community as expected. For example, they do not acknowledge the unique challenges South Asians face, claiming instead that South Asians are not different from Canadians at large. This statement may be politically correct but is definitely not the true reflection of Canadian mosaic in the multicultural context. South Asian Canadians want to believe that these elected officials are assets for the South Asian community and expect that they would do much more for their community and the ethnic minority communities at large.

The profiles presented in this chapter are the incredible stories of South Asian Canadians, second-generation young adults in particular. These profiles reflect dedication, determination, ambition, realistic approach, struggle, and hard work of people of different backgrounds who achieved success in Canada. Their stories are the inspirations not only for fellow South Asians but also for every ethnocultural minority population in Canada. Their stories are the road maps, with every step as a milestone of success. Their optimistic and proactive approach trumped over adversities and brought them success. The second-generation South Asian youths can adopt these stories to guide them forward.

7

What Children of South Asian Origin Think? Opinions about the Key Issues

Second generation is the key link between their parents' culture and a new way of living that is thought of as Canadian. They are the social agents of sociocultural change. The second-generation children of ethnic origins, no matter whether they were born in Canada or abroad, often face intense challenges due to the differences between their cultural background and the community into which they are trying to integrate; all of this is piled up on top of the normal growing pains of youth, making for awkward and complicated situations. Their everyday experience in Canada involves racism and discrimination, or not if subject to debate; although previous literatures suggested that these immigrants and their children face barriers that adversely affect their integration into Canada's mainstream society. The pluralism of a society can only operate well when all of the members of that society (immigrants' children in particular) participate in and identify with that society.

The transition periods (from youth to adulthood), educational attainment, entry into the labour force, career development, and finally the formation of their own family and households for second-generation ethnic minorities including South Asians are the formidable telling stories of the matters that make them distinctive and demanding. A number of key issues were identified, based on previous literatures, and the opinions and perspectives were solicited from a sample of second-generation South Asian youths in Canada. Those youth Canadians openly talked in their own words what they thought about the issues and what were their concerns. The issues are

- job market and future career development
- conflict between parents and children
- cultural conflict between heritage culture and Canadians' culture—bicultural collide
- acculturation and adaptation
- cohesion and inclusion
- racism in everyday life
- mixed marriage

Learning from the second-generation young adults the opinions about these issues, we will be able to compare the results from the published research that are discussed in this book. Addressing these issues and concerns raised will generate greater awareness, inquisitiveness, and meaningful discussions not only among the people of the South Asian communities but also among the Canadian public in general.

The issues were clearly explained in the questionnaire for respondents' better understanding and to help organise their thoughts and write their opinions. Only the well-thought and organised opinions provided by the respondents have been included in the book. To those I sent questionnaire gave me the verbal permission for their opinions only to be published in the book. Therefore, names of the participants were not published in order to protect their identity.

Two groups of young adults participated in the survey: (1) *Generation 1.5* of South Asian origin who immigrated with their parents to Canada at a young age—they spent most of their childhood and adulthood in Canada and are very familiar with the Canadian culture and the official languages, and they have had similar experiences to Canadian born citizens, and (2) *second-generation* young adults who were born in Canada to first-generation parents of South Asian origin. Participants gave opinions in their own words about the issues and their concerns, which are presented below:

Issue #1: Job market and future career development

Labour market discrimination is built in and is justified by an overarching narrative of whiteness. New generation of youth from visible minority immigrants is likely to face greater challenges in entering the job market and securing a stable, career-oriented, and well-paying job. Being a second-generation visible minority youth, what do you think in this context? Keep in mind the fact that you are competing with those white Canadian youths who have the same education, skills, and competencies like yours.

Respondents' opinions:

On a personal level, I have never felt discriminated against in the workforce due to my racial or religious background, but I know many of my peers who have. In my opinion, there will always be people who will show the visible minority some sort of discrimination, but as we grow into a new world where race, religion, sexual orientation, immigrants, etc. are more and more accepted, I think we will be able to rise in adversity and conquer these challenges as they did in the past.

Based on my experience in nongovernmental and legal professional circles, I agree that predominant cultural norms remain that of white Canadians. Speaking about my own experience, I have not had any problems in this respect as I believe I share many of those cultural norms. I have always felt that I was competing on equal terms as my white peers, but I think this is because I have no accent, dress like the majority of individuals and share most of the social and cultural values of the majority. I have noticed that, visible minority or not, those employees who are able to integrate socially with their coworkers are more likely to be overcome barriers associated with being a second-generation immigrant than those who remain socially separate and only interact on a strictly professional basis. The Canadian workplace is one where social and professional lines can be fuzzy.

One more point I would make in this regard is that my parents did not raise me in a strict religious environment and I have never been publicly religious. In the South Asian context, I believe that visible minority youth who are very observant may currently be facing more discrimination due to the rise in anti-Muslim sentiment generally in the Western world. My personal view is that, while we must fight to eradicate all forms of racism in the workplace, and there ought not to be discriminatory barriers for second-generation immigrants to gain and maintain employment, it is necessary for parents and youth to recognize the majority culture in which they are living and integrate. The benefits of living in Canadian society arose from the culture and norms of Canadians and that is why we are here. I am very much against the phenomenon of youth socializing with their ethnic groups only to the exclusion of others, such as is happening in the suburbs of the GTA. It is not healthy for society as a whole, not conducive to social cohesion, and practically speaking, I believe it makes it much harder to obtain employment down the road if the employee cannot participate in the common culture of most workplaces.

Although I have not personally faced any challenges specifically in entering the labour market due to my race or ethnicity, there are other challenges that I face at the workplace and when applying to certain graduate schools. Within the workplace, there are certain social events amongst coworkers that I am unable to attend. Excluding me from these events can often create a negative impression upon my colleagues as they may feel I am an unsociable or unfriendly person. However, this is mainly due to certain events entailing activities that I am not permitted to involve myself within. For example, Christmas parties or other late night parties often involve drinking or going to clubs or bars. These are activities that, as a Muslim, I am prohibited to take part in.

With regard to applying to graduate schools, one barrier that I may face is not particularly well defined, however, it is one that may exist. Many graduate schools are said to have a certain quota of students within the visible minority that they admit every year. This is often assumed because many applications often require an individual to state whether or not they are members of the visible minority. If such is the case, it can restrict my ability to attend a graduate school of my choice.

In the early '90s, we all felt that it was more challenging for minorities to get any jobs, even less paying odd jobs. I remember enlisting with a minority youth organization to get my first job. Things started to change in the late '90s and into early 2000s. There had been a clear shift towards accepting visible minorities in the workplace. We started seeing more and more folks from our community working for high-paying tech jobs. Promotions were handed out to minorities who excelled in their profession. Many of my minority friends even became entrepreneurs starting their own businesses. Finding a job as a minority was becoming less of a concern. I moved to the US right after graduating and found a job pretty quickly. Almost all of my friends were able to find jobs soon after graduating. What helps the situation in our favour is that now we have minorities working as hiring managers and other important positions. Discrimination at workplace is not common as it used to be. You can fight discrimination with education and a strong desire to success. Companies these days cannot ignore qualified candidates even if they come from a different country. I have coworkers who speak very little English but are valuable to company and they are treated that way.

Being an employee of a provincially owned utility (Hydro One), there has been a major change in the demographic of employees being hired. There is an even mix between Caucasians and visible minorities. But when we talk about *the higher level jobs (Directors, VP, SVP, CEO) there are no visible minorities—which is typical in a government owned company; sort of like an old boys club. Yet this does not hinder my future aspirations of obtaining one of these high-level positions. In my eyes, I have the rights skills, drive and enthusiasm to succeed. My employer boasts that they are an equal opportunity employer, so I believe race and religion are irrelevant for my future success in this company.*

If I was not in my current situation and I was looking for employment, then I would have to say that a Caucasian candidate would have the upper hand over a second-generation visible minority—assuming the employer is Caucasian. It's human nature to stick with your own kind, regardless of qualifications. I believe it is our job as visible minorities to assimilate more with the Canadian culture, without compromising religious beliefs. This can be done by being involved in the local community, playing organized sports or socializing with people outside your race. This will definitely help one's chances with future career opportunities through networking.

I do not believe visible minorities face greater challenges in entering the job market. However, I can only speak to my location (Ontario). It seems the opposite, as there appear to be affirmative action policies in place for visible minorities (in both the private and public sectors). That is to say, assuming equivalent education, skills, experience, etc. between a visible minority and a white Canadian, preference may be given to the visible minority.

Personally I do not find racism to be a factor in the job market, particularly in the field that I currently work in. I work in the IT sector and I find that it is quite the reverse. I find more ethnic groups in this field rather than white Canadians. However, having said that, I am merely speaking in terms of second-generation Canadian. I do see a more racist approach to first-generation immigrants, primarily due to the language barriers and not the skill or education level. Going back to my personal experiences being in the job market for the past six years, I do not believe at any point I have experienced any preferential/derogatory treatment due to the colour of my skin or my background.

Working for the federal government for the past 8 years, I have thought about IF this type of discrimination exists. Meaning, I can understand that many first-generation immigrants might have faced that challenge many years ago and that is why they brought initiatives, which helped bring equality in the workplace. However, as we can see, the workplace is still paced by a Caucasian majority and I would think it has more to do with the entirety of the Canadian population. If you were to take a sample of the Canadian population and see what percentage are immigrants and then took the same sample in the workplace and found that there is a large difference, then I would believe that this type of discrimination still exists. Now I am faced with a different challenge than the first generation. My challenge would be dealing with the aftermath of appointments of immigrants to certain positions based solely on the fact that they are a visible minority. For example, if immigrants are appointed to positions that maybe somebody else has a greater ability to fulfill, the organization may discredit my skills/abilities due to this.

I definitely agree with this notion, though I have not necessarily been faced with it yet. I graduated from school and joined the workforce only 3 years ago, so I am still navigating. While it has been tremendously difficult to land a full-time job that is related to the field I studied in, I feel that this problem is ubiquitous among my millennial peers. Job security just does not exist like it used to, and most of my peers—regardless of race—seem to feel the same way. So I am hard-pressed to say that my job troubles lie in the color of my skin, as many of my friends who are white are facing the same issues.

However, I definitely think race offers an unfair advantage or disadvantage depending on what side of the skin-color fence you are on. Although it has not necessarily affected my job hunt so far (although I cannot tell definitely because I don't know what is talked about when someone sees my resume, or after I leave an interview), I have observed some differences in the workplace. The most prominent example is from when I was working in the government—it happened to be at a time when a lot of cuts were taking place in all departments, and mine was no exception. I noticed that all the people let go were those who were visible minorities, and I thought this was too ironic to be a coincidence. I have also heard of stories where one person applies for a job and does not hear back, but then anglicizes his name and is called in for an interview to the same job. It makes me feel that white privilege is indeed alive and well, but I do pray that somehow my competencies will overcome it and not let race impede my effort to becoming successful and having a fulfilling career.

Although I will certainly not argue that systemic discrimination still exists and that as such there are great challenges to visible minorities of all demographics, in my opinion the greatest barriers remain to first-generation immigrants to Canada. For example, the French language requirement is quite an obstacle for a new immigrant who might struggle enough to learn one language but is now forced to learn two lest they be marginalized into lesser paying roles. The second generation, however, at least has the ability to learn French in school. However, that is not to say that second-generation visible minorities (SGVM) are still not hampered as the French requirement has become very rigid, allowing for the preference of francophone over those who must take drawn out and complex

French testing. Add to this, that even according to the Government of Canada, most jobs are acquired through networking or known relationships with people already in positions of power, and challenges certainly do remain for visible minorities who might even have been born here.

Although I agree that there is labour market discrimination, I do not believe that the new generation of youth from visible minority immigrants are likely to face greater challenges in entering the job market and securing a stable, career-oriented, and well-paying job. In fact, I think it is quite the opposite. I feel as visible minorities in Canadian society, we have an advantage in the job market if we have the same education, skills and competencies as our white Canadian colleagues—especially for government jobs due to the employment equity program.

Unfortunately, we are often not bilingual in French and English, putting us back to a disadvantage in the job market. Our first language is our mother tongue (Hindi, Punjabi, Bengali, Urdu, etc.), and we learn English as a second language. On the other hand, those occupying the highest-paying jobs and CEO positions are white, dominant men. I would like to see youth from visible minority immigrants, especially women, taking leadership positions in the government, and in the corporate world. This is precisely, the glass ceiling—the unseen, unbreakable barrier that keeps women and minorities from rising to the top of the corporate ladder. Awareness and education is the first step to creating change.

To some extent, I think being a visible minority works to my advantage. My chances of getting a job might improve because of employment equity.

I am not in the best position to fully analyze this notion. I am still completing my undergraduate degree. I have had a few part-time jobs; however, I feel that it has actually worked to my benefit from being a visible minority. Every office I was hired to wanted to increase the genetic diversity. I asked my supervisors who later admitted to my speculation, saying they wanted to hire staffs that were from all backgrounds to create a good impression. With that being said, we are all second-generation immigrants, with no accents and basic knowledge of French. We dress in a westernized way and know the Canadian culture well enough to relate to each other.

Fortunately, in the government this issue has been acknowledged and there are measures in place to assist visible minorities. In the entry-level positions I did not feel this as much as a second-generation visible minority. There are supportive members who recognize talent and do not discriminate based solely on race. As I have not attempted to climb the corporate ladder to much higher positions, I cannot speak for such higher positions.

On a different note, what I find challenging is definitely having to prove myself as a qualified or capable member without being viewed by others as someone who is simply placed into a position without merit in order to meet the visible minority quota. I believe that first generation will definitely feel a much higher level of discrimination from their counterparts than second generation.

I do not believe being a part of a second-generation visible minority group will dictate the type of career path I'll follow. The most important aspect when entering the labour force is having an education, and having enough experience. Therefore, although I may be a second-generation visible minority youth, I do not believe there will be greater challenges when entering the job market, as long as I have a stable foundation of education and experience.

As a South Asian female, and a visible Muslim as I wore hijab for ten years (including the time of my initial foray into the professional world), I was well aware of the possible labour market discrimination I might face. Surprisingly, this was not an awareness created by experiences I had with other Canadians growing up, white or otherwise. Instead, this fear of discrimination was instilled by my mother. My South Asian mother immigrated to Saudi Arabia in her early twenties, and then to Canada in her early thirties. It took her decades to feel as though she fit in, and so her fears of discrimination, which she herself might have faced, were downgraded to me. Well, she attempted to instil this fear in me anyway. It did not take root. As a confident person by nature, and someone who considered themselves Canadian and as qualified, if not more, than any white or other counterparts, I never hesitated in applications or interviews. I applied more aggressively to jobs to prove my mother wrong as she always admonished me for wearing hijab in fear of job discrimination. When I was employed at a higher-end fashion boutique as a hijab-wearing South Asian, I triumphantly brought the news home to my mother to end all of her fears of my future. And it was smooth sailing from there. Neither my hijab nor my brown skin colour ever seemed to hold me back from any profession. I have worked in private sector, nonprofit sector, and as a Senior Immigration Officer working on refugee cases of all things, and without a second regard to my heritage. However, it is important to keep in mind that these experiences gathered from living and working in Toronto; a city of multicultural hub that consider race as a factor that would be preposterous for any smart HR looking to develop their organisation. The levels of second- and third-generation immigrants here make that a fact I think. I cannot speak the same for other parts of Canada, however, where the multiculturalism isn't as much of a defining factor as it is here in Canada.

I think it can differ according to the type of industry and which part of the country one is working in. Some areas are more culturally diverse than others and are open and accepting of all types of peoples. There are also certain fields of employment that benefit from having employees who visibly mirror the clientele they serve. For example, the nonprofit organizations as compared to corporate business environment could have very different approaches when looking for employees.

As a visible minority, I have actually found my appearance to be an advantage when seeking employment as it allows for a different perspective than the norm, and also due to increasing visible minority/disability inclusion policies.

Issue #2: Conflict between parents and children

As a second-generation visible minority adult, how do you see yourself as a cultural bridge between your parents' ways of living and a new way of living as a new generation of Canadians? Conflict between immigrant parents and their children is by no means inevitable. Second-generation youths feel torn between their desire to fit in with their peers and their willingness to meet their parents' expectations. What is your opinion about this conflict?

Respondents' opinions:

I am quite happy with my current balance of my parents' way of living and my own. I have adopted some of my parents' values (e.g., emphasis on education and importance of the family), enjoy reading post-Colonial literature and considering my parents' journey in life, and maintain certain cultural aspects of life, such as speaking in mother tongue, Indian dance, etc. However, I sometimes feel that I am disappointing my parents by not participating in certain traditions that they value. I do feel some anxiety about not meeting what South Asian parents often consider as "duties," but I have strong personal convictions about leading the life that I feel is right for me, and what I believe to be moral and necessary for my sanity.

I think it is unfair for immigrant parents to raise their children in a totally different culture and expect that they will do everything the way the parents expect. This is for both pragmatic reasons (i.e., it is impossible for a child growing up in Canada to not develop differently so such expectations are unrealistic) and moral reasons (i.e., it is an interference with the autonomy of the children to grow into adults with their own interests and motivations in life). I myself was very lucky to have parents who gave me freedom to develop in my own way. While it did not always seem that way as I was growing up (!), I realize now I was in fact given much room to be both Canadian and Bengali.

This is a huge conflict between the two, as one, generations are set in their ways and have come to a Westernized way of living but also gripping onto their cultural and traditional ways, which they want to embed in their children. And another, as an adolescent youth trying to fit it and grasp all the opportunities that come their way due to being in a more flourished society; so where is the middle ground? Unfortunately, sometimes there isn't one and parent and child have to go through hardships to fully understand where the balance lies. Keeping an open mind and making compromise for one another will be the key to reduce the conflicts.

Personally, I do not often feel that I experience conflict with my parents with regard to fitting in amongst my peers and meeting my parents' expectations. Since my childhood, the majority of my peers have been members of either the South Asian community or of other minority groups because I grew in a neighbourhood which had a predominant immigrant population. Therefore, they were often able to understand the expectations that my parents had of me and I did not find it very difficult to adhere to my parents expectations and maintain a good relationship with my peers. However, not everyone would have been brought up within the same environment as me.

Maintaining positive relationships with peers, whether they are white or of the minority, is important. In such cases, I feel that parents must understand that it may not be possible for their children to fulfill all expectations they may have due to the expectations of their peers, and need to allow a certain degree of leniency. At the same time, children also need to respect that they have a unique cultural heritage. Their parents have been raised with certain cultural values, and their expectations stem from these values. Therefore, children should try to fulfill their parents' expectations and at the same time to avoid committing acts that may be considered taboos in order to uphold their cultural heritage.

Both kids and parents had to make compromises. We had to accept the fact that we couldn't party or stay out late like many of our friends, so we stopped asking for it. Parents couldn't control what we were doing when we went out with friends. It was especially harder when we started University. When we told them we had late classes, they had no choice but to believe us. When many of my friends were from the same community parents felt okay with me spending time with friends or going away on trips with them. Had my close friends been white or not from the same community, parents would have been stricter dealing with us.

Our parents came to Canada for a reason and I believe that is to provide a better life for themselves and their children. The only way of doing this is by assimilating with Canadian culture, without compromising religious beliefs. We as immigrants should embrace the fact that we live in a free country where we can openly practice our own religion and stay true to our roots. Canada is a free country with a multitude of the population practicing their own religion, maintaining their cultural identity and thriving as Canadian citizens. South Asians, unlike other races in Canada, tends to shelter them from the rest of Canada. In order for South Asians to flourish in Canada, we really need to make a solid effort to interact with people outside our race. This will increase our reputation in the Canadian community and provide a better quality of life for our future generations.

This is dependent on the openness and degree of traditional, cultural views of the immigrant parents versus the views of the children and both their abilities to attempt a compromise. The two cultures are completely different, where South Asian cultures are collectivist with emphasis on family/community, while the North American culture is individualistic, placing an emphasis on the individual. There is also a divide in terms of views on gender roles and what is expected from each sex. As a result, there is often conflict, as there is a conflict of ideals in both culture types to begin with. There must be a level of understanding of this fact from both parties, but the immigrant parents will typically need to make more of a compromise, as they are raising their children in a culture that they (should) know is different and can't expect their children to approach life exactly the same as one would in their country of origin. Ultimately, new generation children will have to assume at least some of the Canadian cultural traits in order to succeed in the long term.

There is always a certain gap and there always will be a small gap between parents and their kids. I believe that the environment you grow up in and the society that moulds you sticks with you forever. My parents grew up in a small town in Pakistan and bringing that small town culture to a western country like Canada does have its challenges no matter how hard they try to blend in. A lot of times the eastern and western cultures do clash and that is when kids feel torn. I can tell you from my experiences that the best way to handle this is to establish a compromise between both parties. Kids need to be educated on the importance of keeping and building our culture and parents need to understand that not everything can be passed along. I can also say from my experiences that a lot of *times kids do try to meet their parents' expectations but parents can sometimes not see the results right away and this causes frustration between them.*

For me personally, there was not much of a conflict between my parents' way of living and my own. Having lived in Canada since 1983, they have adapted their lives to fit in with the Canadian population. I did not feel much of a struggle to help them understand my way of living. I have taken much of what they taught me and lived my life according to their values. Personally, my friends impacted my life in more of a spiritual way than my parents.

This is something I definitely relate to, and have so for my entire life. It has been challenging to straddle the line between two cultures. I think it makes it easier if the parents of my generation are more liberal than average, or if the child is not as close to his or her parents. If the parent is not close, then the child will not feel as guilty if they deviate from what the traditional cultural norms may be. If the child is not close, then it is more likely that the parents' expectations are not as stringent as more traditional parents, making it easier for the child to adopt the more lenient host customs.

In my case, my parents were very liberal in wanting the best for me—so anything related to the betterment of my education was always allowed. But dating, staying out late, alcohol, wearing anything sleeveless—those sorts of things that were so apparent among my peers, remained off limits. I didn't necessarily want to dabble in any of these experiences, but as I grew older I found myself wanting more independence—which I think is a common theme among any teenager, white or not. So that is where most of the conflict between parent-child came from in my experience—I mainly fought to stay out late with my friends because I didn't think it was fair that everyone else had no problem, but I had to be home by a certain (relatively early) time. I am really close to my mom especially, and because she has such traditional values and tried to instil them in me from a young age, I never really deviated otherwise because I would feel guilty knowing she wouldn't approve of my actions.

I think the biggest leap of faith she took was letting me go to university away from home and when she saw she could trust me and I wasn't getting into trouble that alleviated a lot of the conflict that had occurred when I was younger. I still partake in more Western habits than my mom ever would have, but I think I do a good job of balancing the two—and because she herself has adapted her viewpoints to accept that it is nearly impossible to impose 100 percent of the customs she grew up with, we don't have any conflict at all these days.

As a SGVM I can certainly speak to this point and state that from my experience, there is a conflict which exists in this regard. While there might be variances between peer group to peer group and household to household, SGVMs must balance the expectations from their friends (and Canadian society) with that of their families. Unfortunately for SGVMs, the expectations are usually at odds making their lives that much more complex, and thus a hurdle that white Canadians are not made to experience. Everything from whom you date, to where you live after university, to how late you stay out, to what career you wish to pursue are all significant points of reflection for SGVMs whereas white Canadians might not give their choices either much thought or paramount to their decision-making process are their wishes alone.

As a shyer, reserved oldest daughter, I often do not feel torn between my desire to fit in with my peers and willingness to meet my parents' expectations. My actions, attitudes and beliefs are often aligned with my parents' attitudes and beliefs. My parents came to Canada in their teenage years and they have assimilated quite well in Western, Canadian society. As my siblings and I grow up, they also adapt to our way of thinking and beliefs. The age difference between my mom and me is not that big, so I often feel like I can talk to her as if she is my older sister. We communicate well and we explain what's going on in our day-to-day life. Interestingly, my mom tells me to be more outgoing!

However, I must say that I am probably the exception. I know some of my South Asian friends, who are also second-generation youth, face a lot of conflicts with their parents and often hide the truth regarding their actions. I still have the traditional beliefs of dressing conservatively, not staying out late at night, and not drinking or clubbing. If I deviated away from these cultural norms instilled in me, I would feel very guilty in doing so—for breaking their trust in me. Nevertheless, lately, I've been demanding more independence and freedom. I hope to move out after completing my degree, and finding myself. This is quite "normal," I would say, regardless of my cultural background. I do believe I am quite well assimilated into Canadian culture; however, I have this ongoing battle where I often feel "too brown" amongst my Native Canadian friends, and "whitewashed" amongst my South Asian friends.

Growing up, I always thought it was really hard to find a balance between my parents' expectations and what I wanted for myself. The hardest part was bridging the collective roots of my parents and my individualist upbringing. However, I am extremely lucky to have the parents that I do because they gave me space to grow. Fortunately, I have come to appreciate the values that were instilled in me as a child and hope to carry them forward to my own family one day. Values like: respect for your elders, being there for each other, and love for family. Although there were times when I hated the process of having to reflect on two worlds and creating a bridge world for myself, I don't think I would be the person I am today without it.

My parents are quite easygoing compared to my South Asian friend's parents. But even with that, there are certain restrictions I had that my other Caucasian friends did not. There was always a constant struggle of my curfew time as I was progressing from my teenage years to my adult ones. I have always been the first one leaving parties because my parents were expecting me at a certain time. Then there are some rules that I have never even bothered to negotiate such as having dates, going clubbing or drinking alcohol because they became my own restrictions on myself. My parents have instilled very reasonable values, which I will continue on. If I ever feel tempted to do anything that they wouldn't do, I always feel guilty about it and then end up talking to them. For example: My parents are vegetarian for religious reasons. I recently started working out and wanted to eat something that is highly nutritious. They would not approve of my dietary choice but I talked it through with them and eventually they agreed. I know a lot of people that end up lying to their parents on where they are because they think their immigrant parents wouldn't understand them. I believe in the opposite. I am always honest on where I am and with whom so that my parents are able to become accustomed to the western culture and are able to understand me better.

Some cross-cultural conflicts between these generations (parents and children) are inevitable. However, once core values are instilled, both generations may learn to find a good balance. Once the two generations differ in these core values, it becomes very difficult to find complacency with regard to any major conflict. When you are younger, it is obviously much harder to accept and find harmony as pressures to be accepted by your peers are often overbearing. As you grow older, many of the values that were instilled in you as a child often may return.

Without a doubt there are evident differences in my parents' way of living in comparison to mine. However, I believe there is a middle point, which joins the two ends. Although there is often a desire to fit in with peers, I firmly stand behind being your own person, and not falling under peer pressure. As well, it is not always easy to meet parents' expectations, however, as young adults all we can do is try our best and work day by day to be the best we can be, not only for our parents, but also for ourselves. We can only hope that our parents will understand our position and assist us along the way.

Conflict occurs regardless of whether our parents had stayed "back home" and raised us or whether they came here. Even "back home," the culture of the *children's generation no longer matches that of our parents' generation. However, if I am able to tease out any conflict that is particular to us being raised Canadian whereas our parents were raised South Asian, it isn't so much a matter of my mother not accepting my behaviour or choices, but more so how much my sisters and I have influenced change in my parents. I've seen my mother grow and go from being annoyed by particular other races, homosexuality, open dating, etc., to being much more tolerant about these issues. A lot of this comes from my mother's own interaction in her workplace with these issues that are more commonly open in Canada. While we were younger, we definitely argued about these issues before. But perhaps our discussions also helped her to become more accepting of others and their way of life. But on the flipside, I'm sure I was very against a lot of the South Asian traditions that I didn't want to accept, that through conversations with my mother as I grew older, I began to understand more as culture customs and respect them for that instead of insisting on my own arrogant view on how things should be done.*

It is completely natural and expected for youth and adults who have grown up in Canada to feel and want to live differently than the way of their parents do. It is a matter of how the children grow up in the new society and culture other than the parents' heritage culture.

It is a difficult process for both parents and children, with parents teaching certain values that may not be congruent with their children's "Western" experiences and understanding. I feel that it is important to negotiate between the values and traditions, finding a balance that meets both the parents' and children's needs. This is easy to say than do in practical life; and requires a lot of patience and a willingness to be flexible and understanding on both ends.

Issue #3: Cultural conflict between heritage culture and Canadians' culture—bicultural collide

Cultural conflict will occur when heritage culture (i.e., immigrants' back-home culture) and Canadian mainstream culture are different. These conflicts are experienced at both groups as well as individual levels of second-generation youth. It is more so when two cultural identities of bicultural individuals are simultaneously important to individual and when individual feels some commitment to each set of cultural norms. Also, a conflict will occur in a situation that pushes the individual to follow only one of the two sets of norms.

What is your opinion on this issue? Do you (as a second-generation visible minority youth) refashion traditional notions in innovative ways?

Are you capable of interpreting and even reframing the dominant narrative in a variety of ways to assert your own sense of identity and Canadianness?

Respondents' opinions:

In Canada, there are many instances where social customs are different from those in back home that led me to adapt the norms over here. This can be traced back to school. In Canada, schools are generally cogendered where both boys and girls study together and are in the same classrooms; there are more interaction between boys and girls in Canada. In some cases, school work involves working in groups where you may be paired with students of the opposite gender. Hence, many of one's close friends throughout school life are of the opposite gender, and boys' and girls' interactions take place. During my undergraduate studies in university in Ottawa, my closest friends amongst my classmates were girls, as they were my friends that I had made in both elementary and high school and thus we developed trust between us. Back home, schools are still either girls' schools or boys' schools. Boys generally refrain from being close friends with girls as it is viewed as a taboo by the society back home.

Another instance where I have refashioned some of the unique cultural norms in Canada has to do with some of the holidays that are celebrated here. Holidays such as Christmas and Thanksgiving are often viewed as cultural holidays in the Western world. Although we do not follow all the social customs that are performed during those holidays, we treat them as occasions for family and friends to get together, enjoy each other's company, and rejoice. As such, spending time with family and friends are some of the core values of Christmas and Thanksgiving in Canada. Therefore, I feel this is one instance where first- and second-generation Canadians, including myself, express our unique sense of Canadianness.

Living as a born Canadian but ethnically different in a Westernized society has been challenging which is different for all. Now, as an adult, passing my adolescent years, I have grown closer to my cultural roots and have a greater sense of appreciation for it. As a youth, the pressure of finding a balance was difficult as there were peer pressures, society norms that had to be followed and a rooted culture that seemed obsolete at times. I've always felt that I had some sense of pride and respect for our cultural ways and took to them in my university days but still managed to keep up with Westernized trends in Canadian living.

At different times in my life, I have followed one set of cultural norms more than the other, but it happened naturally, depending on what was prominent in my life. I believe the personal balance I have achieved is derived from both understanding where I come from—e.g., reading the history of the Indian subcontinent, reading post-colonial literature, as well as speaking to my parents about their histories—but also understanding who I am. I have chosen a very secular approach to integrating my heritage into my life, and I find comfort from those other second-generation youth who have a similar approach. As I grow older, I have also become more comfortable in discussing my background and heritage with white Canadians.

My parents always acknowledged that they didn't understand what it's like to grow up as a Canadian teenager, but they never wanted us to forget the family's heritage. They also believed that the need to integrate in the new country should not override the richness of heritage culture, and that the values they will pass down to us are nonnegotiable. We were taught to respect elders and listen to what they had to say. They wanted us to be part of all the "good" things Canada had to offer and reject all the "bad" things. Religion was important and forced onto us. We naturally gravitated towards Islam and its teachings.

I feel we must balance learning and understanding both our own culture and Western culture. It may be difficult but with proper guidance from parents and friends, it is certainly achievable. My childhood was a combination of both. It was as if I lived in two worlds. A public one, in which our accents, attitudes and ambitions match those of our white peers; and a more private sphere, in which we spoke mother tongue at home and respected value taught by our parents. We attended community events, and at the same time, we played Western sports, i.e., hockey, basketball, tennis. We went to concerts and movies celebrating western culture. We fashioned both western clothes and traditional "desi" dresses. In high school, many of us dressed up in our traditional attires for cultural events. We didn't hesitate even though our "white" friends were there. Again, I think our parents made it easy for us to be proud of our heritage. Once we understood we were different than a white Canadian but not better or worse, it was never an issue of choosing one over the other.

I have not personally experienced the idea of bicultural collide. As stated before, when mixing with different cultures, the only difference would be religious beliefs. For example, Canadians drink alcohol socially—which one can argue is part of Canadian culture. I don't feel pressured to conform to this idea, as it goes against my religious beliefs. I don't feel that anyone should fully conform to a different culture, yet we as immigrants should accept the fact that we live in a new country where we should try and assimilate to our surroundings.

The two cultures are completely different, where South Asian cultures are collectivist with emphasis on family/community, while the North American culture is individualistic, placing an emphasis on the individual. There is also a divide in terms of views on gender roles and what is expected from each sex. As a result, there is often conflict, as there is a conflict of ideals in both culture types to begin with. There must be a level of understanding of this fact from both parties, but the immigrant parents will typically need to make more of a compromise, as they are raising their children in a culture that they (should) know is different and can't expect their children to approach life exactly the same as one would in their country of origin. Ultimately, new generation children will have to assume at least some of the Canadian cultural traits in order to succeed in the long term. Some people may be capable of finding an identity that acts as a compromise between the two conflicting cultures, but ultimately the ability to do so lies in the willingness of the second-generation children to accept that everything may not necessarily follow one particular culture's ideals.

I do in fact "refashion" cultural notions to make them more appealing to nonimmigrant friends. I'm talking about real Canadians. I always try to bring culture to my Canadian friends and colleagues to not only teach them about my culture but to also make both our transitions better.

Having parents from West Indies, they were colonized by the British; therefore, the Canadian culture was not much of a shock to them. If it is not a shock to them, their adaptability to the Canadian culture was seamless and I was raised based on that seamless transition. I personally did not experience any difficulties with having both cultures present in my life in Canada, because most of the cultures and traditions of the British were already present in both cultures I am exposed to.

I think I have done a good job of combining both my cultures. The positive is that I am likely more multidimensional than if I came only from a unilateral culture. The con is that it is quite confusing at times, because it is harder to have a firm stance on certain issues since I can relate to both sides. I think I have the tendency to pick and choose what suits my wants or needs at the time, which again, can bode well for me, but also be frustrating to those around me. It is definitely challenging to not fully belong to either culture, but I haven't necessarily faced a lot of cultural conflict, per se. I don't think I have been particularly innovative in refashioning traditional notions either. I am more of an all-or-nothing type mentality—so I will fully adhere to certain traditional customs, and then fully adhere to other host culture customs. It is not necessarily the right way to do things, but it's the only way I've ever really known to reconcile ambivalent situations—to just choose a side that on instinct feels like the right decision, and then stick to it.

As an SGVM I do believe that because the cultures are so polarized, there are definite clashes that can occur between expectations (i.e., the "Canadian" one and the "traditional" one). And while the degree of the clash will vary significantly depending on the issue, there is certainly an ingrained compromise way of thinking in the mind of SGVMs as they try to reconcile the polarized expectations from both friends and family.

I think I am very much Canadian—but what does it mean to be a true Canadian? I think to be Canadian means to be proud of "who you are" and your cultural background. I am very proud to say that I am an Indo-Canadian, and that I have been able to adapt to numerous environments—whether at school, home, or in the professional workplace, regardless of some of my traditional notions. I do wish I was more outgoing, and let go of some of my traditional notions but they are so ingrained in me that I feel I will raise my kids the same way my parents taught me. Nevertheless, I make my own decisions based on what I feel is the right decision—not that this is the Indian way of doing things or the Native Canadian way of doing things. I have learned to combine traditional notions in innovative ways. For instance, I still dress conservatively, and instead of consuming alcohol, I drink ginger ale in wine glasses.

I identify as a Pakistani Canadian. My parents are not traditional Pakistanis in the sense that they have allowed my siblings and me to make our own mistakes and learn from them. Growing up with two cultures has given us strength. I feel that I have been able to take the best of both worlds and integrate them into my own personal value system. I think the reason I have been able to successfully navigate two cultures is because I allow myself to reflect on and reconfigure dominant pathways.

I don't blame my parents for attempting to push their heritage culture on me because they only want the best for me. They grew up in a time/place where everything was different. Thus they just want to share the experiences they had while they were growing up and offer advice. However, the issue is they are not completely aware of how the circumstances are different. My parents grew up in a time where there was a lot of gender discrimination. Thus, they do not understand the reason why I have so many friends of the opposite gender. They fully trust me but yet feel anxious when I choose to befriend the opposite gender.

I definitely refashion traditional notions in innovate ways in order to keep my parents happy as well as myself. The celebration of various festivals is quite *elaborate and extensive in the South Asian culture. We have westernized every holiday to make it more reasonable, without becoming the social outcast of our community. For example, it is traditional to bring a horse for the beginning of a wedding ritual. Instead, we have changed it to a car so it is more reasonable as there are strict rules in residential areas.*

I believe there was a period in my life where I questioned my cultural identity and wanted to assert myself as a certain way, more traditional ethnocentric. After finding my life partner, I realized that my heritage cultural norms were not so important to me. It was my core values rather than cultural norms that I valued as a person. This helped me to have a better self-awareness and to formulate my identity. It also helped me to become a lot more open-minded to other people's cultural norms including the Canadian dominant culture. I accepted other people's views a lot more easily while always sticking to my core values and norms.

I've seen cultural clashes occur many times throughout my past experiences. In high school, it is often difficult for some students because Canadians have a different way of dressing, eating, behaving and celebrating, in comparison to some students' traditional cultures. In high school, I remember a student feeling uncomfortable because she did not feel like "herself" in her traditional cultural clothing; however, her family forced her to wear it. Within the halls of the school, she always felt different than the rest of the students. Most importantly she just wanted to feel like a "normal" student. It was upsetting to see, because there was a clear cultural clash, and she was torn between the two. However, I think it's necessary to find a place in between. It is not right to completely let go of one's heritage, but also I feel it is necessary to understand the culture of the country you're living in. It's important to remain true to oneself, and true to one's background, but also it's important to be willing to adapt to new cultural norms, and a new way of living.

My cultural conflict led to identity issues that persisted for years, beginning in my early teens until my midtwenties. And even now, in my late twenties, it's not that I've figured out my identity, but more so to just come to terms with its shifting and uncertain state and realized that it doesn't have to have an obvious definition. I am simply a sum of my experiences, a combination of my dual heritages. But in my youth, I remember it being much more complicated. I thought, for a while, that my South Asian identity came first. So I ordered my own description as a Bangladeshi Canadian Muslim woman. But then when I went back to visit Bangladesh in my early twenties, all of my cousins and the people themselves made it obvious that I was a "bideshi," a foreigner, so I realized I was much more Canadian than Bangladeshi. So the order switched to Canadian

Bangladeshi Muslim woman. And then there was a point where I realized my values don't align with the majority of Canadians, and I thought my religion was my most salient characteristic, so then I became a Muslim Canadian Bangladeshi woman. This, unfortunately, is no exaggeration. These were different periods I went through in my identity crisis; the order of the labelling was pivotal in how I perceived myself at the time. But in my late twenties, I've become less religious and more relaxed to define myself and more just accepting of things as they come along. I grew up mostly in Canada and identify as Canadian, my roots are in Bangladesh and my home culture is a merger of Canadian Bangladeshi cultures, and my global life experiences have enriched my perspectives to make these labels a lot less pertinent and a lot less reflective of me. I may initially have been a product of certain countries and heritage, but now through a compilation of globalization in the sense of the books I've read and places I've travelled to and worked in throughout the world, I am no longer limited by my geographical location and culture that was passed down to me.

I feel that there can often be a lot of pressure to follow one set of cultural customs as opposed to another. It is up to the individual to either choose one that fits their values best, or try to find a middle ground. For example, growing up as a female South Asian, I was required to ask my parents for permission whenever I wanted to leave the house for leisure activities. Even though I was an adult, the cultural understanding of my family was that I was not allowed to simply "notify" them that I would be going out, as long as I was living with my parents' home, I would have to ask their permission.

This was difficult for me to accept, as I felt it challenged my maturity as an adult. When asked at what age I would need to be in full control over my social life, I was told that it was not about age, but that when I would get married the responsibility of my social life and my life in general would be transferred over to my husband.

These set of beliefs clearly did not align with my values as an individual, or in the Canadian cultural sense. However, it was the way in which my parents grew up and was what I needed to do. Thus, in order to abide by my parents' rules, wishes and still feel a sense of autonomy, I chose to take a combined approach by using and phrasing my language in a way that both reflects a notification and authorization that they were comfortable with my plans and actions.

Issue #4: Acculturation and adaptation

How do you (as a second-generation visible minority youth) acculturate, and how well do you adapt in the two preferences: (1) a relative preference for maintaining of one's heritage culture and identity, and (2) a relative preference for having contact with and participating in the larger society along with other ethno-cultural groups.

[Acculturation is the process of cultural change that results when two or more cultural groups come into contact as well as the psychological changes that individuals experience as a result of being members of cultural groups that are undergoing acculturation at the group or collective level].

Respondents' opinions:

I feel I have adapted pretty well to the dominant group—it was the culture I grew up in. I have a relative preference for contact with and participating in the larger society along with other ethnocultural groups. While I do maintain aspects of my own culture and heritage, as mentioned above, I like to participate in broader society. I'd like to think the perspectives of different groups can only enrich Canadian society, but we can't do that if we stay clustered in homogenous ethnic groupings. I have also found recently that my own culture has become much wrapped up with religion and not being a very religious person has made it very difficult to maintain strong connections with my own community.

I believe that there are situations that as a second-generation Canadian, I must adapt or acculturate to the dominant norms within Canadian society. Such situations include getting together and playing North American sports, greeting each other with handshakes, trying cuisine from different countries, watching North American movies or international cinema, etc.

However, I am not fully supportive of complete acculturation. Canada is described as one of the most multicultural nations in the world. I feel that this is best expressed as a nation where different cultures are allowed to express themselves in unique ways, rather than acculturate into a single type of culture that is a modification of the already prevailing culture. I believe that it is inappropriate for second-generation Canadians to break cultural taboos in instances where there is an alternative to doing so. In addition, I feel that future generations of South Asian Canadians should continue to maintain cultural practices as this is important for South Asians to express themselves as a distinct ethnic group. This includes celebrating cultural holidays, maintaining their mother tongue amongst future generations (language is the most important aspect of culture in my opinion), and teaching future generations about culture practices, including what is considered appropriate/inappropriate, and other cultural norms.

As an adult, passing my adolescent years, I have grown closer to my cultural roots and have a greater sense of appreciation for it. As a youth, the pressure of finding a balance was difficult as there were peer pressures, society norms that had to be followed, and a rooted culture that seemed obsolete at times. I've always felt that I had some sense of pride and respect for our cultural ways and took to them in my university days but still managed to keep up with Westernized trends on Canadian living.

Growing up in Canada, we had no choice but to learn and accept other cultures. Multiculturalism in Canada is one of the most beautiful things you can experience in life. White Canadians in my opinion are very receptive to other cultures. I rarely felt uncomfortable explaining fasting during Ramadan or not drinking alcohol to my white friends. They always seemed to understand and accept the fact that there were things I couldn't participate in, and it didn't make me any less. I also never judged them for their cultural preference. There was always mutual respect for each other's cultures and religious boundaries. My preference is that you try to learn and celebrate other cultures. You can't truly appreciate your heritage if you are not exposed to others.

Personally, I have no problems adapting to my surroundings. I understand that Canadians come from a wide variety of places around the world, but at the end of the day we are all humans. Everyone has the right to maintain their cultural identity. But in order to be successful in Canada, one must learn how to play the game. It's the small things that make a difference such as socializing with people outside our race, getting involved with your local community, participating in extracircular activities, playing organized sports, going out to eat, etc. The only thing I will not do is go against my religion—which I'm sure no one will have a problem with. We live in Canada for a reason and we must try to take full advantage of the situation.

With respect to myself, my bias lies in that I was raised in the individualistic society that is Canada, so I place preference on being able to live and function myself among Canada's culture. This is because I live and work in this country. Odds are that I will remain in this country. In order for me to properly establish myself and survive in the long term, I will need to favour the individualistic views of the North American culture.

I personally have a very adaptable personality. I try to balance both cultures as best I can. What I mean by this is that when I am with Canadian friends, I adapt to the way they behave and when I am at home with my parents/family

I adapt myself to suit them. It does have its challenges; however, I believe a good balance on both is important.

Living in Canada, maintaining our culture and trying to fit in with the Canadian culture has not posed any difficulty for me. I am still trying to figure out what exactly the Canadian culture is because I feel it is the mix of immigrant cultures that make up what Canada is about. Looking at it from a Caucasian perspective, even then it is a mix of Italian, Irish, Scottish, English and French cultures that make up Canada. During my schooling and even in the workplace people knew I where was from and I never had to show or prove what culture I was trying to maintain. If I did something from my cultural norm, it was usually generally accepted.

My experience with acculturation has been a like a pendulum that has swung back and forth. I grew up within a very cautious and conservative household and I never really questioned it growing up. So as a kid, I had a relative preference for maintaining my heritage. I only started wanting to "experience the other side" when I hit my midteens, which I think is a classically rebellious age. So here, my preference started to shift. I wanted to fit in, felt the peer pressure in order to do so, and started to act out with my family. I thought I had to do or say certain things in order to be liked, and even if I didn't agree or want to, I would find myself playing along sometimes.

Time has taught me that this is obviously not true, and now that the turmoil of teen angst is over, I think my vision is back to being clearer. I have some incredible friends, and in friendship I've learned that quality over quantity is invaluable. I no longer crave wanting to be liked by everyone, I am content with being liked by those I know I can depend on. It is funny what time teaches you—I have learned that my parents were strict with me for a reason, that their rationales and anecdotes of wisdom were indeed wise. Because I have sort of come full circle, I would say that now, I again have a more relative preference for maintaining my heritage culture and identity. I absolutely appreciate the freedoms and opportunities afforded to me by being raised here. However, I find myself more and more not wanting to lose where I come from. A lot of the time I will hear my white friends say something along the lines of "I wish I had a culture as rich as yours." I can envision my teen self retorting, "What are you talking about? We're so constrained!" But now, my response is "I wish you did too!" Because you know what—my culture is beautiful, and I am so proud.

There is a compromising mentality engrained in the SGVM from an early age, and is a mechanism developed to cope from the polar set of expectations they are forced to internally mediate in daily life. As an SGVM I suppose my "acculturation" depends to a large degree on what my personal belief is about that which I am being made to choose between. For example, whether it is a matter of attending mother language school I might be inclined to take that without much protest as I know it is important to learn in order to communicate with my family. However, if on the other hand I am asked to pursue a certain career although I have no interest in it, I would significantly protest. In sum, my ability to adapt may be great, but the degree to which I am willing to do it and become more "Canadian" would depend on the issue.

As a second-generation visible minority youth, I have a relative preference for having contact with and participating in the larger society along with other ethnocultural groups. I would say I am very much Canadian, but I am also very proud of my cultural heritage and identity. I feel that by interacting with other ethnocultural groups, there is so much room to learn and grow as a person. They love learning about my heritage culture, and likewise, I love learning about theirs. I do not choose my friends based on their heritage culture and identity. My friends are actually very similar to me in that we are very accepting to each other and open to their cultures and experiences. In short, my heritage culture and identity are very important to me, but I prefer mixing in with people who are "different" than me. This way, I am able to live a quiet, private life, and also connect with my friends at a one-on-one level not because I have to, but because I want to. To experience the real world, I went to Africa last year pretty much out of the blue, and it was a great self-discovery journey. I thought that I would be a totally different person without any parental control or influence, but I held on to my beliefs and attitudes that have been ingrained into me at a very young age. I mostly follow the traditional cultural norms, but I have expanded myself to a new horizon by interacting with other ethno-groups.

When I was in high school, I could not relate to my Pakistani heritage. I did not want to befriend other Pakistanis or associate myself with others in the community. Much to my own surprise, I have come to appreciate and embrace my Pakistani heritage as I have matured. I realize that there are many cultural norms and expectations that I do not wish to take forward but there are some that I do. I think I have a very balanced view of my culture now and am happy to be an active member of the Pakistani community.

I think it is fairly important to maintain the heritage and identity by keeping some traditions alive. My parents have done a good job instilling some strong values in me. That has led to a stronger self-identity and has really shaped who I am as a person. Although my family isn't very cultural, I still try to engage in as many cultures related events or activities to feel more connected to my South Asian background. I adapt extremely well with others. When I know someone is extremely passionate about a view on a particular topic, I try not to oppose it. I respect everyone's right to an opinion and don't end up imposing anything on anyone.

At first, I only wanted to have friends that were similar to me. We shared our food, talked about the cultural movie industry and had many similar interests. Then, I found that although I was growing closer to my parents and becoming more comfortable with whom I was, they were not. I prefer diversity because the South Asians my age end up hiding a lot of things to their parents by lying on where they are, what they are wearing, etc. Instead of participating in those lies, I try to just stay around people that have a similar mind-set as me. I keep everything in the open, and do not lead double lives. I am not stereotyping this to all of my friends, but just in general, it does happen more than not. On contrary, my parents know where I am at all times and with whom. I have a large array of multicultural friends and that helps keep everything interesting. When we get together, we always share bits and parts of our culture and traditions. I like learning from different people.

I think we try to take what is good from both cultures and implement them in our daily lives. I have learned to become more open-minded such as how I find the Canadian culture to be. (Or the way it was before backlash and ethnocentric behaviours started becoming more prevalent.) I maintain many core religious values and norms instilled in me by my parents' culture and teaching as well.

As a second-generation visible minority youth, I believe I acculturate quite well in the sense that I am more than willing to bring together two cultures into one. I easily adapt to new environments and I love learning about the different cultures. By being a part of two different cultures, I've noticed I'm constantly learning new things, it's truly eye-opening.

In my teens, maintaining my own religious identity was very important, and that separated me from a lot of the activities that the mainstream youth of my generation participated in. I did this consciously and intentionally and do not regret it. As I've grown and my religious values have weaned, I've partaken in a lot more of the activities that are more common amongst Canadians and in those moments, a lot of my culture and previous/changing religious values don't play much of a factor. In those moments, I realize I am more "traditionally Canadian" than I thought. But in my day-to-day activities, what I choose to do in my passing time and whom I engage as friends, while it is multicultural, I still find myself more at ease with those of the same cultural background. I guess we shared the same core values growing up and have more things in common that way.

I believe that maintaining a sense of culture is very important, as it is still a part of our identity. I also believe that it is just as important to respect and participate in the society we live in. However, the amount an individual wishes to adhere to their culture and/or participate in the other should be according to their choice and their values.

Some choose to hold on to their cultural identity through language, clothing, traditions and customs, while others may choose to adopt the "Canadian" way and the English language. While the latter can be looked at negatively and not welcomed by parents, it is not "wrong." Although it is difficult for many parents to accept, it is the genuine reality of raising a family in a different country and culture.

Personally, I value my culture and language, and it is important for me to keep that intact. I also believe in balancing both cultures—heritage culture and many elements of Canadian culture. As such, I use what works from both cultures in my life, and do not practice what doesn't. However, as spirituality and faith is my main guide—that is the lens through which I filter what to keep and what not to use.

Issue #5: Cohesion and inclusion

Social cohesion and inclusion are only possible when all members of the society, including immigrants and second- and other generation Canadians participate in and identify with that society. In some measures of civic participation, recent immigrants and their children are engaged reasonably well with Canadian society. But on other measures, such as a sense of belonging to Canada, there is a gap between immigrants the rest of the population. This gap remains within the second generation despite their progress over time on measures like education and income.

[Cohesion—understood as the quality of relationship between the various individuals and groups constituting a given society where the overlap and convergence of values, experience, and interests is what one may refer to as a distinct identity that is "national," "shared," or "common" in character. It includes the openness of the host society to welcome and accommodate a diversity of cultures. For immigrants, especially the visible minorities and their children, cohesion is about the capacity for reciprocal attachment to and identification with the host society.]

[Inclusion—it is about the removal of barriers to full participation for certain groups and individuals within the host society. Mainly focused on social and economic issues, inclusion often includes measures, immigrants' settlement services, employment equity programs, and to stop discriminatory hiring practices, antiracism activities, and antipoverty initiatives.]

How do you explain these contexts?

Respondents' opinions:

I feel a strong sense of belonging in Canada and this has certainly increased as I lived in different parts of the country, and also was enhanced from travelling abroad and realizing Canada is home. I have a good network of friends that come from all different backgrounds and also I am close with many of my work colleagues. I also volunteer and am involved in community organizations (and have been for years). I truly believe that all of this contributes to my sense of well-being and cohesion. I believe that encouraging new immigrants and second-generation youths to explore their country and communities can increase social cohesion, but there also needs to be a commitment among Canadians to eradicate discrimination based on arbitrary categories such a race. Equity programs, etc. are an important part of this fight, but I do believe that immigrant communities have a concomitant obligation to attempt to integrate into broader society. While employment equity, etc. may improve access to employment, the much wider goals of social cohesion and inclusion can only be achieved through reciprocal efforts by both sides.

In my opinion, there are a few reasons that can explain the gap in the sense of "Canadianness" between immigrants and the rest of the population. First, there are certain issues within society where the views of South Asian cultures and the prevailing Canadian culture are polar opposites of one another. Many of these are important issues, and can create division amongst cultures. This includes issues such as drinking alcohol, attending parties at bars or night clubs, the nature of relationships between males and females, or for females, the types of clothes that are worn in public. This can be viewed as resistance to integration into Canadian culture and create resentment. Other questions have been raised with regard to the appropriateness of wearing cultural or religious items such as the "turban" or "hijab." Differences of opinions on key issues such as these tend to create division in society and the gap in "Canadianness."

Canadians may also view ethnic immigrants as foreigners who usurp their resources and create new competition in the job market. They may feel that they have greater rights in Canada. Furthermore, new immigrants entering Canada bring their culture and heritage into Canada. The introduction of these new cultures into Canada may create a fear within Canadians of losing their culture due to the new norms and practices being brought in by immigrants. This fear is also present within immigrants, who feel that adjusting into a new society with different social customs and norms can cause them to lose their culture. This clash between the two different cultures can create tensions that can be expressed racism.

I think you will get a different answer from each person you interview for this question. Some believe in the "melting pot" concept and some don't. It is a matter of choice. Some are raised as Canadian and others are raised as visible minority Canadians. I was encouraged to embrace all the things that Canada has to offer while not forgetting my family roots. I believe it is important to try and remove barriers that allow you to discover other cultures, language, food, etc. While I believe it is important for organizations to offer social services that cater to immigrants/minorities, it must happen naturally. You can force a company to hire minorities just fill quotas, but the employee will never feel at home. The country has to embrace immigrants as its own and the immigrants have to accept their new country as their own. I find many immigrants don't vote in elections or have any opinions on local and regional politics. Rejecting what the new country has to offer will only make it more difficult to assimilate.

Regardless of where someone is from (i.e., immigrant versus nonimmigrant), there will always be some level for which any person may not necessarily identify with. There are far too many factors and unknowns for any sort of explanation.

I believe that the environment you grow up in and the society that moulds you stick with you forever. A lot of times the eastern and western cultures do clash and that is when kids feel torn. I can tell from my experiences that the best way to handle this is to establish a compromise between both parties. Kids need to be educated on the importance of keeping and building our culture and parents need to understand that not everything can be passed along. I can also say that a lot of times kids do try to meet their parents' expectations.

Interestingly, cohesion and inclusion were easy to come by during elementary, middle school, high school . . . even university to an extent. After the education phase and entering the workforce is where I began to feel less cohesive and included. During my school years, everybody from all backgrounds hung out and we didn't see each other in terms of colour. As adults working in the workforce, I feel this is definitely how we view each other. It is almost like we are forced to be cohesive, inclusive of one another because of the workplace environment, where in the school years this came naturally.

Because I was born and raised here, I have always fully identified with this culture and society. I know my parents would never call it their real home, but I have never felt out of place here. I love Canada Day as much as the next white Canadian and I fully feel that I represent this nation as much as they do. On a daily basis, I don't remember that I am a member of a visible minority—that only happens if I am asked on a questionnaire or if a conversation somehow leads to it (which isn't very frequent). I do know there is still somewhat of a divide, because I see it in others' certain experiences. For example, the classic tale of a highly educated doctor back home who can't find a decent job here really bugs me. I definitely think more measures can be taken to ensure equity in that regard. But if I'm being honest, I have never felt excluded, and I have always felt a good level of cohesiveness. Perhaps the one area that I experience exclusion slightly is the job market, as mentioned above. But this is still based on speculation because I will of course never be directly told that I am not hired for a certain position based on race. Otherwise, I honestly think my adopted country has done a pretty good job of affording immigrant populations many opportunities to call it a new home and have it feel so as well.

In his seminal work Orientalism, *author Edward Said outlines how the Western world develops narrow-minded generalizations about other cultures and simultaneously incorporates these "truths" into their interpretations and/or interactions with other cultures. Unfortunately, this type of thinking is not limited to only non-Canadians as this type of lens distinguishes only by skin color, dress, religion or last name. Therefore, whether or not you are born in Canada, a SGVM will always feel different from their peers or white society at large, as they will consciously (or not) be subjected to prejudgment by the Canadian majority. While questions like "So what country are you from?" could be made without malice, they are nonetheless the sorts of questions which serve to constantly remind SGVMs that they are looked upon as outsiders, regardless of their education or income.*

I feel most immigrants and their children are often engaged reasonably well with Canadian society. Canada is defined by its multiculturalism, and its immigrants and all of its diversity make Canada what it is today. I don't think there's a gap between second-generation immigrants and the rest of the population in terms of education or income. However, for immigrants, i.e., my parents, there is definitely a gap. They struggled to find jobs, have enough money to raise and support their families, and they spent their lives trying to create a better future for us. Foreign-trained doctors coming to Canada have to go through the entire system again, and often cannot practice medicine again. They lose their sense of identity, and have to make new friends from scratch. The struggle is real.

But for us kids born and raised here? Speaking for myself, Canada is my real home, and I feel a sense of belongingness here. Despite being a visible minority, I never felt out of place and I do not believe that the rest of the population looks at me as a visible minority: "Oh hey, that brown girl." We are a country full of colours, and I feel my individuality and uniqueness are desired or at least accepted in Canadian society. In general, however, I sometimes feel excluded due to my quietness and introverted nature, but that does not have to do with myself being a visible minority (although, quietness and shyness is often seen as a good quality to have in my heritage culture; whereas here, it is somewhat frowned upon). All in all, I have always felt a good level of cohesiveness in society. Canada truly is a beautiful country and I would have it no other way.

I think the largest gap is in lower middle-class immigrant households since we have to take loans for our education and these loans impede on our ability to climb up the economic ladder quickly. Having said that, I think these gaps are easily surmountable with enough dedication and lobbying on the parts of immigrants.

I am definitely a proud Canadian. When I was working in a clinic, a lot of patients would ask me where I was from, and I always gave them one answer: I am Canadian. This was not to confuse them as I know they were actually asking about my background, but that's the response I gave because I truly feel like I truly am Canadian. I was born and brought up in Canada and only visited South Asia 2 years ago. Had I visited India more frequently, my answer may have varied. But I only visited it after I had already developed my morals and values, with a more mature self-identity. I am able to speak the national language of Canada, but cannot fluently speak my native language. I feel much more connected with my fellow Canadians than I do with the South Asians back home. I have a good sense of belonging in Canada, and identify it as my true home. Canada is a mosaic of all the cultures all put to one, beautifully arranged. It allows one to celebrate their genetic diversity, all while feeling connected in a larger scale.

I believe that growing up, we were surrounded by students from all backgrounds. The focus was fitting in, in terms of more superficial aspects such as "wearing nice cloths, having lots of friends, partying, excelling in studies or sports. We did not look at one another and discriminate based on race. In the workforce the same theory remained when working in the private sector in more entry-level positions. However, the government environment is different. It is predominately comprised of the baby boomer white/Caucasian population. As many of this demographic did not grow up acclimated to various individuals from multicultures, you definitely notice the variance in treatment and are reminded that you are a minority. In terms of inclusion, there are measures in place to assist minorities; however, cohesion is not always a common practice. There is definitely a narrative to become like the majority in order to be accepted. There remain individuals who dislike minorities regardless of how well adapted they are to the Canadian society, and others who are caring and sensitive towards the needs of minorities, and finally individuals who do not see you as a minority, rather a member of their collective group.

Social cohesion is defined as the willingness of members of a society to cooperate with one another, in order to survive and prosper. With the rising immigration in Canada, there is evident ethnic diversity among the nation; however, there is little evidence of a breakdown in social cohesion. The recent debate in Quebec regarding immigrant groups entering Canada with different cultural and religious backgrounds is concerning, and not the least bit fair. However, regarding the rest of the nation Canada has become a nation full of immigrants, and many Canadians are more than welcoming to the people from different cultural backgrounds. There is a high level of education among Canadian immigrants, and they have adapted well to this society.

I don't find that my circle of South Asian family and friends are necessary for facing issues of social cohesion or inclusion. As most of us, second-generation children, were raised in Canada, and as I come from a circle of families whose parents have made it a mandate to be included in the political world of our country, I have never seen this as an issue really. We have our own cultural and religious activities, and we partake in the greater, general activities of our multicultural cities as well. My father and his friends have always been involved in politics, volunteering in the community with people of all races, and participating in Canada Day celebrations, winter festivals, clubs and sports, the works! I think it's a matter of choice. I can't speak for other circles, but we chose to be a part of this country that we call home.

When people migrate to a new country, they are adapting to a whole new system of life—visually, psychologically, culturally, emotionally, economically, etc. It takes time to understand new cultural norms, practices, understandings, and nuances. There can also be a strong need to hold on to what is known and familiar in order to maintain identity and sense of self in a new and different world. To gain that sense of "home" again, it is completely natural for immigrants to surround themselves with people of similar cultural backgrounds and attempt to recreate that "home" environment in their new country. While this can be a psychological and social mechanism to help manage change, it can make it increasingly difficult to integrate with their new social environment.

Thus, it is understandable that the parents' cultural practices and way of life will, to a large extent, dictate the kind of environment children grow up in and the type of activities they participate in. It takes some time, on the part of the parents and also the children, to open themselves up to new ways of thinking and new ways of participating that they may have not been exposed to or have been comfortable with before, without feeling as though they have changed or abandoned their culture/beliefs/sense of self.

Issue #6: Racism in everyday life

Second-generation children of immigrants are overwhelmingly from ethnic minority groups or visible minority backgrounds, and their everyday experiences include racism, especially at the point of transition from youth to adulthood, and as they complete their education, enter the labour force and try to build the desired career. Research suggests that the second-generation adults may experience more racism than their parents because their linguistic competencies, educational attainment, and high expectations drag them in positions where they are viewed as a challenge to the Canadian dominant group. How do you explain the issue of racism?

Respondents' opinions:

On a personal level, I have never felt discriminated against in schools, university, or at the workplaces due to my racial or religious background, but I know many of my peers who have experienced discrimination. In my opinion, there will always be people who will show the visible minority some sort of discrimination. But as we grow into a new world where people are not discriminated by race, religion, sexual orientation, etc., immigrants are more and more accepted by the mainstream Canadians. I think we will be able to rise in adversity and conquer these challenges as my parents did in the past. Time has changed, and there are differences in interpreting racism or discrimination by our parents' generation and ours as their children. Also issues may be different to different generations.

In my own experience, I have not experienced more racism than my parents. To the contrary, I believe it has been less, but different. It has been more subtle. I explain racism as fear of the unknown and the other, compounded my economic insecurity.

Though I have not consciously experienced racism in Canada, I have seen situations within which another person has been discriminated against or verbally attacked due to their racial or ethnic identity. In my opinion, racism stems from uneasiness against something that is foreign. The main issue is that immigrants or visible minorities are seen as foreign agents within society that may threaten the current social values and practices. This fear or uneasiness intensifies when individuals of different cultures begin to express their own cultures within society. However, these expressions should not be seen as a threat to change the prevailing customs within society. Rather, as a multicultural nation, we should embrace the unique cultural values that immigrants bring to our society.

People who are racist are ignorant, jealous or scared of change. These people are one track minded and are not open to change. We as humans are always going to envy what we don't have; whether that is a nice car, house or job. Second-generation immigrants of ethnic origin who are successful in Canada owe it all too hard work and determination, just like any other Canadian citizen. The fact that race comes into play with how successful a person is just proves my point about ignorance.

Racial and cultural issues loom large among minorities. There's always a fear that someone I am dealing with might be a racist. Sometimes it is overpublicized and used as an excuse. There is no doubt that blacks, Hispanics, Native and Asians (people of color) live daily with the effects of both institutional and individual racism. It has existed throughout human history. I was fortunate in a sense that I don't recall ever being treated differently because of my race. Perhaps I was too naive or blind to see it, feel it. I picked friends who were friendly to me despite my appearance. They didn't care about my skin color or religion. That is not to say that there were no racists in my class or workplace. Much of the attention is focused on individual racist behaviour. However, just as individuals can act in racist ways, so can institutions.

Fortunately, I haven't been part of any institutions that behave in ways that are overtly racist (i.e., specifically excluding people of color from services) or inherently racist (i.e., adopting policies that while not specifically directed at excluding people of color, nevertheless result in their exclusion). Policies laid out by the Canadian and US governments make it difficult for companies to get away with overtly racist behaviour. As I said earlier, employers cannot afford to pick race over talent. You will always be viewed as competitive from your coworker. Race has very little to do with. One may describe an experience as racist while others may not. I don't believe that second-generation immigrants face more racism than the previous one. Time alone has eased the racial tension. When my parents came to Canada in '70s, it must have been much harder to fit in.

Many Canadians had no exposure to foreigners in the past. Nowadays people are more exposed to different countries, languages and religions. We are even seeing minority elected officials. People are less afraid of immigrants.

Luckily, I have no insight on this issue. I say lucky because I have rarely experienced the issue of racism, as I have grown up in very diverse areas. Same goes for my workplace.

I do not feel that racism has affected me in any way, but I am merely speaking from my personal experiences.

I grew up in the predominantly French Canadian neighbourhood and definitely saw racism firsthand. It was generally a small percentage of the population, but it existed. As mentioned before, in my school years, I did not see any real racism... very minor if any... and even in the workplace I never experienced blatant racism. However, I feel there are closet racists that exist who will smile with you while talking bad about people of other cultures behind closed doors.

To be honest, and I suppose this is a fortunate thing, I have never explicitly been faced with the issue of racism. I worked at job once where someone called in to complain about a situation and that somehow took the direction of Muslim-bashing where he blamed immigrant Muslims for a lot of Canada's problems. This was very hard to hear and react professionally, and it is something that when remembered, is still hurtful. But I have never been the direct target of racism, at least not that I know of—which I am very grateful for.

The issue of racism is unfortunately something that is still very much alive and well in Western society. Fortunately, however, instruments like the Charter of Rights and Freedoms, the judicial system and various human rights legislations (and their respective commissions) are avenues prejudiced peoples can go to in order to get the social equality promised to them. And while I truly believe that Canada is one of the most tolerant and progressive societies one could hope to live in, the problem is not only that racism still exists, but rather the manner in which it manifests itself today. While in decades past both employers and establishments could outright deny people on the basis of race alone, today this overt form of racism is not tolerated almost anywhere, let alone Canada. For example, you would hard press to find an employer that would state, "I am not promoting you because you are Indian."

However, what has happened is that racism has become more internalized and systemic and as such the barriers to entry for not just SGVMs, but all visible minorities, are that much tougher to expose. Although one could cite the aforementioned French language requirement as an example of a policy that de facto holds minorities back, not recognizing foreign academic credentials, internal hiring and biases by potential recruiters and employers (particularly as it pertains to one's last name) are all examples of the challenges facing visible minorities in this day and age. A glance at the prevalence of white managers/ executives compared to Canada's population diversity today only confirms such an interpretation.

I personally, thankfully, have never been the direct target of racism. However, I remember, when 9/11 happened, one of my friends was called a terrorist just because she was Muslim. Since 9/11, the media also continues to place emphasis on attacks/suicide bombings done by Muslims, and this, I feel, has unfortunately led to general society blaming Muslims for all the problems we have. Generally, I feel that the white population is very resentful of our success and hard work ethics. They feel we are taking all "their jobs," whether it's in medicine, engineering, or in the government. As a result, I may experience resent and discrimination in the workplace. I'm still in school, and have not entered the workplace so I do not have experience with this. However, I have heard some of my parents' stories where they have directly told them that "it's not fair that all these immigrants are taking our jobs." Unfortunately, they do not see that if they worked harder and did not take everything for granted, there would be a greater balance between immigrants and Native Canadians in the professional workplace—especially in the more challenging fields (engineering and medicine).

I have been fortunate enough to not encounter racism in my everyday life. I rarely think about the colour of my skin and I think that speaks volumes for my experience.

I have never been the target of racism; however, there are many stories I have heard from my parents' experiences, which indicate that racism is still alive and well. My parents constantly have to deal with older generations being ignorant towards their culture. I don't believe it is an issue of the younger generations, but the older ones that still have their stereotypes of different ethnicities etched on to their minds. Another problem is that we are giving entertainers such as Russell Peters the encouragement and appraise to continue to discriminate based on their ethnic backgrounds. If someone else were to say something similar, then that would be considered racism, and they would have been charged for verbal assault.

I have only felt this with very few individuals in the government workplace environment. I believe the more acclimated you are the Canadian culture, the less likely you will be discriminated against as you are viewed more like a contributing member rather than through the racial lens. There are and always will remain the group who were never brought up surrounded by visible minorities and view them as "different" rather than members of the same race. These folks are the ones who will always pose a challenge until they are confronted and forced to view things differently. Racism as a whole is obviously still a major issue as people are afraid of the unknown. Once you start reading blogs and comments online, or listen to certain radio programs and hear the opinion of anonymous callers, you can certainly experience racism at is full capacity.

I've never experienced racism firsthand, but it still exists in many of the less-developed regions and nations throughout the world. That being said, Canada has thrived in this aspect as individuals from all races have contributed to the growth of the nation. Canada is one of the nations, which are most accepting to people of different races and backgrounds.

Thankfully, I grew up mostly in Toronto, where multiculturalism is rampant in a cohesive sense and racist acts are few and far from my experience. However, having traveled, worked, and studied in other areas of Canada where multiculturalism is less obvious, and where I was a visible Muslim, wearing a hijab, and have brown South Asian skin, the differences quickly became obvious. Less obvious racist acts are cases of social exclusion where people treated me differently and assumed that my English or French linguistic abilities or general knowledge was less than their own, which I never did shy from correcting. I found, however, that as soon as I proved myself to be every bit a Canadian as they were in terms of linguistic abilities, education, behaviour, etc., then generally, I was judged more for my personality traits and taken on as an equal. I think my parents face more racism because people don't seem them in equal terms due to their weaker English language abilities or accents. The only few racist acts that I've been victim to have usually been in Quebec, unfortunately, and at the hands of drunk individuals who have accosted me with racist slurs, usually in a religious sense. I don't take intoxicated individuals seriously nor do I take their actions to be representative of Canadians as a whole. Racist individuals will always exist, but they do not stop me from living my life and achieving my goals in Canada. I doubt that in the professional world, racism has stopped me from any promotions or job acquisitions. I am usually judged on my abilities I find.

From my personal experience in schools, university and in the workplace, I have not come across racism so far. I have, however, heard some Canadians who feel as though immigrants and second-generation visible minority youth are "taking over." *I feel that this sort of racism stems from ignorance and a lack of proper understanding.*

World history is about migration, and the history of North America is built upon exploration, invasion, domination and colonization. Thus, when many express such views about visible minorities, they ignore the history upon which the country was built and their own ancestral migration history.

Issue #7: Mixed marriage

The phenomenon of "mixed" marriage is the inevitable result wherever human beings come together to form a common society. In Canada, this is exactly what has been happening in everyday life of ethnic and white Canadians, as we all know that the migration of diversified ethnic and cultural groups has been the story of Canadian life.

The Western perspective of intimate relationships has the importance of romantic love, and that marriage is seen as the union of two individuals who have pursued their preferences and desires. Family approval may be desirable within this perspective, but individuals are expected to take their own decisions and to find their partners without parental assistance. A life partner is not necessarily expected to be from the same cultural, ethnic, or religious group because love possibly can grow between any two individuals regardless of their background.

The South Asian perspective on marriage is somewhat different, where marriage is seen as an alliance of families rather than two individuals only. Family approval of a future spouse is important and necessary, and the adult children of South Asian parents are not encouraged to follow their own decisions like the children in the white Canadian parents. Moreover, partners would not only be expected to have same social status but also be expected to share a common cultural and religious background. As a second-generation South Asian adult, what is your opinion about mixed marriage?

Respondents' opinions:

I don't really have a positive or negative view on mixed marriage—I believe it depends greatly on the man and woman involved and what they prefer. I myself am in a mixed marriage, and I believe that most second-generation immigrant youth in Canada espouse to some degree or another the Western view of marriage as a union of two people who love each other. However, integrating this into our parents' expectations is another story. When I met the person who is now my spouse, I was partially thinking of whether he would be "a suitable boy." I knew whom I married was my choice, but I was also conscious of it being an appropriate person.

It is not always easy to balance the expectations of both parents and your own preferences when you are in a mixed marriage, but I come back to two points I made earlier: (1) parents who migrate with their children should expect that there will be a desire to intermarry, given that the children will be growing up in a completely different culture; and (2) from the perspective of autonomy of the person, an individual ought to be able to make such an important personal decision based on their own values, which often will accommodate, to some degree, some of their parents' preferences.

I think mixed marriage brings an incredible richness to Canadian life. My husband and his family have learned a lot of different things from me because of my heritage. On the other hand, perhaps the most difficult part of this phenomenon is the feeling of immigrant parents that something has been lost if their child does not marry within the culture. There is no easy answer to this.

I believe it is a hit or miss and very situational. Statistically the weight can go either way but this is very dependent on the two individuals and their families. Every marriage goes through different adversities, so added challenges of culture and religion can make it difficult to cope with. Some people are able to surpass the difficulties and become a stronger person where in turn makes the marriage stronger and some people fall to their knees when faced with such challenges. In whoever's lives, where this situation might meet them, it's all dependant on what that person's expectations are, their ability to adapt, their need for identity and how strong their beliefs are, culturally and religiously.

I do not fully agree with complete acculturation of Canadian society. Rather, I feel that the existence of different cultures is important to practice in Canada as a multicultural nation. Opinions on mixed marriage will depend from person to person and one's views with respect to acculturation and the preservation of certain cultural values. Mixed marriages can be very positive because it encourages people of different cultural backgrounds to accept their unique heritages, and can create a union between two cultures. However, mixed marriage will always result in some acculturation. For example, a marriage where the partners have different cultural or religious backgrounds can result in the loss of many of the unique cultural or religious values in the next generation, including language. The future generation may assume more the prevalent "white" culture within Canada. There are certain degrees to which this may occur, depending on the *cultural or religious differences between the partners, as well as their willingness to pass down their cultural values to their children.*

Personally, I would prefer to marry someone with the same cultural and religious background as me. There are certain cultural and religious values that my parents have instilled within me in order to preserve our unique cultural and religious heritage. Therefore, I feel obliged to pass down these values to my children. I feel that marrying someone within my cultural background would make fulfilling this obligation a much easier process. Furthermore, South Asian marriages are alliances between two families than just two individuals. This alliance is much more compatible when the families share the same cultural and religious values. However, even if families do not share exactly the same cultural values, there must be some degree of overlap between the two families' respective values such as religion and language in order for them to be compatible.

My opinion about mixed marriage is that your partner should be Muslim. I don't have any preference about the nationality of the partner. In today's society, youth are going to socialize and eventually find someone they may like. This process is completely different from what past generations have done, i.e., arranged marriage. I'm still of the opinion that this new process should be Halal and the two families should meet and agree.

This was a tough one for me. I agree that the time has changed and we are more accepting of other cultures and values but no matter your background, an interracial marriage will be met with obstacles on both sides. It is especially the case for the generation of people whose parents were immigrants, and they themselves were raised here. To even broach the idea of an interracial marriage will spring forth 100-year-old stereotypes of other cultures you never even knew existed. In my household, it was understood that marrying a non-Muslim was not an option, unless of course, the person converted. Even marriages within different Muslim groups were not encouraged. As we started seeing more and more youths from our generation started marrying mates from outside of the own community, it became a topic of discussions among parents and kids.

I think many parents started accepting the fact that mixed marriages can work. My parents started acknowledging the fact it was a topic that needed to be discussed with open minds. It was important for them to let us know that they were "okay" with mixed marriage as long as the person was a Muslim, educated and came from a "good" family. Ultimately, selecting a partner would be up to us, but we need to care for the family background as well. We accepted the fact that we not only marry our partner but also their family. Many of my friends are currently married to partners who come from different counties, different religious and cultural background. Seeing them happy is good enough for me to think that mixed marriages work.

To preface my response, my bias is due to the fact that I am in a mixed marriage. My opinion is that it, like all things, depends on the people. Various factors come into play. Both parties will need a degree of openness and willingness to accept all parts of one's life. In the context of a mixed marriage, chances are that both parties are doing so, on the basis of a "romantic" union between the individuals. Ultimately, I favour mixed marriages and believe that the individuals should be able to do what they want.

I actually lean more towards our traditional South Asian view in marriage but with a mix of western culture. I believe that marriage is an alliance of both families rather than of two people. However, I do also believe that the two individuals should be in love with each other first before the two families should be involved. As far as mixed marriages are concerned, I lean more towards the two partners having similar cultural and religious backgrounds. I believe this is important not only for the two individuals but for the family as a whole and the kids.

Mixed marriages are becoming more and more common in Canada. I have a mixed marriage and see the challenges that come with it. However, it is a bit of both concepts discussed in the question preface. I feel that parents' opinions are necessary and important, but at the same time it is ultimately the son's or daughter's decision on whom to marry. I agree that love can blossom in every angle, but it takes two people to make that love blossom no matter what background they have. Once an agreement on core values is established between the partners, the rest is manageable. Undoubtedly, parents are great advisors, and should be there for their children and make suggestions. However, the boundary that I see exists between suggestion and enforcement. Saying or telling the children what to do in an authoritarian manner not only diminished the relationship they have with their children if the marriage is not working, but further damage is done. Out of the 10 marriages between family and friends in the past 5 years, only 2 are non-mixed marriages.

Mixed marriage absolutely has always made more sense to me than the South Asian perspective on marriage. I think this is because by the time I understood what relationships were, I had already been influenced by my host culture enough to take on its notion of the importance of romantic love. I was always against the idea of arranged marriage and thought it ridiculous when my mom would suggest the idea of "finding a potential suitor." It made no sense to me how someone else could choose the person I was supposed to spend the rest of my life with, and I consistently scoffed at the idea. Where my mom would talk about "criteria" for her future son-in-law as having to be Muslim and belong to same country of origin, I didn't care at all. I was of the idealistic fairy-tale notion that love is love and you can't choose or arrange whom it happens with. While I still believe this to be true, my perspective has started to be less rigid. As mentioned above, time is teaching me that "Mom is always right" and is proving to be true time and time again. So I accept that I would fully trust my mom's choice for my spouse because I now believe that she indeed would have the foresight, wisdom, and knowledge to be able to choose wisely for me. Arranged marriage, or the South Asian perspective, no longer seems absurd, as the concept of learning to love seems just as valid as falling in love.

This does not negate the fact that I still have to field many questions about arranged marriage, or whether my own marriage was arranged. I still fully see how in awe the Western world is of the concept, and while in my younger days I would have been incredulous with them, now I do think to myself at how rather narrow-minded that is. I wouldn't necessarily say it's a negative stigma—but I do see a sort of "Who are these people?" type look come up on white people's faces when the idea of arranged marriage comes up. It is used as the butt of jokes to make someone feel like a "loser"—like he or she just isn't appealing enough to find someone on their own. It isn't hurtful to me personally, but it does make me wonder if there will come a day where both cultures will fully assimilate—meaning that our South Asian marriage culture won't be a laughing matter to our host culture counterparts.

I think the degree to which one accepts mixed marriage is a reflection of both their families and their own beliefs, and this applies to both whites and nonwhite Canadians. Although SGVMs are usually the ones assumed to have this pressure, one needs to look at the media, their friends, and Western society to see that the vast majority of white people still only marry other white people. If we were truly a colourless society in Canada, it is my opinion that there would be a far greater prevalence of mixed marriages.

Personally, I have no issue with mixed marriages as long as there is some advanced discussion between would-be spouses on major issues (like the religion of one's children). That being said, if two people are committed to each other I do not believe there are any obstacles which justify not marrying outside one's culture, however again I possess this thinking based on having grown up in a liberal household and personally possessing a liberal view on most issues.

In my personal opinion, I do not fully support the western perspective or the South Asian perspective on marriage. I understand both sides of the perspective but instead of agreeing with the "mixed marriage" perspective I have a mixed view about marriage in general. I believe it's very important to have family approval of my future spouse, but he does not necessarily have to share the same cultural and religious background as me. However, I must say, I am attracted to those who look similar to me (known as the familiarity theory in psychology).

Ideally, I would want to marry someone who also shares the same cultural heritage, so I can hold on to my routes, and speak in my mother tongue. Also, he wouldn't be considered an "outsider" in my family, and I wouldn't have to explain to him all of "my" customs and traditions. For instance, it may feel like, "okay, it's Diwali, so we're celebrating my Christmas." I see myself marrying a "brown" guy who has an Indian background just so we share more similarities. However, I am not very religious, so I would prefer if he considers himself spiritual rather than "Hindu, Sikh, Muslim, Christian," etc. All religions have the same underlying morals—honesty, loyalty, and being a good person overall, without intentionally hurting someone. South Asian parents want their kids to marry someone of same (or higher) social status. I do not believe in the caste system whatsoever, so I will not exclude a potential partner based on their caste. Nevertheless, based on all these psychology theories, I think I would marry someone with at least an undergraduate education so we can connect at some intellectual level as well.

I guess I still live in a fairy tale, where I think Prince Charming will come at the perfect time and sweep me off my feet "ha-ha." But realistically, I feel a friend or a family member will introduce me to a potential suitor, and then after getting to know him for at least a year or two, I will decide if he is the "one." The final decision will be mine, and no one can or will force me to marry someone that I cannot love. All in all, I don't believe in "blind love."

In accordance with the South Asian perspective on marriage, I think marriage is a union of two families and it is important to understand the fact that mutual respect between those families is very important for the marriage to be successful. However, I don't think it's necessary for the two partners to share a common cultural background. Religion is really important to me personally. So, I do hope to marry someone who is of the same religion. Culture, on the other hand, is dynamic in my mind so I don't think it would influence my decision to marry or not to marry someone.

Ideally, I would like to meet someone who shares my values and with whom I can envision a shared future. I would like be with and marry someone my parents approve. However, I wouldn't take it upon myself to pass judgement on anyone who has a different opinion on the matter. I think marriage is a very personal decision . . .

I agree with both ideas to some extent. I think the western perspective applies to me more. I do not expect my parents to find a suitable match for me. In this day and age, I believe it is the right of every individual to find someone they connect with. However, it is very important for me to get approval from my family. As explained earlier, they are much more liberal than other South Asian parents. This means they are a little more open with different ethnic backgrounds. I value an individual's education much more than a person's ethnic background. As long as the person shares similar views and values education, I would feel comfortable introducing him to my parents, knowing that they would accept him. In the end, they just want my happiness. On the contrary, if there is a certain side of the family unhappiness with the relationship then that is something that must be resolved prior to forcing a relationship. It is important for both families to approve the new addition to their family. Thus I take parts of both and combine it to form somewhat of criteria to represent my parents' take combined with my own.

This is a very complex question and can be looked at from multiple facets. While I believe that mixed marriages certainly may pose some challenges for the couple engaged, there is also a difference depending on whether or not you belong to a first-generation or second-generation culture and how varied the two cultures are. The more varied they are, the chances are obviously higher for more confrontation with regard to multiple issues. Ultimately, any marriage can work with effort. However, core values and goals of the two individuals must be met and agreed upon. Once these are met, the rest of the issues (generally posed by parents and extended family members) may be effortlessly resolved. It is when the external family become overly opinionated that pressures become overbearing and may hurt the natural family union.

From my perspective, if two individuals truly love each other, they should be allowed to pursue marriage, regardless of race. It is perfectly fine as long as both parties are willing to learn and accept each other's cultures and backgrounds. For me personally, it is very important to get both families approval but beyond that mixed marriage is a matter of choice and love.

I come from a family where one sister married within the same culture and another married completely outside the culture. While at first this may have been cause for unease and it certainly does make relations between the two families more difficult as there is a language and cultural barrier, the difference is that in my family, we put religion before culture. And as both sisters did still marry within the same religion, it trumped any denial or cause for strife in our family. While disagreements occur in many families with mixed marriages, as they did in ours, the basis of the unease was not the different culture. That, if anything, is just a learning curve and slight unease for my parents at first. Personally, I have no issues with it. So long as both parties are respectful of each other's heritage and willing to create a new blending culture at home, I think it's not a deciding factor at all. We must be aware of the fact that when combining families in terms of adaptations, mutual respect for both cultures and values are very important.

I personally do believe in mixed racial marriage. I think that it is beautiful to meld two cultures and from a faith-based standpoint, I believe that intercultural marriage should be encouraged.

That being said, I feel that the process by which this marriages occur, whether it is the "Western" way of the individual choosing, the South Asian tradition of parents choosing, or a mix/balance of both; as long as both parties agree on it and are comfortable with it, it is their prerogative. Statistically and historically speaking, both methods have produced both positive and negative results, so it really depends on the individual and their family.

I do, however, believe in the merits of finding a life partner with which your traditions, beliefs, and social standings align. It is still entirely possible for marriages to work without those, but similar values and practices can certainly make partnerships and relations much easier.

What have we learned from the above opinions?

The followings are the key points extracted from the views and opinions of the second-generation youths of South Asian origin who participated in the survey:

On a personal level, participants faced less discrimination and racism in school and in the job market due to racial and religious background, and they always felt that they were able to compete on equal terms with others including white counterparts, particularly when applying to same level jobs. They also believe that the Employment Equity Program for the four designated groups (i.e., women, aboriginal people, persons with disabilities, and visible minorities) is in fact an advantage for the ethnic minorities in the job market. However, visible minority employees are more likely to experience a hidden or systemic discrimination when it comes to promotion and advancement within the organisation; the "glass ceiling" perspective—the unseen, unbreakable barrier that keeps visible minorities from rising to the top jobs.

In terms of conflict between second-generation youths and their parents, there are significant challenges facing both children and parents. Many think it is unfair for parents to raise their children in a totally different culture and expect that they will do everything in the way parents expect. The two cultures are different—that is, South Asian culture is "collectivist" with an emphasis on family, friends, and community; whereas, the Canadian culture is individualistic, emphasizing the individual. The majority of South Asian youths believe that they need to adopt some elements of the Canadian culture in order to overcome barriers in their day-to-day lives. They emphasize that every second-generation youths of ethnic origin should integrate and assimilate with mainstream Canadian society in order to succeed at par with their white counterparts.

It is clear that for second-generation youths of South Asian origin, bicultural collides are a definite challenge and come in different ways at different times. Teenagers are more apt to lean towards Western cultural norms mainly because of peer pressure, but sometimes it is a lack of understanding. When they grow to adulthood, however, they are more able to strike a good balance between their parents' culture and the Canadian culture, and they handle that balance appropriately. They also come to the realization that they are very much true Canadians while being proud of their heritage and *who they are.*

South Asian youths believe that growing up in Canada requires acculturation with other cultural groups, the dominant white cultural group in particular. They accept that by interacting with other groups, they can learn, share, and grow as good Canadians. At the same time, they feel that their heritage culture and identity are very important to them, and thus they are not in favour of complete acculturation as it may delink them from their traditional values. One very strong message appears to be that, while the South Asian youths don't want to disconnect with the root culture, they do want to live and function well within Canada's multicultural norms at the same time. In fact they are doing well in the acculturation process.

Overall, South Asian youths appear to have fit quite well into the social and economic fabric in Canada. However, perspectives vary according to whether they were born in Canada or abroad. Those who were born in Canada feel strongly that they are no different from their white peers and they fully identify as Canadians and are well integrated into Canadian society. The general view of South Asian youths is that social cohesion worked well in schools because the peers and friends of all cultures and backgrounds mixed together without any barriers and prejudice; it was very natural and spontaneous. Whereas, in the workplace environment, the cohesion among employees of various ethnocultures and backgrounds do not evolve naturally, it is a sort of forced or pseudocohesiveness and inclusiveness that exists among various groups.

South Asian culture and Canadian culture are so polarized that social inclusion is not an easy proposition. Nevertheless, South Asian youths believe that both social cohesion and inclusion is possible if discrimination based on race and colour is eliminated. This can be achieved partly by the strong commitment from the larger society, and partly by ethnic minorities' positive attitude and concrete effort to integrate and assimilate into broader Canadian society.

Generally, second-generation South Asian youths have not experienced blatant racism in their daily lives in Canada, and their experience with their white counterparts have largely been positive, never experienced being treated differently by white peers. Sometimes the issue of racism is overpublicized, or there are overreactions and may be used as an excuse for certain types of behaviour. The majority of the South Asian young adults believe that Canadians are a very tolerant people who welcome ethnic immigrants. Although they hear of verbal racial comments including Muslim-bashing, this is very rare. Unfortunately, racism still exists, but these incidences seem to be minor and mostly hidden. They also believe that the nature and the interpretation of racism are different from generation to generation; certain comments or issues may be derogatory or humiliating in the eyes of the parents, but they are not so in the eyes of their children.

Turning the attention towards mixed marriage, it is observed that this is always a difficult decision for South Asian youths, as it is not easy for them to balance the expectations of their parents with their own preferences. But the overall view about mixed marriage is positive among them. South Asian young adults think that marriage is the romantic union between two individuals, and they are very supportive of mixed marriage. The young generation of South Asian Canadian not only are supportive of intermarriage but also believe that intermarriage is an important factor in order for true integration and assimilation to occur into Canadian society, and that it also brings richness to Canada, which is, after all, "the Canadian mosaic."

The conservative views about marriage are also evident. For example, among Muslims, it is strongly felt that couples must have the same religion. However, the most important message is that mixed marriages (between South Asian and white couples in particular) are very common nowadays in Canada, and South Asian parents are gradually accepting mixed marriages of their sons and daughters.

A Canadian is a fellow wearing English tweeds, a Hong Kong shirt and Spanish shoes, who sips Brazilian coffee sweetened with Philippine sugar from a Bavarian cup while nibbling Swiss cheese, sitting at a Danish desk over a Persian rug, after coming home in a German car from an Italian movie . . . and then writes his Member of Parliament with a Japanese ballpoint pen on French paper, demanding that he do something about foreigners taking away our Canadian jobs.

—Anonymous

Make no mistake. Canada is not a bilingual country. In fact it is less bilingual today than it has ever been.

—Stephen Harper

Canada is a nation of people who came from somewhere else and in this country one was not an alien but simply the arrival at different times. Yet the irony is that the coloured people are always asked by the "White Europeans"—where do you come from? Not the other way around though—the "White Europeans" do think that they should not be asked the question because they belong to Canada as they demonstrate with authority.

—The Author

8

Discussion

The issues I discussed here centred on the key topics that were included in the book. Attempts were made to organise the discussion in order, according to the organisation of the chapters. Yet there might be variation in the flow of discussion while reading, as issues are likely to overlap or intertwined. However, I tried to maintain the continuity of the flow as much as possible.

Immigration

Majority of Canadians support immigration. Surveys and polls consistently show that the majority of Canadians are of the opinion that immigrants make positive contributions to Canada. Polls also suggest that immigration is not a threat to jobs and life Canadians enjoy. Undoubtedly, multiculturalism has been a key debatable issue in many countries in the Western world. In contrast, multiculturalism is the foundation of Canadian values, and Canadians believe that multiculturalism is good for the country. Younger Canadians believe more strongly about it. This support perhaps is the result of positive messages from the government over the years about how immigration helped to build Canada. However, Canada's success in multiculturalism depends upon continued deliberate, thoughtful, and progressive efforts of its population at large to create conditions where all Canadians can prosper.[97]

There are arguments that Canada should reduce immigration levels. But the fact is that the business community, major bank institutions, many construction companies, the Canadian Chamber of Commerce, most universities and colleges, and specialists in the field are all advocating staying the course or even increasing the level of immigration to about three hundred thousand per year. Any drastic reduction could be damaging to the economy and to future growth in many sectors. The fact is immigrants are a positive influence on Canada overall.

Canada is facing a demographic crunch and labour shortage that will hinder the country's future prosperity. In some regions and industries, Canada is already short of educated, skilled workers. With birth rates low and higher life expectancy, those problems are likely to deepen in the years ahead. To face this challenge, a possible solution is to encourage and bring economic migrants—those selected for their skills. With baby boomers approaching retirement, eventually there will be only two workers for every senior citizen. This increases the burden on workers for seniors' pensions and other social programs, slows growth, and makes labour shortages in Canada. A large number of jobs could remain unfilled because of a lack of qualified candidates.

What immigrants do when they come to Canada? They not only fill gaps in the workforce but also pay taxes and spend money on housing, transport, and consumer goods. Data and reports suggest that immigrants' offspring are likely to be the country's best-educated and initiative-taking young people. Therefore, it is important that government should consider this fact very seriously rather than to ignore the issue. Citizenship and Immigration minister Jason Kenney had been promoting his reforms, trying to make it more responsive to the needs of employers and the economy. But he said that he had no intention of boosting the actual number of immigrants Canada admits annually, despite the demands from provincial governments. Public Policy professor Irvin Studin, University of Toronto, said that Canadians are losing the idea of building the country. He further mentioned that Canada should set its target for a population of one hundred million, and thus it would become a more influential consumer market, a more diverse and imaginative producer, a much more robust and self-sustaining culture. This is how Canada's voice would become more prominent and forceful in international affairs.[98]

The shortage of skilled labour in the Alberta oil sands and Saskatchewan potash mines has become a national issue, and that labour shortages are going to be biggest barrier to economic growth. There are labour shortages across the Western Canada and the provinces are bringing temporary workers from various countries. As they arrived and joined the workforce, the colour of workforce changed, said Joe Frieson, demographic reporter of *Globe and Mail*. In Western Canada, provinces are encouraging young people to learn the skills needed by the labour market. The labour market situation was so favourable that anyone who wanted to work found work, and still there would be jobs available. Some estimates suggest that over the next ten years, there would be a million vacant jobs across Canada country.[99]

We generally agree that Canada needs to welcome more of the most capable, productive, and skilled immigrants. But there is a growing debate over the targeted number of immigrants Canada should bring annually. Over the last ten years, the average number accepted roughly 250,000 immigrants. Let us go back for a while. From 1903 to 1913, immigration levels were never lower than the equivalent of 2 percent of the Canada's population. The annual intake hit 400,000 (more than 5 percent of population) just before the start of the First World War. Since then, the Canadian immigration policy was relaxed, but with the exceptions of ethnic immigrants. However, in the 1960s, immigration was opened to people of all races and national origins, and the points system was introduced. In the early 1990s, federal government agreed to fix historical average of 1 percent immigrants of total population as suggested by the late economist Alan Green. Although this is relatively a modest target, the government was not able to meet the target. The 250,000 number that was admitted in 1992 was even more than 30,000 short of 1 percent of population of Canada. Moreover, the gap widened every year since then. To reach 1 percent immigrants at present today, Canada would have to admit about 350,000 people annually. Robert Vineberg, a former director general of citizenship and immigration for the prairie region and a fellow at the Canada West Foundation, said that these numbers may seem large, but at 1 percent of the population, it's not that much, particularly when we have an aging workforce in Canada.[100]

Bill Greenhalgh, chief executive officer of the Human Resources Professional Association, said that Canada needs more immigration than the status quo. He also pointed out that immigrants' qualifications need to be prescreened to get right people. Obviously, the immigration is a matter of huge adjustment and thus the immigrants need reasonable time (at least five to ten years) after arrival to adjust and settle in Canada. As a result, immigrants earn less in the initial stage. McMaster University economist Arthur Sweetman and former StatsCan director Garnett Picot found that recent immigrants earn only about 60 percent as much as the white Canadians at the initial stage, whereas in the late 1970s it was about 90 percent. It is likely that after living in Canada for ten years, immigrants' employment rates and earnings improved considerably. It is important to look at the struggle and sacrifice every first generation of immigrants has been building for the foundation for the future generations. Moreover, the children of immigrants are the greatest asset for Canada in the human capital context. Evidence suggests that the education level of immigrants' children is higher compared to Canadian-born children, and that the children of immigrants outperform children with parents born in Canada.[101]

One may argue that Canada should emphasize inviting and admitting economic-class immigrants who have higher skill levels, lower unemployment, and greater earning power. This is what Immigration minister Mr. Jason Kenney has been promoting. Currently, Canada accepts 150,000 economic immigrants annually. Now if we doubled this number to 300,000, and the other categories (such as refugees, family-reunification cases) keep constant, the total immigration would be in the range of 400,000 people, which would be slightly more than 1 percent of the population. This would mean economic immigrants would be about 75 percent of annual immigration, up from 60 percent at present. This is not a big rise as it looks. Over the past decade, Canada brought more and more temporary workers under temporary foreign worker program. One may argue that instead of bringing higher number of temporary workers, bringing more permanent immigration would be a stable solution. In the long run, however, immigration level must have to rise even higher to sustain population growth. According to population projection done by Statistics Canada, by 2031 there would be negative population growth, meaning more Canadians will die every year than are born. In that case, immigration could likely grow to double of what it is today. Jonah Lehrer (author of the book *Imagine: How Creativity Works*) suggested that not only is immigration beneficial for population growth in Canada but also it brings together the ideas and experiences of immigrants all over the world, which helps innovation, growth, and development. He summarized this by saying, "Ages of excess genius are always accompanied by new forms of human mixing."[102]

Does Canada's immigration system benefits Canada? According to Alan Broadbend and Ratna Omidvar, the answer is yes. The immigration system has been aimed at benefiting Canada for more than one hundred years. In the two great periods of high immigration, the first decade and the last quarter of the twentieth century, immigration policy aimed at bringing in the skilled immigrants needed for the labour market and nation building. Farmers from the United States and Northern Europe were admitted in the early twentieth century, whereas the skilled workers with language, education, and work experience were admitted at the end of the century. Alan and Ratna also pointed out that Canada's immigration system is a success by international standards that simply needs periodic adjustment and maintenance, particularly to avoid the backlogs that have developed during the past decade, due to a lack of such adjustment and maintenance.[103]

The Harper government's transformation of Canada's immigration system is likely to make Ottawa an online matchmaker, connecting the prospecting migrants with Canadian employers. In an interview in 2012, Immigration minister Jason Kenney described the future Web-based "Expression of Interest" system (will be introduced by 2014) as the result of more than five years of reform. It will be an invitation-only route for economic immigrants where prospective arrivals advertise their skills and qualifications on a Canadian government database that will be used by Canadian employers to hire temporary workers. However, one may argue that if this country is so short of skilled labour, why don't we insist corporations to train people by expanding apprenticeship programs? Or is it easier for the government and their corporate supporters to leave young Canadians untrained and unemployed?[104]

Canada is benefited by immigration system, and there are achievements as a result. For example, most of the immigrants receive Canadian citizenship (almost 90 percent), one of the highest rates in the world, said Alan Broadbend and Ratna Omidvar. They argued that it is due to the fact that citizenship is associated with better employment rates because citizenship requirement is a prerequisite for many aspects of civic and political participation. Moreover, citizenship is mandatory for federal government jobs. It is worth noting that federal government is the largest employer in Canada. Although immigrants might initially suffer from lower income, they catch up over time so that the average wage for immigrants comes within a few percentage points of the white Canadians, which suggests that once immigrants are able to get into the labour market, many of them become successful. Similarly, immigrants own homes at nearly the same rate as the white Canadians. Owning a home is one indicator of success in the context of settlement and an indication of the emotional and financial commitment that immigrants make, which is an important factor for successful integration. It is also to be noted that the children of immigrants attain high levels of education and earnings. In fact, second-generation immigrants outperform children of mainstream white Canadians. They attend postsecondary education at higher rates than white Canadians. Research suggests that more than 50 percent of second-generation immigrant Canadians go to university, as opposed to 38 percent of nonimmigrant white Canadians.

In general, Canadians get along each other without prejudice. People of all groups irrespective of colour, race, religion, or gender go to school together or work together. We also notice that immigrants are gradually making inroads into leadership positions in all professions including politics. However, some isolated incidents of interethnic conflict take place, but they are not appreciated by the majority of people because those are contrary to our norms and values.[105]

Counterargument of Immigration

Given the positive arguments on immigration, there are counterarguments on mass immigration in Canada, which are worth noting. Currently, Canada's population is about thirty-five million, a number that has less to do with natural increase but more due do immigration. Canada receives on average 7.5 immigrants per thousand people. This immigration rate is one of the highest in industrialized countries, said Laurent Martel, of the demography division of Statistics Canada. It's twice what the United States receives every year. Martel said that while Canada was recently named the fastest-growing nation in the G8, that growth rate would be in decline without roughly 249,000 immigrants Canada receives each year.

The question is why immigration is a good thing for Canada? Why should we celebrate this population milestone as an accomplishment? If the benefits of mass immigration-driven population growth were apparent, then we would be experiencing them in our daily lives, but that is not the case. These are the questions raised by opponents of mass immigration. Their point of view is a long list of issues that could be looked into thoroughly in a broader perspective. Some issues are being addressed in the following paragraphs.

One of the benefits of immigration is that Canada becomes a more innovative nation. One may argue that this is an assumption but not a quantifiable statement. It draws a connection between innovation and immigration as if the two go hand in hand. To some degree there may be truth in that, but it's not an argument for mass immigration that Canada has been promoting for over the past two decades. The kind of innovative skills Canada seeks can be found with selective immigration. Is it true that Canada would be a world leader in innovative technology but that's simply not the case? Canada has some of the best-ranked schools in the world. The University of Toronto and McGill University rank in the top twenty of the world's best universities. We produce the innovative thinkers that our economy needs. So we don't need to import them as the opponents argued.[106]

Many believe that immigration makes Canada a more productive nation. Again, it may be an assumption but not the reality. Canada's productivity levels are not very impressive compared to other industrialized societies. Indeed mass immigration is a hindrance to productivity by chocking the roadways of Canada's major cities, creating longer commute times for everyone at a loss of an estimated $6 billion in lost productivity. Immigrants provide a ready-made cheap labour force, which is a discouragement of investing in labour-saving technology. It is also thought that the large diaspora communities Canada hosts—the large overseas populations of other nations—help build bridges between our respective countries, opening up economic opportunities for Canadian business. Again this is a not a quantifiable statement, as it is supported mostly by anecdotal evidence, as there is little or no support to this claim. In fact, it is more likely that the benefits mostly flow away from Canada to the home countries of its immigrant communities. We do know Canada's economy losses around $2 billion a year to overseas remittances, or $6.3 billion flow out of the country to the economies of other nations primarily to China, India, and the Philippines. Immigrants are, in a sense, helping to finance Canada's economic competitors.

Nonetheless, immigrants do not necessarily open up foreign markets for Canadian goods. The more likely situation is that they make Canada into a market for foreign cultural goods. The best example of this is Bollywood movies. Canada's South Asian population and their Canadian-born "desi culture" children have created a demand in Canada for Indian-made movies where it didn't exist in the past. This situation is not favourable to Canadian filmmakers. Due to the dominating presence of American films on Canadian screens, it is hard enough already to get screen time for Canadians films and have our stories told. And now they have to compete with an ever-growing demand for Indian-made movies in major urban Canadian markets. This doesn't help the Canadian film industry at all, but it's great for Indian films.[107]

Population growth also means the explosion in populations in places like Toronto, Vancouver, Montreal, and Calgary. Though it might sound exciting to many people to live in a city with a density population in excess of six or more millions, but the reality may not be so true. For example, in Toronto, Vancouver, or Montreal, the gridlock traffic is omnipresent and can drive the commuters crazy. It means not only to cope with the high cost of living in a high density urban centre but also to face fierce competition in the job market. Tokyo, New York, London, Paris, Beijing, Singapore, or Hong Kong are exciting places to visit, but to live there is something else.

Canadians who live in these cities can look forward to have less disposable income in their pockets because taxes and other costs are up in order to meet with the demands of increased population growth, which is mostly by immigration. This is especially hard, since real incomes have been stagnant for workers for the past thirty years. Canada's immigration-driven population growth has not made the nation more competitive, but surely it has made our cities more crowded and costly to live in. Therefore, one may argue that population contraction might not be a bad idea. One of the primary selling points of mass immigration is that we need immigrants to replace an aging workforce. This argument has some merits. However, things have changed in the course of time. Many of the jobs retirees held have been outsourced overseas, which discourages the need to import workers to replace them. Also the fact that the existence of labour-saving technology removes the need to replace a worker once he or she retires. Canada's labour market has moved from labour-intensive industries like manufacturing to knowledge-based economy. As a result, the demand for labours has diminished significantly in Canada. However, if the economy was composed of both a knowledge sector and a manufacturing sector, then an argument could be made for mass-immigration-driven population growth, but that is also not the reality. The reason is that the labour-intensive manufacturing sector has been moved to other countries where from we bring immigrants.[108]

It may be a reasonable argument that population should be allowed to decrease over a period of time and then stabilize. If the population keeps growing but the jobs are disappearing or are less plentiful, then there would be possibility of social unrest. If recent university grads are having a difficult time finding gainful employment according to their interests and skills sets, then new immigrants would likely be a burden. One may argue why Canada insists for rapid population growth. Countries like Japan, South Korea, Singapore, Italy, Spain, France, Germany, and much of Europe have birth rates below replacement levels, yet they do not see the need to increase their immigrant intake quotas. Has the standard of living and the quality of life for Canadians improved with the growth of the population? Are Canadians better off now with a population of thirty-five million than they were with a population of twenty-five million? One can raise these questions. Perhaps in some sectors of the economy they are, but overall, it is debatable.[109]

Immigration policy

By looking at the recent changes in the immigration policies, one may argue that new policies could change the demographics of Canada. Perhaps we are going in the right direction to bring balance between the knowledge based and mass immigration. There have been more changes to Canada's immigration policy in 2012 and 2013 than in the entire history of Canada since its confederation in 1867. Those changes, some already in effect and some still proposed, are likely to have a domino effect on the country, including a significant shift in its demographics. Statistics Canada projected that by 2031, the number of people belonging to ethnocultural groups will double. The projection may not become a reality. But it is a fact that in the past two decades, the majority of the immigrant population in Canada's big cities came mainly from Asian countries, and it is anticipated that this trend will continue.

The immigration policy change, in fact, began with the amendment of the federal skilled workers category in early 2008, at a time when the National Occupational Classification (NOC) list was condensed from more than one hundred professions to twenty-nine. A cap was also introduced for the maximum number of applications. It is to be noted that as of July 1, 2012, Citizenship and Immigration Canada (CIC) has temporarily stopped accepting applications in this category. This, however, does not apply to those with a qualifying job offer or those who are applying when they are under the PhD program. There are changes in the family category as well. For example, parental sponsorship applications were on hold with the introduction of the "super visa." The recently introduced visa category encourages Canadians to invite their parents and grandparents to visit them temporarily, staying no longer than two years at a time. While permanent reunification may be impossible for many families due to this change, restrictions on spousal sponsorships could also have a considerable impact on immigration. Canadians who are planning to get married elsewhere are not sure what is waiting for them because the process is too complicated and cumbersome. This often happens in South Asian communities where arranged marriages are still prevalent and they bring their spouses to Canada.

One of the most important factors in immigration trends is the proficiency in Canada's official languages requirement that has the high priority. Citizenship, Immigration, and Multiculturalism minister Jason Kenney emphasized that Canada needs economic immigrants who speak one of the two official languages and have credentials likely to be recognized so that their transition into Canadian life can happen with limited barriers. He also said that the government wants to facilitate their economic, social, and cultural participation into Canadian mainstream society. This requirement is going to shift in the profile of people who want to immigrate to Canada. British Colombia immigration lawyer Gianpaolo Panusa mentioned that though it appears to be a reasonable approach to ensure that immigrants speak either English or French when they arrive, relatively a high level of English proficiency that the new immigrants have will be an overrepresentation of immigrants from English-speaking countries. In contrast, Canada may no longer be as attractive to people of countries where English is not the first language, such as India and the Far East, Panusa pointed out. So the problem is twofold, he said. First, there are highly skilled individuals from these countries who could contribute to Canada's mosaic even if their English is not good. The second issue is that Canada has expressed the need to increase trade with Far East countries in order to minimize dependence with the United States for trade. It seems logical to bring immigrants from countries with which Canada seeks to trade goods, which may be a positive move to strengthen the relationship between Canada and those countries.[110]

Every year, more than 150,000 foreign workers enter Canada to work temporarily that help Canadian employers to address skill shortages, or to work as live-in caregivers, according to Citizenship and Immigration Canada. But Immigration Watch Canada, a watchdog organisation, pointed out that nearly two hundred thousand new workers were admitted into Canada in 2011, and the program is widely abused by Canadian employers. The Conservative government helped two hundred thousand people jump the queue, while Canadians' brothers, sisters, and parents wait for a long time. This is grossly unfair, said Olivia Chow, New Democrat

Member of Parliament. The government should not bring temporary workers in such a massive scale. Whether or not temporary foreign workers choose to become permanent residents, it is a good thing that the new policies like Canadian experience class has been introduced. Whether or not the Statistics Canada predictions that the ethnocultural community will become a majority group in the major cities by 2031 will come true, immigrants will continue to shape the future of this Canada and its labour market (roughly one in every three people in the labour force could be foreign born). Chow commented that Canada was originally built by immigrants and will continue to be built by them.[111]

Multiculturalism

There are critics that challenge the narratives of Canada as a multicultural country as well as on the notion of American melting pot. Counterargument of melting pot notion is also evident in the literature, which suggested that while some ethnic characteristics erode across generations, many aspects of ethnic identity are retained (Alba and Chamlin 1983, Breton et al. 1990). Both models tend to share a common view that maintaining ancestry and ethnic attachment and identity undermine Canadian or American identities, and that the assimilation of ethnic minority groups into the national identity do not fully take place (Samuel Huntington 2004; Gregg 2006; Cohen 2007). However, there is contrary view that the assimilation effort has controlled the generation gap. For example, children of visible minority immigrants do assimilate in various ways unlike straight-line path followed by first-generation ethnic immigrants (Portes and Zhou 1993). For second-generation children, however, it is important to control the effect of economic condition of the parents and opportunities for higher education. There are critics of multiculturalism in Canada, which insist that maintaining minority ethnic identities undermine the sense of Canadian belonging, but there is not enough evidence to support this view (Jack Jedwab 2008; edited in *Canadian Diversity*).

There could be debate about American melting pot and Canadian multiculturalism on the question of which one is better in terms of national identity. Both notions stand on their own merits. However, one must have to look at it realistically. American melting pot notion encourages a plain flat field where all citizens are melting down to one identity that is Americans—they become Americanized—no matter what colour, race, or ethnic group or what country of origin they are. Is it really the case? In reality, people do not forget their ancestral identity other than American identity such as Italian American, Irish American, Indian American, Egyptian American, Hispanic-American or African American, and so on. Therefore, the American melting pot is not a plain field but comprised of various multiethnic and multicultural groups of people identified as American. Thus, multiculturalism, in fact, exists in United States only unofficially but not as a state policy; whereas, multiculturalism in Canada stands as a declared national policy, and as such, Canadians enjoy certain privileges and benefits through various multicultural programs designed by the government for citizens.

Canadian multiculturalism has two versions—one is the official version, and the other is the unofficial version. Louise Saldanha of University of Calgary has critically explained the difference. Canada was preoccupied with the duality of its "two founding nations," France and England. Prime Minister Pierre Trudeau proclaimed a policy of multiculturalism on July 22, 1988, which became the law of the land. Thereafter, Canada became the first nation to recognise and promote cultural and racial diversity in the national law, which was recognized by the official policy of Canadian Multiculturalism Act—"The freedom of all members of society to preserve, enhance, and share their cultural heritage." The official Canadian multiculturalism was placed within the bicultural and bilingual framework as ethnocultural minority groups, the right to equality with the two founding nations. Therefore, multicultural harmony was institutionalized. Within the government bureaucracy, a structure is given, and the Canadian multicultural mosaic is subsidized by government funding aimed at encouraging us to celebrate "unity in diversity."

However, the unofficial version of Canadian multiculturalism is different than the official version. Saldanha explained that despite being a Canadian citizen for many years, she was looked differently when responded to the question about her nationality as "Canadian." The moral of the issue is that the cultural diversity is guaranteed by the law, but the long-standing culture and social hierarchies remain intact. What it tells is that the multicultural tale of "one heart, many colours" narrates racialized and ethnicized "others" within the national legibility as "colourful" entertainment for established groups who remain unmarked by ethnicity. She further quoted from an essay "Race Consciousness" of a South Asian Canadian Academic, Arum Mukherjee, "My race consciousness, my awareness of the fact that I am non-white in a white country, is certainly not essentialist. I am conscious of being non-white, South Asian (I cannot call myself Indian in Canada though that's what I really am), of being 'Paki,' to the same measure that white Canadians are not conscious of their whiteness. They would rather be 'just Canadians.' But being 'just

Canadian' is a privilege only white people enjoy in Canada. It is we non-whites who are seen as deviants from the norm. So we are tagged with identity cards, some worn proudly, and others with resentment. I can't, of course, speak for all non-white Canadians but I am always conscious of my being non-white and how that fact determines my whole life experience. I doubt I will ever become 'just Canadian,' whatever that means." One may argue that this is a reality in Canada.

Immigrants in jobs

Evidence suggests that new immigrants to Canada are not doing very well at present. Jeffrey Reitz (2011), however, noted that we should not worry much due to the fact that immigrants' grandchildren will do very well in Canada, perhaps will do better than white Canadians. Study reveals that the economic status of second-generation Chinese, South Asian, and other Asian groups is higher than that of the mainstream population in the same age group in the United States, Canada, and Australia. One therefore could argue that immigration benefits are not always immediate, but it takes time, perhaps few generations. Children of South Asian immigrants in Canada are raised with the strong ethics and values pursued by their parents that play a powerful role in their success.[112]

Nick Noorani, founder of the *Canadian Immigrant* magazine, commented that if one asks twenty-five immigrants why they came in Canada, twenty-four of them will say that they came because of their children. They came in Canada to give their children a better life, and a better chance, which they couldn't have back home. It is to be noted that government policy is not entirely shortsighted in terms of immigrants' applications, especially in the case skilled category. Policy makers know that it is not the parents but the children of immigrants who are the future economic assets for Canada. It is like a hidden agenda within the immigration policy. We, therefore, should not look at immigrants as only a current solution but should look at it in terms of generations to come.

Luin Goldring, a sociology professor at Toronto's York University, agrees that the success of second-generation Canadians is the result of a particular kind of upbringing. In commenting on South Asian immigrant parents about its understanding, she said, "If you can't be the professional, try to make sure your kids are." Morton Weinfeld, director of the Canadian ethnic studies program at McGill University, said multigenerational Canadians don't have the same work ethic as immigrants and their offspring.[113] As a South Asian origin living in Canada for thirty years, I echo the same view.

An article "Trending Jobs for Canadian Immigrants in 2013" by Lisa Evans explained the views of Canadian experts about the upcoming job prospects in Canada in the canadianimmigrant.ca website in January 2013. Daisy Wright, career adviser and author of the book *No Canadian Experience*, advises newcomers to do some research about job prospects in all of Canada's regions. She said that while there is fierce competition for jobs in the larger cities, other potential areas will have greater opportunities. She also mentioned that the "Working in Canada" online tool is an excellent resource for the job seekers to review wages, qualifications, and educational requirements for various professions. Evans pointed out that three sectors in particular, such as *natural resources, construction, and health care*, have strong growth potential at present and in the near future. The target group for this article is the newcomers in Canada on their employment prospects. It also gives a good analytical overview of the potential job market in the country where most of the jobs are available currently and will be available in the coming years that Canadian job seekers in general can find productive employment. It would be a smart thing to do groundwork not only for the new South Asian immigrants but also for the second-generation South Asian youths before they choose the field of study and career path in order to take right decision.[114]

In 2011 a study published by the Social Science Research journal reveals that second-generation South Asian and Chinese immigrants in the United States, Canada, and Australia are more successful than the respective mainstream third- and higher-generation white populations. On average, the mainstream population in Canada spends approximately 14.6 years in school, compared with 17.5 years for second-generation Chinese students and 17.3 years for other Asian groups. The study also notes that second-generation Canadians of Chinese and South Asian origins also have higher postsecondary graduation rates. Reitz (one of the authors of the study) commented that from a Canadian perspective, the results are a welcome indication that the children of immigrants are doing well.

With respect to income levels, the story is other way around. Based on 2006 census data, visible minority workers earned only 81.4 cents for every dollar earned by white Canadian counterpart. Research done by the Wellesley Institute and Canadian Centre for Policy Alternatives revealed that earnings of male visible minorities were just 68.7 percent of those who were white males counterpart. The colour code persisted for second-generation Canadians with similar education and age with visible minority women making only 56.5 cents for every dollar white men earned, while minority men in the same cohort earned 75.6 cents. There is a disparity between racialized and nonracialized Canadians, said Sheila Block, director of economic analysis, Wellesley Institute. She mentioned that visible minorities were significantly underrepresented in the public administration—a sector where 92 percent of workers were white. The federal employment equity program has been effective in boosting access and mobility among women and people with disabilities within the federal government, but the representation gap of visible minority persists and speaks for itself the need for targeted hiring, said Galabuzi, a Ryerson University public administration professor.[115]

One of the important challenges facing the country is the proportional representation of visible minorities in the Federal Public Service of Canada, the largest employer in the country. The Federal Public Service has met its targets to hire women, aboriginals, and persons with disabilities to reflect the Canadian population, but visible minorities continue to be underrepresented. The challenge of proportional representation of visible minorities in the public service was one of the topics covered at a conference held by the National Council of Visible Minorities (NCVM) in the Federal Public Service in Toronto. The conference was attended by about two hundred people. Some expressed their frustration that the proportional representation of visible minorities in the public service progress is regrettably slow compared to the rapid demographic change in Canada.

Jacqueline Edwards, former president of the council, said that when one chooses to become a Canadian citizen or an immigrant, that decision should be dependent upon the matters in the recruitment of a public servant. In the hiring process, the only factor should be the education, expertise, and experience, not the colour of their skin. She believes that it is possible to achieve proportional representation of visible minorities in the public service. Max Brault, a human resource manager at Correctional Service of Canada, said that while there has been an increase in visible minorities in the public service, there is still plenty of room for improvement. He also said that there are thousands of individuals from visible minorities who have all the requirements for jobs, but they cannot get the opportunities they deserve. He believes that the government should play a more active role to meet this challenge and said that he does not believe that it is the personal responsibility of visible minorities to overcome the barriers on their career paths in the public service. Instead, it is the government that can and should break down the barriers for the visible minorities to get jobs in the public service.

The government could make an improvement by enforcing current legislation, including the Employment Equity Act. Jacqueline categorically said that there is the Multiculturalism Act that is not enforced, there is the Employment Equity Act that is not enforced, whereas, the Bilingual Language Act is enforced. As part of enforcement and accountability, a position may be created within the Employment Equity Commission, which would report to the prime minister and hold the government accountable to move the agenda forward, she suggested. She argued that Canadians can come together in churches and supermarkets and restaurants, in football fields or hockey stadiums, and it is not an issue in those situations. But whenever there is an issue of authority or an issue of being in a position to make a decision, ethnicity of people become an issue. Mr. Brault argued that it will take years to see the impact of NCVM's efforts to build a representative and inclusive Federal Public Service. Meanwhile, the Perinbam Report ("Embracing Change in the Federal Public Service"—Taskforce on the Representation of Visible Minorities in the Federal Public Service) on the participation of visible minorities in the Federal Public Service and NCVM has brought the visible minority representation as a high-priority issue and made government accountable.[116]

Ethnic diversity

Immigrant families always put culture, tradition, and family experience first in their parenting styles. Immigrants, visible minority groups in particular, have more traditional values and norms that are different than the values of mainstream Canadian culture. Chinese or South Asian parents, for example, emphasize more on behavioural control, disciple, and obedience than the Western Canadian parents. Clashes take place as the children learn the language, new culture, and values quicker than the parents. Gary Direnfeld, a social worker and counsellor, said that it is not a question whether the children will be changed by the host culture, rather how and what degree of change is more important. Aneesa Shariff, psychologist, believes that ethnic identity formation and negotiating between their heritage culture and the dominant culture is a normal and essential part of development. It is important for children to integrate more because they need to get along with their peers and classmates, she said. However, she also mentioned that the process of forming an ethnic identity needs to be resolved during adolescence time; otherwise, it can result in a fragmented sense of self without having a clear idea of who they are. She believes that youth can lead a double life—behaving one way in the home and another way outside of the home, and others may hide their feelings to bend to the wish of their parents, or they gravitate towards counterculture groups. As we can expect, these actions can result in mental problems like depression, anxiety, substance abuse, eating disorders, types of delinquent behaviours, and academic failure. These problems of children are the serious concerns for the family.

It is important that immigrant parents should decide how much they wish to adopt the values of Canadian culture and practice it, and how much they want to retain their own culture. They must also support their children in forming an ethnic identity while encouraging a healthy parent-child relationship. It is not always an easy or a smooth process to go through. It is important to talk about it with the children and come to compromises, and use empathy and open dialogue, and engage in positive activities such as watching movies together and participating in heritage cultural activities, Aneesa suggested. A strong connection to ethnic heritage is important, and at the same time, it is also vital that children and young adults develop a positive identity as Canadians. Parents need to understand and recognize the fact that behaviour in their children is a normal developmental part of adolescents. At the end of the day, parents have to play a central role in all aspects of children's lives. The best chance for developing a strong and healthy relationship with children adjusting to Canadian culture depends on how successfully parents adapt those strategies.[117]

In many ways, second-generation young of South Asian origin are no different to any other young people in Canada. Many listen to the same sort of music, wear the same kind of clothes, do the same kinds of things in their spare time, and have the same kinds of ambitions. However, there are, of course, more serious issues that affect their lives in a distinctive way. There are benefits and pressures of having more than one culture. On the one hand, young South Asians have the best of both worlds—South Asian culture and white culture. Their experience in Canada is richer and more diverse than those who have knowledge of one culture. Nonetheless, they have to balance the demands of living in cultures that conflict with each other. Some South Asian youths feel that they don't fully belong to any culture, never fully accepted in either world. Apparently, it seems that race relations have improved since the parents or grandparents of second-generation South Asians arrived in Canada, but racism is still an issue for many second-generation youths, particularly with regard to job prospects.

The second-generation youths of ethnic origin are living in two conflicting worlds, such as the cultural and familial expectations of their immigrant parents and the social norms of their white Canadian peer group. The relationship between immigrant parents and their young children is very complex, which often leads to a clash of cultures. These youths feel that they are sandwiched between their desire to fit in with their peer groups in the Canadians' mainstream society and their intention to meet their parents' expectations. The act of parenting the young children is very stressful. Most of the time, the factors like their employment and income loss, language barriers, lack of familiarity with Canadian institutions and labour market, cultural values, lack of networking, multiple jobs, retraining and further education, etc. pose big challenges for immigrant parents. Consequently, children do not get the adequate attention and time of their parents to talk about their views and ideas. In many cases, the children also work to contribute to the family income. Female family members may also be required to work outside home to earn money, which is not within their traditional norms for some cultures.

When the young South Asians visit their country of origin, they often experience mixed feelings. When they visit for the first time in their country of origin, it is an opportunity to learn their root culture as well as to build relationships with relatives. Interestingly, their experiences are twofold. While some feel greater acceptance by their peers and relatives in the country of origin, others still feel like foreigners even if they look like everyone else. There was a time not so long ago when young children of South Asians parents living in the Western countries regarded their cousins back home as backward, in dress and in attitudes. This has changed in the course of time, especially in the large South Asian cities, where young children are absorbing Western values rather than practicing entirely the traditional norms and values.

For many South Asian parents in Canada, the main goal in life is to see their children educated and married so they can have a secure future. But the pressure to succeed in life and achieve these objectives can be very stressful to South Asian youths. Many achieve great success as expected by their parents, but others are not so successful and they feel like failures in the eyes of their parents and the extended family members as well. South Asian families are generally conservative than the mainstream Canadian families and may disapprove of things that are considered the style and custom of white Canadian young people. This is especially true in parents' expectations about the way girls should behave. Alcohol consumption, dating, and night clubs can all be bad things in South Asian households. The result of this can be open rebellion, secrecy, or eventual compromise. It can be a struggle for South Asian youths to balance traditional home lives with the demands of living in a secular culture, which has very different values and priorities. The dilemma between tension of parents and keeping up with peers could be very acute among the South Asians children. Many do not share their problems with their parents because they feel that the pressures they face are very different to their parents' experiences when they were young.

We often hear people saying that they came here for the sake of their children. We have reasons to call Canada our home. Everyone has a story to share the challenges faced in the first few years of their arrival here. The transition is difficult no matter if we are prepared or not for change. It is a new beginning. Let us adapt to our new home and try to be Canadian for the sake of our children and grandchildren. By saying this, I do not mean that we should give up our values as an Indian or Pakistani or Bangladeshi or Sri Lankan or wherever we come from. But we must join and applaud our children whenever they feel like a proud Canadian for the right values and reasons. That could happen when they watch the Canadiens or Maple Leafs win, or perhaps watch the Canadian soldiers fight in foreign lands to maintain peace and stability. The avenues are abundant as long as we are smart to grab the opportunity. We need to have conversations with our children, who act as a strong knot that solidifies the family bond. Keep windows open for a meaningful dialogue. This would in turn make them curious towards our own ethnic root and culture. Raising a family in Canada can be challenging and stressful but not impossible.

It is difficult to maintain the extended family system. What usually happens in reality is that both parents work and weekends are taken up with chores, socializing and entertaining, or worship. There is hardly any family time left after all these activities. But we must try to find time to spend with kids and start bonding with them when they are young. Applaud and participate in the sports they like and play, the music they enjoy, or the friends they hang out with. Listen attentively to their concerns. Imagine how difficult it was for us to fit in and how challenges are facing children to adapt between two cultures. It is important to lead them by example and we should be a role model. We must not expect to control but try to correct them when they develop some kind of bad habits you don't like them to adopt. Our children are our future, and the time and effort we spend and sacrifices we make in nurturing them will undoubtedly reward us at the end.

There are opinions in favour of and against mixed marriage in Canada. Proponents of mixed marriage believe that love can overcome difference. So intermarriage by love may be a hope of tolerance and open-mindedness. The supporters of intermarriage also believe that it is the time to transcend old ethnic, cultural, and religious barriers and feel that the wave towards mixed marriage is good for the society at large. This looks very promising by the fact that mass immigration has brought people of various ethnicities and religions closer together where more and more intermarriages are likely to happen. In a multiethnic society, it is likely that people of multicultural origins are lured together by eros, which results to dating and marrying by the fascination of the unknown. One can interpret this interethnic and interfaith marriages are the multicultural element. Statistics Canada data suggest that visible minorities are much more likely to enter into mixed unions, especially among the second and third generation of immigrants. However, there are forces working against mixed unions. In Canada, in many cultures such as Chinese, Arabic, and South Asian, elders are very powerful. It is the norm for parents to encourage arranged marriages between children of same culture, ethnicity, religion, and worldview. Also, tragically though, in some ultraconservative ethnic cultures, opposition to intermarriages ends up in form of "honour killing." Opposition to cross-religious marriages remains strong among many Catholic priests, Jewish rabbis, Evangelical pastors, Sikh priests, and Muslim imams in Canada.

Love marriage is very common among second-generation adults of South Asian origin. Some dating practices are seen among South Asians youths, but it is not as prevalent as other Canadian ethnic groups because majority of the families maintain traditional values. While cross-cultural interracial marriages in the second-generation South Asians are present, the mixed marriages between White Canadians and South Asian backgrounds are becoming more prevalent. Many sociologists view interracial marriage as the best barometer of racial and cultural integration in a society. Intermarriage translates into the fact that people are clearly relating to each other socially to the point where they are getting married. This may also indicate that there is an obvious social and biological blending going on, so the barriers are broken down at that point.

Religion has always been a hot, sensitive, and never-ending issue for debate and discussion. This is more prevalent in the multicultural and diverse society in the context of multiculturalism. With the implementation of *Canadian Multiculturalism Act* in 1988, Canadian society has become increasingly diverse as the act emphasises on the freedom to practice the rights of citizens to their religion without prejudice, fear, and interference. In pursuant of multiculturalism policy, Canada promoted the idea that not only the new immigrants are accepted but also that the immigrants can maintain their heritage, culture, and religion aimed at enriching Canada's cultural mosaic. Although the policy has come under public scrutiny whether it is truly working or not given the understanding of the realities of the immigration and social integration in Canada, the primary focus is to look at the view of the second-generation minorities who have grown up in Canada about the issue of religiosity in the multicultural context.

Religions like Hindu, Sikh, Buddhist, and Muslim in particular are the main multireligious communities that have grown rapidly in Canada since the late twentieth century. Among these communities, Muslim population is more diverse, multiethnic, and multilingual. Muslims in Canada originate from many countries and comprise dozens of ethnoracial and linguistic groups. As they have lived in Canada for decades, the Canadian-born second-generation Muslim youths have grown substantially. Conceptually, we think that the second-generation immigrant youths in general are caught in the middle between the two identities—religious and cultural identities of their parents on the one hand, and the Canadian dominant culture on the other (Rubina Ramji 2008; edited in *Canadian Diversity*).

I talked with many second-generation South Asian youths of Muslim parents who stated that they are exposed to various cultures and religions and Canadian cultures, but they maintain their parents' cultural and religion identity with no fear of marginalization. However, research on second-generation Muslim youths suggests that they exhibit different views towards their religion. While some are highly individualistic who construct their identities and are not carrying on the traditions of their parents in terms of religiocultural preservation, other are extremists, and the rest are in the middle who follow and practice their parents' religious beliefs, customs, and rituals. Beyond these, there is one group of youth who are nonbelievers, although they admit that they are Muslim by birth through their family and cultural background (ibid.). Ramji classified them into four distinct categories—the *Salafists*, the *highly involved*, the *moderately involved*, and the *nonbelievers*.

One may argue that the Islamic belief among the second-generation Muslim youth may have been lost within the larger Canadian population. But study findings, observation, and personal experience gathered from various sources show otherwise; majority of the second-generation Muslim youths are not only adhering to their religion but also involved in and practice their religion. Interestingly, it appears that many of the younger-generation Muslims become *highly involved* or *Salafists,* presumably after 9/11 from strong adherence to and solidarity with religious identity. For example, a male participant in a survey conducted by Rubina Ramji stated the following in explaining why some young Muslims understand Islam in rebellion:

> *I think I may be echoing other people when I say that every generation has its rebellion, and the rebellion in my generation has been something called the Islamic Revival Movement—so the movement that says that our parents' way of following religion was*

> *not strict enough, things like that . . . I see it as just adolescent rebellion, you know, and I think it's if anything, necessary. It's a trend towards going back to the sources, things like that. Uh, specifically things like the "Hijab" and the beard; those are more prevalent in the new generation than in the older ones.*

Many Muslims including the younger generation feel that 9/11 event has brought them more closer to Islam; whereas, the *nonbelievers* do not consider religion is very important and see 9/11 as troubling in the context of Muslim identity. Many Muslims also think that media plays a big role in identifying Muslims as terrorists, and in reaction to that, many of them were more inclined to visibly show their Islamic identity such as wearing *"Hijab"* and keeping beard (ibid.). My personal view is that not only Muslims but also other young South Asians also choose to assert their religious identity because religion plays an important role in the lives of South Asians. However, care should be taken to distinguish between religious assertion and personal view of life, which is something that the young South Asians need to work out for themselves. Moreover, they also should keep in mind that their efforts to become dynamic and innovative towards progression are not blocked by any nonprogressive religious systems or beliefs.

Acculturation, assimilation, and integration

How do immigrants and their children go through the acculturation in Canada? Immigrants move to new countries to build new lives with new cultural and economic opportunities, keeping in mind the welfare of their children. While the sentiment of a new life is pleasant, the realities are that immigrant children face challenges, which are not that pleasant as thought. Sociocultural influences and challenges are immense. Immigrant children face pressure from dominant culture to conform, while parents and extended family expect children to maintain their traditional social norms and values. Assimilation is difficult, and older relatives may disapprove and stick with the native culture that creates further challenges in being accepted by the dominant white culture. Children must learn to deal with the stress of acculturation process in order to find their unique place in the society. The personal characteristics such as emotional maturity, intellect, coping skills, and knowledge are very important factors for adoption of a specific form of acculturation. The following is the opinion of some South Asian youths:

> Our identity is hardly crystal clear. We are Canadian and being Canadian means that we are the norm, but in a multicultural society, what does one assimilate to? We need to figure out where we belong in this country that is made up of so many sub-Canadas. We want to give up the condition of being foreigner, but we hardly can as we are identified as Visible Minorities or Indian—Canadian or Bangladeshi—Canadian. We identify Canadians, but Canadians do not identify with us. We have never come to know what it's like to belong to a community. Our parents did not want their daughters and sons to be Indians or Bangladeshis but they don't want us fully Canadians either. Children of South Asian immigrants are living in paradoxes.

People from all over the world immigrate to Canada for prospect and better future. Many others may have been forced to leave their countries due to fear of prosecution or due to violent political and social conditions in their own countries. Whatever may be the case, individuals and families who immigrate to Canada bring their own cultural ideologies, and they inevitably go through a process of acculturation in the new country. Regardless of which country an immigrant comes from, they typically follow four different ways to adapt to a new culture and society: (1) process of *assimilation*, where individuals do not hold their original cultural identity and characteristics to be important, but value interaction with the other cultures; (2) process of *separation*, where people value the original cultural identity and characteristics and avoiding interaction with the other cultural groups; (3) process of *integration*, which refers to valuing cultural maintenance as well as seeking interaction with other cultural groups; and (4) process of *marginalization*, which refers to a lack of interest in either maintaining the original cultural characteristics or seeking interaction with other cultural groups (Abouguendia and Noels 2001).[118]

For racialized Canadians, integration, assimilation, and the normative assumptions that define Canadian are very complex. It is true that the dominant Canadian culture is regulated by Western values. Adhered to this value, multiculturalism is likely to undermine the aspirations of cultural conventional rules and assumptions of ethnonational dominance (Audrey Kobayashi 2008; edited in *Canadian Diversity*). Visible minority immigrants can look at it in two different ways: (1) dominant culture as being monolithic and normative and thus do not welcome diversity of the society, and (2) Canadian society is highly normative, assimilative, and is regulated by set of European standards and values. Both assumptions seem logical as research suggest. Visible minorities tend to believe that they do not belong to mainstream Canadian society, and the citizens of dominant white society have not gone beyond their adherence to European norms, although they express support the concept of multiculturalism. Obviously, these conflicting views do not show a society that is quite as multicultural as we think it should be.

These views have significant impact on the understanding and experience of the second generation of visible minorities in terms of their identity as full Canadian citizens. Second generation of visible minorities have a dual problem—as they are not fully integrated into the dominant society, Canada becomes the host country while they are the guests in their country of birth; and those born in Canada are, in a sense, oxymoron. Yet there is evidence to suggest that second-generation visible minorities are capable of adapting, aligning, and interpreting the dominant cultural narrative in a variety of ways and project their own identity and Canadianness. At the same time, they can redefine and reframe the traditional norms in innovative ways and act as a bridge between their parents' domestic culture and the new way of living in Canada (ibid.).

Yet second-generation children see conflicting identity as they grow up and become aware of both their heritage culture and dominant white culture; neither of these is entirely their own. For their parents, personal and cultural identity is closely linked to the country of origin; but for their children, it is very difficult to choose a culture they can think their own. Yet they are forced to choose their own identity given the fact that the external environment will have an impact in the process of acculturation. In the social context, the second-generation visible minority children face challenges of "colour" and "race" while integrating with wider Canadian society. This brings the question of resiliency, the capacity to cope effectively with the internal stresses of their vulnerabilities. Evidence from various research studies on immigrant children suggests that discrimination becomes a reality in the lives of second-generation visible minority children (N. Arthur et al. 2008; edited in *Canadian Diversity*).

Whenever the second-generation children face discrimination, they respond proactively. For example, they find extensive education in today's knowledge economy as the key factor to combat labour market challenges where systemic discrimination against visible minorities prevails. They also have adopted strategies to neutralize discriminatory acts by ignoring the importance of those acts. One smart way of doing so is the bicultural integration—that is, their strong motivation to retain their cultural heritage and intention to participate in the mainstream society. This is a smart and very practical approach because it enables them not only to turn adversities into opportunities for growth and advancement but also to promote self-esteem, reduce risks, and enhance good relationships with their own ethnic groups as well as with Canada's mainstream society (ibid.). Adapting this approach, second-generation children of ethnic origin would be capable to establish them as a true Canadian while maintaining their root culture and familial values.

There are conflicting views about the Canadian identity and belonging among racialized second-generation children. Jeffrey Reitz and Rupa Banerjee, analyzing *Ethnic Diversity Survey* data, found that racialized second-generation youth experienced racial discrimination at the highest level. This made national headlines in 2007. They also pointed out that racialized second-generation youth are less likely to feel that they belong to Canada, and therefore, their sense of Canadian identity is diminished. This suggests that they are likely to witness lower level of social integration compared to all young people in Canada. Interestingly, this result is persistent even after controlling the level of income. There are two major theories about life trajectories of the second-generation Canadians: (1) second-generation youths are more likely to feel a stronger sense of belonging and Canadian identity than first-generation youth; and (2) although second-generation youth make headway in economic success and social integration, many of them, especially the visible minority groups, are at the poverty level and not very successful in social adaptation (Lori Wilkinson 2008; edited in *Canadian Diversity*).

Canadian identity

One would likely to argue that the longer the people live in Canada, the higher the sense of Canadian identity. Although this is subject to the lifestyle they lead in Canada, it is important to remember that identity (either individual or national) is dynamic (it evolves from one's understanding, perseverance, and achievement), which change over time; it takes the form as one wants to be and prepares and secures a place for himself/herself in the society. The view on racism among minority immigrants, especially among second-generation youths, may likely to change with the change of time and scope. However, one of the most prominent discourses that emerged in a study done by Meghan C. Brooks (2008) is that second-generation participants believe racism is an issue in Canada. He further commented that being Canadian is about mixing and matching identities, accommodating social constructions of race, religion, and culture, standing with one leg on either side of the world—that is, ancestral heritage and the mainstream culture. They understand that belonging in Canada is dependent on a number of factors such as strong footings and places in the dominant society in which their contributions can be noticed, recognized, rewarded, and valued. Evidences are available from numerous literatures, but it is important that they should be accompanied by strong push for policy that will address racism.

Canada is preparing for 150th anniversary in 2017. Like mainstream Canadians, ethnic communities also are going to celebrate the sesquicentennial by focusing on Canadian values. But what would be their understanding and experience about it? Most likely it would be the good, the bad, and the ugly, said Tobi Cohen, of *PostMedia News* (tcohen@postmedia.com). Ascension of two Sikhs to the federal cabinet, the Chinese head tax, and the ongoing impact of immigration on Canada's first inhabitants who remain isolated and marginalized are the diverse range of experiences he mentioned. Yet the anniversary is a moment of celebration and reflection and, of course, a time for change—focusing more on what unites Canadians regardless of race, religion, ethnicity, language, or country of origin.

Frank Dimant of B'nai Brith Canada said that the two languages, French and English, dominated during Canada's centennial. But many communities are now living in isolation, none more so than the aboriginals. He also noted that during late sixties, Montreal was the home to 120,000 Jews and considered the "centre of the Jewish future in Canada," but that number has been reduced to a "geriatric community" of about 75,000. He argued that the strong hand of the Quebec government in trying to control the language is a tremendous discouragement to immigrants. Dimant said that B'nai Birth is already looking into Canada's 150th event, which will bring different religious and ethnic communities together. One can think that reassessments of Canadian patriotism, a focus on the poor and marginalized, and a celebration of Canadian values, along with others, are the themes to be addressed and touched upon, he hopes. He thinks that Canada has served as a role model in the world for the ability of multicultural groups to exist side by side, and it is something Canadians should be proud of. It is, therefore, important that we should address the key challenges facing Canada and work hard to mitigate them in order to unite Canadians as opposed to what divides them.

Around the time of the confederation, the vast majority of newcomers came from England, Ireland, and Scotland and were largely of Christian descent. Historic census data suggests 44 percent of Canada's 3.3 million citizens were Roman Catholic, while just 2 percent were of "miscellaneous creeds." All thirty-six so-called Fathers of Confederation, according to

Library and Archives Canada, were white men. When Canadians started preparing for its centennial, the British Isles, remained the chief source of newcomers, though immigrants from Italy were adding significantly and were considered Canada's racial diversity. The country was also welcoming significant numbers from Greece, Portugal, and Commonwealth countries, such as India, although the British and French were still considered the dominant groups. In 1971 Canada became the first country to adopt multiculturalism as an official policy. The concept was included the Charter of Rights and Freedoms in 1982, and the Multiculturalism Act finally became law in 1988. Today, the Philippines, China, and India are Canada's chief source countries for new immigrants, and the latest census data suggests Canadians speak more than two hundred different languages. One in five Canadians speaks neither French nor English at home. It would be very exciting to witness the sesquicentennial fireworks on July 1, 2017, when visible minorities will comprise one-fifth of the Canadian population, as predicted by Statistics Canada.

Sikhs have been a part of Canadian society for more than a century. Canadian exclusion laws kept them out for several decades, culminating with the *Komagata Maru* incident of 1914 in which a boatload of passengers from Punjab, India, were turned away at the border. At the same time, about ten Sikhs fought in the Canadian Forces during the First World War. They have a very long and proud history in Canada. For them, the 150th anniversary is a good opportunity to highlight the country's successes on the multicultural front.

In 2008 Canada's fast-growing Chinese community also marked 150 years in the Great White North, beginning with the British Columbia gold rush in the 1850s and continuing with the construction of the Canadian Pacific Railway. At the time, the Chinese Canadian National Council (CCNC) launched an online cultural project showcasing the work of Chinese Canadian writers, musicians, videographers, and artists. Last year, an award-winning Canadian documentary dubbed *Lost Years* also chronicled the last 150 years of Chinese diaspora. It told the family history of Kenda Gee, a Chinese Canadian man who retraced the steps of his great-grandfather—who sailed for Canada in 1921 only to face racism, Chinese head tax, and exclusionary laws that prohibited Chinese family reunification.

Alice Choy, CCNC national director, said that her organisation recently published a book about the Chinese experience in Canada and that efforts are ongoing to collect more stories and photos, which could result in a second publication. The 150th anniversary is an opportunity to promote integration and build bridges within Canada's Asian communities, she commented. There are many differences between Mandarin and Cantonese speakers within China and even more differences between those who come from Cambodia, Laos, and Taiwan. She emphasized that everyone should be together, communicate well, and know about other people's cultures. Every country has taboos, something that we don't understand, but it is important that we understand each other, integrate, and build up an inclusive environment.[119]

Culture

INDOlink website has reviewed studies in the United States, Canada, England, Western Europe, and Australia, and all of them came up with one key conclusion that most of the problems that arise between two cultures are from the odds or conflicts between each other. For example, boys and girls at Canadian schools learn about independence and to be critical thinkers. In contrast, South Asian children learn the virtues of collective responsibility and respect to the elders in the family. Parents of South Asian children have the dilemma about children's freedom, as they are confused at how much freedom they will allow their children. Parents' main concern is for the girls, who tend to encounter many difficulties at school due to contrasting values of family and school. Much of the difficulties arise from sexual control of youth, girls in particular. Issues surrounding sexuality have become the potential area of intergenerational conflict within the South Asian immigrants. Most often this becomes a community problem in various forms such as "youth issues," "the second-generation problem," "cultural issues," etc. Of course, the community considers any individual sexual behaviour of its youth (particularly girls' sexual behaviour) as potentially destructive of the integrity of the group. Shamita Das Gupta, assistant professor of psychology at Rutgers University in Newark, USA, pointed out that girls' discontent revolves around the issues of dating, marriage, and the choice of a partner.[120]

India-born psychologist Kauser Ahmed of New Jersey said that South Asian parents hope that their children can function in the American culture well to adopt appropriately within the workplace, retaining the core South Asian culture. However, for their children growing to adulthood in North American culture, but without incorporating any Western values and ideals, is not realistic. He further pointed out that South Asian girls find that the compromising of relationships between their parents and the outside world is the most difficult aspect of their bicultural lives. Many South Asian young girls who identify themselves as American or Canadian feel that living with two different lives and engaging in relationships that are kept hidden from their families are very difficult. It is likely that those girls who try to manage both worlds live with constant guilt and a sense of fracture in their lives. Helen Ralston, of Saint Mary's University in Canada, acknowledges that the primary concern for the majority of South Asians girls is the relationships with boys. She noted that parental rules of relationship with boys are only acquaintanceship with a boy classmate who might call the daughter at home about an exam or homework. However, when the daughter accepts to go out with a male partner, it is not permitted. But the rules are different in the case of a son. For example, a son can go out with girls and can bring his girlfriend at home; a daughter cannot do the same. But the daughters of South Asian immigrant women are not passive and silent who are caught between two cultures and confused about their identity. In contrast, they are very active, dynamic, and articulate creators with fluid sense of identity. They consciously choose how they will present themselves within the family and community and to the world.[121]

While talking about the youth, Dr. Sehdev Kumar, professor emeritus at the University of Waterloo, stated that youth is a time for adventure, exploration, and romance, something out of the ordinary, something heroic. At the same time, the youth suffers from security, yet they are not completely shattered if something does not work. There is certain mixed feeling between seeking adventure and the unknown on one hand, and security and the known on the other. In the midst of these, a new zest of life and creativity can emerge. Without adventure, little can be gained. Parents and teachers must pass the torch of life to the new generation to carry forward as it is seemed right. Parents should not load burden on the shoulder of the second generation with old dreams and expectations. That is not true freedom. Freedom of thought, imagination, and dreams, worth, and meaning of life are precious gifts to cherish and to pass on from one generation to another. Dr. Kumar was always in fear of those who cherish freedom and are uncontrolled in their imagination and dreams by orthodoxy or traditions or expectations of others. To live in that freedom is a courageous act, he said.[122] It is so true that any youth must learn and excel in their life.

Second generation of South Asian origin

The stories of South Asian Canadians, particularly the second generation, are built through the experiences of successful and unsuccessful people. It is, however, important to follow the path of those who become successful in Canada. One has to keep in mind that our lives are our messages that we need to pass on to others who want to thrive. For first generation of South Asian Canadians, it is important that they inspire their children to keep on working hard by focusing on the right things of life. For example, Rathika Sitsabaiesan, MP, Scarborough-Rouge River and the first Tamil Canadian in Parliament, had a bad experience of racism because of her skin colour when she came to Mississauga from Sri Lanka. But her father inspired her with his love for social activism, and because of her father, she and her sisters were involved in community building from a very young age. Likewise, success stories of second-generation South Asian are driven by the inspiration of their parents along with the hard work and dedication.

The second generation is the future asset to Canada's economy in terms of education, skills, official languages proficiency, diversity, and cultural bridges for Canada's leadership in the globalized economy. Research suggests that overall many individuals from the second generation are doing well in terms of employment and income. However, results change when factored by racialized and mainstream disaggregation of data. For example, those who belong to racialized groups notably fall behind compared to the general population. The conventional wisdom tends to project a brighter future for the second generation, given the fact that they are hardworking, dedicated, and adhere to a set of Canada's dominant values. These basic narratives incorporate a vision of the host society, which is ready to embrace diversity and provide opportunities for upward social mobility for each and every second generation of Canadians. This promise, however, does not come true for the second generation who belong to racialized groups. Current demographics indicate that economic growth with the increase of labour force in the near future will significantly rely on immigrant population. So creating conditions for inclusion of immigrant population in the economy and society in building the path for their sense of belonging and active civic engagement is very important (Alfia Sorokina et al. 2012).

Given the inequalities on socioeconomic indicators between the racialized and mainstream second generations of Canadians that persist in Canada, it is obvious that many racialized second-generation Canadians feel that the sense of belonging as Canadian is still partial. It is also true that the second generation of ethnic origin are the prospective candidates for bridging the gap between racialized and dominant society in all walks of life in Canada. So ensuring socioeconomic growth, prosperity, and upward mobility of the second-generation Canadians of ethnic origin are the important narratives for successful social integration and inclusion of this group of Canadians into the mainstream society.

One of the ways the second-generation South Asians can help themselves and work to prosper in Canada is to create a common platform where they could collectively address challenges they face in bridging the economic and cultural gaps between South Asians and the mainstream Canadians. The initiatives must be taken by the youths in the form of youth forum, which would develop programs and short- and long-term projects. The main objective of those programs and projects would be to assist second-generation youths who struggle with social inclusion, depression, peer pressure, education, and job mentoring. These would encourage them to meet the high academic and professional job expectations. The focus should be to empower youths so that they can talk openly about their collective as well as individual experience and challenges. The youth forum as such would provide services, as a group, to the youths according to the needs and guide them to work strategically and smartly to meet challenges face the South Asian youths. However, individual success is always the priority and perhaps the main focus for those who are capable to do so by his or her individual strength, capacity, knowledge, skills, and competencies.

It is recommended that second-generation South Asian young adults learn lessons from the stories of successful Canadians of South Asian origin presented in part 2, chapter 6 in the book. Those stories are the reflection of dedication, struggle, and hard work of people who achieved great successes, which could be the model not only for South Asians but also for all ethnic minority population in Canada. Their successes would be the inspiration to others and would multiply. One final note: when others can make things work in their life, you can make it too. One needs to follow the footsteps of successful people and not to deviate from the end goal.

The perspectives of different cultural groups can enrich Canadian society, but we cannot achieve that if we stay clustered in homogenous ethnic groupings.
—A second-generation Canadian
of South Asian origin

*Ethnicity does not replace Canadian identity.
It is Canadian identity.*
—Harold Troper

9

Conclusion

This book aims to highlight the real-life stories, experiences, and quotes from many immigrants of South Asian origin in order, first, to draw some general conclusions on the South Asian immigrant experience; second, to offer valuable lessons to the second and subsequent generations of South Asian immigrants; and third, to sensitize the Canadian society at large to the issues and implications of immigration in order to generate serious debate that has forward-looking policy implications. Given the negative immigration related developments in similar countries elsewhere, notably in France, Italy, Germany, and Australia, it is imperative that Canada's diverse democratic society does not repeat the same mistakes. Societal forces should be familiar with the important issues at stake and their implications for a stable and prosperous Canada. In the following paragraphs, I offer no recommendations or any immediate policy prescription. Rather, what I have stated are the real concerns about the conditions of Canada's ethnocultural population, South Asian immigrants and their children in particular.

Canada's ethnically diverse population is referred to as a cultural mosaic. South Asians are the largest ethnic population representing one-quarter of the total visible minority population in Canada. Additionally, the ethnic diversity of the South Asian Canadians reflects the cultural, linguistic, and religious diversity among themselves. The size and variability of the South Asian population make them a significant segment of the Canadian multicultural mosaic, and who have adopted many mainstream Canadian values and cultural norms while keeping their heritage and cultural and core family values intact. Things change with time not only at the societal level but also at the family and individual level. For example, incidences of divorce are on the rise among South Asians due to increased access of women to education, labour market participation, and other social and economic resources. Another key change observed is intermarriage; either between second-generation South Asian adults and white Canadians, or between South Asians and people of other ethnic origins. These intermarriages mostly occur among the second generation.

First-generation South Asians have a history of accomplishments in Canada's nation building and continue to perform well and to be proud Canadians. Their contributions in Canadian politics, economy, culture, arts, and music are highly acclaimed, as noticeable from the contributions of notable South Asian Canadians in this book, many of whom are award winner including the Order of Canada. A good number of South Asians succeeded in Canadian politics, both at the federal and provincial levels reflected by seats held in Canada's House of Commons and Senate. Many second-generation South Asians were equally successful in Canada. Although they, individually or collectively, are not strong enough yet to influence mainstream media and public opinion that drive public policy change; nonetheless, they have a track record of hard work, disciplined life, entrepreneurship, and academic and professional excellence. One hopes that South Asian youths will influence the course of progress in the Canadian society. It may be noted that South Asians are playing an important role in their source countries' economies in the form of long-term investments, technology, and knowledge transfer in various fields such as science, IT, and medicine, philanthropic contributions to communities back home, influencing public opinion about their home countries through Canadian media and politics, and most importantly, foreign remittance to South Asian countries.[123]

Cries of "unity in diversity" alone will not eradicate discrimination and subtle racism in Canada, as noted by Angela Aujla. The national identity of many second-generation South Asians, though born and raised in Canada, continues to be the subject of scrutiny; they are categorized as visible minorities by the dominant white culture that continues to see them as not being "real" Canadians, notwithstanding the government's effort to promote multiculturalism.[124] Although Angela talked only about South Asian women, it may apply to all South Asians irrespective of gender. In a sense, they are singled out as the "other" in disguise. Therefore, many South Asians feel pressured to assimilate themselves with the dominant culture. This study points that assimilation process begins at two different times; for some it starts early life, for others it starts with intermarriage that may not necessarily be between a South Asian and a white Canadian, but could also be between a South Asian and an individual of another ethnic minority. The notion of acculturation has become an important issue in the context of intercultural relations in the culturally pluralistic Canadian society.

As noted in the book, the acculturation process has a mixed record among South Asians; while some are successful, many others are not. The same is true with regard to social and psychological integration into the mainstream society. South Asian immigrants have to keep in mind that the more integrated into the mainstream society they become, the higher their success in social inclusion and sense of belonging, which in turn brings economic, social, and political success, and minimizes chances of social exclusion and marginalization.

The view of minority youths including those from South Asia reveals that ethnocultural identities do not necessarily undermine Canadian identity. Rather they think that a positive interaction between national identity and particular group memberships build the foundation of a unique identification as Canadian. The positive attitude of these young people is also observed at the neighbourhood level. Research cited in the book suggests that the second-generation youths have a strong sense of cohesiveness within the locality shaped by their interaction with neighbours, and that they also contribute reciprocally to shape the neighbourhood.[125] Although the interpretations on these issues vary among the youths, they seem to have a clear idea as to which works for them best.

As discussed earlier, discrimination is a reality in the lives of ethnic minorities. But there are ways and means to overcome or avert it. For example, a higher level of education can give them competitive advantage. When that is achieved, they gain strength to participate in mainstream society and to retain their heritage culture at the same time. This ability allows the minority youths not only to transform odds into opportunities for desired success but also to reduce risks, build confidence, and develop positive relationships with mainstream society and strengthen bonds with their ethnic community.[126]

Friendship and social network building are two important qualities that help in the competition and may be considered as prima facie evidence of many successes in life. Understanding and adopting these two elements in the struggle for recognition of credibility and to establish the Canadian identity are of particular importance. Maureen Kelly, a colleague at McGill University, once remarked that it is very important that one makes a network of friends with mainstream Canadians in order to be visible and known to a wider circle of important and notable people to whom one can demonstrate one's credibility. She argued that this was helpful not only for one's career but also for a feeling of being included in the Canadian mainstream society. One would also feel psychologically strong and not feel isolated and helpless. This is a part of social integration into the mainstream society too. It may be noted that this was the first lesson I learned within the first two years of my arrival in Canada. I continue to promote this strategy till today.

Entrepreneurship is an important route to overcoming challenges especially in the job market. Entrepreneurship can be through a family business or through individual effort. Transfer of an established business from a parent to the second-generation youth is relatively easy and convenient compared to establishing a new business. Whatever may be the case, entrepreneurship is a potentially promising area that South Asian youths should consider seriously. Ratna Omidvar, president of Maytree, has strongly encouraged the second-generation ethnic minority youths to become entrepreneurs. "We were entrepreneurs by default, you are entrepreneurs by design and by purpose. Your trajectory will be different from ours."[127] Coincidentally, she mentioned Reza Satchu as one of the most successful entrepreneurs, whom I have described in the book. I would invite the interested readers to explore the activities of Reza Satchu and other successful South Asians entrepreneurs' profiles in chapter 6 of this book. They reinforce the picture of ethnic minorities in Canada being hardworking and innovative in nature.

However, success in entrepreneurship is not without difficulties. Ethnic minorities have to be contending with language challenges, insufficient knowledge about different businesses, cultures and markets, rules and regulations, and insufficient networks and capital. Recognizing this, the government of Canada has instituted programs to help new immigrants and entrepreneurs to overcome those barriers and become successful. New immigrants should take full advantage of these programs. The government's vision of these programs is that successful entrepreneurs will create jobs and build wealth for themselves, for their families, for their communities, and ultimately for Canada.

This book has attempted to capture the stories of second-generation children of South Asian origin in Canada, *what* changes they brought about in their lives especially in areas of education, career, and economic and social integration, and *how* they succeeded in achieving their desired goals. Below are some conclusions that might be drawn from the narrative in this book:

- Second-generation children of South Asian origin are the cultural bridge between their parents' way of living and Canadian lifestyle, a sort of mix of parents' heritage and culture and of Canadian mainstream culture. Yet many youths seem to be torn between the two paradigms.
- Second-generation children of South Asian origin amply demonstrate their capacity to deal with the dominant Canadian cultural narratives as well as to secure their ethnic identity and Canadianness side by side.
- However, ethnic identity can be a barrier to a full Canadian identity. The twin identity of *visible minority* and *Canadian* is a dilemma that exacerbates the divide. Notwithstanding the above, the majority believe that ethnocultural identity does not necessarily diminish Canadian identity.
- It is clear that in the acculturation process, majority of second-generation South Asian adults choose *integration strategy* rather than *assimilation strategy* or *marginalization strategy*.
- The second-generation South Asian youths, in general, are very proud to be Canadian and positive about Canadian multiculturalism. They appreciate multiculturalism because they feel that they are not judged by their peers, coworkers, and neighbours by their race, religion, and ethnicity. Overall, the diverse population get along fairly well and live in harmony in Canada.
- The first-generation South Asian immigrants faced much discrimination and racism, and that continues to this day, though to a lesser degree. Second-generation youths were much more capable of handling discrimination and racism appropriately.
- Intermarriage between South Asians in Canada and other Canadians was taboo in the past but now is very common and more acceptable to parents. However, second-generation South Asian youths prefer the traditional view of marriage, particularly within the same religion.
- Career-oriented South Asian young adults consider *education* as the key to their success in the job market and in building social networks.
- Studies show that the children of South Asians and Chinese immigrants outperform mainstream white Canadians in school. Among the reasons cited are (a) parents encourage their children

to perform better in order to minimize employment challenges that they had to face, and (b) they work hard both in school and at home instead of wasting time hanging around with their peers or playing video games.
- o While discrimination, both overt and subtle, exists against ethnic minorities in Canada, one must continually strive to get the better of it. Attributing failure to the presence of discrimination will not change things for the better. It is far more advisable to trace the paths of successful people and abjure the unsuccessful ones. The key to success is *hard work* and *perseverance*.

I recall the advice of a sociology professor, Uli Locher, from McGill University who strongly emphasized that hard work was the key to success. He argued that there were brilliant students but were not successful because they were not hardworking people. I tried to pass this invaluable piece of advice to the next generation of young Canadians.

As a South Asian immigrant living in Canada for thirty years, I was able to gain a lot of insights by talking, observing, and experiencing the differences and similarities within the Canadian multicultural society. My understanding is that the ethnic minority immigrants who want to be successful in life must recognize, accept, and adopt the differences and similarities, and capitalize on their ability to integrate the best elements from different cultures to create new hybrid ideas and ways of thinking. This is important for immigrants because hybridism does not necessarily favour one culture over another but builds on the best elements and preferences of each of the culture.

10

References

Aurther N., Chaves, A., Este, D., Frideres, J., and Hrycak, N. 2008. "Perceived Discrimination by Children of Immigrant Parents: Responses and Resiliency." Edited in *Canadian Diversity*: "The Experiences of Second Generation Canadians"; vol. 6:2, Spring 2008. *A Publication of the Association for Canadian Studies.*

Ana M. Ferrer; Garnett Picot; and W. Craig Riddell, 2012. "New Directions in Immigration Policy: Canada's Evolving Approach to Immigration selection." Working Paper No. 07 Canadian Labour Market and "Skills researcher Network.

Alfia Sorokina, Paul Chung, Clara Jimeno. 2012. "Social and Economic Inclusion for All? The Rise and of the Second Generation Canadians and Challenges for Racialized Groups." Social Planning Council of Ottawa.

Audrey Kobayashi. 2008. "A Research and Policy Agenda for second Generation Canadians." Edited in Canadian Diversity: "The Experiences of Second Generation Canadians"; Vol. 6:2, Spring 2008. *A Publication of the Association for Canadian Studies.*

Abella, R. S. 1984. "Report of the Royal Commission on Equality in Employment." Ottawa. *Ministry of Supply and Services.* Edited in "Cultural Diversity in Canada: The Social Construction of Racial Differences." *Strategic Issues Series*; Peter S Li, Professor of Sociology, University of Saskatchewan; Research and Statistics Division, 2000.

———. 1987. "Employment Equity—Implications for Industrial Relations." *Kingston Industrial Relations Centre, Queen's University.*

Andrew Parken and Matthew Mendelsohn. 2003. "A New Canada: An Identity Shaped by Diversity." *Centre for Research and Information on Canada*. The CRIC Papers. Greg Baeker. 2002. "Sharpening the Lens: Recent Research on Cultural Policy, Cultural Diversity and Social Cohesion." *Canadian Journal of Communication*; vol.27 (2002).

Anoul Dey, Michael Marin, Philippe-Oliver Giroux, Sadia Rafiquddin, Eric Tribe, and Paul M. Yeung. 2012. Prospering Together—Addressing Inequality and Poverty to Succeed in the Knowledge-Based Economy." *The Action Canada Rask Force on Inequality, Poverty, and the Knowledge—Based Economy. www. Prosperingtogether.ca*

Assanand S, Dias M, Richardson E., and Waxler-Morrison N. 1990. "The South Asians." In N Waxler-Morrison J, Anderson, and E. Richardson (Eds.), "Cross-cultural caring: A handbook for health professionals." *Vancouver, BC: UPC Press.* Edited; "Rights-Based Education for South Asian Sponsored Wives in International Arranged Marriages"; Noorfarah Merali. *Interchange, Vol. 39/2,* 2008.

Almeida, R. 1996. "Hindu, Christian, and Muslim families." In M. McGoldrick, J. Giordano, and J. K. Pearce (Eds.), *Ethnicity and family therapy.* New York: Guilford. Edited in "Ethnic Identity and Parenting Stress in South Asian Families: Implications for Culturally sensitive Counselling." Aneesa Shariff. 2009. *Canadian Journal of Counselling, Vol. 43.*

Aneesa Shariff. 2009. "Identity and Parenting Stress in South Asian Families: implications for Culturally sensitive Counselling." *Canadian Journal of Counselling, Vol. 43.*

Ali M and K. Kilbride. 2004. "Forging New Ties: Improving Parenting and Family Support services for New Canadians with Young Children." *Ottawa: Human Resources and Skills Development Canada.* Edited in "Parents and Teens in Immigrant Families: Cultural influences and Material Pressures" by Vappu Tyyska. *Canadian Diversity; Vol 6:2, 2008. A Publication of the Association for Canadian Studies.*

Anisef P, K. M. Kilbride, J. Ochocka, and R. Janzen. 2001. "Parenting issues of Newcomer families on Ontario." *Kitchner: Centre for Research and Education in Human services and Centre of Excellence for Research on Immigration and Settlement.* Edited in "Parents and Teens in Immigrant Families: Cultural influences and Material Pressures" by Vappu Tyyska. *Canadian Diversity; Vol. 6:2, 2008. A Publication of the Association for Canadian Studies.*

Aujla Angela. 2000. "Others in their own land: Second-Generation South Asian Canadian women, racism, and the persistence of colonial discourse." Canadian Woman Studies 20.

Ayse K. Uskul; Richard N. Lalonde and Sheila Konaur. 2010. "The Role of Culture in International Value Discrepancies Regarding Intergroup Dating." *Journal of Cross-Cultural Psychology*, 2011. Available at: http://jcc.sagepub.com/content/42/7/1165.

Arora, P., and Viswanath, K. 2000. Ethnic media in the United States: an essay on their role in integration, assimilation and social control. *Mass Communication and Society*, 3(1).

Abouguendia, M., and Noels, K. A. (2001). General and acculturation-related daily hassles and psychological adjustment First-generation and second-generation South Asian immigrants to Canada. *International Journal of Psychology*, 36(3), 163–173.

Alba, R., and M.B. Chamlin. 1983. *"A Preliminary Examination of Ethnic Identification among Whites."* American Sociological Review 48. Edited in "The Rise of the Unmeltable Canadians? Ethnic and National Belonging in Canada's Second Generation." Vol. 6:2, Spring 2008. *A Publication of the Association for Canadian Studies.*

Breton, R., QW.W.Isajiw, W.E. Kalbach and J.G. Reitz. 1990. *"Ethnic Identity and Equality: Varieties of Experience in a Canadian City.* Toronto: University of Toronto Press. Edited in "The Rise of the Unmeltable Canadians? Ethnic and National Belonging in Canada's Second Generation." Vol. 6:2, spring 2008. *A Publication of the Association for Canadian Studies.*

Bagley Christopher. 1987. "The Adaptation of Asian Children of Immigrant Parents: British Models and their application to Canadian Policy" in Milton Israel. (Eds.). The South Asian Diaspora in Canada: Six Essays. *Toronto: Multicultural History of Society of Ontario*, 1987.

Brettel C. B, Hollifield J. F. 2000. "Migration Theory: Talking Across Disciplines." Edited in "Understanding Migration: International Migration Theories" by Aleksandra Tomanek, 2011. Available at: http://understandingmigration.blogspot.ca/2011/03/international-migration-theories.html

Baptiste, D. A.1993." Immigrant families, adolescents, and acculturation: Insights for Therapists." *Marriage and Family Review;* 19. Edited in "Ethnic Identity and Parenting Stress in South Asian Families: Implications for Culturally sensitive Counselling." Aneesa Shariff. 2009. *Canadian Journal of Counselling, Vol. 43.*

Berry, J. W. 2001. "A psychology of immigration." *Journal of Social Issues;* 57. Edited in "Ethnic Identity and Parenting Stress in South Asian Families: Implications for Culturally sensitive Counselling." Aneesa Shariff. 2009. *Canadian Journal of Counselling, Vol. 43.*

Baht, V., Mihelj, S., and Pankov, M. 2009. "Television, news, narrative conventions, and national Imagination." *Discourse and Communication*, 3(1).

Buchignani Norman. 2012. "The Canadian Encyclopedia @ 2012 Historica Foundation of Canada." Available at: http://www.thecanadianencyclopedia.com/

Buchignani N, Indra D, and Srivastiva R. 1985. "Continuous Journey: A Social History of South Asians in Canada." *Toronto: McClelland and Stewart*. Edited in "Calculated Kindness"; Global Restructuring, Immigration and Settlement in Canada; *Rose Baaba Folson;* edited.

Becklumb Penny and Elgersma Sandra. 2008. "Recognition of the Foreign Credentials of Immigrants." Parliamentary Information and Research Service; *Library of Parliament; PRB 04-29E*.

Cohen, A. 2007. *"The Unfinished Canadian: The People We Are."* Toronto McMillan. Edited in, "The Rise of the Unmeltable Canadians? Ethnic and National Belonging in Canada's Second Generation." Vol. 6:2, Spring 2008. *A Publication of the Association for Canadian Studies*.

Charles M Beach, Alan G Green Worswick. 2011. "Towards Improving Canada's Skilled Immigration Policy: An Evaluation Approach"; *Policy Study 45*; C.D. Howe Institute, October 2011.

Conference Board of Canada. 2009. "Immigrant-Friendly Business: Effective Practices for Attracting, Integrating and Retaining Immigrants in Canadian Workplaces." Ottawa. Edited in "Towards Improving Canada's Skilled Immigration Policy: An Evaluation Approach"; Charles M Beach, Alan G Green Worswick. *Policy Study 45; C.D. Howe Institute*, October 2011.

———. 2010. "Immigrants as Innovators: Boosting Canada's Global Competitiveness." Ottawa. Edited in "Towards Improving Canada's Skilled Immigration Policy: An Evaluation Approach"; Charles Beach, Alan G Green Worswick. *Policy Study 45; C.D. Howe Institute*, October 2011.

Cheung, L. 2005. "Racial Studies and Employment Outcomes." Ottawa: *Canadian Labour Congress*.

Chanda Rupa. 2008. "The Skilled South Asian Diaspora and its Role in Source Economies." *Indian Institute of Management, Bangalore; Economics, Our Scholars*. Available at: http://southasiandispora.org/the-skilled-south-asian-dispora-and-its-role-in-source-economics

Conseil des Relations Interculturelles. 2009. *A Fair Representation and Treatment of Ethno-Cultural Diversity in Media and Advertising: Quebec Chronicle World. Teen-age Black Journalists Target UK Racism*. 2011. Chronicleworld.org

Changing Black Britain. Retrieved March 4, 2011, from http://www.chronicleworld.org/archive/voices.htm.

Cheung Leslie. 2006. "Racial Status and Employment Outcomes." Research Paper # 34. *Canadian Labour Congress.*

Carolan, M. T., Bagherinia, G., Juhari, R., Himelright, J., and Mouton-Sanders, M. 2000. "Contemporary Muslim families: Research and practice." *Contemporary Family Therapy, 22*(1). Edited in "Ethnic Identity and Parenting Stress in South Asian Families: Implications for Culturally Sensitive Counselling." Aneesa Shariff. 2009. *Canadian Journal of Counselling, Vol. 43.*

Creese G, I. Dyck, and A. McLearn. 1999. "Reconstituting the Family: Negotiating Immigration and Settlement." *Vancouver: RIM Working Paper*; No. 99-10. Edited in "Parents and Teens in Immigrant Families: Cultural influences and Material Pressures" by Vappu Tyyska. *Canadian Diversity; Vol. 6:2, 2008. A Publication of the Association for Canadian Studies.*

Dion, K. K., and Dion, K. L. 2001. "Gender and cultural adaptation in immigrant families." *Journal of Social Issues, 57*(3). Edited in "Ethnic Identity and Parenting Stress in South Asian Families: Implications for Culturally Sensitive Counselling." Aneesa Shariff. 2009. *Canadian Journal of Counselling, Vol. 43.*

Dosanjh, J. S., and Ghuman, P. A. S. 1998. 'Child-rearing practices of two generations of Punjabis: Development of personality and independence." *Children and Society; 12.* Edited in "Ethnic Identity and Parenting Stress in South Asian Families: Implications for Culturally sensitive Counselling." Aneesa Shariff. 2009. *Canadian Journal of Counselling, Vol. 4 Diversity Watch.* 2004. Diversity Watch—Ryerson University School of Journalism. Retrieved March 4, 2011, from http://www.diversitywatch.ryerson.ca/home_miller_2004report.htm#Why Douglas S. Massey, Joaquin Arango, Graeme Hugo, Ali Kauaouci, Adela Pellegrino, and J. Edward Taylor. 1993. "Theories of International Migration: A Review and Appraisal." *Population and Development Review, Vo. 19, No. 3, 1993. Published by Population Council.* Available at: http://cis.uchicago.edu/outreach/summerinstitute/2011/documents/sti2011-parks-theories_of_international_migration.pdf

Dua E, 2000b. *"The Hindu Women's Question: Canadian Nation Building and the Social Construction of Gender for South Asian Canadian Women."* Edited in *"Calculated Kindness"* by Rose Baaba Folson, 2004.

Drummond D and F Fong. 2010. "An Economics Perspective on Canadian Immigration." *Policy Options 31* (July-August). Edited in "Towards Improving Canada's Skilled Immigration Policy: An Evaluation

Approach"; Charles M Beach, Alan G Green Worswick. *Policy Study 45; C.D. Howe Institute*, October, 2011 *Development Bank*, June. Edited; "Combating the Social Exclusion of At-Risk Groups"; Research Paper; November 2005. Meyer Burstein. *PRI Project*; New Approaches for Addressing Poverty and Exclusion.

Dua E. 2000. "The Hindu Woman's Question: Canadian Nation Building and the Social Construction of Gender for South Asian-Canadian Women." In Agnes Calliste and George J. Sefa Dei (eds.), *Antiracist feminism, Critical Race and Gender Studies*. Halifax: Fernwood Publishing. Edited in "Calculated Kindness"; Global Restructuring, Immigration and Settlement in Canada; *Rose Baaba Folson*.

Electoral Firsts in Canada—Wikipedia, the free Encyclopedia. Available at: http://en.wikipedia.org/wiki/Electoral_firsts_in_Canada.

Evans, D. 2005. *Journalism—Homing Instinct*. Diana Evans Official Website. Retrieved March 4, 2011, from http://www.dianaommoevans.com/dianaevans_journalism_hominginstinct.asp.

Farver, J. M., Narang, S. K., and Bhadha, B. R. 2002. "East meets west: Ethnic identity, acculturation, and conflict in Asian Indian families." *Journal of Family Psychology*, 16(3). Edited in "Ethnic Identity and Parenting Stress in South Asian Families: Implications for Culturally Sensitive Counselling." Aneesa Shariff. 2009. *Canadian Journal of Counselling, Vol. 43*.

Gigna, Clément. 2013. "For Canada, immigration is a key to prosperity." http://www.theglobeandmail.com/report-on-business/economy/economy-lab/for-canada-immigration-is-a-key-to-prosperity/article.

Gregg A. 2007. *"Identity Crisis: Multiculturalism, A Twentieth Century Dream Becomes a Twenty-First Century Conundrum."* Walrus. Edited in "The Rise of the Unmeltable Canadians? Ethnic and National Belonging in Canada's Second Generation." Vol. 6:2, Spring 2008. *A Publication of the Association for Canadian Studies*.

Ghose Ratna. 1983. "Sarees and the Maple Leaf: Indian Women in Canada." In Kurian and Srivastava. Edited in "Calculated Kindness"; Global Restructuring, Immigration and Settlement in Canada; *Rose Baaba Folson*.

Guoxuan, C., Halle, D., and Zhou, M. 2002. Médias en langue chinoise aux Etats-Unis : immigration et assimilation dans la vie américaine. *Qualitative Sociology*, 25(3).

Green Alan G and David A Green. 1995. "Canadian Immigration policy: The Effectiveness of the Point System and Other Instruments"; *Canadian Journal of Economics*, vol. 28(4b). Edited in "Towards Improving Canada's Skilled Immigration Policy: An Evaluation

Approach"; Charles M Beach; Alan G Green and Christopher Worswick. *Policy Study 45; C.D. Howe Institute*, Oct. 2011.

———. 1999. "The Economic Goal of Canada's Immigration

Guillemette Yvan and William B. P. Robson. 2006. "No Elixir for Youth: Immigration Cannot Keep Canada Young." Backgrounder 96. Toronto: C.D. Howe Institute. Edited in "Towards Improving Canada's Skilled Immigration Policy: An Evaluation Approach"; Charles M Beach, Alan G Green Worswick. *Policy Study 45; C.D. Howe Institute, October* 2011.

Gupta, T. D. 1996. "Racism, and Paid Work." Toronto: Garamond Press. Edited in "Racialized Youth, Identity and the Labour Market"; Canadian Diversity: "The Experiences of Second Generation Canadians"; Vol. 6:2, Spring 2008. *A Publication of the Association for Canadian Studies.*

Giguère B, J. Gonsalvas, and R. N. Lalonde. 2007. "Where are you really from? Identity Denial among South Asian and East Asian Countries." Paper presented at the annual convention of the Canadian Psychological Association, Ottawa (June). Edited in "When Might the Two Cultural Worlds of Second Generation Biculturals Collide"? By Richard N. Lalonde and Benjamin Giguère *Canadian Diversity; Vol. 6:2, 2008. A Publication of the Association for Canadian Studies.*

Goodwin R, and D. Cramer. 2000. "Marriage and Social Support in a British-Asian Community." Journal of Community and Applied Social Psychology 10. Edited in "When Might the Two Cultural Worlds of Second Generation Biculturals Collide"? By Richard N. Lalonde and Benjamin Giguère *Canadian Diversity; Vol. 6:2, 2008. A Publication of the Association for Canadian Studies.*

Harold Troper, 2012. "The Canadian Encyclopedia"; 2012 *Historica Foundation of Canada*

Huntington, S. 2004. *"Who Are We? The Challenges to America's National Identity."* Simon and Schuster. Edited in "The Rise of the Unmeltable Canadians? Ethnic and National Belonging in Canada's Second Generation." Vol. 6:2, Spring 2008. *A Publication of the Association for Canadian Studies.*

Hynie M, R. N. Lalonde, and N. Lee. 2006. "Parent-Child Value Transmission among Chinese Immigrants to North America: The Case of Traditional Mate Preferences." Cultural Diversity and Ethnic Minority Psychology 12. Edited in "When Might the Two Cultural Worlds of Second Generation Biculturals Collide"? By Richard N. Lalonde and Benjamin Giguère *Canadian Diversity; Vol. 6:2, 2008. A Publication of the Association for Canadian Studies.*

Health and Welfare Canada. 1989. "Charting Canada's Future: A Report of the Demographic Review." Ottawa: *Health and Welfare Canada*. Edited in "Towards Improving Canada's Skilled Immigration Policy: An Evaluation Approach"; Charles M Beach, Alan G Green Worswick. *Policy Study 45; C. D. Howe Institute*, October 2011.

Held D., A. McGrew, and D. Goldblatt, 1999. "Global Transformations: Politics, economics and Culture." *Oxford: Polity Press*. Edited in "Calculated Kindness"; by Rose Baaba Folson, 2004.

Hoffmann-Nowotny H.J. 1989. "Weltmigration: Eine Soziologische Analyse." In Kälin, W and Moser R. (Editors). *Migration aus der Dritten Welt: Ursachen und Wirkungen. Haupt*, Bern, Stuttgart. Edited in "In Brief Overview of Theories of International Migration." Available at: http://www.glopp.ch/C1/en/multimedia/C1_pdf1.pdf

Ibrahim, F., Ohnishi, H., and Sandhu, D. S. 1997. "Asian American identity development: A culture specific model for South Asian Americans." *Journal of Multicultural Counseling and Development, 25(1)*. Edited in "Ethnic Identity and Parenting Stress in South Asian Families: Implications for Culturally sensitive Counselling." Aneesa Shariff. 2009. *Canadian Journal of Counselling, Vol. 43*.

Jacob Jedwab. 2008. "The Rise of the Unmeltable Canadians? Ethnic and National Belonging in Canada's Second Generation." *Canadian Diversity; Vol.6:2, 2008. A Publication of the Association of Canadian Studies*.

Jeffrey G Reitz. 2005. "Tapping Immigrant's Skills: New Directions for Canadian Policy in the Knowledge Economy." *IRPP Choices;* vol.11; no.1; February, 2005.

Jerome H. Black and Bruce M. Hicks. 2006. "Visible minority Candidates in the 2004 Federal Election"; *Canadian Parliamentary Review* 29:2 (2006); Jerome H. Black; "Ethnoracial Minorities in the Canadian House of Commons: An Update on the 37th Parliament"; *Canadian Parliamentary Review 25* (2002).

Jain R. 1983. "Indian Communities Abroad: Themes and Literature." New Delhi: *Manhor Publishers*. Edited in "Calculated Kindness"; Global Restructuring, Immigration and Settlement in Canada; *Rose Baaba Folson*; edited.

Jacqueline A. Gibbons. 1990. "Indo-Canadian Mixed Marriage: Context and Dilemmas." Polyphony, Vol. 12. Available at http://www.tgmag.ca/magic/mt33.html

Jeffrey Reitz, 2011. "Racial Minority Immigrant Offspring Successes in the United States, Canada, and Australia." *Population Change and*

Life Course Strategic Knowledge Cluster. Population Studies Centre, The University of Western Ontario, London.

Kappu Desai. 1990. "Ethnic Communities and the Challenge of Aging." *Polyphony, Vol. 12; 1990.* Available at: http://www.tgmag.ca/magic/mt32.html.

Karen Bird. 2007. "Patterns of Substantive Representation among Visible Minority MPs: Evidence from Canada's House of Commons." Paper prepared for the *ECPR Joint Sessions of Workshops,* Helsinki, May, 7–12, 2007.

Kilbride, K.M; Anisef, P; Baichman-Anisef, E; and Khattar, R. 2004. "Between Two Worlds: the Experiences and Concerns of Immigrant Youth." Edited in "Immigrant Youth and Employment: Lessons Learned from the Analysis of LSIC and 82 Lives Stories." *Statistics Canada, Research Data Centre at McMaster University. RDC Research Paper No. 29.*

Kunz, J. L. 2003. "Being Young and Visible: Labour Market Access among Immigrant and Visible Minority Youth." Ottawa: *Human Resources Development Canada.* Edited in "Immigrant Youth and Employment: Lessons Learned from the Analysis of LSIC and 82 Lives Stories." *Statistics Canada, Research Data Centre at McMaster University. RDC Research Paper No. 29.*

Kazimi Ali. 2011. "Undesirables: White Canada and the *Komagata Maru.*" *Douglas and McIntyre;* Vancouver, BC, Canada. Available at: www.douglas-mcintyre.com

Kwak K, and Berry J. W. 2001. "Generational Differences in Acculturation among Asian Families in Canada: A Comparison of Vietnamese, Korean, and East-Indian Groups." *International Journal of Psychology,* 36(3), 2001.

Kurian, G., and Ghosh, R. 1983. "Child rearing in transition in Indian immigrant families in Canada." In G. Kurian and R. P. Srivastava (Eds.), Overseas Indians: A study in adaptation. New Delhi, India: Vikas. Edited in "Ethnic Identity and Parenting Stress in South Asian Families: Implications for Culturally sensitive Counselling." Aneesa Shariff. 2009. *Canadian Journal of Counselling, Vol. 43.*

List of House Members of the 41st Parliament of Canada—Wikipedia, the free Encyclopedia. Available at: http://en.wikipedia.org/wiki/List_of_House_members_of_the_41st_Parliament_of_Canada

List of senators in the 41st Parliament of Canada—Wikipedia, the free Encyclopedia. Available at: http://en.wikipedia.org/wiki/List_of_senators_in_the_41st_Parliament_of_Canada

Lori Wilkinson. 2008. "Visualizing Canada, Identity and Belonging among Second Generation Youth in Winnipeg." Edited in Canadian Diversity: "The Experiences of Second Generation Canadians"; Vol. 6:2, Spring 2008. *A Publication of the Association for Canadian Studies.*

Lee Hansen, Marcus, 1961. "The Atlantic Immigration, 1607–1860." *New York: Harper.* Edited in "Calculated Kindness by Rose Baaba Folson, 2004.

Li P. S. 1992a. *"The Economics of Brain Drain: Recruitment of Skilled Labour to Canada, 1954–86."* In Vic Satzewich (ed.), Deconstructing a nation: Immigration, multiculturalism and racism in 90's Canada. Helifax, Nova Scotia: Fernwood Publishing; Edited in "Cultural Diversity in Canada: The Social Construction of Racial Differences." *Strategic Issues Series*; Peter S Li, Professor of Sociology, University of Saskatchewan; Research and Statistics Division, 2000.

Lee E.S. 1966. "A Theory of Migration." *Demography, Vol. 3.* Edited in "In Brief Overview of Theories of International Migration." Available at: http://www.glopp.ch/C1/en/multimedia/C1_pdf1.pdf

Michael Dewing. 2009. "Canadian Multiculturalism." Parliamentary Information and Research Service; *Social Affairs Division; Library of Parliament*; PRB 09-20E Winter E. 2001. "National Unity versus Multiculturalism: Rethinking the Logic of Inclusion in Germany and Canada." *International Journal of Canadian Studies 24* (Fall / Autumn).

Meyer Burstein. 2005. "Combating the Social Exclusion of At-Risk Groups"; Research Paper; *PRI Project*; New Approaches for Addressing Poverty and Exclusion.

Mahtani, M. 2001.Representing minorities: Canadian media and minority identities. *Canadian Ethnic Studies/Etudes Ethniques au Canada*, 33(3).

McAdoo Harriet and Young-Shi Ou. 1993. "Socialization of Chinese American Children." In Harriet Piper McAdoo (Ed.). Family Ethnicity: Strength in Diversity. *London: Sage Publications, 1993.*

Massey Dauglas S. 1990. "Social Structure, Household strategies, and the Cumulative Causation of Migration." *Population Index, 56 (1).*

Miu Chung Yan, Sean Lauer, and Surita Jhangiani, 2008. "Preliminary Understanding of Challenges in Entering the Job Market: Experience of new generation youth from visible minority immigrant families." *Canadian Diversity*; vol 6:2. Spring 2008; "The Experience of Second Generation Canadians." A Publication of the Association for Canadian Studies. Metropolis.

Nafiza Islam. 2012. "Ekushey February: International Mother Language Day." *South Asian Generation Next.* Available at: http://

www.sagennext.com/2012/02/23/ekushey-february-international-mother-language-day

Oreopoulos P. 2009. "Why do skilled immigrants struggle in the labour market? A field experiment with six thousand resumes from Metropolis British Columbia." Edited in "Immigrant Youth and Employment: Lessons Learned from the Analysis of LSIC and 82 Lives Stories." *Statistics Canada, Research Data Centre at McMaster University. RDC Research Paper No. 29.*

Peter R. Grant and Shevaun Nadin. 2005. "The Difficulties Faced by Immigrants Facing Ongoing Credentialing Problems: A Social Psychological Analysis." Paper Presented at the *Tenth International Metropolis Conference*, Toronto, October. 2005. Policy: Past and Present." *Canadian Public Policy 26 (4)*. Edited in "Towards Improving Canada's Skilled Immigration Policy: An Evaluation Approach"; Charles M Beach, Alan G Green and Christopher Worswick. *Policy Study 45; C.D. Howe Institute*, Oct. 2011.

———. 2003. "What is the Role of Immigration in Canada's Future? In Canadian Immigration Policy for the 21st Century"; Edited in "Towards Improving Canada's Skilled Immigration Policy: An Evaluation Approach"; Charles M Beach, Alan G Green Worswick. *Policy Study 45; C.D. Howe Institute*, Oct. 2011.

Patrick Grady. 2011. "How are the Children of Visible Minority Immigrants Doing in the Canadian Labour Market"? *Global Economics Working Paper* 2011-1.

Picot Garnett. 2008. "Immigrant Economic and Social Outcomes in Canada: Research and Data Development at Statistics Canada." *Catalogue No. 11F0019M No. 319. Statistics Canada* Edited; "How are the Children of Visible Minority Immigrants Doing in the Canadian Labour Market"? Patrick Grady (2011). *Global Economics* Working Paper 2011-1.

Picot Garnett and Feng Hou. 2008. "Immigrant Characteristics, the IT Bust, and Their Effect on Entry Earnings of Immigrants." *Catalogue No. 11F0019MWE2008315. Statistics Canada.* Edited in "How are the Children of Visible Minority Immigrants Doing in the Canadian Labour Market"? Patrick Grady (2011). *Global Economics* Working Paper 2011-1.

Picot Garnett and Arthur Sweetman. 2005. "The Deteriorating Economic Welfare of Immigrants and Possible Causes: Update 2005." *Catalogue No, 11F0019MIE2005262. Statistics Canada.* Edited in "How are the Children of Visible Minority Immigrants Doing in the Canadian

Labour Market"? Patrick Grady (2011). *Global Economics* Working Paper 2011-1.

Pendukar K. 2005. "Visible Minorities and Aboriginals in Vancouver's Labour Market." *Working Paper Series; Research on Immigration and Integration in the Metropolis.* Edited in "Immigrant Youth and Employment: Lessons Learned from the Analysis of LSIC and 82 Lives Stories." *Statistics Canada, Research Data Centre at McMaster University. RDC Research Paper No. 29.*

Pendukar K and Pendukar R. 1998. "The Colour of Money: Earnings Differentials among Ethnic Groups in Canada." *The Canadian Journal of Economics; 31(3)*. Edited in "Immigrant Youth and Employment: Lessons Learned from the Analysis of LSIC and 82 Lives Stories." *Statistics Canada, Research Data Centre at McMaster University. RDC Research Paper No. 29.*

Perreira, K.M; Harris. K.M; and Lee, D. 2007. "Immigrant Youth in the Labour Market." *Work and Occupations*, 34(1). Edited in "Immigrant Youth and Employment: Lessons Learned from the Analysis of LSIC and 82 Lives Stories." *Statistics Canada, Research Data Centre at McMaster University. RDC Research Paper No. 29.*

Palameta, B. 2007. "Economic Integration of Immigrants' Children." *Perspectives;* October, 2007.

Picot, G. and Hou, F. 2003. "The rise in low-income rates among immigrants in Canada." Statistics Canada. Catalogue no. 11F0019MIE.

Phinney, J. S. 2003. "Ethnic identity and acculturation." In K. M. Chun, P. B. Organista, and G. Marin (Eds.), Acculturation: Advances in theory, measurement, and applied research. Washington, DC: *American Psychological Association.* Edited in "Ethnic Identity and Parenting Stress in South Asian Families: Implications for Culturally Sensitive Counselling." Aneesa Shariff. 2009. *Canadian Journal of Counselling, Vol. 43.*

Piore Michael J. 1979. "Birds of Passage: Migrant Labour in Industrial Societies." *Cambridge: Cambridge University Press.*

Ratna Omidvar and Ted Richmond. 2003. "Immigrant Settlement and Social inclusion in Canada. Perspectives on Social Inclusion"; *Working Paper Series.* January 2003.

Richard N. Lalonde and Benjamin Giguère. 2007. "Culture, Identity and Family Allocentrism in the Interpersonal Relationships of Second Generation Immigrants." Paper presented at the *annual convention of the Canadian Psychological Association.* Ottawa (June). Edited in "When Might the Two Cultural Worlds of Second Generation Biculturals Collide"? By Richard N. Lalonde and Benjamin Giguère *Canadian*

Diversity; Vol. 6:2, 2008. A Publication of the Association for Canadian Studies.

Reitz Jeffery, 2004. "Canada: Immigration and Nation-Building in the Transition to a Knowledge Economy. In Controlling Immigration: A Global Perspective"; Edited in Wayne A Cornelius, Takeyuki Tsuda, Philip L. Martin and James F Hollifield. Stanford, CA: *Standard University Press.*

Rajiva Mythila. 2004. "Racing Through Adolescence. Becoming and Belonging in the Narratives of Second Generation South Asian Girls." *Doctoral Dissertation.*

———. 2006. "Identity and Politics: Second Generation ethnic Minority Women in Canada." *Master's Thesis.*

Richard N. Lalonde and Benjamin Giguère. 2008. "When Might the Two Cultural Worlds of Second Generation Biculturals Collide"? *Canadian Diversity; Vol. 6:2, 2008. A Publication of the Association for Canadian Studies.*

Ravenstein E.G. 1985. "The laws of Migration." *Journal of the Royal Statistical Society, Vol. 48 (June).* "In Brief Overview of Theories of International Migration." Available at: http://www.glopp.ch/C1/en/multimedia/C1_pdf1.pdf

———. 1989. "The laws of Migration." *Journal of the Royal Statistical Society, Vol. 52 (June).* "In Brief Overview of Theories of International Migration." Available at: http://www.glopp.ch/C1/en/multimedia/C1_pdf1.pdf

Rubina Ramji. 2008. *"Creating a Genuine Islam: Second Generation Muslims Growing Up in Canada."* Edited in Canadian Diversity: "The Experiences of Second Generation Canadians"; Vol. 6:2, Spring 2008. *A Publication of the Association for Canadian Studies.*

Skuterud, M. 2010. "The visible minority earnings gap across generations of Canadians." Canadian Journal of Economics. Cited in "Colour by Numbers: Minority earnings in Canada 1996–2006"; by Krishna Pendakur and Ravi Pendakur. Forthcoming, Journal of International Migration and Integration.

Stan Kustec, 2012. "The role of migrant labour supply in the Canadian labour market." *Citizenship and Immigration Canada, Research and Evaluation.*

Statistics Canada, 2012. "The Canadian Immigrant Labour Market: 2008–2011." The Immigrant Labour Force Analysis Series. Catalogue no. 71-600-X.

Statistics Canada, December 2012. "Study: Canada's immigrant labour market, 2008–2011." *The Daily*—December 14, 2012. Component of Statistics Canada catalogue no.11-001.

Stalker P, 2001. "No-Nonsense Guide to International Migration." *London: Verso.* "Calculated Kindness"; Rose Baaba Folson, 2004.

Sampat Mehta R. "International Barriers"; *Canada Research Bureau; Harpell's Press, 1973*

.Statistics Canada, 2008. "Canada's Ethnocultural Mosaic, *2006 Census Catalogue No. 97-562-X*

———. 2007. "Immigration in Canada: A Portrait of the Foreign Born Population, 2006 Census"; *Cat. # 97-557-XIE.*

———. 2007. "The Canadian Labour Market at a Glance"; *Labour Statistics Division; Cat. # 71-222-X.*

Siemiatycki Myer. 2005. "Canadian Issues: Immigration and the Intersections of Diversity." Edited in "Towards Improving Canada's Skilled Immigration Policy: An Evaluation Approach"; Charles M Beach, Alan G Green Worswick. *Policy Study 45; C.D. Howe Institute,* Oct. 2011.

Simon Julian L. 1989. "The Economic Consequences of Immigration." Oxford: Blackwell Publishers. Edited in "Towards Improving Canada's Skilled Immigration Policy: An Evaluation Approach"; Charles M Beach, Alan G Green Worswick. *Policy Study 45; C.D. Howe Institute,* October 2011.

Studin Irvin. 2010. "Canada—Population 100 Million." Global Brief, June. Available at http://globalbreif.ca/blog/category//features. Edited in "Towards Improving Canada's Skilled Immigration Policy: An Evaluation Approach"; Charles M Beach, Alan G Green Worswick. *Policy Study 45; C.D. Howe Institute,* October 2011.

Sweetman Arthur and Warman Casey. 2010. "A New Source of Immigration: The Canadian Experience Class." *Options Politiques,* July-August, 2010.

Sen Amartya. 2000. "Social Exclusion: Concept, Application and security, Social Development." Paper No. 1. *Office of Environment and Social Development, Asia*

Silberman, R; Alba, R; and Fournier, I. 2007. "Segmented assimilation in France: Discrimination in the Labour Market against the Second Generation." *Ethnic and Racial Studies,* 30(1). Edited in "Immigrant Youth and Employment: Lessons Learned from the Analysis of LSIC and 82 Lives Stories." *Statistics Canada, Research Data Centre at McMaster University. RDC Research Paper No. 29.*

Siddiqui Haroon. 2004. "South Asians." *Lecture delivered for The Annual Asian Heritage Month*—Lecture presented in association with Innis College, University of Toronto, the Centre for South Asian Studies and the Hong Kong University Alumni Association of Ontario; May 18, 2004.

South Asian Outlook. Available at: http://www.southasianoutlook.com/issues/2008/november/ten_south_asians_in_canada's. Saman Malik. 2011. "Reconfiguring the joint family." Available at: http://www.suhag.com/living/reconfiguring-the-joint-family/

Segal, U. A. 1991. "Cultural variables in Asian Indian families." *Families in Society, 11*, 233–241. Edited in "Ethnic Identity and Parenting Stress in South Asian Families: Implications for Culturally sensitive Counselling." Aneesa Shariff. 2009. *Canadian Journal of Counselling, Vol. 43*.

Sharma, A. R. 2000. "Psychotherapy with Hindus." In R. S. Richards and A. E. Bergin (Eds.), Handbook of psychotherapy and religious diversity Washington, DC: *American Psychological Association*. Edited in "Ethnic Identity and Parenting Stress in South Asian Families: Implications for Culturally sensitive Counselling." Aneesa Shariff. 2009. *Canadian Journal of Counselling, Vol. 43*.

Shams, M. 2001. "Social support, loneliness and friendship preference among British Asian and non-Asian adolescents." *Social Behavior and Personality, 29(4)*. Edited in "Ethnic Identity and Parenting Stress in South Asian Families: Implications for Culturally Sensitive Counselling." Aneesa Shariff. 2009. *Canadian Journal of Counselling, Vol. 43*.

Swearer, S. M. 2001. "Review of the stress index for parents of adolescents." In B. S. Plake and J. C. Impala (Eds.), The mental measurements yearbook (14th ed.,). *Lincoln, NE: Buros Institute of Mental Measurements*. Edited in "Ethnic Identity and Parenting Stress in South Asian Families: Implications for Culturally Sensitive Counselling." Aneesa Shariff. 2009. *Canadian Journal of Counselling, Vol. 43*.

Shields, J, K. Rahi, et al. 2006. "Visible Minority Employment Exclusion: The Experience of Young Adults in Toronto." *Policy Matters*. Toronto: CERIS, Metropolis. Edited in "Racialized Youth, Identity and the Labour Market"; Canadian Diversity: "The Experiences of Second Generation Canadians"; Vol. 6:2, Spring 2008. *A Publication of the Association for Canadian Studies*.

Stark O, Bloom D. E. 1985. "The New Economics of Labour Migration." *American Economics Review, Vol. 75*. Edited in "Understanding

Migration: International Migration Theories" by Aleksandra Tomanek, 2011. Available at: http://understandingmigration.blogspot.ca/2011/03/international-migration-theories.html

Tran, K. 2004. "Visible Minorities in the Labour Force: 20 years of change." *Canadian Social Trends*; Summer 2004. Edited in "Immigrant Youth and Employment: Lessons Learned from the Analysis of LSIC and 82 Lives Stories." *Statistics Canada, Research Data Centre at McMaster University. RDC Research*

Tran Kelly, Kaddatz Jennifer, and Allard Paul. 2005. "South Asians in Canada: Unity Through Diversity." *Canadian Social Trends*; Autumn 2005; Statistics Canada; Catalogue No. 11-008.

Tyyska Vappu, 2008. "Parents and Teens in Immigrant Families: Cultural Influences and Material Pressures." Edited in "Canadian Diversity: The Experiences of Second Generation Canadians"; Vol. 6:2 Spring 2008. *A Publication of the Association for Canadian Studies.*

Talbani, A., and Hasanali, P. 2000. "Adolescent females between tradition and modernity: Gender role socialization in South Asian immigrant culture." *Journal of Adolescence, 23*, Edited in "Ethnic Identity and Parenting Stress in South Asian Families: Implications for Culturally sensitive Counselling." Aneesa Shariff. 2009. *Canadian Journal of Counselling, Vol. 43.*

Tyyska Vappu. 2006. "Teen Perspectives in Family Relations in the Toronto Tamil Community." *Toronto: CERIS, Working paper*; No.45. Edited in "Parents and Tens in Immigrant Families: Cultural influences and Material Pressures" by Vappu Tyyska. *Canadian Diversity; Vol. 6:2, 2008. A Publication of the Association for Canadian Studies.*

———. 2005. "Immigrant Adjustment and Parenting of Teens: A Study of Newcomer Groups in Toronto, Canada." In "Youth—Similarities, Differences, Inequalities." Edited by V. Puuronen, J Soilevuo-Gronnerod and J. Herranen. Joensuu. *Finland: University of Joensuu; Reports of the Karelian Institute*, No. 1/2005. Edited in "Parents and Teens in Immigrant Families: Cultural influences and Material Pressures" by Vappu Tyyska. *Canadian Diversity; Vol. 6:2, 2008. A Publication of the Association for Canadian Studies.*

Ungerleider, C. S. 1991. Media, minorities and misconceptions: the portrayal by and representation of minorities in Canadian news media. *Canadian Ethnic Studies/Etudes Ethniques au Canada*, 23(3).

Wallerstein Immanuel. 1974. "The Modern World System, Capitalist, Agriculture and the Origins of the European Economy in the Sixteenth Century." *New York: Academic Press.*

Wood J. R. 1983. "East Indians and Canada's New Immigration Policy." In Kurian and Srivastava. Edited in "Calculated Kindness"; Global Restructuring, Immigration and Settlement in Canada; *Rose Baaba Folson*; edited.

Wakil, S. P., Siddique, C. M., and Wakil, F. A. 1981. "Between two cultures: A study in socialization of children of immigrants." *Journal of Marriage and the Family, 43(4)*. Edited in "Ethnic Identity and Parenting Stress in South Asian Families: Implications for Culturally sensitive Counselling." Aneesa Shariff. 2009. *Canadian Journal of Counselling, Vol. 43*.

11

Annex 1: Stories of South Asian Immigrants

South Asian Singles Want to Mingle[128]

By Pradip Rodrigues

Thousands of South Asian parents no longer have to worry about getting their children hitched. This is the **DIY (Do it yourself) generation**, who are taking matters in their own hands and finding their partners, friends and lovers without any "help." While arranged marriages are still prevalent among large sections of South Asians in Canada, it is clearly falling out of favor among a growing number of well to highly educated South Asian men and women. While many conservative-minded parents are unhappy with their grown-up children dating and attempting the complex job of finding their partners, a growing number of better-educated parents see this development as not only inevitable but also beneficial. Furthermore, finding reliable partners from the Indian sub-continent is trickier today than in earlier times. Fewer good matches are willing to settle down in Canada given India's booming economy and those who are eager to escape could be getting married for all the wrong reasons.

One parent of a 23-year-old girl says, "I had an arranged marriage and always thought I'd find a husband for my daughter, but my daughter is now soon to buy a condo downtown with her boyfriend. Am I upset? Initially yes, but times have changed and it is not right to impose a stranger on our daughter, better she does it her way. She has a well-paying job and more importantly an independent mind of her own." There are many South Asian women, who aren't about to settle for a groom from back home just based on caste and money. Sonia Kumar, in her early 30s, is single and quite happy being that way until she finds "the right person." Armed with an MBA from Schulich School of Business, York University, she is currently a sales representative with a Communications firm and an active member of NetIP, a non-profit organization that brings South Asian professionals in the GTA together and provides a platform to network. Being part of this organization has put Sonia and hundreds of other single professionals in contact with friends and potential like-minded partners. "I have met many South Asians through NetIP over the years, I haven't found the right person, but I have made many very good friends. I am in no hurry to settle down and neither is my family pressuring me to do so. They are more concerned about my general well-being and happiness." Sonia's younger brother on the other hand, views relationships a little differently. "Many of my friends, including my brother, use dating sites. I don't because I have access to people through NetIP. Sites like Plentyoffish.com have netted him a different date every weekend," she reveals.

Single South Asian men tend to keep all options open. Some even arranged marriages as a last resort. Some young professional men on dating sites can be extremely open to dating anyone and everyone, who might show the slightest interest because more often than not, they are simply looking to sow their wild oats on a Friday night as opposed to seriously seeking a compatible partner. Many South Asian single women attest to this fact. Sonia Kumar adds, "I avoid dating sites because quite often the men are either much younger or not serious about a serious relationship with anyone." But then again, there are plenty of South Asian women, who are looking for dating options with no strings attached.

Mishal V, a twenty years plus single man admits he isn't ready to settle down just yet when there is such a wide dating pool available. "Heck, even my parents' generation would not want to settle for boring arranged marriages when you have so many fun encounters possible."

Geeta Chopra, a realtor and host on a TV show is single and excited about meeting new people all the time. Her work brings her in touch with plenty of young single people and needless to add a few dates as well. "I'd say 60 percent of second generation South Asians prefer finding partners through dating or matrimony sites. Half of these people are serious and the other half, semi-serious. I don't care either way because even if I meet a non-serious person, quite often I could get a friend out of the encounter," she said. Many young South Asians have lived in households witnessing first hand their parents' loveless relationship or have seen some unhappy marriages when a partner is imported from "back home." This is not to say that the choices they make will be separation-proof, but at least they have a say in the whole process.

Pooja, a 27-year-old professional says, "How can you know the true nature of a partner in an arranged marriage? Both persons are on their best behavior, saying all the right things to make a good impression until the proposal is accepted and marriage happens. When you date a person and get to know him or her over a period of time, you at least make your choice based on what you see with no pressure or expectation of any long-term commitment. Living-in before marriage is better for some personalities looking for an escape clause," she stated.

Fiza Shah (a school teacher an actor/professional dancer) married the man she fell in love with at University. "I am a regular Muslim while my husband is Ismaili. It was an issue with my parents for a while but they quickly got over it. Many of my friends aren't that lucky," she says. Often, a girl might fall in love with a boy but one or both might end up having to choose between their partners of another faith or culture or the happiness of their parents. And while some serial daters might one day succumb to the ease of an arranged marriage, dating, for now, remains somewhat like a sport. You don't know how the date will turn out and neither will you know how the evening might end. It is a real thrill for the brave, the bold and the beautiful, certainly not for the faint hearted!

South Asian Doctor Who Received One of the Highest Canadian Awards for Research[129]

Pradip Rodrigues

When the "Influenza A (H1N1)" pandemic hit Canada back in 2009, among the many researchers studying it closely was Dr Deepali Kumar, a physician-scientist at the University of Alberta. Last year, the startling results of her study published in the prestigious infectious disease journal, the Lancet Infectious Diseases caught the attention of the Royal College of Physicians and Surgeons of Canada, who awarded her the 2011 Gold Medal in Medicine, Canada's most prestigious prizes in Canadian medicine. Dr Deepali Kumar, physician-scientist at the University of Alberta.

Following the pandemic what Ms. Kumar did was to work closely with 26 hospitals, mostly in North America and a few in Europe, and study the data on the pandemic. What she found was when the flu shot vaccine was administered to vulnerable patients, who'd undergone an organ transplant within 48 hours; they did not require to be moved to ICU. Up until that point, a patient displaying signs of H1N1 was placed under observation while undergoing a battery of tests, typically she found a delay in administering the vaccine by five days resulted in a 5 to 30 percent higher mortality rate among vulnerable patients, who suffered lung damage and a 5 to 30 percent higher mortality rate. As a result of her study, transplant patients, who are brought into hospitals with flu-like symptoms, are administered the vaccine as a precaution without waiting for the customary tests. Lives are being saved and more will continue to be saved thanks to Ms. Kumar's research findings.

Deepali and her husband Atul Humar, also a physician-scientist, live in Edmonton, Alberta with their three adorable kids, Sapna 11, Sonika, 8 and Saurav, 6. Their work-life balance is in sync as they juggle responsibilities of instilling values and teaching ethics to their children and working closely together on projects. Deepali came to Canada as a young girl with her parents, both academicians, who after moving around the country on work, finally settled down in Ottawa, where she grew her roots. "I lived in Mississauga before coming to Edmonton," she said, "but we found the commuting to Toronto General Hospital too difficult given their young children and when the option to work at the University of Alberta came up, they jumped at the opportunity given the university's reputation." In recent years, the University of Alberta is considered a centre of excellence in influenza research in transplant patients.

Coming from the same cultural and social milieu, both husband and wife are keen to expose their children to the same cultural and social diversity that they experienced growing up in Ottawa. "My children attend Hindi school and have made many Indian friends there; we teach them about Hindu culture and make them aware of their heritage. At the same time it is important to put yourself out there and be part of the mainstream. I think it is important to have good communication skills and one needs to communicate effectively in an open society like Canada," she adds. Dr Kumar's demeanour often betrays the two sides of her personality. Sure she can be the intense workaholic concentrating on her research between 9 am and 5 pm, but between 5 pm and 9 am, is when she pursues the other important things in her life, one of which is taking in at least one Bollywood movie a week. "I love Bollywood movies," she admits, "my kids enjoy them too, especially the movie *Bodyguard*." Deepali also admits to another thing—she did grow up considering becoming a Bollywood actress as an alternate career path. Deepali is currently working on creating an effective flu shot vaccine best for transplant patients. This physician-scientist South Asian couple are going places and you will be hearing more about their contributions to science.

Making Community Work a Passion[130]

By Asma Amanat

"I think it's important for employers to see immigrants as coming to the table with assets, not deficits. Having employees with global experience that speak multiple languages, makes Canadian businesses more competitive globally, and opens up new markets to individuals such as newcomers and immigrants they may not have been able to reach before. I know a lot of my friends and colleagues are looking to alternative ways of connecting via online or dating events. It seems to be working."

Munira Ravji's family migrated to Canada from Nairobi, Kenya in the mid-1980s. As a pharmacist, her father enrolled into the University of Saskatchewan to upgrade his certifications to practice in Canada. The family later moved to London, Ontario, where Munira's father opened his own pharmacy. After finishing her studies in Montreal, she started her business—offering PR consulting and project management to not-for profit organizations. A few years ago Munira moved to Toronto, where she worked with numerous youth, arts and community organizations. At the core of this is her involvement with Maytree Foundation initiatives for immigrants. As she puts it, "I have so much respect for immigrants making the move to Canada. Seeing my parents struggle, and prevail has inspired me to support and encourage others who are taking the giant leap of faith and starting from scratch in Canada." She wishes to empower new Canadians to enable them to offer their talents to the Canadian society and be accepted and prosperous in the process. Having worked in close proximity with new Canadians, Munira feels that lack of access to certain positions and opportunities can hold visible minorities and women back. A number of factors affect their possibilities, she feels, including family dynamics, income levels, and the lack of the right kind of social networks. In her view, a combination of changing the dynamics of the country's education system as well as corporate and societal values can provide solutions to this problem.

Speaking about the often-dreaded "Canadian experience" and English-language education for new immigrants, Munira says, "I think it's important for employers to see immigrants as coming to the table with assets, not deficits. Having employees with global experience that speak multiple languages, makes Canadian businesses more competitive globally, and opens up new markets to individuals such as newcomers and immigrants they may not have been able to reach before." Her advice to immigrants, especially skilled ones, is to tap into local programs like the ones offered by TRIEC and to employers to utilize comprehensive and free resources such as hireimmigrants.ca and the roadmap tool to support the process of recruiting, retaining and promoting skilled immigrants. Munira tells Generation Next that one of the most exciting aspects of her job is working with major corporations across Canada that are focusing on skilled immigrants who have already settled in cities across Canada. As she says, "All of the major banks, as well as consulting firms are already championing the need and benefits to hiring skilled immigrants. We hope to continue growing these relationships with major corporations, as well as small to medium enterprises to help them to prepare for a looming labour shortage, as well as to strengthen their existing teams and organizations by connecting them to qualified international counterparts."

As an Ismaili Muslim, Munira is the external communications chair for the Ismaili Muslim Council of Ontario. She feels that as a young professional, her experience and ideas are valued in the organization. "Besides taking on leadership roles across the Council's many portfolios, there are also groups and networks that are focused on bring young Ismaili professionals together either to network and socialize, or encourage professional development and capacity building," she says. The discussion moves to Canada's multiculturalism, which Munira feels is incredible. However, she feels Canada is yet to figure out "how to leverage this diversity instead of making it token." In order to make the country's multicultural claim more authentic, there has to be fair representation across sectors in terms of leadership, she believes. Referring to the South Asian community, she says there's still room for the community to be more active in the political arena, which she suggests can be done by encouraging emerging leaders to run and getting seniors out of their homes to participate in political campaigns.

At a more personal level, Munira loves her current role. She says with exuberance, "I have the opportunity to speak publicly about something that I am passionate about (skilled immigrant employment), and collaborate with some of the most celebrated leaders and experts in my industry. It's also really inspiring to be a part of such an important movement and watch the momentum grow across Canada. I don't think I will ever stop volunteering!" Given the level of today's youth involvement in various activities, does Munira think it's a challenge to find Mr. or Miss Right? Munira tends to agree that there might not be "enough in-person spaces in which to meet other like-minded individuals in a meaningful and authentic way," but also adds, "I know a lot of my friends and colleagues are looking to alternative ways of connecting via online or dating events. It seems to be working." So where will Munira Ravji be ten years from now? In her own words she said, "I hope to continue being as happy and content as I am now—surrounded by family and friends, maintaining a meaningful career, and giving back as much as I can. In the next 10 years, I hope to see all this hard work and innovative thinking materialize into the kind of Canada we envision now; something that is sustainable and harmonious, something to really be proud of.

A Passionate Advocate for Renewable Energy[131]

By Asma Amanat

"There has been some opposition to some wind farms and it's due partly to misinformation spread by groups that are not happy with the wind farms. There's a misconception that electricity costs have gone up due to renewable energy, but the costs are actually due to upgrading the transmission system because it's so old. These upgrades need to take place regardless of what form of energy is added and that's what is causing some of the increased costs."

"I think the Ontario government has shown exceptional leadership in renewable energy. The Feed-in-Tariff program is the only one of its kind in North America and is modeled on Feed-in-Tariff program in other countries. Regardless of which party is elected this fall, I would like to see this sort of leadership for renewable energy. I focused my attention on my career and academic development and when I have a family I will be a lot older than my parents were when they started a family . . . I will be a lot older when my children are in their teens, much older than I would prefer to be but I couldn't think of any other way to get myself on an upward career track. I felt I had to focus on one major thing first."

"Environmental sustainability is part of Gandhian principles. Another principle is equality for all people so that everyone has the same opportunities," says Adarsh Mehta, Development Director at Acciona Wind Energy Canada. Inspired by the ideals of Mahatma Gandhian the stint in Nepal to help less fortunate, Adarsh is more "culturally inclined." She incorporates the Gandhian philosophy in her day-to-day life, believing that Gandhian ideals "can be extended to any religion really. So it's more cultural and spiritual base that I stick to and not so much a religious base," she shares with Generation Next.

With an undergraduate degree in Applied Math and Computer Science and a Master's degree in Applied Maths, Adarsh's area of focus was environmental fluid dynamics. "So, that's really when the whole environmental awareness started and I was modelling wind flow over complex terrain for my thesis," she says. It was this wind flow modelling that really got her into the wind industry. While wind energy and other sources of renewable energy has recently become a controversial subject, Adarsh believes that the opposition is mostly because of misinformation and lack of long term thinking. "There has been some opposition to some wind farms and it's due partly to misinformation spread by groups that are not happy with the wind farms. What we're trying to do at the industry level is to create more awareness about the benefits of wind energy. We're also trying to correct misinformation about costs to the ratepayer. There's a misconception that electricity costs have gone up due to renewable energy, but the costs are actually due to upgrading the transmission system because it's so old. These upgrades need to take place regardless of what form of energy is added and that's what is causing some of the increased costs," she explains.

Adarsh's experience working in the industry is quite different. "We're talking about the long term benefits and we should always talk about the long term benefits because humankind is going to be around for the long term. We're trying to build an economy, not an industry. There might be some short term job losses but I would actually say its net positive. We're creating more jobs than we've lost and a lot of people who lost jobs are from the manufacturing sector; we've put some of those folks back to work already. So those jobs that were lost were lost prior to any renewable energy program, because of an economic recession in an entirely different sector. We're creating jobs for them in the renewable energy sector," she tells us. This may sound like endorsing Ontario Premier Dalton McGuinty. Without any hesitation, she proclaims admiration for Ontario's renewable energy policy. "I think the Ontario government has shown exceptional leadership in renewable energy. The Feed-in-Tariff program is the only one of its kind in North America and is modeled on Feed-in-Tariff program in other countries. So I really do applaud Ontario for that. This is the sort of leadership that we hope will stay. Regardless of which party is elected this fall, I would like to see this sort of leadership for renewable energy," she says.

At the federal level, the story is quite different. "We tried very hard to get federal government engagement. They did not renew the Eco Energy program for renewable energy. That expired in March of this year and that was the last time they had given out any funds from that incentive program," says the Chair of Can WEA Board of Directors. A far as the impact of Harmonized Sales Tax (HST) goes; the wind industry hasn't really been impacted. "It doesn't really make us any more or less competitive," she tells us. The benefits of renewable energy may be multipronged, but like other communities, very few South Asians understand it. "I actually don't see there being enough awareness in the South Asian community. There are so many things that South Asians can be doing to help with sustainability in our environment; we have the confidence, and capability and capacity to do that and we just need to put it to good use," responded Adarsh when asked how well aware South Asian community is when it comes to awareness of sustainable energy. One reason is that the first generation of South Asian immigrants are unaware of it. The younger generations have more awareness because they are being educated in the Canadian curriculum which includes study of renewable energy.

Wind industry is a field where there are still very few women or representation from visible minorities. When Adarsh went to Canadian Wind Energy Association Conference in 2004, there were 300 people. Of these there were only a handful of women. The number of women since then, she feels, has grown to about 25 percent. As a young woman in a unique field where there are very few women, Adarsh is "trying to encourage young women to pursue opportunities that have not traditionally been on their radar." At an individual level, Adarsh has encouraged a group of friends, all career women in Ottawa, to put resources together to send a young girl from a Child Haven home to college for Engineering. "That has meant a lot to me, I encourage young women to bring themselves up," Adarsh tells.

As a young professional with a full time career, starting the family took back seat for Adarsh. Pressure of establishing a career took precedence. "I focused my attention on my career and academic development and when I have a family I will be a lot older than my parents were when they started a family . . . I will be a lot older when my children are in their teens, much older than I would prefer to be but I couldn't think of any other way to get myself on an upward career track. I felt I had to focus on one major thing first," she shares. Nonetheless, Adarsh attributes her success to motivation given to her by a former Vice President at the Canadian Wind Energy Association. "And had it not been for his encouragement, I'm not sure that I would actually be here at the moment," Adarsh says gratefully. "He kind of gave me the encouragement to get involved in the wind energy industry at the industry level, not just with my company. So I started getting involved in caucuses, focus groups and committees that the Canadian Wind Energy Association has organized to resolve certain issues and develop strategies. I was elected to the board of directors of the Canadian Wind Energy Association in 2008. A year later I was elected to the board executive committee as Vice-Chair and then I was elected Chair of the board. So it has been an upward progress and I really have to thank the friend that encouraged me to get there," she says.

Making an Exciting Future in Hollywood[132]

By Asma Amanat

Sandy Sidhu, an aspiring young artist is playing a recurring role as Dr. Mehta in the military science fiction television series, *Stargate Universe*. Sandy Sidhu and her co-stars launched *Afternoon Tea* at Toronto International Film Festival (TIFF) in 2011. The film was selected for 2011's Shorts Cut Canada Programme at the 36th TIFF. *Afternoon Tea* is among the 40 short films selected.

Born and raised in BC, Sandy first entered the spotlight by representing her hometown as the Nanaimo Princess Ambassador from 2003 to 2004. Sandy has received a degree in Cell Biology and Genetics at the University of British Columbia. What does Cell Biology has to do with acting, you may wonder. "Some might find that the polar opposite of acting but I've always been creative. I started doing theatre when I was fourteen years old and I've been drawing since I was a kid," she explains.

As a young artist who has embarked on a challenging career, Sandy believes that the South Asian artists can make it to the mainstream. For herself, she tells Generation Next "I see an exciting future ahead. Increasingly you see more and more South Asians on screen. Just the other day I saw *30 Minutes or Less* with Aziz Ansari. There are numerous TV shows airing right now that have main cast members who are South Asians, and looking at blockbuster hits like *Slumdog Millionaire* and *Bend It Like Beckham* you can see the demand. It's a fortunate time to be in the industry as just twenty years ago it would have been a very different landscape and most likely much more difficult to attempt. "I definitely think there's acceptance. Sure, the North American industry hasn't quite got to the point of seeing a South Asian Batman yet (And that is something I'd love to see). If there any barrier then it's up to people in my generation to break through those and make it happen," she adds. While the mainstream may be open to visible minorities, are communities like the South Asian community open to accepting the community's newest stars? "The South Asian

Community is incredibly supportive. There might be more apprehension or fear to attempt a career so different, but I think that's about it. And that's a universal feeling, not one limited to just our community," she stated.

As a young actress, Sandy believes that getting good roles may be a bit of a challenge.

". . . It would be having stronger characters and not just being boxed into roles that are just the girlfriend, the wife. Not that those roles can't be fascinating themselves but to stretch people's current expectations and explore different aspects of a woman's psyche. I'd also love to continue to see more film projects with a woman that completely carries the film." As far as the stereotypes like arranged marriages go, Sandy says "although I wouldn't choose to be in one, I have nothing against arranged marriages because I know people who've had success with it."

How about social issues like honour killings?

"I have zero tolerance for it. It's appalling and nonsensical. I grew up with the mentality that we choose our love, that we choose our passions, and that to live our life with freedom is a basic human right we all deserve to have without consequences," she says strongly. At an individual level, how does she see the relationship between fate and hard work?

Sandy tells: "I believe in both. You can't sit around expect things to just happen for you. I think it's a fusion of working hard and having faith it'll all work out the way it's meant to."

Cultural Divide Still Exist Here[133]

By Asma Amanat

She was born in Lahore in 1962; she moved with her family first to Britain and then about a year later, at age three, to Canada. Rukhsana has eleven books published and others under contract. She has appeared on television and radio numerous times, has been featured at international conferences in Denmark, Mexico, Singapore, Italy, and South Africa, and has presented all across Canada and the United States. She tells tales of India, Persia, the Middle East, as well as her own stories. In an interview with Generation Next, Rukhsana talks about her life, writings, and aspirations.

Tell us about your journey to being a writer.

My father had chosen to live in Canada because he wanted to get away from those cultural influences which said girls are expendable. He also wanted to raise us as Muslims, and he wanted a good neighbourhood. It turned out to be very difficult. Because we stuck out so much, we were persecuted from day one. If it hadn't been for that negative treatment, I don't think I would have become a writer because my growing up was so horrible that I went to books to escape.

Your stories have enabled children of all cultures to connect with cultures of Eastern origin. Your speech and articles talk about assimilation of Muslim culture into the mainstream (particularly the West and Canada). In your opinion, does the cultural divide in Canada still exist?
Yes. The cultural divide still exists in Canada. It's not as bad as it was earlier, but it's definitely still there. I think what frightens me the most is that I see ethnic enclaves more and more. Within the Muslim community, it's like they're withdrawing into their own communities and that can lead to disenfranchisement and even radicalism. I actually think that the best way forward is to get more involved in mainstream community, let our voices be heard, rather than less involved. And that can happen best through the sharing of stories.

How do new immigrants become a part of the mainstream? What advice would you like to give to the new immigrants who are struggling hard to carve a niche for themselves?
I think the best advice I can give is to be yourself and don't be ashamed. It is part of the Canadian charter of rights and freedoms that Canada has to respect religious freedoms and not discriminate on the basis of race or ethnicity. So you can basically dress in accordance to your beliefs and you'll find that the vast majority of Canadians will accept and respect that. But in return, we immigrants have to respect that in other communities and ethnicities as well. It goes both ways and sometimes I find immigrants who have come from more homogenous societies, where they didn't have to come face to face with people of other mindsets and races, have a hard time accepting differences in others. They can actually be quite racist and not even realize that they're being racist because they see racism as a top down sort of phenomenon, only perpetrated by white people towards non-whites. The other piece of advice I'd give is really really learn English!

You've written in one of your articles—"Muslim children in particular suffer from a sense of insecurity and inferiority—at least I did. While growing up I felt as though all the bluster of the Muslim leaders in the masjid arose because they couldn't make it in mainstream circles. They couldn't be a 'someone' in the 'real' world so they had to build their little

hill in the Muslim community and stand atop it proclaiming themselves king. Pathetic! I didn't want to be like that. I wanted to think bigger. I thought, if I'm going to make it, I want to make it in the mainstream because after all, I didn't want to limit myself to writing only for Muslim children. I wanted my stories to be for everyone."—Does that mean that you are against any kind of ghettoization?

Yes, kind of. There's nothing wrong with people having their communities and clubs and such. But I see too many Muslims and immigrants basically becoming kind of schizophrenic, in that they go to work in the mainstream but socialize only in within their own little communities. Open it up people! Reach out and make friends with all kinds! You can learn so much!!! And they can learn so much from you too!

What has been the response from the community?

It's neat and positive. Occasionally when I go places in the Muslim community I get recognized. In fact the only negative response I can recall was from some yahoo who was trying to get me to join a petition trying to change Islamic law so he could go out and drink and dance and party and stuff. I told him simply there was nothing stopping him from doing all that, but I did not believe that Islam should be changed to accommodate the lifestyle he wanted to live. He could take it or leave it. That's the beauty of freedom of choice.

How do you deal with criticism?

I always take any criticism I receive very seriously. First I ask myself does this person have merit in what they're saying. Am I really guilty of what they're accusing me of? And I try my very best to answer the question honestly. I consider myself a work in progress. I can always be improved!

In Canada too, we sometimes see the same division—Indians and Pakistanis have their own groups? What's your opinion on multiculturalism in Canada?

Honestly I think multiculturalism has been best for Canada. I remember when Pierre Elliot Trudeau first introduced the idea that we Canadians would be a mosaic where everyone had a right to retain their cultural identity and still be respected! I prefer it to the melting pot idea of America. But the problem arises when enough people from a certain demographic come and start "sticking to their own kind." I know it's more comfortable to just stick to your own kind, but it doesn't lead to a harmonious society. I came across one idea in Singapore that I actually admire. They have a policy in Singapore that no one ethnic group can occupy any apartment building. There has to be a diverse ratio of ethnicities in each apartment building. It seems a bit of a pain, but the idea is that it forces people to live together and tolerate one another.

Entrepreneur and lawyer Meleni David is dedicated in providing excellent legal services to her clients and their families who have experienced personal injuries. Sri Lankan-born Meleni is a recipient of the Top 25 Canadian Immigrants of 2012 Award and the National Ethnic Press and Media Council of Canada Award from the lieutenant governor. In a conversation with Generation Next, the lawyer extraordinaire speaks about her challenges and the road to success.[134]

Although I agree the industry was a male dominated one, I don't see any reason for it to continue to stay that way. I am planning to do everything I can to succeed in this field and groom and train other female lawyers in my office to be successful.

My advice to new immigrant women is to believe in them and believe in the power they hold within themselves. It is their duty to bring up their children to the best of their ability but their lives do not end there. They should have a purpose in life and with the right direction and help and support from their families they need to go after their dreams and career.

When did you immigrate to Canada from Sri Lanka, and under what circumstances?
I immigrated to Canada in 1995. I left Sri Lanka due to Civil War and fear of persecution. I wanted to get away from the war zone to make a peaceful life for myself and my family.

A brief overview of your struggle in the country—how did you mange to accomplish what you are today?
I faced persecution as a member of minority group in my country. I could not finish my education, could not work without fear and could not have a peaceful life. I managed to succeed because of God's blessings, my family's support and my determination. And, Canada gave me the opportunity that I was looking for.

As a leading female lawyer in Canada—do you believe the industry to be essentially a male-dominated one?
Although I agree the industry was a male dominated one, I don't see any reason for it to continue to stay that way. I am planning to do everything I can to succeed in this field and further and to groom and train other female lawyers in my office to be successful in this area. The

niche was carved for me by God. I am a god-fearing person and always do the right thing and I am honest in all my dealings. I take pride in the reputation I have gained in my community as not only an expert in my field but also as a respectful and honest professional.

How did you mange with two kids, home and school back then?
It is all in you. You have the power to decide how you want to live your life. Life is not a bed of roses. You have to focus on what you want in life, you have to be determined not to change the course and prepare to make sacrifices along the way to achieve your goal. My life was exactly like that. Lots of challenges, lot of negative feedbacks, lot of heart aches and self doubting moments, and not to mention the sacrifices day and night for seven years. But, I was determined to go through the hurdles along the way with the least trouble to people around me and my family in particular. I wanted my children to never miss out their childhood just because I went back to school. My husband and my parents were pillars for me throughout my school days. I also had the Almighty's blessings every step of the way in my life.

What advice would you give to all those new immigrant women who are struggling hard to juggle between home and career?
Women are a special species created by God with special powers. They care for others throughout their lives and they are very happy doing so. They can juggle many things all at once and they are good at what they do. My advice to new immigrant women is to believe in them and believe in the power they hold within themselves. It is their duty to bring up their children to the best of their ability but their lives do not end there. They should have a purpose in life and with the right direction and help and support from their families they need to go after their dreams and career. May be once their children are grown up or otherwise. But it's left to them to make it happen. Especially in Canada there are many opportunities for new immigrants. They can attain their goal with the right mind-set and sacrifice.

What advice would you give to internationally-trained professionals who feel frustrated when their credentials don't work here?
Well, first of all they come to this country for a reason and I am hoping that is for a peaceful life and they have at least attained that when they start their life here. You can't have everything in life all at once, without any hardship. In my opinion life would be too boring then. I also believe you don't appreciate things in life when you get them without much effort. As

a professional, when you find out after coming here that your credentials don't work here then it is in you to make it work here. "Your credentials won't work here" is not written in stone. It may be in a piece of paper you receive by mail. It is all in you to start working towards your career, with everything you have, till you receive a piece of paper saying "your credentials have been approved. You are qualified to practise in Canada." You might face hardship, you might face negativity sometimes even from you own family. But in the end, it will be all worth it. So work on it. It is an attainable goal and you can do it if you really want to do it. I did it.

At any point, would you like to go back to your home country?
I would go back if I am able to live the life I had before the civil war. That, certainly, is not going to happen anytime soon. So, I won't give up hope; at the same time I don't long for it. Most of us who immigrated to Canada have a peaceful life here. But my country is beautiful. It was called a taste of paradise.

You have helped shaped the life of seven foreign-trained lawyers and two foreign-trained doctors. How did you do so?
I hired them to work in my law firm and encouraged and accommodated them to continue and upgrade their studies. When they completed their studies, they went on to open their own practices. When foreign-trained lawyers worked in my office, they got to work in their field and it reduced time for them during their licensing process. For doctors too, if they are working in their field even though it is a law office (primarily because our law firm specializes in Personal Injury Law), they are able to summarize all the medical information on our clients' files.

My Art Reflects Life of a South Asian Woman[135]

By Asma Amanat

"I think my experiences in life are reflected in my art. It reflects the lives of South Asian women, with a special focus on Pakistan. My work concerns with issues of marriage, relationships and independence of thought. It's about the pressures which middle class families face—like those of dowry, choice in marriage and the concept of 'Chand si Bahu' or perfect appearance."

Sumaira Tazeen is a contemporary miniature painter, educationist, and a curator. She received her BFA in miniature painting from the National

College of Arts, Lahore, in 1996. Since 1996, her work has been featured in various group and solo exhibitions in Pakistan, United States, Canada, and United Kingdom. She's also taught for seven years as an associate professor at Indus Valley School of Art and Architecture, Karachi. Born in Hyderabad (Pakistan), Sumaira now resides in Oakville, Ontario. As she points out, her artworks are a "depiction of a path running parallel with her life." She has always looked at her art "through the eyes of a woman, who is conscious of the issues prevalent in society and is keen to bring a positive change in them." Sumaira is a recipient of several awards, some of them being Charles Wallace Trust fellowship 2004 and DIFD Scholarship award for 2003–2004. Besides traditional and contemporary styles of miniature paintings, she also dabbles into sculpture, video, and installation art. In a conversation with Generation Next, the artist talks about the concerns reflected in her work and life as a South Asian artist in Canada.

When did you move to Canada?
I moved to Canada in March 2012 due to personal reasons. Also, Pakistan's political situation has made lives difficult for many to live in peace; there is lot of frustration in almost every aspect (be it security or the economy). All these factors have pushed people to move away from a beautiful country which has rich natural resources, a distinct culture and a strong history. Besides that, I have more opportunities to explore and expand my career as an artist. I am planning to do my master's in fine art next year. This was something I always wanted to do but couldn't just because there are no good graduate programs and I had no money to apply in international universities at that time. Here in Canada, I am quite satisfied with my progress so far.

Tell us something about your initial days in Canada. Was it a smooth ride?
Thank God it wasn't bumpy as such. It was actually a smooth sailing. I had commissioned a painting to complete, so had no financial issues. My husband has got a good job. He is a food technologist and works for quality control in a coffee plant. I started a part time job but decided very soon that it is not my forte, but the job gave me a good understanding of the Canadian culture and work environment. Now I want to work as a self-employed visual artist. I am participating in shows. My art video got selected to be shown soon at Celebration Square in a show named *The Gaze*. It's a project organized by AGM and Mississauga city culture division. I recently gave a presentation at the department of Fine Art, Queen's University, Kingston Ontario. I'm also planning for my MFA in 2013.

You've said that your work is "about the pressures and anxieties I have, as a woman in this culture. It is about the dreams of a bride who awaits the happiness in life. It is about expressing one's own feelings"—what are your concerns "as a woman" that your art works reflect?

I think my experiences in life are reflected in my art. It reflects the lives of South Asian women, with a special focus on Pakistan. My work concerns with issues of marriage, relationships and independence of thought. The pressures which middle class families face are those of dowry, choice in marriage and the concept of "Chand si Bahu" or perfect appearance.

As a woman artist, how difficult was it to establish you in the competitive art industry?

It was not difficult fortunately to mingle in the art circle. I was lucky enough to get the opportunities (of course I put in efforts for it and tried my best to give to the community). When I started, I was the only miniature painter in Karachi. I started almost all the miniature painting departments in universities and art colleges. I introduced miniature as Neo Miniature there.

You've said: "The research in my art practice has always questioned the marriage practices in our society; the criteria setting the standards of good and bad!" Would you call your art "feminist"? Is it an activism of sorts?

Yes it is about questioning the norms of the society. Maybe it's feminist but it's not purely feminist. That's because I sometimes do not agree with pure feminist theories. My ideas are built up on my own experiences.

What do you think of the international art scene? Are South Asians able to carve a niche for themselves here in Canada?

Yes there is a great room for that. Artists are already merging in the scene but definitely a lot needs to be done, especially introducing miniature painting as Neo Miniature (not traditional craft). This art form has a lot of future and it's booming internationally. I think an artist should be open to the ideas and mediums of the fast moving world.

Art is a major form of investment. Do you think in all this it is being reduced to mere business? Do people really understand "art" in the true sense of the word?

Yes it is investment too and there is a commercial aspect attached to it, which is not bad, but maintaining that balance in every aspect of life is important. As far as understanding art is concerned, I would say that yes there are people who take art as an art form.

South Asians are creating waves at Christie's—one of them being Tyeb Mehta. What's your opinion on the art scene in the subcontinent?

I think art scene in South Asia especially Pakistan and India is booming internationally. Apart from the seniors like Sadeqain, Jamil Naqsh Souza, M F Husain and Tyeb Mehta, the young artists have been getting recognition too. Maybe it's because of the current political situation in the countries especially Pakistan and the type of work the artists produce is inspired by it. For instance, Imran Qureshi, Rashid Rana, Aisha Khalid, Hamra Abbas, Risham Syed (there is a big list), and from India Subodh Gupta, Riyas Komu and Dibanjan Roy.

What feedback have you received from the community so far?

So far it's encouraging. I'd like to see more South Asian artists doing well in Canada. I want to endorse miniature painting as an art form/medium of expression in art institutions. Also, I want to introduce South Asian art and culture in the youth of today because I feel that art students are only familiar with Western art mediums and history.

Sunny Uppal Puts Canadian Values in Action[136]

By Samuel Getachew

The Historica-Dominion Institute has a "mission to help all Canadians come to know the fascinating stories that make our country unique." In past years, it has hosted programs such as Heritage Minutes, the Heritage Fair, and the Canadian Encyclopedia to fulfill that ambitious public service. Last month, at the central library in Ottawa, it hosted a well-attended event to mark Asian Heritage Month in Canada. The topic focused on the children of first-generation Asian Canadian immigrants. Sunny Uppal was one of the speakers at this important event along with Ontario Conservative MP Michael Chong. Uppal reflects with Generation Next on his experience as a public servant, his first-generation—South Asian—immigrant experience as well as gives advice for South Asians who may want to emulate such a fulfilling Canadian (immigrant) journey.

You have achieved much at such a young age. The TD Canada Trust Scholarship for Outstanding Community Leadership as well as the attainment of your graduate degree from Ivy League Columbia comes to mind. Share with us your academic journey so far?

During my senior year of High School (at Milliken Mills High School in Markham, Ontario), I was quite involved in numerous leadership activities. It was during this time that I was awarded the TD Canada Trust Scholarship for Outstanding Community Leadership. It was a pivotal moment for me, as it demonstrated that a significant institution within the country felt I was deserving of an award given to only 20 students a year across Canada. Moreover, not only did the scholarship value academic excellence, but specifically looked for young Canadians who were committed to giving back to their communities in an innovative and effective manner. I started my post-secondary education at The University of Western Ontario, where I obtained my Honours Bachelor of Science degree in Biology. During my years at Western, I developed a real interest in environmental studies—largely due to the fact that the subject incorporated a significant amount of science, however, also had a political and diplomatic component with respect to globally managing the issues.

I pursued my Master's Degree at Columbia University, where my focus was on environmental health policy. The school provided a fantastic opportunity to learn about key environmental issues that affect human health from a policy perspective. Furthermore, I took advantage of being at a University with numerous graduate programs, and ended up enrolling in classes ranging from toxicology to the study of climate change and public health. Furthermore, having the chance to study in New York City and living at the International House (a historic residence for international graduate students in New York) broadened my experience, as it allowed for me to meet many interesting individuals pursuing incredibly diverse career paths.

You have had an interesting immigrant's journey to Canada that is perhaps not unique in a multicultural country such as Canada.

My family's immigration journey begins with my grandparents, who left India in the early 1970s and arrived in Toronto. Their story was not uncommon in the sense that they had to work incredibly hard and make significant sacrifices to establish themselves in Canada. My father spent most of his formative years growing up in Toronto, and married my mother through an arranged marriage (not uncommon in India) in 1983. My brother and I were both born in Toronto, but grew up in a joint family with both my parents and grandparents. It was a full house, but also a home that struck a great balance between both Canadian and Indian traditions. I always look back at this time with a great deal of appreciation as both my parents and grandparents worked incredibly hard to ensure that I was given the opportunities they never had—namely, the pursuit of a higher education and the opportunity to have a career that I was passionate about.

Share with us your experience with the United Nations Economic Commission (for Europe's Convention on Long-range Transboundary Air Pollution)

I began my career with the United Nations as an intern at their office in Geneva, Switzerland. I specifically worked for the UN Economic Commission for Europe (a regional commission under the Economic and Social Council). Within this commission, my specific area of work focused on the Convention on Long-range Transboundary Air Pollution. After my internship concluded, I was provided the opportunity to work as an International Consultant for the same group. My role focused on capacity building, specifically assisting the countries of Eastern Europe and Central Asia in developing the policy, technical and legislative tools to implement and ratify the Convention. This opportunity provided me with a great deal of experiences including extensive travel to the region and the chance to learn about new cultures. However, most importantly, it truly taught me that providing assistance in an effective manner can generate a significant difference with respect to any area of work—including the environment.

You once told the *Globe and Mail* how you always carry Canadian values of global outreach and capacity-building, explain.

Growing up in Canada, I increasingly became aware of the important role this country has played in the international landscape with respect to assisting those countries and people that are less fortunate than us. However, the opportunity to work internationally and focus on environmental capacity building efforts in Eastern Europe and Central Asia really put these Canadian values into action. There were numerous occasions where officials from these regions would express their positive opinion and views on Canada, and all that we stand for. Their comments always focused on the fact that we as a country, and as a people, are known to help and generously offer our skills and expertise wherever we can. Furthermore, in my current role with the Canadian government, I get the opportunity to work with other countries on environmental issues ranging from building strategic policies to international negotiations, and I'm proud to say that we continue to be a constructive and effective partner in international dialogues.

You were one of two recent speakers in Ottawa on the occasion of South Asian Month. Your presentation focused on your experience as a first generation immigrant. Why do you think such an event is important?

I had the opportunity to speak in celebration of Asian Heritage Month in Ottawa this past May. The event was organized by the Historica-Dominion Institute's Passages to Canada program. This particular engagement focused on the stories of children of first-generation Asian-Canadian immigrants (such as me). I felt it was important to participate as sharing our stories and experiences allows for other Canadians to gain further insight into the sacrifices and challenges our parents and grandparents faced, and how in turn, that has influenced our values and goals in this country. Also, it was a great opportunity to reflect on my own life thus far and take stock of all the challenges and positive experiences my family and I have experienced in Canada, and how their decision to leave everything and immigrate to Canada was the best decision they ever made.

If you have any advice for young South Asians who may want to emulate such an experience—what would that be?

My interaction with the South Asian community in Canada continues to be a great source of pride. Many have and continue to accomplish fantastic things in all aspects of life. For young South Asian Canadians, I wish to convey that they should pursue their areas of interest. As the global economy increasingly becomes competitive, the generations to come will face a great amount of challenges with respect to succeeding. As such, being passionate about your career is crucial to your success—you truly should strive to be in a position where you are excited to go to work every morning. Beyond this, I would also advise them to never forget the shoulders they stand on.

Knowledge of Law Essential for Combating Human Rights Violations[137]

By Asma Amanat

Qasim Ali has an impressive academic background. He immigrated to Canada in 2000. With a Bachelor's degree in Kinesiology and Health Sciences from York University, he is a second-year law student in the Canadian and American Dual JD program at the University of Windsor and the University of Detroit, Mercy. He intends to be a judge at the criminal division of the Third Circuit Court in Detroit, Michigan. In addition, he is also coordinating the establishment of a legal newsletter at University of Windsor which will focus on comparing and contrasting South Asian systems and legislations with their Canadian counterparts. He is also involved in various political and social justice organizations namely, Journalists for Human Rights, Frontier College, JVS Toronto, and Pakistan Tehreek-e-Insaf Canada. Here is Qasim's interview:

Describe your early days as a journalist at the Journalists for Human Rights at York University—what work were you involved in and how did it influence you to pursue law?

If asked about writing and journalism in my first year of undergrad, I would definitely not see myself interested because of my weak writing and communication skills. But it is by far the most rewarding and maturing experiences. In my third year at York University, I decided to volunteer at the community newspaper, *Excalibur*, as I saw it as a good way of improving my writing skills and as a good experience for my professional growth. Within a year I had contributed a few news articles and I was faced with the opportunity to be with a new and growing journalism group on campus, Journalists for Human Rights. JHR was affiliated with the Canadian based international non-profit which trains journalists around the world so as to advocate for human rights and social justice. I got involved and within an year I was the president and was able to write about and contribute equity and justice related features to the local newspaper and to helm the 3rd annual *R!OT*, a student magazine highlighting the positives of student organizations on campus while combating human rights violations. I was able to involve ten student organizations and it was a positive experience to all of us.

Pursuing law had always been a dream, and I was highly influenced by the Lawyers' Movement in Pakistan, which I researched and wrote about while at JHR at York University. As I wrote in my personal statement, law is one of the only fields which you can apply to every aspect of our lives and it is also a field which has produced more leaders and human rights activists than any other field. Once I was in my first year of legal studies, I understood that knowing the law and thinking like a lawyer are two of the most important aspects when trying to combat human or civil rights violations.

Please tell us about your latest endeavour—studying American and Canadian law at the University of Windsor.

I am currently in my second year at the Dual JD program and I am ecstatic at the opportunity I have to pursue a legal degree in two of the most advanced legal systems in the world. It is a lot of work, as we are studying two different systems and laws at the same time and are doing it in the same duration as the students who are pursuing only one degree, however, I believe that the skills we get through this workload will help us immensely in our legal careers.

What similarities and differences do you find between American and Canadian law? How do they complement and co-heave together?

There are two very different systems and there are countless differences. The only similarity is that both legal systems have their roots in the English law. American law originated and evolved from the common law, which is what we have in Canada. Canadian law relies heavily on common law, laws made by the judges through court decisions, while American law heavily relies on codified laws, made through legislations. Another difference between the systems is that the American legal system has 52 jurisdictions, while Canadian legal system only has one. For example, each state in America has their own legal codes, while the federal government has another. In Canada, the laws are divided up between the provincial and federal government and they both have jurisdiction over different issues.

What challenges do young lawyers face these days in terms of securing and finding worthwhile employment?

In the increasingly globalized world we have today, having knowledge of two legal systems is always a positive; it makes you more desirable than other law students. Also, the American legal system is a lot more advanced in certain areas of torts and evidence, for example, many lawyers in Canada rely on American decisions when looking at issues which we have never faced before.

What advice do you have for young lawyers or students wishing to pursue law in the future?

Volunteer. Show the world that you exist, as the legal profession is 90 percent marketing. Making a difference in your locality is one the best ways to get the best references and to show the law schools that you are more than just books. The difference between good lawyers and the great lawyers is that they are known, as almost everyone can research and present the law as anyone else.

Encouraging Women to Become Resilient and Resourceful[138]

By Asma Amant

My message to women and girls in Canada is that I understand the struggles faced by newcomers; my family arrived in Canada from Uganda in the early 1970s, fleeing discrimination. Throughout my career I've looked for ways to help bring the voices of women and newcomers to the forefront, so we can learn from their experience and be guided by their expertise.

Mina Mawani has been appointed as president and CEO of the Canadian Women's Foundation (CWF) after Beverley Wybrow, president and CEO of CWF for the past twenty-two years, announced her retirement.

CWF's website describes its mission and vision as "We invest in the strength of women and the dreams of girls. The Canadian Women's Foundation raises money to end violence against women, move women out of poverty and build strong resilient girls through funding, researching and promoting best practices. We are a leading voice for women in Canada."

Mina is taking this dedication of CWF's to its next chapter with her leadership. "Mina is an accomplished leader who is passionate about women's equality issues," said Patricia Rossi and Julie George, co-chairs, board of directors, Canadian Women's Foundation. "She brings with her more than 15 years of experience and an impressive track record of visionary leadership in non-profit, hospital and government organizations. Mina is an exemplary leader to guide the next exciting chapter of our work to improve the lives of women and girls in Canada."

Mina was most recently the chief development officer at Civic Action where she was a member of the executive committee responsible for overall strategy and operations. Mina is best known for successfully leading transformation as CEO of the Aga Khan Council for Canada, where she realigned program planning and funding models to build organizational capacity and contributed to planning for a new Ismaili Centre and Museum in Toronto. Mina has also held key roles at the Ministry of Health and Long-Term Care, KPMG, and PricewaterhouseCoopers.

A strong believer in giving back to community, Mina serves on several boards including Women's College Hospital (current chair of the Governance and Nominating Committee) and the advisory board for the UN Women National Committee. Generation Next asked this inspiring young woman to respond to our questions. Here are her responses:

The Canadian Women's Foundation's goal to move women "into confidence" seems quite broad. What does it mean to you?

At the Canadian Women's Foundation, we help women realize their potential and to take a positive approach to learn and recognize their "hidden" assets, which often helps women take those first steps out of poverty. Similarly, confidence helps empower women to feel safe and gives them the strength to speak out against violence and to share their stories.

Moving girls into confidence is also an important part of our work. As girls enter adolescence, from ages 9 to 13, their confidence declines sharply and they experience higher rates of depression. This may be an outcome of the widespread sexualization of girls and women in our society where girls believe their value comes from their sexual appearance rather than their intelligence or other qualities. So we help girls move into confidence by funding dynamic programs that help them stay safer, improve their mental health, challenge stereotypes and successfully navigate adolescence.

I think confidence is a critical part of the solution to making fundamental changes within our society. To help move women into confidence is not a broad term rather a term that implies a fundamental shift in the way we, as women, think about ourselves and our place in our communities. If women learn to notice all of our assets, and I don't mean financial assets, but things like our friendships, our families, and our skills, we can view ourselves in a more positive light and we will be able to tackle the many challenges we face.

Many people think of Canada as a society where women have equal rights and that there is no big need of organizations such as the Canadian Women's Foundation. How do you address this attitude and mindset?

In our society, gender inequality is visible in many areas, including politics, religion, media, cultural norms, and the workplace. The face of poverty in Canada is a woman's face with 12% of all women in Canada living in poverty. Some groups of women are also more likely to live in poverty like visible minority women, Aboriginal women and single mothers. Similarly, violence against women remains a serious problem in our country. On any given day in Canada, more than 3,000 women along with their 2,500 children are living in an emergency shelter to escape domestic violence.

At the Canadian Women's Foundation, we take a positive approach to address root causes of the most critical issues facing women and girls; we study and share the best ways to create long-term change and bring community organizations together for training and to learn from each other. We carefully select and fund the programs with the strongest outcomes and regularly evaluate their work. Helping women creates safer families and communities, and a more prosperous society for all of us. So our work is critical in helping empower women and girls in Canada to move them out of violence, out of poverty and into confidence.

What are the greatest needs of women, and which ages of women does the Canadian Women's Foundation serve?

Women and girls face high levels of violence, and are more likely to be poor. When you help a woman move out of poverty and out of violence, research shows that it has a "ripple effect"—the benefits flow outwards to her children, her family, and her entire community. Improving women's equality is an intelligent investment in a better world. We fund programs that support women and girls of all ages from coast-to-coast-to-coast.

Many newcomer women are vulnerable and do not seek help or refuse it when they get it. How does the Canadian Women's Foundation encourage them to seek help especially when these women are uncertain of their legal status in Canada?

The Canadian Women's Foundation believes that when you give an abused woman a chance for a better life, she can escape the violence and begin to rebuild her life. We fund programs across Canada that provide women, regardless of their legal status, with counseling, legal advice and safety planning. We target our support to women and girls who need it most—in many cases, that means newcomer women and racialized women. Many of these programs do outreach to newcomer communities and help women understand her rights and her legal status. For example, the self-employment programs we fund help women who are new to Canada to become financially independent as quickly as possible. We also fund many programs that help newcomer women to speak out against violence by telling their own stories in their own way, and to work in their own communities to bring about change. Each program we fund takes a different approach to encouraging newcomer women to seek help, regardless of her legal status in Canada.

As a new President and CEO, what is the message that you want to share with women you serve and women who need assistance but are afraid?

The Canadian Women's Foundation provides funding to grassroots community organizations so women can have access to resources. In many countries, there are no resources for women to reach out so many women who need assistance are afraid but I want to let them know that we are here for them—this is why the Foundation exists—to help those who are vulnerable and afraid. We help empower these women to become resilient and to look forward to a better future for themselves and their children. I want to increase awareness among those who are afraid and let them know we are here and that there are programs that can help and offer support.

Violence against women happens in all cultures and religions, in all ethnic and racial communities, at every age, and in every income group. My message to women and girls in Canada is that I understand the struggles faced by newcomers; my family arrived in Canada from Uganda in the early 1970s, fleeing discrimination. Throughout my career I've looked for ways to help bring the voices of women and newcomers to the forefront, so we can learn from their experience and be guided by their expertise.

What Can Us South Asians and Canadians Learn from Each Other?[139]

By Baldev Padam

Canada's natural beauty and breathtaking landscapes, vast distances and rich resources have allured many from other countries and continents centuries ago to reach and settle here. Inward flow of people from abroad continued and as a result today one-fifth of 35 million people, were not born here. Many Chinese Indians, Philippines, Pakistanis other immigrants from Asia landed here in recent decades and brought their diverse cultures and social etiquettes here along. Canada has rightly been called the land of immigrants.

Canada, the other United Nations

That made this country globe's ethnic and cultural mosaic and with legitimate pride Canada avers that diversity instead of making it weaker and a divided country has molded it into a compact and stronger nation. Keeping their respective identities intact, people live cordially here. As a result some call it a dream land while others term Canada as the other United Nations of our world. Its grandeur tempted South Asians too, who essentially started reaching here in last quarter of the 20th century, whereas Punjabi's struggle to land here began much earlier. The tale of *Komagata Maru* boat, hundreds of Punjabi passengers from it weren't allowed to land here in 1914, and faced British police firing back home, killing many of them, is too tragic to mention. Though *Komagata Maru* voyage ended in tragedy but that didn't deter Punjabi spirit to accept things lying low. Their perseverance and efforts succeeded in the long run and today they are part-and-parcel of Canada's mainstream life. Thank God, national prides and prejudices, with advent of new century and globalization, have been consigned to the dustbin of history. In such a backdrop, I landed here as immigrant in the year 2001, with my own expectations and qualms about the country and my anxieties ending as the plane landed at Toronto Airport. I found here things excellent and people courteous.

Courtesy and courtesy everywhere

The saying: "First impression is the last impression" holds good for new arrivals from South Asia who, after reaching Toronto Airport, find, to their pleasant surprise, that custom officials at immigration counters are soft spoken and well-behaved. The officers won't ever let you feel down, harassed or uncomfortable while checking your documents and asking other relevant questions. The new immigrants, thus, leave the airport gleefully taking pleasant memories of their first landing. Back home, custom officials at the airports normally evoke dread among ordinary citizens. During my visit to India last year I, however, observed that things at Delhi Indira Gandhi International airport were better now than before but still they lack in some areas and need long way to go to match Canadian style courtesies.

After becoming accustomed to routine life here one realizes that courtesy and discipline of life doesn't end at the airport but begin with it. It is ubiquitous: One finds it while boarding a public transit, entering into a Cineplex, visiting a hospital or going to malls and plazas. In fact everywhere, people stand in queue and wait for their turn to get things done. The health cards and other documents needed by new immigrants are delivered hassle free. Courtesy in Canada is par-excellence when apparent strangers exchanged a "Hi" smilingly while meeting one another on streets, in parks or on the lake shore. This is quite refreshing for newcomers. "Thank you," responded by "You're welcome" are common courtesies observed here always. Holding the door open for others to let them in is a unique Canadian gesture, seen rarely elsewhere. Some of the incidents when Mississauga Transit drivers helped me to board another bus on the way to my destination are still fresh in the memory. Compared to that, what we often find while riding a roadways lorry back home is disgusting.

Western perception of Eastern culture

Western people have a stereotypical perception of South Asia that is orthodox and goes back to colonial era. Situation has undergone a change after India won freedom in 1947. With dawn of the 21st century and due to globalization, India, along with China, are the fast emerging economy of the world and the Indians in course of time have made deeper impact on economic, social and political life in UK and North America. These people are painstaking diligent and have proved their mettle in academics and look ahead to capture job market here. President Barack Obama has time and again cautioned US youth of Indian's imminent assault on America's jobs if Americans failed to come up to their level.

Paradoxically, the fact also remains that the cultural assimilation of the South Asians with the West is not very much in insight in Canada. The immigrants bring to Canada their own way of life and cling to that fastidiously; particularly the elder rural immigrants who often are seen in groups just chatting in parks, around places of worships, wearing apparels that even back home are being discarded by the younger generation. In fact, Eastern people are not ready to leave their ghettoes and Westerns are unwilling to come closer to them, their isolation is complementary.

In the end

It however has been observed by many, that youth both from East and West could well turn the tide in near future and proves Rudyard Kipling wrong, whose famous lines "Oh East is east, and West is west and never the twain shall meet," may not hold good for long. Younger whites slowly, but surely, are getting closer to lilting bouncy Bollywood music and folk dance, like Bhangra, and have developed taste for Indian foods like samosas and Tandoori chicken and other cuisine. Indian students doing well in studies invite both their admiration and envy. The Eastern and Western youth seen mixing freely at university level is a welcome sign. Needless to mention, India's yoga has already been accepted widely by North America that is likely to narrow down the gap between two cultures in the long run. It is clear that none would like to say goodbye to one's culture, yet people of all colors, shades and races, including the first nation, together could make Canada look like a bouquet made up of colorful flowers. Let Canada be like a comfy global village full of its diverse tolerant population living here in peace.

Hip-Hop: Voice of Social Change: Deejay Ra[140]

By Asma Amanat

Have you been watching mainstream TV channels? Lately there have been quite a few talented South Asians making it into the mainstream media industry. Of these, two young names are Raoul Juneja, a.k.a. Deejay Ra, and Dilshad Burman. Hosted by Dilshad Burman, V-MIX is a weekly, half-hour program that explores the world of urban arts and entertainment. Profiling recording and performing artists from the South Asian community in Canada and internationally, the series will feature music videos, interviews, music commentators, DJs, writers, stage artists, comedians, and choreographers. Prominent Toronto-based producer Deejay Ra is on the show every week, bringing viewers the latest music news updates. Generation Next got up close with these two young talents from the South Asian community to know about them in depth. The interview with them reveals not only their personalities but also how they see life and issues surrounding South Asian community:

Please tell us a bit about your academic/family background?
My Dad's side of the family comes from a business background, whereas my Mom's side has a military and education background. So growing up I was able to see my Dad's family very active in New York's financial sector. I also was able to see the history of my Mom's family in India's military sector, along with their family now running schools in India. A love for the arts and a dedication to charity work was the common ground, so my studying Media at Western as well as being active in the Canadian charitable world seems like a combination of these backgrounds!

Why showbiz?
I never got into Media thinking of it as showbiz, the typical American celebrity TV show was never of interest to me. My Media background started out in hip-hop which I always thought of as a voice for social change, as the art form originally was. Moving more towards the South Asian music scene and then my eventually being able to bring both worlds together through V-MIX has always seemed like more of a cultural commitment, to bring great multicultural music (and arts in general) to the forefront.

Have you gone through the periods we hear in interviews of celebrities like Amitabh that in the beginning no one was willing to give work but they persisted and are legends now?
I think artists have to deal with a lot more rejection than Media personalities do, when it comes to Media personalities I think I've learned it's more about putting your time in and not limiting yourself. When I was researching universities to attend, I wanted to make sure I could host a college radio show wherever I chose. The universities in Toronto had waiting lists of over 1000 people to host shows on their college radio stations, so I chose to go to Western where I was offered my own show the moment I contacted them. I've still had to do many different Media related jobs over the past ten years to get to where I am today, but I'm really happy to see many of my other TV colleagues who put similar time in also reaping the benefits.

What's your family's reaction to your profession choice?
My family was always very supportive but when I started out, I was one of the only prominent South Asian Canadians in the global hip-hop

scene, so I think they knew it would be difficult for me to make my mark doing something that hadn't been done before.

Is it a profession where you can make money?
I feel the Media and Arts professions are ones where you make very little money starting out, but if you're lucky enough to get the right opportunities, you can make a lot of money doing what you love. We've seen that in the success of colleagues of mine like Russell Peters and Panjabi MC, whom I knew when they were only starting to make their mark on the world.

Is there a fair representation of visible minorities in channels like City TV, OMNI etc.?
Canadian channels like Citytv and OMNI Television have a fantastic representation of visible minorities both with content and staff—even fifteen years ago when I moved back to Toronto from New York, I grew up watching their talent like Monika Deol and Karen Johnson who were very inspirational and groundbreaking for those times. In addition to our focus of South Asian artists on VMIX, we love to highlight partnership between visible minority artists of all cultures. Plus there's amazing diversity even among the South Asian talent we see on our Citytv and OMNI channels today, representing all aspects of the South Asian diaspora!

What in your opinions are issues of young South Asian professionals?
I notice young South Asian professionals who were born and raised in Canada like myself are constantly striving to find a balance between their Canadian and South Asian cultures, but it's very possible if you're authentic to yourself.

Which are popular clubs for South Asian youth to visit?
I never was a club DJ, I always stuck to DJ'ing on the radio so I would only visit clubs when Canadian hip-hop artists I wanted to see were performing. I feel most South Asian youth in Canada are listening to the same music the average Canadian youth is listening to, so they are normally attending the same popular clubs as everyone else.

In spite of growing number of South Asian artists, very very few have really made a mark. What's the reason in your opinion?
The "contemporary" South Asian music scene as I call it is still a brand new industry especially in North America, before V-MIX we didn't even have a dedicated TV show in North America supporting contemporary

South Asian music. Apache Indian in the 1990s was really the first South Asian urban music artist to make a mark globally, and now in the 2000s we've seen M.I.A. and Jay Sean achieve huge international successes. The common denominator with all of these artists is they are all from the UK, where they have had outlets like the BBC Asian Network for over a decade. We believe that V-MIX is one of the first big steps to seeing more South Asian artists make a mark like they deserve to.

Do you feel generation gap between your parents and your generation?
I feel there is always a generation gap but artists like Raghav have helped bridge the gap between our generation and our parents' generation, doing music for today's youth but incorporating classic Indian songs into their mixes, so both kids and parents can enjoy together. We saw the same with Abhishek Bachan rapping in "Bluffmaster" which helped a lot of parents understand better what hip-hop music was all about.

Where do you see yourself in ten years?
Ten years ago I was getting my start in the industry in a big way, interviewing celebrities like Russell Peters on the radio and artists like Panjabi MC on television. I feel it's a blessing I'm doing the same thing now ten years later, helping promote a whole new generation of artists while also paying tribute to those who helped pave the way for the hip-hop and South Asian music scenes we have today. I would be happy if ten years from now I'm still involved in the TV industry in any capacity, whether in Canada or internationally.

When New Immigrants Succeed, All of Canada Wins[141]

By Asma Amanat

Murali Murthy is the author of the bestselling *The ACE Principle—15 Success Principles to Absorb, Comprehend and Excel in Every Area of Life*. A creative director and advertising strategist, Murali Murthy holds a master's in communications and has held senior positions at various agencies including JWT, TMP, Bozell, and Bates in diverse markets across North America, Europe, and Asia. He has also developed and directed award-winning sites and interactive projects for Rogers, Scotiabank, TD Canada Trust, and RIM, to name a few. Murali also volunteers his time with CAMP (Communications, Advertising, Marketing Professionals), one of Canada's first voluntary organizations for the marketing fraternity. As the chairperson, he helps new Canadians integrate into the job market sooner by providing industry-tested tools, resources, and mentorship. In a conversation with Generation Next, he talks about his role as a mentor and his passion for guiding people to success.

When did you come to Canada?
My wife and I arrived in Canada in April 2002. It has been an eventful journey of a decade. I came to Canada from Dubai and though I had a good job there, like all immigrants of course, I made the move to come to Canada for better future prospects for me and my family. I now live my wife and two sons in Markham, Ontario.

Tell us something about your journey to being a mentor and coach in Canada?
I am passionate about helping the people I work with, take great pride in my service and am very diligent about my commitment to deliver extraordinary results. I coach clients in the areas of personal high performance, team development, coaching and leadership. I help my clients achieve this through effective private consultations and one-on-one mentoring for individuals, entrepreneurs, organization heads and business leaders. My teachings are always based on the proven ACE Principles, show everyone how they can do more and be more. It was a smooth ride—as I was anyway helping new immigrants integrate into society each month through the CAMP sessions—so a lot of rich experience was gained in the process.

As a mentor and coach, what qualities do you wish in your subjects?
The first thing I look for is acceptance. The ability to accept that they may not know everything—they may have been high achievers back home but in a new country there may be things they need to learn and adapt. Humility—the willingness to learn, to change, to adapt and to work. And yes, an attitude of gratitude. Effective mentoring is an engaging process that requires patience and perseverance to change deeply held belief and introduce new habits and new ways of thinking. That's why when clients and immigrants adhere to the above traits, then my mentees dramatically increase their professional credentials and go on to accomplish career and personal goals.

What advice would you give to new immigrants who face a tough time getting recognized in a foreign country?
Times are tough but we are tougher. Never forget that back home wherever you come from, you were among the cream. Average people don't

make it to Canada. You had to score a high 67 points—that was possible because you were excelling in your job and community. Never let go of that winning feeling. It's a matter of time before you understand the country, understand what it takes to succeed and then win.

Isn't there enough proof—that for every immigrant not succeeding, there's also someone who is succeeding at the same time. Why don't we look to the successful people for inspiration—so many immigrants continue to succeed, all you need is to look to them for inspiration, learn from them and excel. Absorb their success habits, comprehend and excel. Remember, our lives are the result of what we observe, how we interpret and how we apply that information each moment.

I call it **The ACE Principle**™. Learn how to *Absorb, Comprehend* and *Excel* in every field that you choose. Success is all around you. **Absorb. Comprehend. Excel . . . ACE your life!**

Based on my experiences with new immigrants, I was able to write an entire book. *The ACE Principle* book is precisely about that. You can learn more at www.poweroface.com.

What has been the response to your book *The Ace Principle* from the community?

Tremendous—people from all sectors, from all walks of life are buying it and reading it because there's something for everyone. The chapters have been designed in an easy to read format, so any and everyone even if they read just one chapter or one section, they will get the message.

Some people face a "subtle discrimination" in the job market too.

I understand there is a "situation." But instead of lamenting about the "situation" why don't we strive to find a "solution." At the end of the day, I can have reasons or I can have results.

To rephrase the Scotiabank tagline—You are much more powerful thank you think. When I landed in the country, I studied the successful immigrants and I found there was a pattern to their success. I studied the unsuccessful ones and I found that there was a pattern there too. I decided to follow the successful ones. The fact is, high achievers think, talk, behave and act differently than other people. And what separates them from unsuccessful people can be attributed to fundamental characteristics that are illuminated in their successes—over and over again. To quote, Steve Jobs: We are here to make a ding in this universe. Or another quote comes to mind, Mahatma Gandhi's—Your life is your message. Everyone's life is a message. The question is—is yours worth emulating?

How was the idea of CAMP conceptualized?

In 2005, a group of 12 immigrant professionals founded CAMP a networking organization of internationally trained communications, advertising, and marketing professionals. Based in the Toronto Region CAMP became Canada's first networking organization for newcomers in these fields, established on the principle of immigrants helping immigrants. Over the years, CAMP has assisted over 1000 members in meeting their career objectives through networking events, educational forums and professional development opportunities. Now independent, CAMP is diligent about organizing monthly meetings with industry speakers, allowing members a chance to meet and hear from those established in their fields in Canada.

What is your vision for the future?

I believe that the purpose of life is life with a purpose. The CAMP website proudly says: "Integrate. Inspire. Innovate." I believe when new Canadians succeed, all of Canada wins. Our common dream is for Canada's continued development and growth, where international skills and talent is recognized and productively utilized. We celebrate members' successes by getting them to share their winning strategies that helped them get the breakthrough they were seeking. At the end of the day, talk is cheap. I could talk all day but if I don't show results through CAMP no one would take us seriously. I am proud to say, we consistently deliver results; we are proud of helping new Canadians find jobs in their fields and hold their dignity intact.

Undeterred by Challenges[142]

By Asma Amanat

Bahi Krishnakhanthan is an enthusiastic motivation speaker, facilitator, and psychotherapist. Her transpersonal and transformational approach to therapeutic counselling and a client-centred therapy helps people deal with issues that prevent them from living a fulfilled life.

Bahi has been awarded the 2008 Caring Canadian Award by the governor-general of Canada, and the 2005 Woman of Distinction in the region of Durham among several high-calibre women. She was also presented the 2006 National Leadership Award from Canadian Federation for Business and Professional Women for her exemplary leadership of improving the economic, political, employment, and social conditions for women. Bahi's compassion and upbeat attitude make her a great role model for many. In a conversation with Generation Next, she takes us through the several challenges she faced in Canada such as cultural, language, gender, and as a single parent, and the success story that she is today.

When did you come to Canada?

I came to Canada in 1982 from Sri Lanka. I left Sri Lanka for better economic conditions and further my accounting career. I was surprised when I was selected by the Canadian government on "Merit Point system" and was issued "Landed Status" visa to come here.

You've been a single parent and a victim of domestic abuse. Tell us about your journey to being a motivation speaker, facilitator and psychotherapist today.

I met someone here in Canada and got married within three years of being here. I came to Canada on "Merit Point System" all alone from Sri Lanka in 1982. My marriage lasted for 2 short years. In the first year, I had a baby daughter and she died. In the second year, I had my infant son and fled from my own home because of domestic abuse for our safety.

It was difficult being a single parent without any family here. Having to support my infant all alone without any financial or other help was challenging. I returned to work within 3 weeks of delivering my infant son (after Caesarian surgery) to support us. During tough times, I was promoted in my accounting job to financial controller, became self sufficient and bought my own home, etc. I also met two missionary families who gave spiritual support and stood by me through the challenging times. It was Grace (unmerited favor of the Universe) working in my life like everyone else. Somehow it appeared that the challenges seemed to continue. One winter snow storm day, I met with a life threatening car accident and lost my health. Though it took many years of rehabilitation therapy, my return to job with Canada Revenue Agency as a Corporate Tax Auditor was unsuccessful and I lost my job. I felt a great loss once again.

My spiritual quest gave me much strength, a new direction and aliveness. I went to school and became a Spiritual Psychotherapist. I joined international speaking organization and was honored as Public Speaking Champion within short period because of my story. I also enjoyed taking volunteer leadership with non-profit organizations and it led me to receiving Governor General's award, Woman of Distinction Award, National Leadership Award—for improving economic, employment, social and political conditions of women, etc. In fact, when I surrendered to the Universe—Life Force, my life took on a new direction and propelled me.

Tell us something about your initial days in Canada as a new immigrant. How did you sail through?

I faced cultural, language, social, gender and other barriers as a new immigrant. Winter weather was also challenging in Edmonton, Alberta. However, my dreams were bigger than the barriers that I faced, which helped me to sail through. I found mentors who helped me find success. I took risks to leave my City job in Edmonton to take a job in Ontario and moved. I found ways to integrate into the community. I joined recreational organizations and participated in new recreational activities; joined non-profit organizations and volunteered in the community. I took evening and weekend courses to get my Canadian accreditation here.

What advice would you give to newcomers who face a tough time getting their degrees recognized and eventually getting their dream jobs? What are the qualities they should possess?

It is important to stay focused in what they want. If their dreams are bigger than the barriers they are likely to succeed. Finding mentors can be helpful. Talk to other immigrants who have gone through tough times. In fact, I had additional challenges being a single parent, coming out of a bad marriage, living in fear, living alone, health challenges, etc. It is important for us to stay connected to our Higher Self (divine) through this process. We will get directions, comfort, meet right people, engage in right activities, be protected, etc.

Do you think the Canadian policies towards immigrants especially foreign trained professionals are fair?

Some leave their country by choice and others leave out of necessity due to major disasters in their homeland. It takes time and patience to settle in a new country. This could be frustrating to some foreign trained professionals based on their profession. In most professions, the regulating body gives some exemptions to foreign trained professionals resulting in fewer courses to take. This was my personal experience.

How do you deal with immigrants who are frustrated when they are unable to find a foothold in Canada?

Several cultural, immigrants, religious and other organizations did invite me to speak at their events. Schools and colleges also did invite me to speak at their special or regular events. I have shared my personal experiences, struggles, triumphs, etc. It's through listening to their frustrations, strategizing their priorities with time lines, connecting with relevant organizations and groups, finding their core problems, reconnecting with their self, finding ways to nurture them through this difficult times, etc.

What in your opinion are the key needs of new immigrants today, and how do you think they can be addressed?

I find the key issues are culture shock, language and social barriers and finding the right job. The new immigrants need to find the right support system through their cultural, social and other organizations to integrate into the community and finding hope in the Canadian system.

My Works Critically Examine My Environment[143]

Posted by Administration, South Asian Generation Next

Tazeen Qayyum is a contemporary miniature painter who received her BFA in Visual Arts from the National College of Arts Lahore, Pakistan in 1996. A contemporary visual artist based in Oakville, Canada, her work has been shown internationally in both solo and group exhibitions and has received several critical reviews in media. Along with paintings, Tazeen has created gripping performance-based works, "artist books" and site specific installations. Tazeen moved to Canada in early 2003 with her husband. "It seems that the real reasons for our move keep unfolding with every new achievement in life, but back then the motivation was to explore the world, learn new things and further our education," she says.

In Tazeen's opinion, her work is a comment on "aggressive global politics and the subsequent suppression of difference." As a practicing Canadian artist of Pakistani origin, she believes in creating thought-provoking works and critically examines her lived environment. "In my paintings, an image of a cockroach appears repeatedly to simultaneously attract and repulse; commenting on human rights violations and fatalities as a result of war. A dead cockroach appeared in my work back in 2002 when the US and its allies launched the war on terror full force, when people are killed like insects, we question our own insensitivity and the diminishing value of human life. Since then my work and narrative developed as we witnessed how the war progressed and its consequent effects. I borrow the language of entomology, and reference insect museum displays, to explore how categories and classifications parallel the agendas of political propaganda."

As a woman artist, Tazeen believes the Canadian arts industry is quite competitive for all artists irrespective of gender. She still does not consider herself "established" within the mainstream arts here. "As a practicing professional artist, for over 15 years now, I have somewhat established myself within the South Asian contemporary arts globally, and to some extent a small niche within Canada, but I still have a long way to go," she points out.

Tazeen has participated in numerous International group shows, one of which is "A Thousand and One Days: The Art of Pakistani Women Miniaturists"—a large scale group exhibition curated by three international curators; Salima Hashmi, Duccio K. Marignoli and Enrico Mascelloni in 2005. The show was showcased at the Honolulu Academy of Arts, Hawaii and Musee des Beaux, Rouen, France. The exhibition and the accompanying publication focused on contemporary women artists of Pakistan who were making noticeable contributions towards the development of contemporary expressions within the country against all odds.

Art is a major form of investment. Tazeen's work too has been featured at Christie's and the Sotheby's South Asian Modern and Contemporary Art auction in New York. "I personally disapprove of the current trends and the impact of auction houses on South Asian arts and artists," says Tazeen, "I do not believe that art auctions and the sale of one's work are true representation of the quality of work nor a true measure of art appreciation. At the same time auctions do not have a positive impact on the artistic growth of young and mid-career artists." She adds that the auction houses should focus on senior artists with established careers spanning over several decades. "What we are seeing is a trend to sell and resell new works of young artists at misleading prices, which is damaging the artists' career and the credibility of the auction."

Tazeen feels Canada offers a wonderful support system for the arts through its many grants in the arts and other opportunities. She tells us that compared to South Asian countries where it is fairly tough to grow your work without limitations and patronage, the artists have far better opportunities here to grow their work conceptually, upgrade their skills, take on new projects, access information and new materials. One thing that the South Asian artists should understand though is that the ways to excel here are different, and "it is important for them to first get an understanding of the processes here." Several artists of South Asian background are doing wonderful work here, "one should always focus and concentrate on continuously improving and developing the quality of the work, success will follow naturally," Tazeen advises.

In the past two years Tazeen was able to undertake a number of projects that stretched the boundaries of her art practice. Along with painting, she created new works in sculpture, installation, performance and most recently created 12, one-of-a-kind, "Artists' Books." She envisions keeping experimenting and growing her work both "conceptually, critically and esthetically." "I would like to believe that my work is well respected within the community and the number of exhibition opportunities I get offered reflects the feedback," she signs off.

Avish Sood: Looking at Marketing and Sports[144]

By Asma Amanat

As South Asian community grows in Canada, it hides within itself very talented gems. These gems are its second generation. Passionate about their choices, these young men and women are integrated into the Canadian fabric and making a mark in the Canadian landscape through their hard work and perseverance.

One such example is Avish Sood. Avish has a unique career choice, but a choice he is absolutely dedicated to. With bachelor of commerce from University of Toronto's Rotman School of Business, a postgraduate degree in sport and event marketing from George Brown College, and education from Darden School of Business from University of Virginia in Foundations of Business Strategy, Avish has worked in sports marketing for the last few years. Avish is a sponsorship sales coordinator for Toronto Pan American Games. He was corporate partnerships and business development intern for Toronto Blue Jays, sponsorship director for Canada Cup Floorball Championships, account manager at Alkaso International, and junior accountant at Rogers Sportsnet. He was also president and cofounder and board of directors of University of Toronto Sports and Business.

Here is Generation Next's interview with this very talented young man:

Tell us a little about your family background.

I've grown up in a pretty traditional family with two older sisters helping pave the way for my growth. My parents, originally from India, are two of the most hard-working people I will ever meet and they have set the standard in terms of how each of us strives to be. Our family continues to remain close and no matter how busy we are, we will always find some time to catch up and enjoy each other's company.

Are you more passionate about marketing or sports?

I've grown up always wanting to play in the NBA but when I realized that wasn't an option, I knew I needed another way to be involved with the sport that I love. My passion for marketing is foremost, but being in such an exciting industry certainly plays a role into how I approach work each day. As my career continues to grow, my love for both marketing and sports will play a key role in my success.

With digital media continuously changing sales in today's world is a tough field to be in. Do you agree or has its nature changed?

Social media has taken the world by storm, and as such there are countless opportunities for business development and relationship building. With information available at your fingertips, it's much easier to find the decision-makers of an organization and reach out. Although technology has created a more competitive landscape, each sales person has an incredible platform to allow them to learn about their best prospects and build foundational relationships with them. Despite all of these recent changes, sales continues to be based on providing value and being genuine. If you do those two things, you will be successful.

Do you believe the South Asian community will be passionate about events like the Pan Am games especially given the fact that new immigrants are shaping much of the GTA now?

Multi-sport games always attract a wide-ranging and diverse audience. With such a cultural host city in Toronto, the Pan Am/Parapan Am Games have an incredible opportunity to bring people together of all different backgrounds as unified Canadians, including South Asians. I am very excited to play a role in the event, as 2015 will truly be a remarkable year for the province of Ontario.

Is the attitude toward sports different in your generation from your parents' generation?

Older generations didn't have as much free time and they truly had a different set of priorities compared to us. With so many different ways to be involved through fantasy, broadcast and social media, our generation has really built a closer relationship with sports that can't be compared to others.

How popular do you think are sports like ice hockey in your generation in the South Asian community?

Despite being integral to the Canadian culture, hockey is a very expensive sport to be involved in. I've seen many South Asian kids get involved in basketball and soccer because they didn't have the financial resources to purchase all the associated equipment for hockey. Despite this, players like Nazem Kadri and Manny Malhotra have been great ambassadors for hockey's multi-culturalism and have helped spark a new generation of hockey players. You can count on more South Asian youth getting involved in the sport in the near future!

Tell us about the University of Toronto Sports Industry Conference.

The conference was created by Natan Levi, Adrian Kania and me three years ago. Our goal at the time was to provide opportunities for students interested in a career in sports business. Despite being one of the most prestigious schools in the world, the University of Toronto didn't have any opportunities for students passionate about following this career path. Fast forward a few years later, and the event has become Canada's largest student-run sports conference. The event attracts students from all over North America, and has hosted some of the most esteemed professionals in the business. This year's conference president Malcolm Mo has been doing an incredible job leading the event, while bringing on some incredible speakers for the event in March. Our goal was to really "Turn Dreams into Careers," and I think that we are all living proof that if you want something bad enough, you can achieve it.

Whom do you consider your mentor, a key influence on your personal and professional life?

As entrepreneurs, my parents are my biggest influence as I have seen their hard-work and persistence first-hand each day that they lived in this country. After I told my mom I wanted to quit my stable accounting job and pursue a sports marketing career, she fully believed in my vision with no questions asked. Not many Indian parents would have done that, but mine truly believed that I was capable of anything as long as I was passionate. The traditional roots my parents have set for me that revolve around being humble, dedicated and loyal will always be instilled in both my personal and professional life.

What are some of the challenges that South Asian youth such as you face, and how can they overcome them?

You will face challenges each day of your life, but the key is to not let this prevent you from moving forward with your career and personal development. There are so many resources that can help you establish yourself professionally but it's up to you to take advantage of them. One of the biggest challenges that will come up throughout your life is distraction. It's incredibly easy to postpone your work and get involved with the wrong types of people, so you can't lose sight of your end goal. As lame as it sounds, write down your goals, place them somewhere visible and make sure you take active steps to achieve them. To quote Ashton Kutcher, "Opportunity looks a lot like hard work"—don't let any job be beneath you since it might just be a stepping stone to help you land that coveted dream job. Make sure you are taking active steps to following your dream, even if it doesn't always seem like the path will lead anywhere.

Mina Khtaria: Looking to Lead by Example[145]

By Sabrina Almeida

Meet Mina Khtaria, a national finalist for the 2014 Miss Universe Canada Pageant, who hopes to inspire South Asian girls to follow their dream wherever they may lead. She will represent British Columbia at the pageant in Toronto, where she will be competing with over fifty delegates from across the country for the title. Born and raised in the small town of Port Alberni, British Columbia, Mina is the youngest daughter of immigrant parents. As a first-generation Indo-Canadian, "family and heritage" have always been important to her.

Here are excerpts of the interview.

What inspired you to take part in the competition?

I've been doing pageants for a few years now. I've always been modelling and performing and being in front of a crowd so I just wanted to keep going with it. I've participated in Miss BC, Miss India-Canada before and currently I have the title of Miss Asia-Pacific 2013 for Canada.

Are you a student?

Yes, I am pursuing a Bachelor of Arts Degree in Sociology at the Kwantlen Polytechnic University. I'm also a CFL cheerleader for the BC Lions. Other than that I've just been focussing on this pageant and doing all the prep work.

What do you like to do?

I'm really into health and fitness so I love working out. I love going outdoors and hiking or doing any physical activity such as running, swimming, outdoor yoga, etc. I also like spending time with my friends and family.

What is your career path?

I would want to end up doing something that I would really love. I love modelling right now and doing pageants but with that I want to inspire girls especially of the South Asian community to follow their dreams. I find that in our community there are a lot of cultural boundaries so I want to encourage those girls to go after what they really want instead of falling into cultural pressures and doing something that they don't love.

What are these cultural boundaries you are referring to?

I am referring to family tradition or not having support of the family when they want to do something that they are passionate about. I'm a cheerleader, a model . . . I've been to Mumbai to model . . . I travel a lot, all around the world. I find that a lot of girls are always asking me, "how can you just get up and do that" because they don't have the support from their family. We need the community to realise that when you doing something that you *love* and are passionate about it really makes you happy and that's when you are *going* to have success in your life.

Would you agree to an arranged marriage?

I personally would not. I'm born and raised in Canada so I'm Indo-Canadian. My Indian roots are my culture which I *love* and adore but at the same time I'm Canadian. That (arranged marriage) is an Indian tradition . . . since I'm Canadian it is not for me.

What would you like people to know about you?

I'm outgoing and energetic. I love travelling around the world and meeting people and learning about their cultures. It is something that I hope to do for many, many years. I like working with *people* on one-on-one basis.

What draws you to people?

I just *love* that there are six billion people on this earth and every single person is different. So when you meet someone it is always going to be a different experience. I just love that.

Mina's desire to connect with other cultures and help people led her to western Africa where she taught English and volunteered in an orphanage for six months. She has also hosted a South Asian television talk show and contributed to the health and food columns for an ethnic magazine.

Mina recognizes that the opportunities available to young women in Canada are unique in the world and wants to lead by example to promote a positive self-image and the value of a healthy lifestyle. She views life with no limits and wants to share her unique perspective with others. She wishes that "young women will regain their confidence and have the passion to follow their dreams" wherever they lead.

Set Career Goals[146]

By Nadia Chowdhury

At a very young age, many individuals dream of incorporating their passion, goals, and beliefs into a viable career. Just like these individuals, Abira Rajalingam's journey and interest in becoming a public servant started at the tender age of four, when she first arrived in Canada. Abira fondly remembers the kindness and thoughtfulness that Canadian officials showed her and her family in terms of thoroughly explaining the immigration process to them and assisting them in settling into this new country by providing them with multiple programs and services. That is why Abira is committed to give back—especially in the area of immigration, citizenship, and public administration.

Abira Rajalingam shared her thoughts with Generation Next's Nadia Chowdhury:

Please tell us a bit about yourself.

I completed my Bachelor of Arts degree from York University and majored in Political Science and minored in History. Currently, I am pursuing my Master's degree in Public services, while working at the Region of Peel as an Assistant Technical Analyst, researching, planning, promoting and educating citizens in the Region of Peel about Public Works program such as water and wastewater treatment and water efficiency. I have also been involved in several extracurricular activities such as volunteering as a Teaching Assistant and Activity Coordinator at a local public school, where I developed and implemented new social programs for children, led community projects, monitored budgets, conducted community information sessions, while preparing classroom displays and bulletins.

How has the field of public policy and administration changed over the years, in your opinion?

The internet and social media is increasingly utilized as a tool for public educational and awareness purposes. Several federal agencies in Canada utilize Facebook and Twitter to improve service delivery and distribute information about services and programs to Canadians. For instance, Human Resources and Skills Development Canada (HRSDC) utilized Twitter to inform and educate immigrants about upcoming employment opportunities. This method of communication is beneficial for two reasons. The first being cost effective and the second being efficient service.

The Public policy and administration field has become more "citizen focused"; the Canadian federal government has put forth more effort in consulting and collaborating with citizens and delivers services through their preferred method of choice. There is effective partnership between governmental departments and private enterprise to implement and carry out effective services to Canadian citizens at a lower cost to the Canadian government through PPP (triple P).

As a woman of color in Canada, how do you find accessing employment and work in the public service field? How involved and accessible is this field to young people of color in today's Canada?

Since 2001 the accessibility of employment opportunities for women of colour within the public service field has definitely become much easier. The Canadian Human Rights Commission in contrast conducts compliance audits of federal departments, crown corporations and businesses regulated by the federal government. With these regulations in place, we can definitely see that accessibility of employment opportunities for young people of colour especially women has gotten better and easier over the past few decades and would continue to get better.

What advice do you have for those aspiring to study policy and administration in the future?

The first thing that I would advise students to do is to set career goals and objectives by doing a lot of research. Public policy is a broad field and students would not necessarily be able to learn everything about the field. By choosing a specialization in one specific area of the field, they would become expects on that subject matter, enhancing Canada's policies and meeting the needs of Canadians. Students should also look into the degree and specialization programs that are offered by post secondary institutions along with internship and co-op opportunities. Co-op opportunities are beneficial for two reasons. The first reason being that it gives students an opportunity to get an idea of the nature of work they would be performing in the near future. The second reason being experience, employers in most instances hire individuals based on experience and through co-op opportunities students are able to gain the experience required and many other skills sets that are essential for public servants.

I would also strongly encourage students to volunteer with different organizations and NGOs. The experience they gain from this is valuable as they will be serving the public, while getting a better understanding of public service and the nature of work that the public servants perform on a daily basis.

The MomShift: Providing Real-Life Relatable Success Stories for Postbaby Career[147]

By Asma Amanat

Reva Seth continues her journey to provide hope and inspiration to young mothers who want to go back to work, citing examples of real-life mothers who have achieved success. A lawyer who turned her back to a career at Bay Street is now the mother of three boys, an author, a journalist, and an entrepreneur. In her second book called *The MomShift*, Reva looks to provide everyday women with examples of moms who have taken up careers after being mothers, and are successful at that. She believes that success stories of women such as Marissa Meyers or Sheryl Sandberg are inspirational but not something many moms relate to. Therefore, in her book *The MomShift*, she has interviewed more than five hundred women who have been successful in postbaby career and can be a great source for millions more to create their own postbaby career success stories. She is also the founder of the MomShift, an online and media campaign showcasing and sharing the stories of women from a variety of professional and personal backgrounds who all achieved greater career success after starting their families and counter to the usual story we hear.

Generation Next got an opportunity to interview Reva Seth. Here it is for our readers:

How difficult and frustrating was it for you to transition from a career in law to public relations and corporate communications?

I started my career as a Bay Street lawyer and I left it long before I had children—instead, I made the decision based on the realization that while I had enjoyed law school, the practice of law was completely different and not actually the right personality fit. In some ways it was easy decision since I knew I would probably only ever be an average lawyer and certainly not a happy one. But it was also incredibly difficult to leave an established and clear career that was well paying and that I had spent years investing in— the transition wasn't easy at all, since I personally kept comparing myself to what my friends in law were earning or doing—and feeling like I was getting left behind—even though I was the one who had decided I didn't want to do what they were doing.

When I'm speaking on this topic, I often use that period in my life as an example of how we need to stop ourselves from this kind of thinking and instead, really appreciate that we are all on our own individual journeys, and that there is no timeline or right way to proceed—it's all about finding what works for our own goals, personalities and ambitions and not letting others—whether it's friends, family or the cover of a business magazine define what "success" looks like for us.

How did you work your way up?
One of the lessons in the book is the idea of working smarter and more strategically—I didn't work my way up—after a year at the bottom of the PR rungs, I was told that even though I could clearly do more, the policy was that you had to spend a certain amount of time in each role before you could be promoted. After my son was born, on the advice of one of my then bosses, I left the agency and returned to work with them as a consultant and not an employee—this meant I could take much bigger roles and projects immediately (freed from the artificial promotions path) and as well, also consult to other clients. It was a great piece of advice and the start of my successful consulting practice.

How do you cope when there is a mistake or something doesn't quite go your way?
I try not to dwell on it and instead move on to the next thing—I mean you know mistakes and professional rejection are going to happen since that's just part of the process. I mean I probably should focus more on what I can learn from each experience but really, I just tend to think about what the next move I can make.

Do you think any of what you have accomplished so far can be done without a supportive spouse?
I think I'm very lucky in that I have a supportive partner with my husband Rana. However, in the book I look at how a supportive spouse is an incredible asset when it comes to career success and kids but I also deliberately look at successful women who either didn't have a supportive spouse or who are single parents whether by choice, or as a result of divorce.

From having the first baby to the third, how have you evolved? Have your expectations from yourself changed?
It's a cliche to say it but still its true—that for me having kids has made me a better person—I talk about it in the book how I personally didn't fully grow up until I became a mother and how I had this idea that adult life was always something that would happen later. Rana and I have had three boys in 7 years, so by the third, everything is much lower key.

Have you challenged some of your own notions that my kids will never do this and they start doing exactly what you don't want them to do (especially in public?)

To be honest I don't think I had many notions about what my kids will never do—mostly because I was a pretty difficult child at all stages, so I had low expectations based on my own behaviour! I think the most important point on this is that all parents need to give other parents a break—we are all trying our best and if you see someone's kid totally acting out at the mall or on the subway, before you judge them, keep in mind that you have no idea what challenges that family might be facing or what has happened before that point.

Do you think mothers get to do 8 hour work in 5 hours?

Certainly many of the mothers I interviewed referenced how they worked more efficiently after becoming parents.

Have you been disappointed by the quality of say family literacy centres and other such projects initiated by the government to help young families?

The biggest disappointed is the consistent frustration on our inability to find better solutions to the challenges of finding affordable, accessible and quality child care solutions.

Do you think there is enough support for stay-at-home moms from the governments and corporations once they decide to get back to work?

I think it is certainly starting to improve since governments and organizations of all sizes are starting to realize that stay at home moms looking to transition back to the workplace are an under leveraged talent pool—one of the goals of my book *The MomShift* is provide women with a range of choices and options on the different ways that they can do this by sharing the stories of how other women from a diverse range of personal and professional backgrounds have successfully transitioned back to the workplace.

Women who have careers like law etc. can get back to work after a few years, admittedly with quite some difficulty, but then there are women who are bachelors only, do you think workplaces take them and then pay them what they deserve?

I think it very much depends on the individual situation—what *The MomShift* does show women, is that regardless of what their educational background might be—they do have more choices than they think—and the book shows them examples of how volunteer work, entrepreneurship or consulting work can all be ways to help them overcome the challenges they might face when they are transitioning back to the workforce.

There are enough young women out there who will tell you that successful career first, family later. Do you think the approach is wrong and actually successful career, marriage and motherhood can complement each other?

I regularly have the opportunity to speak with younger women who aren't yet mothers but who are thinking about this issue—and the most common question I am asked is when is the right time to have a baby. For my book, I spoke with over 500 women who all achieved greater career success after children—and the good news is that there really is no right way or time to have a baby. Women today have more choices than ever when it comes to how they create the families they want and the careers they want—and what *The MomShift* does is show you stories of what that can look like—so the reader can find ideas that they can use in their own lives. And yes, I do think motherhood can certainly complement a career—so many women I interviewed told how becoming a mother helped their careers—and my own story is just one example of that—where I started my first successful business and sold my first book only after I became a parent—even though they were goals that I had had for some time.

In the world we live in, do you believe that both parents can work traditional 9–5 jobs and still raise kids especially when there are vaccination appointments, baseball games to take kids to, school calling because one of your kids is sick and needs to stay home for a few days?

The book provides many examples of the different ways that yes, this is possible and certainly doable since this is what the majority of Canadian families currently are doing (70% of Canadian mothers are working mothers)—but *The MomShift* also shows the importance and advantages of both individuals and companies re-imagining how a work day and career should look. I am a strong advocate of increased flexibility for everyone—not just parents. Given the technology choices we have, the strain and delays of commuting, all of us should start to expand our views on what the traditional "work day" should look like. I also believe there are structural and systems changes that we can make that start to better reflect the reality that fewer families are structured in a way that has one person at home—the school day is just one example of this.

Do you get an impression that workplaces don't understand challenges that new or young mothers face at home, and consequently women's ambitions do become hindrance?

What I hope to address with this book is current cultural framework that sees children and a successful career as always being in conflict—what my research showed is that this is not actually the case—but media overwhelming still focuses on either the challenges women face or extreme examples of career success—Sheryl Sandberg for instance is very inspirational but her story and example are not actually that helpful to the majority of working moms. Research that I reference in my book shows that when women see examples of success that are more relatable and attainable it increases their own personal ambition.

Don't women feel guilty about having ambitions to grow in their career and then not being able to be mothers who get to spend a lot of time with their kids, watching them grow and seeing their firsts?

Working mom guilt is a very real issue and so is working Dad guilt—I think it is just part of being a parent to feel like maybe you should be doing something differently or something more. Ultimately, career ambition, family life, what your children might need from you and how you define what being a good parent looks like—these are very individual questions that we all need to answer for ourselves. One of the most important lessons that I have learned from my five years of research and 500+ interviews is that the more successful and happy women I spoke with were that [who] were confident about defining what a successful family and career life looked like for them, at this time and being open to it changing as their ambitions and families evolved.

South Asian Community Issues and What It Must Do[148]

By Asma Amanat

Many times politicians do not acknowledge the unique needs of cultural communities suggesting that they are the same as the broader community. While this may be true for certain issues, the statement is not necessarily reflective of deeper understanding of the needs of the diverse communities. Ontario's health-care providers are now realizing that diverse communities have certain beliefs and values that have an impact on how they access health care. This is a good first step; however, much more needs to be done.

Having South Asian elected officials at federal and provincial level is an asset for the South Asian community; however, these officials can do much more to raise the issues of the largest visible minority—the South Asian community—in their respective legislatures. We asked South Asian elected officials at the federal and Ontario level to reflect upon the positive aspects of the community and to highlight the areas where South Asian community can do better to be part of the Canadian society.

What is interesting about the South Asian community is that while its votes are frequently courted by the politicians, this community often remains neglected. Targeting "very ethnic" ridings is just one example. However, both the federal and the provincial governments make little effort to impart information in this community. While the mainstream media is flooded with advertisements about the health-care system, Foodland Ontario, Human Resource Skills Development Canada, Department of Finance, and so on, the South Asian media is not considered to be worthy of our government's dollars. No wonder South Asian community has very little knowledge about the health-care system, the tax benefits, legal system of Canada, and the benefits offered by the government to its citizens.

While we are "applauded" for taking the government's message back to the community, elected officials of South Asian descent state that the government has to spend resources equally. A survey conducted by Peel Newcomer Strategy Group indicates that the poverty among immigrants is higher, and they earn less when compared to average Canadians. The report also suggests that services in Peel region are not catching up with its development. We must note that many of these ridings are represented by the South Asian elected officials.

We must also emphasize that these South Asian MPs and MPPs are in a position to address many of the issues. To name just the few, these representatives can raise the awareness of Canada's role in Afghanistan, bridge gaps between Canada and the South Asian countries, and address radicalization among our youth. And this needs to be done beyond just paying lip service.

Generation Next contacted all MPs and MPPs of South Asian descent for this story. Many did not respond, but those who responded are presented below:

"With hard work barriers will be broken down."
MP Deepak Obhari (Vancouver South)

The Prime Minister and I will be inaugurating "Year of India." (It has already been inaugurated.) Pakistan is Canada's important ally in our efforts in Afghanistan; we have helped communities' post civil war in Sri Lanka. Bangladesh's foreign Minister was in Canada just a few days ago, and we had productive discussion on mutual interests. To build stronger ties between Canada and these South Asian countries, local communities can act as a bridge. The links of the local communities with the South Asian countries are very valuable to us. I would like to see the South Asian community engaged overall—culturally, economically, and politically businesswise. Their contribution is multi-dimensional.

There is a glass ceiling. As we highlight the disparities, things will change. There is resistance to change. But barriers are broken down every day and more and more people from visible minorities are serving at higher executive positions. When there is democracy people thrive and have the right to do what they choose to do. But people must understand that the laws of the country cannot be broken. If they are broken there will be consequences. Beyond that Canada is a free country where people can do whatever they want to do.

"Second generation is stranded."
MP Navdeep Bains (Brampton South)

Our real success lies in representing more than the South Asian communities. We represent our national interest. The South Asian community has fair amount of political influence. I frequently hear concerns regarding education, child care services, healthcare and infrastructure. Many of the issues are related to the second generation people, that is taking care of their elders and parents, making sure that their kids are doing well. This second generation can act as a bridge to understanding mutual interests, which will lead to the development of stronger sense of belonging and participation. As a community, we must hold our community leaders to a higher standard.

"Let's address operational challenges of places of worship."
MP Gurbax Malhi, (Bramalea-Gore-Malton)

The over 1.3 million Canadians of South Asian descent has made significant contributions to the development and general welfare of Canada. Our South Asian origin community is working hard and giving back to its new country. It includes business people, lawyers, doctors, politicians, and individuals performing in numerous other professions. In every field, Canada has been and continues to be greatly enriched by the contributions of its South Asian background community.

Let us resolve to reinvigorate the dialogue and work together toward more sustainable operational models to address the operational challenges faced by some of our places of worship. Let us not engage in infighting, but collaborate to seize the opportunities that will help us realize a brighter and even more prosperous future for ourselves and for our country. Well known for its ingenuity and ambition, our community has much to offer to Canada and the world.

"Political influence transitioning from ceremonial to substantive."
MPP Dr. Shafiq Qaadri (Etobicoke North)

One of the great benefits of having so many members of the community elected is the signal sent worldwide. The political influence exerted currently is moving steadily from soft and ceremonial to hard and substantive. Of course, different parties move at their own rate, some quite reluctantly.

"Treat the new generation better."
Ontario Minister of Government Services Harinder Takhar (MPP from Mississauga Erindale)

The greatest strength of the South Asian community lies in the importance we place on education. There are many issues which the newcomers face. The newcomers' issues are the recognition of foreign credentials, finding a job and the right resources to help them. The community that has lived here longer holds on to the old customs in the new country. The aging population needs senior centres where other seniors can meet each other. Pension and protection of properties back home is another issue the community faces.

The old and the new generation need to work together. The old generation needs to understand the new generation better and understand that they cannot be treated the way we were treated back in the day forty or fifty years ago.

"Let's work together and stop leg pulling."
Liberal MP Ruby Dhalla (Brampton Springdale)

As the Member of Parliament for one of the most multicultural, multilingual, and multireligious communities in Canada I have seen firsthand the contributions of immigrants, especially those from the South Asian community who have helped build the foundation of our country. In fact, in Canada's Parliament the Punjabi language is the fourth most common spoken language by Parliamentarians. These achievements are a reflection of the dedication, hard work and vision of the South Asian community and serve as a reminder of the many barriers broken, and sacrifices made by those that have come before us. The South Asian community is to be commended for its entrepreneurial spirit, its passion for political participation, and charitable contributions which in my riding of Brampton-Springdale resulted in the Brampton Civic Hospital naming their wards in honour of the followers of the Sikh faith through the establishment of the "Guru Nanak Emergency Services Department." I believe a weakness of the community that needs to be improved is the "leg pulling" that occurs. The entire community needs to make a better effort of working together on common issues and challenges facing the Diaspora.

It will only be by working together that we can work to ensure there is greater representation of the Diaspora in decision making capacities on boards, organizations, and elected office so that issues such as foreign credential recognition is addressed to ensure that professionals immigrating to Canada have their credentials recognized and accredited. In fact, to address this issue one of the first initiatives I undertook when I was elected was to bring forward a private member's motion that called on the government to work in collaboration with all stakeholders to create a separate department for Foreign Credential Recognition. Since this motion was passed in parliament there has been much progress and I hope moving forward there will be more with the cooperation and support of the community.

"Please be on time."
Liberal MP Sukh Dhaliwal (Newton-North Delta)

I believe that the South Asian community is very strong when it comes to the role of the family and the loyalties that bind us all together. Through multi-family households and large extended families, generations are brought together, so that our grandparents and uncles and aunties are all pseudo parents to children and cousins when growing up.

South Asians are also extremely business oriented, and there seems to be an intrinsic inclination towards entrepreneurship and enterprise within the bloodline. Ingenuity breeds the ideas, hard work solidifies success, and South Asians have never shied away from putting effort into their efforts. With this success comes the spirit of generosity, which South Asians tend to offer freely due to an appreciation of their good fortune in Canada, and their understanding of the way many have to struggle in their countries of origin.

Finally, I think that South Asians are very strong when it comes to political activism. For those that have originated from India in particular, the largest democratic system in the world has left a lasting mark when it comes to comprehending the importance of getting involved in the political process.

The only weakness that I can think of off the top of my head is our tardiness when comes to showing up to appointments or scheduled events! In terms of South Asian youth, the most important piece of advice I can offer is that they should follow their interests, and spread their enthusiasm, talents and work ethic as broadly as possible. South Asian young people being involved in a variety of activities, causes and fields is an extremely positive thing.

"South Asian social life's attached to places of worship."
MPP Kuldip Kular (Bramalea-Gore-Malton)

South Asian community brings energy, ambition, determination, drive and passion to Canada. South Asian newcomers understand that in order to succeed they have to struggle. They are industrious people. Sometimes we have issues like divisions in the South Asian community just like any other community. Coming from countries where the government denies its citizens a lot of things, we try to get things done faster.

Many South Asians try to settle down in the areas that we can call ghettos but the South Asian social values are aligned with the mainstream social culture. Being in the government, we cannot just put resources for the South Asian community, we put the funds where they are needed. As South Asians, our main social life is attached to our faith, so we take our challenges and issues to gurdwaras, mandirs and mosques. Sometimes things like corruption charges happen at the places of worship.

"Get involved in broader society."
Conservative MP Tim Uppal, (Edmonton–Sherwood Park)

One of the strengths of the South Asian community is its history in Canada that dates back to one hundred years. South Asian community is well integrated in the society with the focus on building their family and the network. Their hardworking skills and family values are well suited for the Canadian society.

It is true that in some areas the South Asian community is ghettoizing. It is very important that the South Asian community holds on to its traditions and cultures; it's a good thing. But we have to make sure that the community has the language and the cultural skills to communicate with its neighbours outside of their comfort zone.

"The political influence of the South Asian community can be much more."
Liberal MP Ujjal Dosanjh (Vancouver South)

The South Asian is not that well organized nationally at least. There are organizations like Indo Canada Chamber of Commerce, Canada-India Foundation but there is lack of consistent perception of the needs of the South Asian community. I don't believe that given its vast numbers, the South Asian community has political influence as it could have.

Although there are South Asian MPs and MPPs, some of us are individually more ambitious and perhaps more participating, but I believe the community has a potential to be very strong and be more effective voice in the Canadian political system.

As representatives from the largest visible minority in Canada, we do count. Witness the recent appointments to the upper chambers both in England and Canada. All parties know that cultivation of multicultural communities must be part of a successful election coalition.

"Canada is home. We will live and die in Canada; we must realize that."
MPP Yasir Naqvi MPP (Ottawa Centre)

The South Asian community is very hardworking, very focused and determined. We place a lot of emphasis on education as there is cultural tendency to be doctors, engineers, lawyers and accountants. Though education is becoming expensive, it's far cheaper than any country in the world and Ontario has the best graduation rate in the G8 countries.

The South Asian community must realize that Canada is home. This is where we live and this is where we will die. Members of the South Asian community should get involved beyond the ethno-cultural organizations to the broader community based organizations in the neighbourhood we live in. When our community grows, we all grow. Our youth should take ownership of the community to instill the change; that's where belonging, acceptance and inclusion comes from.

Second-Generation South Asian Political Leaders Please[149]
By Pradip Rodrigues

At the Liberal Leadership Convention I talked to and listened to dozens of delegates, almost all of whom were first generation South Asians.

They happened to either be ardent supporters of one of the major political parties in Canada, harboured political ambitions or simply got involved in politics as a means of gaining access and respect within the community.

Second-generation South Asians were hard to find. I did manage to talk to one second-generation South Asian delegate whose father is a well-known community leader and very politically and social connected. While the father has assiduously courted and built support in the community and allies in the political sphere, his son came as a delegate albeit reluctantly, it was a result of his father's request. This delegate said his father is very keen he get into politics, given he is born Canadian, well-integrated and can connect with the mainstream, but the 25-year-old is still uncomfortable and it is doubtful that he would ever aspire to do what his father does so well. Upmeet Sidhu is his name and he tells me that most South Asians of his generation aren't inclined toward politics.

He gave me a few reasons, first, unlike his parents' generation who gravitated toward small businesses, his generation are mostly professionals with 9–5 routines. If they are married, they want to spend time with their wives and family, not spend endless hours evenings and weekends schmoozing and networking on behalf of some political candidates or parties. Most South Asians aspiring to hold public office in Canada or associate themselves with political parties are first-generation immigrants. This was understandable in earlier times given the fact that they came in their youth and second-generation South Asians were either children or teenagers, now of course they are now adults and their parents are ageing but this is one generation that wants to have little or nothing to do with politics and this is bound to have an impact in the years to come.

There are a several politicians and candidates of South Asian descent who are nothing short of embarrassments. Not only do they lack in-depth understanding of Canadian politics, but they lack the oratorical English skills so necessary to appeal to all Canadians and not just Canadians of South Asian descent. They more often have grown up in India, have gotten into some small business and then have gotten involved in politics as a means of networking and furthering their own businesses.

At the Liberal Leadership Convention I met scores of young volunteers and delegates supporting the other leadership candidates, most of them were White, university educated and politically tuned in. I met one of Kathleen Wynne's delegates from Northern Ontario, a 22-year-old named Beth. She got involved to make a change and raise an issue—Autism. Her autistic brother requires help and her two parents have both gone to different provinces to work as there were no jobs for them in her community.

Many of the other young delegates and volunteers were activists involved with many social issues including environment.

Second generation South Asians in Canada by contrast aren't quite inclined toward social issues and even less inclined toward politics to make a difference. They are too busy working to buy bigger houses and build impressive fortunes, and if at all they get involved in community issues, it would most likely be organizing a Bollywood dance show. While there are a few articulate South Asian politicians like MPP Jagmeet Singh, who I understand also speaks passable French and grew up in Canada, most are visible minorities with pronounced Indian accents and often the ones who've grown up here and have Canadian accents usually sound and act like they were politicians not even from India originally but in India.

But times are changing, our population is increasing rapidly, we now have a significant number of South Asians who were born and grow in Canada. They should be the ones now to speak up not just for our community but for all Canadians. And South Asian voters should think more in the interests of what's good for the country rather than what's good just for the South Asian community. We need second generation leaders who can bring changes in terms of social and economic integration, who can position themselves as Canadian politicians rather than community politicians.

12

Annex 2: South Asian Marriage

Marriage is one of the most significant events that South Asians experience in their lives. When focusing our attention into South Asian families, such a life-changing event can have a significant impact not only on each family, but also on the bride and groom. A big transition takes place in the lives of both the bride and groom, particularly for the South Asian bride.

Both the bride and groom go through emotional, physical, and financial adjustments in their new lives, and the bride undergoes severe stress because of the transitioning and balancing of traditional and Western expectations. First and second generations of South Asians are continually faced with many intergenerational and cultural challenges that make this journey even more complex. Regardless of cultural or religious belief, the institution of marriage has greatly affected the women. Based on traditional values, roles, and beliefs, the married South Asian woman's status evolves as her status in the community is usually elevated. The marriage process—from searching for the potential mate to family (and partner)—leads to the fact of uniting of two families rather than uniting of two individuals.

In a traditional family, whether it is an "arranged marriage" or an "arranged introduction," if parents choose their son's or daughter's future partner, many potential conflicts and decisions are made without knowing or understanding the needs that newlyweds require in order to successfully adjust and prosper. In these families, the bride is expected to move from her family to her husband's family and dwellings. Although it might be a financially viable arrangement, we tend to neglect just how emotionally stressful this transition is for the bride. She must adjust to a different family dynamic along with all the other changes in her life. In doing so, the bride must undergo many struggles. In fact, this is one of the most critical times in her life during which she is most vulnerable to emotional and mental distress leading to mental health issues. Many conflicts may lead to anxiety, grief, loss, trauma, crisis, and adjustment disorders. When these issues are coupled with anger, depression, and social isolation, they become even more complex. Serious experiences such as self-harm, suicide, domestic violence, and divorce are likely to follow, if not prevented from the beginning.

South Asians who have experienced these intergenerational and cultural struggles themselves support women and couples during these times. South Asian women are gradually starting to receive preventative and compassionate support now more than ever before. Undoubtedly, the main objective is to make the transition between "being single" to the "marriage" as easy as possible and to work towards a successful and thriving union. What can each couple (especially the bride) do to overcome these hurdles to a peaceful marriage? Here are some helpful tips that a South Asian couple in westernized world can follow to keep a marriage happy, peaceful, and long lasting:

- Know yourself well, calm, and cool. Prepare for a lifelong commitment. Know your likes, dislikes, preferences, and personality.
- Determine your as well as your potential partner's dreams, goals, and aspirations.
- Give yourself time to contemplate, to dream, and to financially, mentally, and emotionally prepare for this big change in your life.
- Though it seems westernized for some, but meet several people before choosing your potential mate. Experience through meeting is important in order to have a relationship for a reasonable duration prior to deciding on "the one." The idea behind this is to fully understand each other's values, beliefs, attitudes, and behaviours that base a person's expectations and lifestyles before making the commitment for a long-term relationship.
- Know what your future family and in-laws' expectations are from you (especially for brides moving into her extended family's dwellings). What family type do your in-laws fit into? Is it traditional, progressive, or a westernized family, and how will this affect you? Each type of family will have its own struggles to adjust to and overcome.

- Observe how your prospective mate reacts to stressful events. Most likely each of you will have tough times, and how you tackle these challenges will predict your future coping mechanism and solution.
- Resolve pending financial, emotional, or mental health issues that could be detrimental to your life or your partner's life.

Marriage, like all relationships, takes considerable time and effort to sustain and nurture. This unity of two families and of two unique human beings is an incredible journey. Along the way, a couple will face many successes and downfalls, but if they are courageous enough to fulfill one another's needs first and then their own, then each life partner may discover a far greater truth than each may have found apart.[150]

The wedding customs and rituals

The word "wed" is derived from the ancient Greek word for "pledge." And that is exactly what a wedding is, no matter what country it takes place in, no matter what culture it is a part of. To wed is to pledge yourself to another, and marriage is the most solemn pledge we make in our lifetimes.[151]

South Asian weddings are very bright, colourful, and traditional events, filled with ritual and celebration that continue for several days. The traditional wedding is about two families being brought together socially, with as much emphasis placed on the families concerned coming closer as the individuals involved. Many of the wedding customs are common among Hindus, Jains, Sikhs, and even Muslims.

Indian wedding

Due to the diversity of Indian culture, the wedding style, ceremony, and rituals vary greatly among various states, regions, religions, and castes. While the Christians of India usually follow a more or less Western wedding ceremony, the Indian Hindus, Muslims, Buddhist, Jains, and Sikhs follow traditions quite different from the West. In certain regions, it is quite common that during the traditional wedding days, there would be a "Titak" ceremony (where the groom is anointed on his forehead), a ceremony for adorning the bride's hand and feet with henna (called *mehendi*) accompanied by *Ladies' Sangeet (music and dance)*, and many other prewedding ceremonies.

Another important ceremony followed in certain areas is the "Haldi" program, where the bride and the groom are anointed with turmeric paste. All of the close relatives make sure that they have anointed the couple with turmeric. In certain regions, on the day of the wedding, the bridegroom, his friends, and relatives come to sing and dance to the wedding site in a procession called "Baraat," and then the religious rituals take place to solemnize the wedding, according to the religion of the couple.

While the groom may wear traditional *Sherwani* or *Dhoti* or Western suit, or some other local costume, his face, in certain regions, is usually veiled with a mini curtain of flowers called "Sehra." In certain regions, the bride (Hindu or Muslim) always wears red clothes, never white because white symbolizes widowhood in Indian culture. In Southern and Eastern states, the bride usually wears a red "Sari"; but in northern and central states, the preferred garment is a decorated skirt-blouse and veil called "Lehenga." After the solemnization of marriage, the bride departs with her husband. This is a very sad event for the bride's relatives because traditionally she is supposed to permanently "break off" her relations with her blood relatives to join her husband's family. Among Christians in the state of Kerala, the bridegroom departs with the bride's family. The wedding may be followed by "reception" by the groom's parents at the groom's place.[152]

A Pakistani wedding typically consists of four ceremonies on four separate days. It may consist of three days if the first function called "Mehndi" is done in a combined manner by both the bride and groom's family. The first function is Mehndi in which the families get together and celebrate the upcoming wedding function. On this day, it is customary to wear green, yellow, orange, or other vibrant colours. The bride-to-be gets her hands painted with henna, and songs and dances go on throughout the night. The next day is "Baraat," which is hosted by the bride's family. This event is usually held in a reception hall, and the groom comes over with his family and friends; a large feast is given. The bride's friends and relatives are also present, and the Baraat event can be considered the "main" wedding event, as it is the largest one out of all the events. Then there is the holy ceremony of "Nikah," which is performed by a religious *Pastor* or *Imam*, after which bride and groom are declared as husband and wife. The Next day there is a function of "Walima" in which the groom's family is the host and the bride's family come over for a big feast. On her wedding day, the bride-to-be can wear any colour she wants, but vibrant colours and lots of traditional gold jewellery are typically worn. It is customary for the bride to wear traditional clothes such as a *lahnga, shalwar kameez,* or *sari*. These weddings are also typical of the Muslim community in India.[153]

Two types of marriages are prevalent in Bangladesh—Muslim marriages and the Hindu marriages. Although there are a number of rituals that are different in these two weddings, they have a lot in common as well. Both the wedding ceremonies in Bangladesh are celebrated in a befitting manner.

Wedding preludes

Nearly two days before the wedding day, a premarriage ritual takes place at the bride's home. It is a "henna" ceremony, where the new bride's hands and feet are embellished with henna. In Bangladesh it is often termed as the "Mehendi Sondha." It is an informal gathering of the women folks of the family, mostly the bride's relatives and close friends. The next day—that is, the morning before the wedding day—a ritual called "Gaye Holud," or turmeric ceremony, takes place at the bride's home. As part of the ritual, the groom's family, except the groom, comes to the bride's house and presents her gifts, mostly saris, jewelleries, sweets, and other traditional gifts. The groom's family also brings in turmeric paste, which is put all over her face and her body. The ceremony is commonly followed by both Hindus and Muslims in Bangladesh. The same turmeric is then taken for the groom, and the same ritual is celebrated at the groom's house. The idea behind the "Gaye Holud" is that the turmeric paste cleans up and brings brightness of the skin.

Wedding in Bangladesh

The wedding preludes are more or less the same for both the Muslims and Hindus. However, the wedding rituals are quite different. For Muslim, on the day of wedding, the couple is made to sit close to each other in the presence of a Muslim priest called a *kazi*. Both the bride and the groom are surrounded by their respective relatives and friends. The kazi asks for consent from the bride and the groom and, with their consent, sanctifies the marriage. The family of the groom has to give monetary compensation to the bride. This is known as "Mahr." The couple offers sweets to each other after this ceremony. The marriage ceremony is followed by music, dance, and a grand feast. A "Walima," or a wedding reception, is normally organized the next evening at the groom's place. The couple dresses traditionally and greets their friends, relatives, and all the invitees. A wedding feast is arranged at the occasion.

It is, however, important to be mentioned that an Islamic Bangladeshi marriage differs in several ways to Islamic marriages that are held in other countries with predominantly Muslim population. The wedding processes and customs are quite unique in their own way in Bangladesh. The cultural fusion has its influence on several aspects of an Islamic Bangladeshi marriage. Though Bangladesh is basically a Muslim country, Muslims here follow several customs of their Hindu counterparts. In a traditional marriage, the prewedding ceremonies, food, dress, and rituals differ considerably from the normal Muslim traditions that are held in other countries. They reflect to a large extent with the heritage of Bengal. Bengali cultural aspects have impact on the marriage of Muslim population in Bangladesh. In other words, Muslims in Bangladesh like to celebrate the weddings with a touch of a Bengali tradition.

In a conservative Islamic marriage, there are separate events for men and women. It is not so in a Bangladeshi Muslim marriage. The wedding is spread for three days and is thoroughly enjoyed by all men and women who participate in the events. Women are not seen veiled in the Muslim Bangladeshi marriage. One of the ceremonies that are common to both Hindu and Muslim marriages in Bangladesh is the Gaye Holud, or turmeric ceremony. In other Muslim countries, the Henna ceremony takes place in place of Gaye Holud. However, Henna ceremony is also common, in addition to Gaye Holud, among many Muslim marriages in Bangladesh. All men and women who participate in the Gaye Holud ceremony apply turmeric paste on the Bangladeshi bride and the Bangladeshi groom. Celebrations take place at both the bride and the groom's place. Women are not restricted from singing and dancing. The Bangladeshi bride and the groom do not meet after the turmeric ceremony is over, till their marriage. All the gifts from the groom's side are given by the elders from the groom's side to the bride.

Conservative Islamic marriages are short and simple in comparison to the marriages that are held in Bangladesh. Bangladeshi Muslim marriage has more colour, flavour, and extravaganza in the customs and traditions that are followed. People go to any extent to make the Bangladeshi marriage ceremonies more colourful, attractive, and memorable. Sari is the most preferred bridal costume in all Bangladeshi weddings. It is usually draped in a distinctive style. An Islamic priest, after taking the consent of the bride and the groom, solemnizes and also registers the marriage in both Bangladeshi and other Muslim marriages. Women participate in many of the events in a Bangladeshi wedding unlike a conventional Muslim wedding wherein women are restricted in many events and customs. Because of the long-standing thousands of years of liberal culture and the ethnic Bengali

Heritage, the marriage in Bangladesh has acquired a unique flavour. The customs like "Bor Jatri," "Bor Boron," "Subho Dristi," "Bidaay," "Bou Bhaat and Badhu Boron," and "Phool Shojja," which are observed in the Hindu marriage, are part of Muslim marriage in Bangladesh. These marriage customs are observed in both Muslim and Hindu marriages because of their intrinsic value within the Bengali culture, which are very common among Hindus and Muslims in the Bangladesh.[154]

For Hindus in Bangladesh, the groom and his family ("Bor Jatri") arrive at the bride's house on the wedding evening. The groom is greeted ("Bor Boron") with bells and conch shells by the bride's mother. The wedding is performed in the presence of the priest, who chants the "Mantras." The bride is seated on a low wooden stool and is lifted and taken around the groom in seven complete circles ("Saat Paak"). After the circles are completed, the bride and groom exchange garlands of flowers three times ("Mala Badal"). After garlanding one another, the bride and the groom are made to look at each other in front of all the assembled invitees ("Subho Dristi"). Also seven circular rounds are taken by the couple around the fire, thereby solemnizing the occasion. The groom put vermillion ("Sindoor") on the bride's hair parting and forehead as a symbol of marriage worn by Hindu women thereafter.

Postwedding rituals: the farewell ("Vidaay") ceremony takes place the next day when the bride leaves her paternal home to move to the groom's place; it is a mixed moment of joy and sorrow as the bride is bid adieu with blessings of her parents and relatives to start a new life with her husband. After the couple reaches the groom's house and the initial welcome ceremony is over, they are separated for the night ("Kaal Ratri"), probably to get a fresh and sound sleep and prepare for the next day's "Bou Bhaat" and "Badhu Boron" ceremony. A "Bou Baran" ceremony—that is, welcoming the new bride—takes place at the groom's house. A reception is held the next evening at the groom's place to treat the guests. Finally, the couple is adorned with flowers and left together alone in their room to enjoy conjugal bliss on a bed laid with flowers ("Phool Shojja").[155]

Sri Lankan wedding

Like India, Sri Lanka is also a confluence of many religions—Hindu, Buddhist, Muslims, and Christians—and their marriage customs and rituals vary accordingly. During ancient times, pre-Buddhist Sinhalese marriage laws and customs would have been similar to those prescribed in the Hindu laws of Manu. With the advent of Buddhism in the island during the third century BC, the legal position of women underwent a significant improvement. The Sinhalese customs and rituals have also undergone a vast change from the *Kandyan* times. *Kandyan* society was an extremely licentious where both men and women had full freedom to cohabit with whomsoever they pleased. Sexual morality hardly ever mattered, and polygamy (a man taking more than one wife), polyandry (a woman taking more than one husband), and concubinage were all recognised as legal. Group marriages and trial marriages were also commonplace. Divorce was also very easy, as the *Kandyan* law recognized that either men or women may dissolve the marital tie at their will and pleasure.

Buddhist wedding, which is very prominent in Sri Lanka, is influenced by the Hindu culture, which gives prominence to *Nekath*, the auspicious time. The *Nekath* is derived from the horoscopes of the bride and the groom, which are based on their dates and times of birth. Of the many traditional events that take place during a Buddhist wedding, the "Poruwa" ceremony is the most important. The Nekath strictly guides the ceremony. Poruwa is a beautifully decorated wooden platform on which the traditional Buddhist marriage ceremony takes place. This event is called the "Poruwa Siritha" (ceremony). The Poruwa Siritha appears to have existed in Sri Lanka before the introduction of Buddhism in the third century BC. Through the ages, many innovations have been introduced to the Poruwa Siritha. By and large, the men and women of present-day society realize the value of their heritage and are motivated to protect and preserve traditions of their past for posterity. The Poruwa Siritha was as valid custom as a registered marriage until the British introduced the registration of marriages by law in 1870. Today's Poruwa Siritha has been influenced by both up-country and low-country customs of Sri Lanka.

<u>Wedding procession</u>: *Poruwa* is an elevated and beautifully decorated wooden platform on which the traditional Buddhist marriage ceremony takes place. When arranged on a grand scale, the groom is escorted to the wedding location by drummers and typical *Kandyan* dancers in procession, and even an elephant is decked up for the procession. The bridegroom and party assemble on the left of the *Poruwa*, and the bridal party on the right. The bride and groom enter the *Poruwa* leading with the right foot. They greet each other with palms held together in the traditional manner.

<u>Auspicious seven</u>: The ceremony starts when the couple offers seven betel leaf bundles to the gods, thereby requesting the gods to protect the lives of seven generations originating from their marriage. The bride's father places the right hand of the bride on that of the groom as a symbolic gesture of

handing over the bride to the bridegroom. The groom's brother hands a tray to the groom with seven sheaves of betel leaves with a coin placed in each. The groom holds the tray while the bride takes one sheaf at a time and drops it on the *Poruwa*. The groom repeats this process. This is a custom carried out to remember seven generations of relatives on each side.

Golden knot: The groom's brother hands a chain to the groom who in turn places it on the bride's neck. The bride's maternal uncle then enters the *Poruwa*, ties the small fingers of the bride and groom with a gold thread, and then pours water over the fingers. The water poured and the earth on which it falls are intended to be the lasting witnesses to the marriage. The uncle then turns the couple clockwise, three times, on the *Poruwa*.

Mother care: The groom presents to his bride a white cloth, which in turn is presented to the bride's mother. This is an expression of the groom's gratitude to his mother-in-law for bringing up his bride. Next, the groom's mother presents the going-away *saie* to the groom. The groom hands it over to the bride, and she in turn gives it to her mother.

Chathurthi karma: The bride's mother will then present a plate of milk rice and *kavum*, cooked with special ingredients befitting a marriage ceremony, to the bride who feeds a piece of each to the bridegroom. The bridegroom feeds the bride in return.

Shining bright: As the newlyweds step down from the *Poruwa*, helped by a couple from the bridegroom's party, the *Shilpathipathi* (master of ceremonies) breaks a coconut into two. The bridal couple lights a traditional brass oil lamp to signify their resolve to keep the home fires burning.[156]

Wedding in Nepal

The wedding customs of Hindu and Buddhist are most popular among marriage traditions and ceremonies of various ethnic groups and castes of Nepal. The majority of the population in Nepal is Hindu and Buddhist. Both of them deeply believe in traditional marriages, as it is supposed to last a lifetime. It is an unshakable and traditional conviction that such marriages lead to much conjugal happiness and success. It emphasizes on mutual respect and discourages the practice of divorce.

Traditionally, weddings in Nepal are arranged by the respective families. It is not uncommon for matches to be decided when the two individuals are still children. However, child marriages in Nepal are illegal, and the couple therefore waits until adulthood to complete their marriage rites. Traditionally families in Nepal consider a number of factors before arranging the marriage. These factors may include caste, religion, ethnicity, and also the consideration of ties between families in an effort to build allegiances. It is important that arranged marriage and forced marriage in Nepal are not confused. It is not normal practice for families in Nepal who are arranging marriages to force their offspring to marry someone that they do not wish to marry. The offspring are also consulted, and it is important that they consent to the marriage. There is a slow shift away from arranged marriages to "love' marriages (i.e., individuals now have more freedom in Nepal to chose whom they wish to marry without family interference). There is also a shift in Nepal towards marriage across castes (which traditionally was strongly resisted) and across ethnic groups.

Hindu marriages in Nepal are often arranged with the assistance of a priest, who analyses the horoscopes of the couple to ensure that they are compatible, and they typically take place during the days of selected months of the year (such as from mid-January to mid-March, mid-April to mid-June, and mid-November to mid-December). Buddhist weddings in Nepal are often quieter occasions, with a focus on ceremonial events. The weddings are usually extremely large, sometimes encompassing whole villages and large numbers of extended family. Buddhist marriages are performed at monastery. Traditional dress is worn by both bride and groom, and lama (monk) does all customary *puja* (worship) to solemnize the wedding. The butter lamp is lit at the monastery during wedding day, which is very attractive. The music played during this occasion is traditional and different from modern music, which makes environment pleasant and soothes the mind.[157]

Sherpa[158] weddings and marriages in Nepal differ to Hindu and Buddhist weddings quite considerably. Sometimes the marriage rites for the couple are completed years in advance of the actual wedding ceremony, and consequently, the couple may even have their children attend the wedding.[159]

Wedding in Myanmar

In Myanmar the marriage ties are social rather than religious. The Myanmar custom is to do court marriage in front of the honourable judge by signing officially before celebrating ceremony. The formal word for marriage in Burmese is called *Mingala Saung*; the word "*mingala*" comes from the Pali language, "*Mangala*." It generally means "auspicious," lucky, or good chance of success. The word *"saung"* means "to carry"; and together it means the couple will carry with them this *Mangala*.

Traditionally, a marriage is recognized with or without a ceremony when the man's *Longyi* (sarong) is seen hanging from a rail of the house or if the couple eats from the same plate. Weddings are traditionally avoided during the Buddhist lent, which lasts three months from July to October. Buddhist monks are not present to conduct the wedding and solemnize the marriage, as they are forbidden to officiate a marriage, which is considered a worldly affair (*lokiya*). However, they may be invited to bless the newlywed couple and recite a protective *Paritta* (protection or safeguard from certain afflictions). Typically, the bride and groom arrange an almsgiving feast to the monks the morning of the wedding to gain merit. A master of ceremonies, typically a Brahmin, is hired to preside over the ceremony. The bride and groom sit on cushions next to each other. At the beginning of the wedding, the Brahmin blows a conch shell to commence the ceremony and joins the palms of the couple, wraps them in white cloth, and dips the joined palms in a silver bowl. The Burmese word for "to marry" is "*let htat,*" which literally means "to join palms together." After chanting a few Sanskrit mantras, the Brahmin takes the couple's joined palms out of the bowl and blows the conch shell to end the ceremony. Afterward, entertainers start performing dances and music, and the wedding is ended with a speech by a guest of higher social standing.

To become a married couple in Buddhism is known in Burmese as *yay-set-sone-deir*, meaning of which is likened to the cohesion of one drop of water with another drop of water. It is the *Kamma* (action) of the incumbents (the husband and the wife) and not the destiny that caused meeting together, and getting married was a prior arrangement by an external entity who has control over one's fate. The mutual agreement to live as *Lin* and *Mayar* (husband and wife) to a Buddhist couple is following the moral application of self-abstinence as laid down in the Five Precepts (*Sila*). The observance of maintaining the Five Precepts is a wholesome act of moral and ethical development in raising a family. The Five Precepts are not imposed by God or a divine being as a commandment. It is a self-regulating and is conducive to character building. The denial of any of the Precepts is not considered a "sin," as there is no such thing in Buddhism. Among Buddha's followers, it is very important that married couples follow and practice his teachings to raise a family. Among hundreds of different categories of love in Buddhism, the most important ones are *Metta* (loving kindness), *Karuna* (compassion), and *Mudita* (sympathetic joy).

These attributes of love are the key to a happy, successful, and lasting marriage. It is true, though, that the perceptions can be influenced, conditioned, or tainted by personal views and thoughts, which could either be right or wrong. According to Buddhism, the right view (*Samma Ditthi*) is one of the constituent categories of wisdom called *Panna* (insight). In this regard, the ethical aim is the pragmatic performance of duty by husband, wife, and children, which must be conceived rightly, because events in life may lead to beneficial, pleasant, and agreeable outcomes, or to harmful and detrimental consequences. Thus, rather than expecting divine intervention for solution, Buddhist couples follow the guidelines of Buddha's teachings by searching inwards through *Vipassana* meditation and take refuge in the *Buddha, Dhamma, and Sangha* for guidance, wisdom, and understanding in their daily lives to achieve a life of harmonious living, which itself is *Mangala*, a blessing.[160]

Intermarriage

Intermarriage couples are likely to share some common values, aspirations, and expectations (although they come from different ethnic, social, or cultural backgrounds), which are important elements in building social cohesion and contributing to social integration in a multicultural society like Canada. As such intermarriage is considered as one of the positive measures of the dissolution of social and cultural barriers because it is the result of intimate social interaction between people of two different ethnicities. While intermarriage in the United States is considered to be an important element in the "melting pot" theory of assimilation, it is still a very effective means of ethnic intermixture because it breaks down ethnic exclusiveness and thus very closely mixes various ethnic populations (particularly ethnic minorities and mainstream population) more effectively than any other social process.[161]

It is, however, important to note that the tradition of intermarriage had a long history for millennia in South Asia. Indo-Iranian nomadic groups know as Aryans, from Central Asia, migrated to India more than three thousand years ago and settled particularly in the northwestern and northeastern parts of the subcontinent. Persian, Indo-Scythians, Indo-Hephthalites, Indo-Greeks, and Mughals married local women in that region during Antiquity and the Middle Ages.

Interethnic marriages between European men and Indian women were very common during colonial times. According to the historian William Dalrymple, about one in three European men (mostly British, as well as Portuguese, French, and Dutch, and to a lesser extent Swedes and Danes) had Indian wives in colonial India. One of the most famous intermarriages was between the Anglo-Indian resident James Achilles Kirkpatrick and the Hyderabad's noblewoman and descendant of Prophet Mohammed, Khair-un-Nissa.

During the British East India Company's rule in India, in the late eighteenth century and early nineteenth century, it was initially fairly common for British officers and soldiers to take local Indian wives. The six-hundred-thousand-strong Anglo-Indian communities have descended from such unions. There is also a story of an attractive Gujjar princess falling in love with a handsome English nobleman, and the nobleman converted to Islam so as to marry the princess. The sixty-five-thousand-strong Burgher community of Sri Lanka was formed by the intermarriages of Dutch and Portuguese men with local Sinhalese and Tamil women. Intermarriage also took place in Britain during the seventeenth to nineteenth centuries, when the British East India Company brought over many thousands of Indian scholars, *lascars,* and workers (mostly Bengali) who settled down in Britain and took local British wives, some of whom went to India with their husbands. In the mid-nineteenth century, there were around forty thousand British soldiers, but less than two thousand British officials present in India.[162]

History repeats itself but in different forms. In twenty-first century, the world has turned into a small global village, and close interaction and contact between people of varied cultures, religious faiths, colours, languages, and traditions is a normal phenomenon. Nonetheless, in a country of immigration and increasing diversity such as Canada, intermarriage is very common. In the last few decades, people from South Asian countries migrated in large numbers to the Western world including Canada. While the first-generation immigrants from South Asian countries largely remained as isolated groups, the children of first generation and the second generation of South Asian diaspora were more integrated into the mainstream society, and that the intermarriages were a very common outcome. These South Asians across North America are marrying non-South Asians at higher rates than before.

On the contrary, South Asians, in general, were and still now are traditional. They tended to marry within the same religion, socioeconomic status, and caste. Majority of them who immigrated to Canada would like to keep intraethnic marriage traditions in order to avoid cultural dilution. Many South Asians also worried that interethnic marriages could create distance between first-generation parents and their grandchildren to the extent that it would affect the social and cultural identities of the grandchildren who would be of mixed or multiethnic parents. Perhaps a new blending culture will evolve in a multiethnic society as a result. Who knows? We perhaps are going to experience this sooner than later.

Ethnic intermarriage in Canada between South Asians and white Canadians has become a statistical reality in recent time. They are most popular among the young—the rate of mixed unions is almost double the national average among younger adults generation. More and more visible minorities including South Asian adults of different world views are dating and marrying white Canadians, and therefore more Canadians are having wedding rituals that blend traditions from multiple worldviews as a result. Moreover, the fact is that merging of two cultures brings a unique understanding of the institution of marriages and unions. Even the ceremonies become more vibrant. The more diverse the cultures, the more interesting it become.

While intermarriage among South Asians was seen as taboo in the past, it is very common nowadays, and the parents are also gradually accepting those marriages. This is perhaps a new emerging as a reflection of social integration into mainstream Canadian life. Parents are accepting because the younger generations no longer want to live under the strict rules of elder generation. There is a Canadian Bengali girl whose story would perhaps represent the broader experience of South Asians regarding intermarriage. She (an economist by profession) married a white Canadian, which ended in divorce after eighteen years, but cultural differences was not the reason for the split, as she told. She married again a white Jewish man. Interestingly, some of her friends who were shocked by her first marriage had a white son-in-law. "They no longer see me as horrible or a groundbreaker or anything else. In fact, I think Indians have become more accepting," she said.[163]

As the intermarriages gain popularity among the younger generation, many South Asians still consider intermarriage is a defiance of tradition. Many fear that marrying someone from a different racial community would likely to take their children away from their own culture. Obviously, there are predictable clashes of cultures and other problems in the interracial marriages. Yet such problems not necessarily undermine or weaken intermarriage. According to Arpana Inman, professor of sociology and South Asian studies, Lehigh University, Pennsylvania, intermarriages are just as healthy as any other marriage.[164]

One important message for interracial couples is to learn how to adapt to another culture when they enter into it. This is very important in a multicultural society where couples can go beyond their cultural, racial, and religious differences, and share common values and aspirations in the name of love. However, blending two cultures has never been easy. Interracial couples can follow some good advice. Be bold and confident about your relationship, as you built it by heart, although your relatives and friends do not accept your relationship; ignore others' skepticism about your intermarriage or relationship; be committed to your relationship; and have patience as one day parents and others will accept your relationship and marriage. It is important to note that the main challenge in the intermarriage is the religious practices, but the positive aspect is that the couples in intermarriage are prepared for the challenges they face, and they agreed to make compromise and are open to change.

Intermarriage couples in Canada—some examples

The following are some examples of intermarriages in Canada that are close match with the ceremonies of South Asian wedding customs including wedding outfits.

Chris is Scottish, English, and Welsh. Nafeesa is South Asian. Her family are Ismaili Muslims who came to Canada as refugees fleeing Uganda after Idi Amin's expulsion order. The Vancouver couple was married in a civil ceremony at the Ismaili Jamatkhana in Burnaby officiated by Ismaili priests.[165]

Megan is white. Sunny is South Asian from Kapurthala in India's Punjab region. They met on an online language buddy site in 2008. Three months after they started chatting, Sunny sold his motorcycle to pay for a plane ticket for Megan to visit him in India. The rest, as they say, is history (or you can read it here). The couple had just celebrated their second-year wedding anniversary. They live in Fort St. John, but are in India this month visiting Sunny's parents.[166]

Rob is Hindi from Fiji. Dessa is Scottish Hungarian. The couple met in Surrey and have been together for more than eleven years.[167]

Teena is South Asian. Ken is Chinese. They live in Vancouver. The couple, both from immigrant families, met at work. Ken was an articling student at accounting firm KPMG, and she worked for the city of Richmond, a client. They have four kids they affectionately describe as "Chindus."[168]

Mursal is Afghan Canadian. Raymond is German and First Nations.[169]

Brent is Irish and British. Stephanie is half Chinese Indonesian, half East Indian. They live in Richmond. "I've always loved and cherished my mix," said Stephanie. Stephanie said her grandmother, her dad's mom, took a strong stand and let her son marry for love, not push for an arranged marriage. When Brent and Stephanie got married this July, "my Indian and Chinese sides both embraced his family with open arms—a truly magical and eclectic 'Canadian' wedding," said Stephanie.[170]

13

Annex 3: Glossary of Prominent Immigrants of South Asian Origin[171]

Amit Chakma (born in 1959) is the tenth president of the University of Western Ontario. Born in southeastern Bangladesh and a member of the Chakma ethnic minority, he moved away from his tribe to study chemical engineering at the Algerian Petroleum Institute in Algeria. In 1977 he graduated at the top of his class. He then moved to Canada and earned MSc and PhD in chemical engineering from the University of British Columbia.

From 1988 until 1996, he taught chemical engineering at the University of Calgary. In 1996 he moved to the University of Regina as dean of Engineering. He then served as Regina's vice president of Research from 1999 to 2001. During his time at the University of Regina, Dr. Chakma was named to Canada's one of the top 40's lists. He became vice president of Academic and Provost at the University of Waterloo in 2001. His research interests are natural gas engineering and petroleum waste management. On July 1, 2009, Dr. Chakma succeeded Paul Davenport as the University of Western Ontario's president. Having left the University of Waterloo, he has been noted for his service to both the university and the academic and business community of Kitchener-Waterloo. His goal as president of Western University is to position the school among the top-one-hundred universities in the world.

Ian Hanomansing (born in 1961) is a Canadian television journalist with the Canadian Broadcasting Corporation (CBC). He currently reports for CBC Television's nightly newscast—*The National*. Hanomansing was born to a Hindu Indian family, in Port of Spain, Trinidad and Tobago, but grew up in Sackville, New Brunswick. He attended Mount Allison University for his undergraduate education and then studied law at Dalhousie Law School. While in university, he was one of the country's most successful debaters and the top speaker at the Canadian National Debating Championship.

As a reporter, Hanomansing has covered a number of stories, including the 1989 Exxon Valdez oil spill, the 1992 Los Angeles riots, the 1994 Stanley Cup riot, the handover of Hong Kong from Great Britain, and five Olympic Games (Atlanta, USA, 1996; Nagano, Japan, 1998; Salt Lake City, USA, 2002; Torino, Italy, 2006; and Beijing, 2008). As an anchor, he led Canada-wide coverage of the Northeast Blackout of 2003 and, most recently, the 2006 shootings at Dawson College in Montreal, Quebec. From 2000 to 2007, he was the anchor of the national segment of the defunct newscast *Canada Now*; following that program's cancellation, he was the coanchor of *CBC News: Vancouver*, CBUT's supper hour newscast, from 2007 to 2010. He has been a reporter with the CBC since 1986 and was one of the network's main reporters for the 2008 Beijing Olympics. In addition to his other duties, Hanomansing cohosted *Hemispheres*, a weekly international documentary program on CBC Newsworld, coproduced by the Australian Broadcasting Corporation. Hanomansing and his role as newscaster is often the object of satire in the CBC comedy *This Hour Has 22 Minutes*, in which he is portrayed by cast member Shaun Majumder. In the March 24, 2009, episode of *This Hour Has 22 Minutes*, Ian Hanomansing himself portrayed Shaun Majumder being interviewed by Shaun Majumder portraying Ian Hanomansing. On November 28, 2008, Hanomansing won the Gemini Award for the Best News Anchor in Canada, beating Kevin Newman and Peter Mansbridge.

Deepa Mehta, LLD (born on January 1, 1950, in Amritsar, Punjab, India,) is a Genie Award–winning Indian-born Canadian film director and screenwriter, most known for her *Elementary Trilogy, Fire* (1996), *Earth* (1998), and *Water* (2005); among which *Earth* was submitted by the Indian government for Academy Award for Best Foreign Language Film, and *Water* was submitted by Canada for Academy Award for Best Foreign Language Film, making it Canada's first non-French Canadian film to receive a nomination in that category. She also cofounded Hamilton-Mehta Productions with her husband, producer David Hamilton, in 1996.

After completing her graduation, Mehta started making short documentaries in India, and in time she met Canadian documentarian Paul Saltzman, who was in India making a film and whom she was to later marry and migrate with to Canada in 1973. Once in Canada, she embarked on her film career as a screenwriter for children's films. She also made a few documentaries, including *At 99: A Portrait of Louise Tandy Murch* (1975). In 1991 she made her feature-film directorial debut with *Sam & Me* (starring Om Puri), a story of the relationship between a young Indian boy and an elderly Jewish gentleman in the Toronto neighbourhood of Parkdale. It won honourable mention in the Camera d'Or category of the 1991 Cannes Film Festival. Mehta followed up with *Camilla,* starring Bridget Fonda and Jessica Tandy, in 1994. In 2002 she directed *Bollywood/Hollywood,* for which she won the Genie Award for Best Original Screenplay.

Mehta directed two episodes of George Lucas's television series *The Young Indiana Jones Chronicles.* The first episode, "Benares, January 1910," aired in 1993. The second episode was aired in 1996 as part of a TV movie titled *Young Indiana Jones: Travels with Father.* Mehta also directed several English-language films set in Canada, including *The Republic of Love* (2003) and *Heaven on Earth* (2008), which deals with domestic violence and has Preity Zinta playing the female lead. The film premiered at the 2008 Toronto International Film Festival. Mehta is currently collaborating on the screenplay for *Midnight's Children* with the novel's author, Salmon Rushdie. British Indian actor Satya Bhabha will play the role of Saleem Sinai, while other roles will be played by Shriya Saran, Seema Biswas, Shabana Azmi, Anupam kher, Siddharth Narayan, Rahul Bose, Soha Ali Khan, Shahana Giswami, and Darsheel Safary. The film is scheduled to be released in 2012.

Zarqa Nawaz (born in 1968 in Liverpool, England) is a British Canadian freelance writer, journalist, broadcaster, and filmmaker of Pakistani origin. She was raised in the Toronto area and attended Chinguacousy Secondary School. Initially, Nawaz planned to go to medical school. She completed a bachelor of science degree from University of Toronto. She completed a second degree in journalism at Ryerson University in 1992. She worked with CBC Radio, CBC Newsworld, CBC Televison's *The National*, and CTV's *Canada AM,* and was an associate producer of several CBC Radio programs, including *Morningside.* Her 1992 radio documentary *The Changing Rituals of Death* won multiple awards at the Ontario Telefest Awards. Stating that she became "bored of journalism," she took a summer film workshop at the Ontario College of Art and Design and began working as a filmmaker, using comedy to explore the relationships between Muslims and their neighbours in contemporary North America. She has described the goal of her production company, FUNdamentalist Films, as "putting the 'fun' back into fundamentalism." Her use of humour in the television series *Little Mosque on the Prairies* attracted media attention ranging from CNN and *The Jerusalem Post* to *The Colbert Report* even before it aired, prompting the CBC to broadcast it months ahead of its original schedule.

Nawaz's CBC show *Little Mosque on the Prairie* was inspired by her documentary *Me and the Mosque*. Nawaz felt that mosques would be run differently if imams were recruited from North America instead of being brought from overseas where cultural differences, especially when it came to women, affected how the imams behaved with their congregation.

Aditya Jha, LLD, is a celebrated Indo-Canadian entrepreneur, philanthropist, and social activist with active involvement in Canadian public affairs. His business portfolio consists of several start-ups and turnarounds. He also runs several philanthropic initiatives through his private charitable foundation (POA Educational Foundation), promoting education and nurturing entrepreneurship to equalize the access to opportunity for those not so fortunate. Jha takes special interest in nurturing prosperity and financial independence among Canadian First Nations (aboriginal) communities and individuals through education scholarships at top Canadian universities and a project (Project Beyshick) that nurtures entrepreneurship. He is the cofounder and outgoing national convenor of the Canada India Foundation—a public policy organization. He is winner of the Top 25 Canadian Immigrants Award (2010), inductee to the 30 Most Influential Indo-Canadians Power List (2009), and recipient of Honourary Doctorate of Laws from Ryerson University—the highest honour conferred by the University. Aditya Jha was born to a Hindu family in Bihar, India.

Shuman Ghose Majumder (born in 1974) is a Canadian technologist, entrepreneur, and author. He is the former click fraud czar at Google, the author of works on digital distribution including the Open Music Model, and cofounder of TechAIDs.

Early in his career, he created the first real-time collaborative graphic design application as a software engineer at Groupeware. He was later cofounder of a software development firm and a management consultant with Mckinsey & Company and IBM. He was one of the early product managers for AdSense, led the launch of Link Units and AdSense for Feeds, and was part of the team that launched Gmail. He was the recipient of two Google Founders' Awards for significant entrepreneurial accomplishments. He is coauthor of *CGI Programming Unleashed* (Macmillan, ISBN 1-57521-151-1, 1997) and a contributing author to *Crimeware* (Symantec Press, ISBN 0-321-50195-0, 2008).

Munir A. Sheikh, PhD, is a Canadian public servant, economist, academic, and the former chief statistician of Canada. He is currently a distinguished fellow and adjunct professor at Queen's University. On November 30, 2010, the provincial government appointed Sheikh and Frances Lankin to lead the Commission for the Review of Social Assistance in Ontario. Born in Pakistan in 1947, Sheikh received a master of arts in economics from McMaster University in 1970 and earned his doctorate in economics from the University of Western Ontario in 1973. Sheikh began his public service career as an economist with the Economic Council of Canada from 1972 to 1976. After a brief stint with the National Energy Board between 1976 and 1978, he joined the Department of Finance and rose to the rank of senior assistant deputy minister in 2000.

Between 2001 and 2006, he held senior positions with Health Canada, the Privy Council Office, and Human Resources and Social Development Canada. He has also taught at the University of Ottawa and Carleton University. Later in his career, Sheikh oversaw a $100 billion tax reduction policy and helped craft the 2005 budget. He was praised by a former colleague as "the best economist in the federal government."

Aftab Mufti is a professor of civil engineering at the University of Manitoba and president of ISIS Canada. He was born in Pakistan in 1940. He graduated from the NED Engineering College, Karachi, in February 1962, and worked as a structural engineer for the Karachi Port Trust for one year. In September 1963 he was admitted to McGill University, Montreal, Quebec, and graduated with a master of engineering in 1965 and a PhD in 1969. During this time he also worked on the Canadian Theme Pavilions for Expo 67 as a structural engineer for deStien and Associates of Montreal.

In 2010 Dr. Mufti was awarded the Order of Canada "for his contributions to and leadership in the field of civil engineering, notably for researching the use of advanced composite materials and fibre optic sensors in the construction and monitoring of bridges and other infrastructures" (2011). Aftab Mufti was honoured by the International Society for Structural Health Monitoring of Intelligent Infrastructure (ISHMII) at its December 2011 conference (SHMII-5), as it inaugurated the Aftab Mufti Medal for high achievement and innovation in civil structural health monitoring. Dr. Mufti is held in high esteem for his lifetime of influential engineering accomplishments and dedication to the development of structural health monitoring as a recognized field within civil engineering. Dr. Mufti is also the editor in chief of the *Journal of Civil Structural Health Monitoring*. His international leadership and vision had shaped the field globally. With colleagues in the Americas, Europe, and Asia, Dr. Mufti cofounded ISHMII and became its first president. The initial recipients of the Aftab Mufti Medal are Dr. Urs Meier, past deputy director general of

EMPA, the Swiss federal laboratories for materials testing and research, and Dr. Jan-Ming Ko, an emeritus professor of structural engineering of the Hong Kong Polytechnic University.

Tahmena Bokhari is a Pakistani Canadian beauty pageant titleholder and social worker. She was born in Toronto, Ontario, Canada. She won Mrs. Pakistan World 2010 in Toronto and became the third Pakistani woman in history to represent women on an international platform. After winning Mrs. United Nation International 2010, she became the first Pakistani woman to win an international pageant title for Pakistan.

She obtained her master's in social work from the University of Toronto and subsequently traveled abroad, working with orphans, victims of poverty, and natural disaster survivors. She worked in the relief efforts following the October 8, 2005, earthquake in Kashmir, including serving as a counsellor and translator for foreign doctors. As a college professor, Bokhari teaches social work at Seneca and George Brown colleges. She has worked as a consultant to governments and organizations, and as a public speaker and writer in the Grater Toronto Area. She focuses on diversity, women's movement, health (particularly cancer), and issues involving immigrants and settlement. Bokhari is a strong advocate for ending violence against women. She has spoken out on the murder of a young Pakistani woman, Aqsa Parvez, which occurred in Mississauga, Ontario, in 2007, and has challenged the term "honour killing" popularized by the media since this murder. Bokhari has also written about the issues of violence along with other social issues in her quest to work towards social justice.

Following another high-profile case of the Shafia family, Bokhari stated, "Like in the case of Aqsa Parvez, it is too easy to blame one man or one family. This family and this man are a product of society, and we are all responsible. There is a range of violent acts and gender-based hate against girls and women that we condone every day, but somehow when women get killed and it makes the news, we are left shocked. The murder of women is just the next step in a long range of socially acceptable norms and mores that we don't challenge. The conversation we need to be having is about the manifestations of patriarchy we see in various aspects of our lives, including religion, culture, language, and media." In addition, Bokhari is a strong advocate for diversity and inclusivity as well as a trainer and consultant on these issues.

Yasir Naqvi, MPP, is a politician in Ontario, Canada. He was elected to the Legislative Assembly of Ontario in the 2007 provincial election, representing the riding of Ottawa Centre. He is also the president of the Ontario Liberal Party.

Naqvi was born and raised in Pakistan and immigrated to Canada with his family in 1988 at the age of fifteen. Naqvi is a graduate of McMaster University and the University of Ottawa Law School. He was called to the bar in Ontario in 2001 and began practicing law at Flavell Kubrick LLP, specializing in international trade law and eventually becoming a partner. He continued his practice with Lang Michener LLP after that firm merged with Flavell Kubrick LLP in 2005. He left Lang Michener in 2007 to join the Centre for Trade Policy and Law at Carleton University. The *Ottawa Citizen* named Naqvi as one of its People to Watch in 2010, with a profile in the January 9, 2010, *Saturday Observer* headlined "Yasir Naqvi, he's a firecracker." *Ottawa Life* magazine also included him in its Tenth Annual Top 50 People in the Capital list for 2010. In a September 2011 column, Adam Radwanski of the *Globe and Mail* called Naqvi "possibly the hardest-working constituency MPP in the province."

He was appointed parliamentary assistant to Rick Bartolucci, the minister of Community Safety and Correctional Services, in the cabinet announcement of October 30, 2007. On October 3, 2008, he was named parliamentary assistant to the minister of Revenue Dwight Duncan. On June 24, 2009, a cabinet shuffle moved John Wilkinson into the role of minister of Revenue, and Naqvi was kept on as his parliamentary assistant. On September 2, 2010, Naqvi was appointed parliamentary assistant to the minister of Education Leona Dombrosky.

Sudarshan (Sudi) Devanesen, CM (born 1943), is an Indian Canadian family physician and educator, public health activist, and member of the Order of Canada. In 1972 he immigrated to Canada. After briefly practicing at Janeway Children's Hospital at Memorial University of Newfoundland in St. John's Newfoundland, he moved to Toronto, Ontario, and resumed studies to respecialize as a family physician. He began study at St. Michael's Hospital and the Faculty of Medicine of the University of Toronto in 1973; he would eventually become chief of family and community medicine at St. Michael's and is today an associate professor at the University of Toronto. He was medical director of the Broadview Community Health Clinic from 1980 to 1989. He also served as physician for the Fred Victor Centre, a downtown Toronto mission serving the homeless, and on the board of directors of Casey House, a hospice serving HIV/AIDS patients.

He earned his master of clinical science from the University of Western Ontario in 1990 and is a fellow of the College of Family Physicians of Canada. An advocate of holistic medicine, his practice integrates the medical and biopsychosocial models of health care. Particularly concerned with prevention of disease and interested in cardiovascular disease, he became founding president (1994–1997) of a South Asian community council of the Heart and Stroke Foundation of Ontario, and has both studied and educated on the risks of cardiovascular disease in the South Asian community in Canada. He was appointed member of the Order of Canada on May 30, 2001, and invested with the honour on December 4, 2001. His citation into the order called him "a positive role model and mentor to hundreds of medical residents, family physicians and nurse practitioners."

John Beamish Dossetor, OC (born 19 July 1925), is a Canadian physician and bioethicist who is notable for cocoordinating the first kidney transplant in Canada and the Commonwealth. Born in Bangalore, India, he attended Marlborough College in Wiltshire before receiving a BM and BCh from St. John's College, Oxford, in 1950. In 1955 he immigrated to Canada to accept a position at McGill University. In 1958 he coordinated the first kidney transplant. From 1960 to 1969, he worked at the Royal Victoria Hospital. In 1960 he joined the University of Alberta as a professor of medicine, director of the Division of Nephrology and Immunology, and codirector of the Medical Research Council, Transplantation Research Unit of the University of Alberta Hospital. From 1985 to 1996, he was the director of the Bioethics Centre in the Faculty of Medicine (later named the John Dossetor Health Ethics Centre).

He is a cofounder of the Kidney Foundation of Canada. In 1994 he was made an officer of the Order of Canada. He was awarded the 125th Anniversary of the Confederation of Canada Medal. He lives in Ottawa, Ontario.

Vim Kochhar (born in September 21, 1936) is a Canadian businessman and former senator, the first person of Indo-Canadian heritage appointed to the Senate of Canada on January 29, 2010. Vim Kochhar obtained an engineering degree from the University of Texas and came to Canada in 1967. He retired from the Senate on September 21, 2011, upon reaching the mandatory retirement age of seventy-five.

Rotary Cheshire Homes (RCH) was founded in the early 1980s by Joyce Thompson and Vim Kochhar. RCH offers housing to persons who are deaf-blind. Vim Kochhar set the wheels in motion to develop housing for physically disabled persons. As a member of the Toronto-Don Valley Rotary Club, Kochhar enlisted the help of his fellow Rotarians in organizing the first Great Valentine Gala in February 1984. Over 1,200 people attended, raising over $239,000. Due to the success of the gala and the need to distribute the funds raised, Kochhar founded the Canadian Foundation for Physically Disabled Persons (CFPDP).

Irshad Manji ('Irshād Mānjī, Gujrati: Irshād Mānjī; born in 1968) is a Canadian author, journalist, and advocate of a "reform and progressive" interpretation of Islam. Manji is director of the Moral Courage Project at the Robert F. Wagner Graduate School of Public Service at New York University, which aims to teach young leaders to "challenge political correctness, intellectual conformity and self-censorship." She is also founder and president of Project Ijtihad, a charitable organization promoting a "tradition of critical thinking, debate and dissent" in Islam, among a "network of reform-minded Muslims and non-Muslim allies." Manji is a well-known critic of traditional mainstream Islam and was described by the *New York Times* as "Osama Bin Laden's worst nightmare."

Manji's most recent book, *Allah, Liberty and Love*, was released in June 2011 in the United States, Canada, and other countries. On Manji's website, the book is described: *"Allah, Liberty and Love* shows all of us how to reconcile faith and freedom in a world seething with repressive dogmas. Manji's key teaching is 'moral courage,' the willingness to speak up when everyone else wants to shut you up. This book is the ultimate guide to becoming a gutsy global citizen."

Manji's previous book, *The Trouble with Islam Today* (initially published as *Trouble with Islam*), has been published in more than thirty languages, including Arabic, Persian, Urdu, Malay, and Indonesian. She was troubled by how Islam is practiced today and by the Arab influence on Islam that took away women's individuality and introduced the concept of women's honour. Manji has produced a PBS documentary, *Faith Without Fear*, chronicling her attempt to "reconcile her faith in Allah with her love of freedom." The documentary was nominated for a 2008 Emmy Award. As a journalist, her articles have appeared in many publications, and she has addressed audiences ranging from Amnesty International to the United Nations Press Corps to the Democratic Muslims in Denmark to the Royal Canadian Mount Police. She has appeared on television networks around the world, including Al Jazeera, the CBC, BBC, MSNBC, C-SPAN, CNN, PBS, the Fox News Channel, CBS, and HBO.

Salim Mansur is an associate professor of political science at the University of Western Ontario in Canada. He is a columnist for the *London Free Press* and the *Toronto Sun*, and has contributed to various publications including *National Review*, the *Middle East Forum*, and *FrontPageMag*. He often presents analysis on the Muslim world, Islam, South Asia, and Middle East. On two occasions, Fatwas (religion edicts) were issued against him, calling for his death.

Mansur was born in Kolkata, India, and moved to Toronto, Canada, where he completed his doctorate studies in political science. Mansur is a member of the board of directors for the Center for Islamic Pluralism based in Washington DC, a senior fellow with the Canadian Coalition for Democracies, a group that seeks to support democracies and placed particular emphasis on calling for the Canadian government to adopt a pro-Israel stance. Mansur writes that, from Algeria to Indonesia, from Central Asian republics to Sudan, the entire Muslim world "has turned its back on modernity." He says the Muslim world must stop blaming the West for its own ailments.

Dr. Hargurdeep Saini, also known as Deep Saini, is a notable scientist and is a vice president of University of Toronto. Additionally, he is currently also the principal of the University of Toronto's Mississauga campus. Professor Saini was previously the dean of the Faculty of Environment at the University of Waterloo, Ontario.

Saini began his academic career in Canada in 1982 when he joined the University of Alberta as a postdoctoral fellow; he has been the dean at the University of Waterloo since 2006. Dr. Saini is a noted plant physiologist and is the past president of the Canadian Society of Plant Physiologists and the Federation of Canadian Plant Science Societies; Saini also visited India as part of Ontario Premier Dalton McGuinty's "Clean Tech Mission to India." He is currently a member of the NSERC's "Biological Systems and Functions" grant selection panel, the associate editor of the *Canadian Journal of Botany* (since 2003), and has also served as consulting editor of the *Journal of Crop Production* (1997–2000).

Haroon Siddiqui; born in Hydrabad, India. At Osmania University in Hyderabad, he earned degrees in science and journalism. In 1963 he joined the Press Trust of India as a reporter and copy editor. When his father fell ill, Siddiqui briefly left journalism to manage his father's company, which he did until 1967.

While at the Press Trust, he met Roland Michener, then Canada's high commissioner to India who encouraged him to immigrate to Canada. By 1968 he had taken a job at the *Brandon Sun* in Brandon, Manitoba, reporting on municipal and provincial politics from 1968 to 1978. In 1978 he joined the *Toronto Star*, becoming foreign affairs analyst in 1979, news editor in 1982, and national editor in 1985. From 1985 to 1990, he was the national editor, responsible for coverage of federal and provincial affairs. From 1990 to 1998, Siddiqui was the *Star*'s editorial page editor; and on his departure from that position, he was given the title of *"Editor Emeritus"* and a twice-weekly column, which focused on national and international politics as well as cultural and Muslim issues. He has written from a left-of-centre perspective on such issues as the war in Iraq and terrorism. He is the past president of PEN Canada and chair of International PEN's Writers-in-Exile Network. He is on the board of directors of the Calmeadow

Foundation (a microcredit lender), the Canada Club of Toronto, and the advisory board of the Ryerson University.

He shared a 1983 National Newspaper Award for spot news reporting. In 1992 and in 1998, Siddiqui received a Professional Man of the Year award from Indo-Canadian Chamber of Commerce, and a media award from the Canadian Islamic Congress. In 2000 and 2001 he became a member of the Order of Ontario for crafting "a broader definition of the Canadian identity," inclusive of our First Nations, French Canadians, and newer Canadians.

Chandrakant Shah, Ont, MD, FRCP(C), FAAP, SM (Hyg.), is a Canadian doctor, researcher, and social activist. Dr. Shah is the clinical coordinator of Anishnawbe Health Toronto, where he has been a staff physician since 1996, providing primary health care to Toronto's aboriginal community as well as people who have been marginalized, such as the homeless, the unemployed, and children living in poverty. He is also a consultant with Peel Public Health, honourary staff of the Hospital for Sick Children, and courtesy staff at the St. Michael's Hospital (Toronto). He is professor emeritus of the Dalla Lana School of Public Health at the School of Medicine, University of Toronto. His textbook, *Public Health and Preventive Medicine in Canada*, is widely used by Canadian undergraduate and graduate students from a range of health disciplines. He is recipient of several awards including the Order of Ontario and the Outstanding Physicians of Ontario award (2007) by the Council of the College of Physicians and Surgeons of Ontario for excellence and coming closest to meeting society's vision of an "ideal physician."

Ali Velshi (born October 29, 1969) is a Canadian American television journalist best known for his work on CNN. He is CNN's chief business correspondent, anchor of CNN's *Your Money*, and a cohost of CNN International's weekday business show *World Business Today*.

Born in Nairobi, Kenya, and raised in Toronto, he is the son of Murad Velshi, the first Canadian of Indian origin elected to the Legislative Assembly of Ontario, and his wife, Mila, who grew up in South Africa. He is an Ismaili Muslim of Indian descent and earned a degree in religious studies from Queen's University in Kingston, Ontario, in 1994. In 2010 Velshi was awarded the Queen's University Alumni Achievement Award.

In 1996 Velshi was awarded a fellowship to the United States Congress from the American Political Science Association. In this capacity, he worked with Lee Hamilton, a Democratic representative from Indiana. Being Muslim, Velshi regularly acknowledges his Islamic background and perspective when discussions involve Islam. Velshi has strongly defended the Muslim community's right to build a mosque and Islamic centre

(Park51) near Ground Zero in New York City. Velshi has also been critical of Peter King's hearings on Islamic radicalization in the United States as a form of Islamophobia and branding King as "naive." Velshi supports the separation of mosque and state and rejects "Political Islam," which requires the implementation of Sharia law. He has been in turn accused of downplaying the role that mainstream Islam jurisprudence, scholarship, and interpretation play in the development and application of radical Islam and branding negative statements about Islam as biased.

Anne Marie Abeyesinghe Mediwake (born 1975 in Kandy, Sri Lanka) is a Canadian television news anchor. Formerly coanchor of Global Toronto's 6:00 p.m. *News Hour*, she was hired in September 2009 by the CBC News Network. In October 2010, she became coanchor of CBC News Toronto's supper hour newscasts, alongside Dwight.

Her parents immigrated to Canada from her native Sri Lanka when she was just a child. They settled in southern Alberta, and she started her television career in Lethbridge in 1993. Six years later, she moved to Toronto where she was a reporter for CTV. While at CTV, she cohosted the award-winning *21©*, a current-affairs program aimed at Canada's younger generation, and reported for *Canada AM* and *CTV National News*.

Manjushree Thapa (Kathmandu, 1968) is a Nepali writer. She began to write upon completing her BFA in photography at the Rhode Island School of Design. Her first book was *Mustang Bhot in Fragments* (1992). In 2001 she published the novel *The Tutor of History*, which she had begun as her MFA thesis in the creative writing program at the University of Washington. Her best-known book is *Forget Kathmandu: An Elegy for Democracy* (2005), published just weeks before the royal coup in Nepal on February 1, 2005. The book was shortlisted for the Lettre Ulysses Award in 2006. After the publication of the book, Thapa left the country to write against the coup. In 2007 she published a short story collection, *Tilled Earth*. In 2009 she published a biography of a Nepali environmentalist, *A Boy from Siklis: The Life and Times of Chandra Gurung*. The following year she published a novel, *Seasons of Flight*. In 2011 she published a nonfiction collection, *The Lives We Have Lost: Essays and Opinions on Nepal*. She has also written as an op-ed contributor to the *New York Times*. During the fall and winter of 2011, she was writer-in-residence at Berton House in Dawson City, Yukon.

Prof. Vern Krishna is the first South Asian and academician to be elected to the position of treasurer (head) of the Law Society of Upper Canada in their 205-year history. The treasurer is the head of the Law Society and presides over Convocation, which is the governing body of the Law Society of Upper Canada.

Before being elected as treasurer in June of 2001, Professor Krishna served as a bencher of the Law Society for ten years. As a bencher of the Law Society, he has held high-profile positions such as chair of the Finance and Audit Committee, a member of the Strategic Planning Committee, as well as being appointed to the Board of the Lawyer's Professional Indemnity Company. Professor Krishna received his bachelor of commerce in the United Kingdom and his MBA and LLB in Alberta. He also received his LLM from Harvard University and his DCL from Cambridge. Professor of Law at the University of Ottawa, he is a member of the Ontario, Alberta, and Nova Scotia Bars.

Professor Krishna was awarded the title of Queen's Counsel and is a fellow of the Certified General Accountants of Canada, fellow of the Royal Society of Canada, and also a recipient of the Governor General's 125th Canada Commemorative Medal. He is a published author and has written extensively on tax and financial issues and served as executive director of the CGA Tax Research Centre at the University of Ottawa. He is the author of several leading works in taxation including the *Fundamentals of Canadian Income Tax* (sixth edition) and *Canadian International Taxation*. He is the editor of *Canada's Tax Treaties* and managing editor of *Canadian Current Tax*, a monthly publication on tax matters. He is the author of several leading works including *Canadian Corporate Law Reporter, Canadian Current Tax, Canada's Tax Treaties, and Ontario Law Reports*.

Rohinton Mistry was born in 1952 in Mumbai, India. He earned a BA in mathematics and economics at the University of Mumbai. He immigrated to Canada with his wife in 1975, settling in Toronto, where he studied at the University of Toronto and received a BA in english and philosophy. While attending the University of Toronto, he won two Hart House literary prizes (the first to win two), for stories that were published in the Hart House Review, and *Canadian Fiction* Magazine's annual Contributor's Prize for 1985. Two years later, Penguin Books Canada published his collection of eleven short stories, *Tales from Firozsha Baag*. It was later published in the United States as *Swimming Lessons and Other Stories from Firozsha Baag*.

When his second book, the novel *Such a Long Journey*, was published in 1991; it won the Governor General's Award, the Commonwealth Writers Prize for Best Book, and the WH Smith/Books in Canada First Novel Award. It was shortlisted for the prestigious Booker Prize and for the Trillium Award. It has been translated into German, Swedish, Norwegian, Danish, and Japanese, and has been made into the 1998 film *Such a Long Journey*. His third book, and second novel, *A Fine Balance* (1995), won the second annual Giller Prize in 1995, and in 1996, the Los Angeles Times

Book Prize for Fiction. It was selected for *Oprah's Book Club* in November 2001 and sold hundreds of thousands of additional copies throughout North America as a result. It won the 1996 Commonwealth Writers Prize and was shortlisted for the 1996 Booker prize. His literary papers are housed at the Clara Thomas Archives at York University.

Tariq Hussain (born on December 24, 1968) is a Canadian singer-songwriter and radio personality. Usually credited as Tariq, he has released four albums in his musical career, is currently a host for CBC Radio 3, and a member of the eclectic musical ensemble Brasstronaut.

Tariq was born in Cowansville, Quebec. His father, a Pakistani immigrant, was a Muslim who asked that pop music be banned from the household. It was only after his father's death that Tariq began playing guitar, at age fourteen. At Bishop's University, he studied theatre arts. He started devoting most of his time to a music career upon moving to Calgary, Alberta, in 1995.

For most of his musical career, Tariq was based in Calgary, but moved to Vancouver when he joined Radio 3. He is presently a member (guitarist) with the Vancouver-based band Brasstronaut, which formed in 2007.

Wajid Ali Khan (born on April 24, 1946 in Lahore, British India, now Pakistan) is a Canadian businessman and politician. Until 2008, he was a member of the Canadian House of Commons, representing the riding of Mississauga-Streetsville as a Conservative member of Parliament. Along with Yasmin Ratansi, Khan was the first Muslim member of Parliament (MP) to be elected for the Liberal Party. In the October 14, 2008, federal election, Khan lost his reelection bid to Liberal candidate Bonnie Crombie by 4,725 votes.

Shaun Majumder (born on January 29, 1972) is a Canadian comedian and actor. He was born in Burlington, Newfoundland, and Labrador to a European descended mother from Newfoundland and a Bengali Hindu Indian father formerly from West Bengal. He started his entertainment career as an announcer for the YTV game show *CLIPS* and soon was hosting the network's popular morning kids' show *Brain Wash*, where he was known as Ed Brainbin. He also hosted the "Slime Tour" segments on the popular game show *Uh Oh!* Eventually he joined *This Hour Has 22 Minutes* in 2003 and also hosted fifteen episodes of the *Just for Laughs* specials on television and participated in the comedy festivals in Montreal. He was also a star of *Cedric the Entertainer Presents*, aired in the United States on the Fox network, and appeared in an NFB documentary on aspiring Canadian comics, *The Next Big Thing*. Majumder has also starred in the CBC comedy pilot *Hatching, Matching and Dispatching* and the short film *Plain Brown Rapper*, as well as playing Kumar's brother in the 2004 comedy *Harold and Kumar Go to White Castle*.

In 2010 he had a guest starring role as Benny Natchie in *Republic of Doyle*, and for two years (2010–2011) starred in the TV series *Detroit 1-8-7* as Detective Vikram Mahajan. In the summer of 2011, Majumder was cast in *The Firm* in the recurring role of Andrew Palmer, the lawyer at the firm who befriends Josh Lucas's character, Mitch McDeere. In 2013 Majumder stars in a TV show called *Majumder Manor*. It documents his own quest to develop the tourism potential in his picturesque hometown of Burlington, Newfoundland.

Shyam Selvadurai (born on February 12, 1965) is a Sri Lankan Canadian novelist who wrote *Funny Boy* (1994), which won the Books in Canada First Novel Award, and *Cinnamon Garden* (1998). He currently lives in Toronto with his partner, Andrew Champion.

Selvadurai was born in Colombo, Sri Lanka, to a Sinhalese mother and a Tamil father—members of conflicting ethnic groups whose troubles form a major theme in his work. Ethnic riots in 1983 drove the family to immigrate to Canada when Selvadurai was nineteen. He studied creative and professional writing as part of a bachelor of fine arts program at York University. He recounted an account of the discomfort he and his partner experienced during a period spent in Sri Lanka in 1997 in his essay "Coming Out" in *Time Asia*'s special issue on the Asian diaspora in 2003.

In 2004 Selvadurai edited a collection of short stories: *Story-Wallah: Short Fiction from South Asian Writers*, which includes works by Salman Rushdie, Monica Ali, and Hanif Kureishi, among others. He published a young adult novel, *Swimming in the Monsoon Sea*, in 2005. *Swimming* won the Lambda Literary Award in the Children's and Youth Literature category in 2006. He was a contributor to *TOK: Writing the New Toronto, Book 1*. In 2013 he released a fourth novel, *The Hungry Ghosts*.

Adnan Virk is a sports anchor, currently for ESPN. He was previously an anchor for Maple Leaf Sports and Entertainment's Raptors NBA TV, Leaf TV, and Gol TV. Until June 2009, he hosted several programs on *The Score* and was previously an associate producer for Sportscentre at TSN. He was also the cohost of *Omniculture* and *Bollywood Boulevard* at Omni Television.

In 1972 his parents immigrated to Canada from Pakistan. He was born in Toronto but spent his formative years in Morven, Ontario, a small town just outside of Kingston. After graduating from high school, he took radio and television arts at Ryerson University. In 2009 he joined Maple Leafs Sports and Entertainment (MLSE) as a host and reporter for Raptors TV, Leafs TV, and Gol TV Canada. He left in April 2010 to join the ESPN family of stations in Bristol, Connecticut. It is planned that starting the 2013 MLB Season, he will anchor *Baseball Tonight*, replacing Steve Berthiaume.

Philip Michael Ondaatje (born on September 12, 1943), Order of Canada, is a Sri Lankan-born Canadian novelist. He won the Booker Prize for his novel *The English Patient*, which was adapted into an Academy Award-winning film.

Ondaatje's work includes fiction, autobiography, poetry, and film. He has published thirteen books of poetry and won the Governor General's Award for *The Collected Works of Billy the Kid* (1970) and *There's a Trick With a Knife I'm Learning to Do: Poems 1973–1978* (1979). *Anil's Ghost* was the winner of the 2000 Giller Prize, the Prix Medicis, the Kiriyama Pacific Rim Book Prize, the 2001 Irish Times International Fiction Prize, and Canada's Governor General's Award. *The English Patient* won the Booker Prize, the Canada Australia Prize, and the Governor General's Award, and was later made into a motion picture, which won the Academy Award for Best Picture. *In the Skin of a Lion*, a fictional story about early immigrant settlers in Toronto, was the winner of the 1988 City of Toronto Book Award, finalist for the 1987 Ritz Paris Hemingway Award for best novel of the year in English, and winner of the first Canada Reads competition in 2002. *Coming Through Slaughter* is a fictional story of New Orleans, Louisiana, circa 1900 loosely based on the lives of jazz pioneer Buddy Bolden and photographer E. J. Bellocq. It was the winner of the 1976 Books in Canada First Novel Award. *Divisadero* won the 2007 Governor General's Award. *Running in the Family* (1982) is a semifictional memoir of his Sri Lankan childhood.

Surjeet Kalsey was born in India. She relocated to Canada in 1974 and currently lives in British Columbia. Kalsey is a poet and short story writer, editor, translator, and counsellor. With most of her writings appearing in Indian and Canadian publications, readers can easily venture out and explore the diversity of Surjeet Kalsey's works.

She received a master's degree in English and Punjabi literature from Punjab University, Chandigarh, and a master's in creative writing from the University of British Columbia. Surjeet's master's thesis from UBC was titled "Karma-Shakti Therapy: An Indigenous Healing Model." She has edited and translated books and poetry. One translation appears in the Punjabi issue of *Contemporary Literature in Translation* (1977). Surjeet has also edited and translated an anthology of poetry, *Glimpses of Twentieth Century Punjabi Poetry* (1992). Kalsey's poems and short stories have appeared in numerous literary magazines. She has also written and directed plays on violence against women.

She has published books in both English and Punjabi—a book of poetry in Punjabi, *Paunan Nal Guftagoo* (1979) and *Speaking to the Winds* (1982) and *Footprints in Silence* (1988) in English. Surjeet has taught at the Vancouver Community College since 2001. She also works as a counsellor for battered women and continues to write. Many of the works by Kalsey reflect women's issues in Indo-Canadian life. Violence against women and violence within the family are but a few of the issues that emerge in her plays, poetry, and short stories. Although little has been written about Surjeet Kalsey, she delivers a powerful spirit in poems such as "Disowning Oneself," where she speaks of the struggle of women and their desire to be free. Tree and leaf analogies in Surjeet's poems describe emotions such as bliss and jealousy and portray the struggle of women.

Not only do Indo-Canadian women have to struggle within their own homes and communities for basic freedoms, but they also have to deal with racism. This comes across vividly in "Saffron Leaves," in which Kalsey talks about race relations and diversity. Although Kalsey writes much about women disowning themselves and struggling in the world, she holds out hope. "Visions" is a powerful poem about the strength and power of women to change much of what's wrong with the world, unlike "Selection" in which she speaks of the infanticide of female babies. Surjeet Kalsey is a champion of women's and children's rights. The invitation has been extended and the door opened for readers to learn about Surjeet Kalsey's poems, short stories, and plays.

Ajmer Rode is a Canadian author writing in Punjabi as well as in English. His first work was nonfiction *Vishva Di Nuhar* on Einstein's Relativity in dialogue form inspired by Plato's *Republic*. Published by the Punjabi University in 1966, the book initiated a series of university publications on popular science and sociology. Rode's first poetry book, *Surti,* influenced by science and philosophical explorations, was experimental and, in the words of critic Dr. Attar Singh, "has extended the scope of Punjabi language and given a new turn to Punjabi poetry." His most recent poetry book, *Leela*, more than one thousand pages long and coauthored with Navtej Bharati, is counted among the outstanding Punjabi literary works of the twentieth century.

Ajmer Rode is regarded the founder of Punjabi theatre in Canada. He wrote and directed the first Punjabi play, *Dooja Passa,* dealing with racism faced by minorities. This was followed by his full-length play *Komagata Maru* based on a significant racial incident in British Columbia's history. Though it lacked professional direction, the play generated considerable publicity inspiring theatrical interests in the Indian Canadian community. His most recent English play, *Rebirth of Gandhi,* was produced at Surrey

Arts Centre Canada) in 2004 to a full house. Among Rode's significant translation is *The Last Flicker,* an English rendering of a modern Punjabi classic novel *Marhi Da Diva* by Gurdial Singh, who recently won the Gyan Peeth, India's highest literary award. The translation was published by the Indian Academy of Letters in 1993. Currently Rode is member of an international team of translators rendering Sufi songs from Urdu, Punjabi, and Hindi into English; the project based in Los Angeles aims to produce a large multilingual book of original and translated songs sung by late Nusrat Fateh Ali Khan, the legendary Sufi singer of the twentieth century.

An active member of the Writer's Union of Canada, Ajmer Rode was on its national council in 1994 and later chaired its Racial Minority Writers Committee. Currently, he is coordinator of Vancouver's Punjabi Writers Forum, the oldest and influential Punjabi writers association in Canada. He has been founding member of several other Indian Canadian literary and performing arts associations including Watno Dur Art Foundation and India Music Society, founded to promote classical Indian music in North America. He was the first secretary of Samaanta, an organization to oppose violence against women, and is now on the advisory board of Chetna, a Vancouver-based organization promoting minority rights and opposing casteism. He has served on Canada Council and British Columbia Arts Council juries to award literary grants.

Rode was given the Best Overseas Punjabi Author award by the Punjab Languages Department, India, in 1994. Guru Nanak Dev University honoured him with the Prominent Citizen (literature) Award and the G. N. Engineering College honoured him with the Poet of Life Award the same year. In Canada he has been honoured with awards for Punjabi theatre and translation.

Ashok Mathur was born in Bhopal, India, and immigrated to Canada with his family in 1962. At first they settled in Nova Scotia, but by 1968 they were in Calgary, where he began working on a variety of small press and art projects. Mathur completed his PhD in English at the University of Calgary, focusing on antiracism inside and outside the academy. His first book, *Loveruage,* was published in 1993 by Wolsak and Wynn. His novel *Once upon an Elephant* was published by Arsenal Pulp Press in 1998. His second novel, *The Short, Happy Life of Harry Kumar,* was published by Arsenal Pulp Press in fall 2001. His forthcoming book is titled *A Little Distillery in Nowgong* and is based on Parsi history and diaspora. He currently is head of Critical and Cultural Studies at the Emily Carr Institute of Art and Design in Vancouver.

Raindra Maharaj is the author of *The Amazing Absorbing Boy, A Perfect Pledge,* and *Homer in Flight,* among other works. He has published in various literary journals and anthologies, written reviews and articles for the *Washington Post*, the *Globe and Mail*, and the *Toronto Star*, written a play, *Malcolm and Alvin*, for CBC Radio, and cowritten a screenplay for the film *Malini*. His books have been nominated for the Commonwealth Writers' Prize (twice), the Chapters / Books in Canada First Novel Award, the Rogers Writers' Trust Fiction Prize, and more recently, the Bocas Prize and the Trillium Award. Born in the Caribbean. He lives in Ajax, Ontario.

Suwanda H. J. Sugunasiri was born in Tangalla in Sri Lanka in 1936. On a US Fulbright Scholarship at the Ivy League University of Pennsylvania, he came to Toronto in 1967. Earning a PhD in 1978, he joined the University of Toronto's Faculty of Divinity in the early 1990s where he found himself "teaching Christian students to be better Christians." He founded Nalanda College of Buddhist studies in 2000. A columnist for the *Toronto Star* and a poet with three publications, he has just published his first novel, *Untouchable Woman's Odyssey* (2010). He has published poetry in English and fiction in Sinhala and edited a collection of short stories and a monograph on South Asian literature in Canada. Other nonfiction works include works on multiculturalism in Canada and a couple of works on Buddhism.

Priscila Uppal was born in Ottawa in 1974 to a Brazilian mother and a South Asian father. She completed a double honours, BA in English and creative writing from York University in 1997, an MA in English from the University of Toronto in 1998, and a PhD in English literature from York University in 2003. She currently lives in Toronto where she is a poet, fiction writer, academic, and professor of humanities and English at the undergraduate and graduate levels at York University. She is also a member of the board of directors of the Toronto Arts Council. Her creative and academic interests frequently intersect, and she has published work that explores the tensions and dynamics between women (particularly in closed societies: schools, nunneries), the nature of human violence, sexuality (including infertility), multicultural clashes (ethnic, religious, geographical), revisionist mythmaking (classical myth, biblical myth, historical figures), illness (physical, psychological, cultural), mourning rituals and the expression of grief (towards individuals, communities, abstract concepts), the world of readers and the dangers and benefits of reading and the imagination, the world of sport and sport aesthetics, as well as the nature of the artistic process, among other things. She has also collaborated with visual artists in the past (Tracy Carbert, Daniel Ehrenworth) and plans on more collaborative projects in the future. She lives with poet and critic Christopher Doda.

She is the author of nine books of poetry: *Summer Sport: Poems* (2013), *Winter Sport: Poems* (2010), *Successful Tragedies: Selected Poems 1998–2010* (Bloodaxe Books U.K. 2010), *Traumatology* (2010), *Ontological Necessities* (2006), *Live Coverage* (2003), *Pretending to Die* (2001), *Confessions for a Fertility Expert* (1999), and *How to Draw Blood from a Stone* (1998); the novels *To Whom It May Concern (2009)*, and *The Divine Economy of Salvation* (2002); and a critical study on elegies, *We Are What We Mourn (2009)*. She is also the editor of several anthologies and essay collections, including *The Exile Book of Canadian Sports Stories* (2009), *The Exile Book of Poetry in Translation: Twenty Canadian Poets Take On the World* (2009), *Barry Callaghan: Essays on his Works* (2007), *Red Silk: An Anthology of South Asian Canadian Women Poets* (2004), and *Uncommon Ground: A Celebration of Matt Cohen.*

Her works have been published internationally and translated into numerous languages including Croatian, Dutch, French, Greek, Italian, Korean, and Latvian. In 2010 she was CANFund poet-in-residence during the Vancouver Olympics and Paralympics. Priscila Uppal's works have been taught in several countries, where she has also read and lectured at literary festivals, universities, colleges, and reading series. She is a frequent guest on radio, television, and in print media, and has designed and led writing workshops for over a decade.

Uma Parameswaran—poet, playwright, and short-story writer—was born in Madras and grew up in Jabalpur, India. Parameswaran read extensively drawing motivation from epic poetry and Greek theatre through her schooling and during the India-China war of 1962. Receiving the Smith-Mundt Fulbright Scholarship, Parameswaran moved to the United States to study American literature at Indiana University, earning her MA in creative writing. She completed her PhD in English at Michigan State University in 1972. Currently she is a professor of English at the University of Winnipeg. Since settling in Canada, Parameswaran has devoted much of her writing and efforts in the literary field to creating an identifiable South Asian Canadian diaspora. Other areas of research are English Romantics, postcolonial literatures, and women's literature.

Moyez G. Vassanji, CM (born on May 30, 1950), is a novelist and editor, and a citizen of Canada. Vassanji's identity easily straddles three continents.

M. G. Vassanji was born in Kenya and raised in Tanzania. He attended the Massachusetts Institute of Technology and the University of Pennsylvania, where he specialized in nuclear physics, before moving to Canada as a postdoctoral fellow in 1978. From 1980 to 1989 he was a research associate at the University of Toronto. During this period he developed a keen interest in medieval Indian literature and history, cofounded and edited a literary magazine (the *Toronto South Asian Review*, later renamed the *Toronto Review of Contemporary Writing Abroad*), and began writing fiction. In 1989, with the publication of his first novel, *The Gunny Sack*, he was invited to spend a season at the International Writing Program of the University of Iowa. In 1996 he was a fellow of the Indian Institute of Advanced Study in Shimla, India.

M. G. Vassanji is one of Canada's most acclaimed writers. He has published six novels, two collections of short stories, a memoir of his travels in India, and a biography of Mordecai Ritchler. His work has appeared in various countries and several languages. Vassanji has been nominated for the Giller Prize for best work of fiction in Canada three times, winning twice. He has also been awarded the Commonwealth Regional Prize (Africa) and the Governor General's Prize for nonfiction. His work has also been shortlisted for the Rogers Prize, the Governor General's Prize in Canada for fiction, as well as the Crossword Prize in India. His most recent book, set in Tanzania, will be published in Canada in 2012. He is a member of the Order of Canada and has been awarded several honourary doctorates.

Anosh Irani (born in 1974) is an Indian Canadian novelist and playwright. An Irani was born and raised in Mumbai. After working in advertising in India, he moved to Vancouver in 1998 to study and pursue writing.

His first full-length play, *The Matka king*, premiered in October 2003 at the Arts Club Theatre Company in Vancouver. His play, *Bombay Black*, won four Dora Awards, including Outstanding New Play. Irani was also featured in *Quill and Quire* as one of a handful of young Canadian "writers to watch." He published his debut novel, *The Cripple and His Talismans*, in 2004. This dark fable won critical acclaim for its magic realist depiction of the seedy beggars' underworld of India. Irani's second novel, *The Song of Kahunsha*, was chosen as a CBC Book Club one pick and was selected for the 2007 edition of *Canada Reads*, where it was championed by Donna Morrissey. *Kahunsha* is a story about the abandoned children of Bombay, struggling for survival and to hold on to hope amid the violence of the 1993 racial riots. His third novel, *Dahanu Road*, was published in 2010. His latest play, *My Granny the Goldfish*, premiered at the Arts Club Theatre Company's new venue, the Revue Stage, in Vancouver on April 16, 2010.

Tarek Fatah (born on November 20, 1949) is a Canadian writer, broadcaster, and a secular Muslim anti-Islamist activist. He is the author of *Chasing a Mirage: The Tragic Illusion of an Islamic Stat* published by John Wiley and Sons. In the book Fatah challenges the notion that the establishment of an Islamic state is a necessary prerequisite to entering the state of Islam. He suggests that the idea of an Islamic state is merely a mirage that Muslims have been made to chase for over a millennium.

Fatah's second book, titled *The Jew Is Not My Enemy: Unveiling the Myths that Fuel Muslim Anti-Semitism*, was published by McClelland and Stewart in October 2010. The book won the 2010 Annual Helen and Stan Vine Canadian Book Award in Politics and History. In May 2009 Fatah joined CFRB 1010. Later that fall, he joined John Moors's morning show as a contributor. Currently, he hosts *The Tarek Fatah Show* on Sunday afternoons. He also has a weekly column in the *Toronto Sun* and is a frequent guest on the Sun News Network.

Fatah is the founder of the Muslim Canadian Congress and served as its communications officer and spokesperson for several years, and was frequently quoted in the press as a result. Fatah advocates gay rights, a separation of religion and state, opposition to *sharia law*, and advocacy for a "liberal, progressive form" of Islam. Some of his activism and statements have met with considerable criticism from Canadian Muslim groups. He is a staunch critic of Pakistan in his articles and columns, which have earned him much controversy. In February 2013, the website of the *Toronto Sun*, where Fatah contributes his articles, was blocked in Pakistan. According to reports, the block was likely due to Fatah's unsparing critiques of Pakistan published in the tabloid. Fatah is also banned from making public speeches or lectures in Pakistan.

Suresh Joachim Arulanantham is a Tamil Canadian film actor, producer, and multiple Guinness World Record holder who has broken sixty world records set in several countries in attempts to benefit underprivileged children around the world. He has captured the public's attention by breaking world records in many categories. He currently holds more than twenty records, including the World's Fastest Movie from script to screening in eleven days, twenty-three hours, and forty-five minutes.

Nelofer Pazira is an award-winning Afghan Canadian director, actress, journalist, and author. She grew up in Kabul, Afghanistan, where she lived through ten years of Soviet occupation before escaping with her family to Pakistan. From there, they immigrated to New Brunswick, Canada, more than twenty years ago.

In 1996 Nelofer attempted to return to Afghanistan—still under Taliban rule—to find a lost childhood friend. Although unsuccessful, Nelofer became the star of *Kandahar*, a highly acclaimed feature film (presented at the Cannes Film Festival in 2001) that was based on her journey. She was awarded the Prix d'interprétation by the Festival du Nouveau Cinéma de Montréal for her performance in Kandahar. She also assisted UNESCO as a goodwill ambassador in their cultural work inside Afghanistan. She has been a jury member at a number of film festivals including those of Locarno, Geneva, Sao Paulo, Edinburgh, and Montreal. Nelofer later performed in, coproduced, and codirected *Return to Kandahar*, which won the 2003 Gemini Award in Canada and also appeared in Chrisgtian Frei's documentary, *The Giant Buddhas*. In 2008 she directed and produced *Audition*, a documentary about images and cinema in Afghanistan, which premiered at the Hot Docs Canadian International Documentary Festival. She is the writer and director of *Act of Dishonour* (2010), a feature film about honour killing and the plight of returning refugees.

Nelofer has directed a number of documentaries and has worked for the Canadian Broadcasting Corporation (CBC) in CBC Television and CBC Radio. Her radio documentary *Of Paradise and Failure*, about the fate of a young suicide bomber and his family, was the winner of the Silver Medal at New York's media award ceremony. She has written for the *Toronto Star*, the *Independent* of London, the British film journal *Sight and Sound*, and many other publications. Nelofer founded a charity, the Dyana Afghan Women's Fund (www.dawf.ca), named after her childhood friend who died during Taliban rule. It provides education and skills training for women in Afghanistan. In 2006 Nelofer's memoir *A Bed of Red Flowers: In Search of My Afghanistan* was named winner of the Drainie-Taylor Biography Prize.

Nelofer is a frequent speaker at international conferences as well as universities and colleges including Carleton University and George Washington University, and was a keynote speaker at the Religion, Culture, and Conflict symposium at Trinity Western University. She defended Joseph Boyden's novel *Three Day Road* in *Canada Reads 2006*. She is a past president of the influential freedom of expression movement PEN Canada. In 2009 she accompanied the governor-general of Canada, Michaelle Jean, as a cultural delegate in state visits to Slovenia, Croatia, and Greece. Nelofer holds a degree in journalism and English literature from Carleton University (Ottawa), and a master's degree in anthropology/sociology and religion from Concordia University (Montreal). She has also received an honourary doctorate of law from Carleton. Recently, she received an honourary doctorate of letters from Thompson Rivers University in Kamloops, British Columbia. She established her own film company, Kandahar Films, in 2001.

Sheema Khan was just three years old when she emigrated with her family from India to Montreal. They wanted a country with a good education system and work opportunities. But mostly, they wanted to leave behind the sectarian violence between Hindus and Muslims in their Calcutta home. Canada was that land of promise for them.

Sheema Khan is a patent agent who holds several patents of her own in drug delivery systems. She has a PhD in chemical physics from Harvard and took a year off to do social work before continuing her studies at Massachusetts Institute of Technology. Sheema Khan writes a monthly column for the *Globe and Mail* on issues pertaining to Islam and Muslims, and is the author of *Of Hockey and Hijab: Reflection of Canadian Muslim Women*. She has served on the Board of the Canadian Civil Liberties Association (2004–2008) and is the founder of the Canadian Council on American-Islamic Relations (CAIR-CAN) and its former chair (2000–2005). She testified as an expert witness on Muslims in Canada before the O'Connor Inquiry and has appeared before a number of parliamentary committees. In addition, she has spoken at numerous NGO conferences and government agencies on issues of security, civil rights, and Muslim cultural practice. She is married, the mother of three, and a faithful follower of Islam who started wearing a hijab after much soul-searching. She loves hockey (the Canadiens, of course), and plays soccer once a week with a women's team near her home in Kanata. Most recently she has become a public advocate for Muslims in Canada, particularly women who find their rights and points of view not always heard.

Raheel Raza (born 1949 in Pakistan) is a Muslim Canadian journalist, author, public speaker, media consultant, antiracism activist, and interfaith discussion leader. She lives in Toronto. She has been compared to Asura Nomani and Amina Wadud for her controversial views on Islam. She is the author of *Their Jihad, Not My Jihad: A Muslim Canadian Woman Speaks Out*. She opposes terrorism committed in the name of Islam. She also is an outspoken adversary of what she has called "inequality toward Muslim women." As a result, she has received death threats.

In August 2010 Raza, along with Tarek Fatah, both from the Muslim Canadian Congress, opposed the Muslim community centre, Park51, located near the World Trade Center site, or *Ground zero*. "We Muslims know the . . . mosque is meant to be a deliberate provocation, to thumb our noses at the infidel. The proposal has been made in bad faith, as '*Fitna*,' meaning 'mischief-making' that is clearly forbidden in the Koran . . . As Muslims we are dismayed that our co-religionists have such little consideration for their fellow citizens, and wish to rub salt in their wounds and pretend they are applying a balm to sooth the pain."

Raza is a freelance writer. In 2000 she received an award from the Canadian Ethnic Journalists and Writers Club. She has written for the *Gobe and Mail*, the *Toronto Star*, *Khaleej Times*, *Guld News*, *FrontPage*

Magazine, and the *Commentator.* She has also lectured at York University in the portrayal of Muslims in the media.

Glenda Braganza (born in 1978 in Halifax, Nova Scotia) lives in Montreal, Canada, and is a Canadian television and stage actress who has appeared in several Canadian and American television shows and films. After graduating from Concordia University in 2001, she worked and received critical praise in several productions on the Montreal stage, including *Jennydog, Jane Eyre,* and at the Montreal Fringe. Her various performances earned her the Montreal English Critics Circle Award as the Best Actress of 2003–04. She most recently starred as Gina Green in the Hollywood made-for-television film *10.5: Apocalypse,* which was about a natural disaster to hit the United States; it starred Dean Cain and Beau Bridge. She has also been on Canadian television with a featured role in the Stephen Surjik film *Tripping the Wire,* and on American television with a recurring role on the Independent Film Channel original series *The Business.*

Naranjan S. Dhalla, CM, OM, FRSC, is a Canadian cardiovascular research scientist focusing on cardiovascular pathophysiology and therapy of heart disease. Dr. Dhalla is recognized as a world leader in heart research. His laboratory employs a variety of experimental models to investigate a wide range of cardiovascular diseases at the subcellular and molecular levels.

Born in Ghanieke, Punjab, India, he received a bachelor of science in physics and chemistry from Punjab University in 1956, an AIC in chemistry from the Institution of Chemists in Kolkata, India, in 1961, a master of science in pharmacology from University of Pennsylvania in 1963, and a PhD in pharmacology from University of Pennsylvania in 1965.

In 1968 he joined the University of Manitoba as an assistant professor in physiology. In 1972 he became an associate professor and a full professor in 1974. In 1991 he was appointed a Distinguished Professor of Physiology. From 1996 to 2006, he was the director of St. Boniface Research Centre's Institute of Cardiovascular Sciences. He currently serves as the executive director of the International Academy of Cardiovascular Sciences.

Dr. Dhalla also served the International Society for Heart Research as secretary general from 1972 to 1988 and as president elect, president, and past president from 1989 to 1998. He is credited for expanding the reach of the ISHR by establishing chapters in Russia, China, Japan, India, and South America, and in many other countries of the world. In 1997 he was made a member of the Order of Canada, Canada's highest civilian honour, for having "distinguished himself in the field of cardiovascular research." In

1996 he was awarded Manitoba's Order of the Buffalo Hunt and the Order of Manitoba in 2002. In 2000 he was made a fellow of the Royal Society of Canada. In 2007 he was granted heraldic arms from the Canadian Heraldic Authority with the motto "Satayam Shivam Sundaram" or "Truth Purity Beauty." In 2009 Dr. Dhalla was awarded a honourary doctorate from Punjab University, Chandigarh, India.

Lata Pada, CM (born 1947), is an Indian-born Canadian choreographer and Bharatanatyam dancer. Pada is the founder and artistic director of Sampradaya Dance Creations, a dance company that performs South Asian dance. She is also the founder and director of Sampradaya Dance Academy, a leading professional dance training institution that is the only South Asian dance school in North America affiliated with the prestigious, UK-based Imperial Society for Teachers of Dancing. Pada is known as an influential figure in South Asian-style dance in Canada.

In December 2008 she was made a member of the Order of Canada for her contributions to the development of Bharatanatyam as a choreographer, teacher, dancer, and artistic director, as well as for her commitment and support of the Indian community in Canada. Lata was also recently appointed as adjunct professor in the Graduate Faculty of Dance, York University, Toronto. On June 18, 2012, Pada was awarded the Queen Elizabeth II Diamond Jubilee Medal for her outstanding contributions in promoting South Asian dance in Canada.

Pamela Leila Rai (born in 1966 in New Westminster, British Columbia) is a former freestyle, butterfly swimmer from Canada, who competed for her native country at the 1984 Summer Olympics in Los Angeles, California. There the resident of Delta, British Columbia, won a bronze medal in the 4 x 100 meter medley relay, alongside Anne Ottenbrite, Reema Abdo, and Michelle MacPherson. Rai represented Canada as a youth from 1976 to 1979 and was a member of Canada's National Swim Team from 1980 to 1987. Rai competed in many international events over the span of her career. Other notable awards include University of Victoria Athlete of the Year, City of Victoria Athlete of the Year, Hapoel Games silver, Pan American Games silver, and Commonwealth Games gold medals. Rai swam for the University of Victoria in British Columbia, Canada. She graduated with a degree in sociology and went on to attain an education degree from the University of British Columbia. Rai is high school special education teacher and a certified yoga instructor trained in Netala, India, in the Sivanada Yoga lineage. Rai owns and operates Silent Motion Yoga Vedanta Centre on Vancouver Island, Nanaimo, British Columbia. Rai is a member of the BC Sports Hall of Fame, the Swim BC Hall of Fame, and the University of Victoria Sports Hall of Fame. Rai is the first woman of Indian ancestry and the first Indo-Canadian of any gender to win an Olympic medal.

Monita Rajpal (born in 1974 in Hong Kong) is a Canadian CNN International news anchor, based at the network's Hong Kong office where she anchors *NewsCenter with Monita Rajpal* and *Talk Asia*. Previously, she anchored *World One* along with Zain Verjee. She also hosted the art programme *Art of Life*. For her work on the *Art of Life* program, Rajpal has reported from Havana, Cuba; Rajasthan, India; Beijing and Shanghai, China; Champagne, France, the Monaco Grand Prix, and the Venice Carnival. She also hosted a half-hour special on the fashion designer Tom Ford in which she was granted exclusive access to him and his home. She has also interviewed designers Alberta Ferretti at her headquarters in Cattolica, Italy, as well as Donatella Versace as part of a half-hour special Rajpal hosted on the 2006 Academy Awards. Also for *Art of Life*, Rajpal interviewed tennis great Boris Becker, cosmetics giant Aerin Lauder (of Estee Lauder), Olivier Krug (of Krug Champagne), and the LVMH chief, Bernard Arnault.

Since joining CNN in 2001, Rajpal has anchored many leading global and breaking news stories. In 2007 Rajpal interviewed former Russian president Mikhail Gorbachev, former vice president Al Gore, and the former Pakistani prime minister Benazir Bhutto, along with reporting on Tony Blair's departure from government. Rajpal joined CNN from CityTV in Toronto, where she was a general assignment reporter and anchor. As a CityTV reporter, Rajpal covered various stories for the channel's primetime nightly news, including federal elections, education strikes, municipal politics, and the city's homeless population. In addition to her work at CityTV, Rajpal anchored the primetime news show at Cable Pulse 24, CityTV's twenty-four-hour news channel.

Melinda Shankar (born in 1992) is a Canadian actress who is best known for playing Alli Bhandari beginning in season 8 of *Degrssi: The Next Generation* and Indira "Indie" Mehta on *How To Be Indie*. She started her acting career at age ten, appearing in TV commercials, print ads, and some theatre work. She costarred in *Harriet the Spy: Blog Wars*, a Disney Channel Original Movie alongside Jennifer Stone as Janie Gibbs, Harriet's best friend. She was born and raised in Ottawa, Canada. Shankar currently resides in Toronto, Canada.

Jaggi Singh (born in 1971 in Toronto, Canada) is one of Canada's most high-profile antiglobalization and social justice activists. Singh lives in Montreal where he works with groups such as Solidarity Across Borders (a local migrant-rights organization) and the No One Is Illegal collective, among others. Singh graduated from St. Michael's College School of

Toronto and attended the University of Toronto. He also attended the University of British Columbia.

Manoj Sood (born on May 5, 1962) is a Kenyan Canadian film and television actor. Manoj immigrated with his family to Canada in 1964 when he was eighteen months old. He grew up in Calgary, Alberta. Later, he went to filming school in St. Michaels University School in Victoria, British Columbia. Manoj Sood was born in Mombasa, Kenya, but grew up in Western Canada. Manoj entered the entertainment world in 1994 and has been working steadily for the past twelve years. Manoj, much to his surprise, landed a supporting role in *American MOW* after his very first audition. Up until then his only acting experience had been from his acting classes. Since that day Manoj has appeared in more than forty television and feature film productions. He has appeared on popular television shows like *Da Vinci's Inquest*, *The Dead Zone*, *Romeo*, *Little Mosque on the Prairie*, and *Dead Like Me*, as well as numerous others. Manoj has also acted in popular films such as *Meltdown* (2004) (TV) and *Rat Race* (2001).

Veena Sood is a Canadian-based film and television actress of Punjabi descent. She works in both the United Kingdom and Canada. She starred in ITV's *Compulsion* featuring Ray Winstone and Parminder Nagra. She has also starred in the UK film *Nina's Heavenly Delight*, as well as the Canada/UK film *Touch of Pink*, which received a standing ovation at the Sundance Film Festival. She cofounded Calgary's Loose Moose Theatre Company, best known for their improvisational theatre work. She also performs one-woman improvised shows at Canadian and UK comedy festivals with her character, "the Maharani." She used to cohost CBC Television's women's talk show *In the Company of Women*.

She has been seen on television in recurring roles in the series *Hope Island*, *Battlestar*, *Caprica*, *Little Mosque on the Prairie*, *Endgame*, and *Continuum*, and is a sought-after actress on the Canadian comedy television scene. Sood has also appeared in the feature films *Connie and Carla*, *Helen*, *50/50*, and *The Big Year*. She is sister to Ashwin Sood, Sarah McLachlan's drummer and ex-husband, and Manoj Sood, who plays Baber on *Little Mosque on the Prairie*.

Has won several awards for her acting work in Canada, including a Jessie Richardson Award (theatre) and a Leo Award (television). She has a great ear for accents, having had to do a Scottish/Punjabi accent for *Nina's Heavenly Delight*.

She was born in Nairobi, Kenya, and grew up in Calgary, Alberta. Currently, Veena continues her improvisational theatre work as the coartistic director of Keith Johnstone's *The Life Game*. Sood voiced Ms.

Harshwhinny, the Equestria Games inspector, in the animated TV series *My Little Pony: Friendship Is Magic*.

Moez Surani (born in 1979) is a Canadian poet. He is the author of the poetry collections *Reticent Bodies* and *Floating Life*. He currently lives in Toronto where he is the poetry editor for the *Toronto Review of Books*.

Poems from Surani's debut collection, *Reticent Bodies*, began appearing in 2001, when Canadian poet Todd Swift published the anthology *100 Poets against the War*. Surani's *Realpolitik*, which was initially published under the pseudonym "d. m.," was selected as part of this critique of the Iraq War. In 2001 he won the Kingston Literary Award for his short story *In Times of Drought*, which depicts the journey of two siblings who walk from Afghanistan to Iran. That year, Surani also won Queen's University's richest writing prize, the Helen Richards Campbell Memorial Scholarship for excellence in creative writing. From 2002 to 2008, his poetry was published in Canada and abroad. The *Dublin Quarterly* selected his poem "Alley Dolle" as their choice for their 2005 poem of the year, citing its "movement and music." His poem "Chopping Wood on Ivan's Farm" won third prize in *Arc Poetry Magazine*'s 2008 Poem of the Year contest.

Reticent Bodies was published in fall 2009. Poet and critic Jcob McArthur Mooney stated that the book is a return to the Canadian romantic mode of Leonard Cohen and Irving Layton. In the *Journal of Canadian Poetry*, another review praised the book for its expressiveness. In 2008 Surani received a Chalmers Arts Fellowship to visit his ancestral homelands, India and East Africa. During this trip, Surani wrote "Kilimanjaro Journal" and the poem "Are the Rivers in Your Poems Real," which won the *Antigonish Review*'s Great Blue Heron Poetry Prize in 2010. That award's jury citation states that the poem "dramatizes the tension between the world of the collective myth and poetic imagination on the one hand and individual experience and empirical decision on the other."

Between 2008 and 2011, Surani lived and traveled extensively in Asia, Europe, and Africa. In July 2010 Surani walked the Camino Santiago across northern Spain. In 2011 Surani began writing book reviews. His reviews include work by Chilean novelist Robert Bolano and the English religious historian Karen Armstrong.

Surani's second poetry collection, *Floating Life*, was published in spring 2012. The book's themes have been characterized as travel "connections made and left behind, and, above all, the fleeting nature of experience." In interview, Surani said that *Floating Life*'s leitmotif is a divestment of personal power. Surani has defined poetry as "the residue of living."

Drona Prakash Rasali (Nepali: द्रोण प्रकाश रसाली, born in Humin, Palpa district of Nepal) is an active member of Nepali Diaspora, who was elected as the deputy regional coordinator for Americas (DRC) in the International Coordinating Council (ICC) of the Nonresident Nepalis Association (NRNA) for the period, 2009–2011. He ran and lost the election for the position of regional coordinator (RC) for Americas in the NRNA International Coordinating Council (ICC), 2011–2013. He has served as the advisor to NRN-Canada National Coordinating Council since 2008[11] as well as the advisor to the NRNA International Coordinating Council (ICC) for 2011–2013.

After completing his doctoral degree from the University of Manitoba, he worked in a national epidemiological project studying food safety systems (through pork traceability, to be specific) in Canada, which involved both veterinary and public health. In 2005 he was appointed as a provincial chronic disease epidemiologist in the Saskatchewan Ministry of Health. After his seven-year public service there, he moved to take his current role as the director, Population Health Surveillance and Epidemiology at British Columbia's Provincial Health Services Authority.

Dr. Drona Rasali, a lifetime member of the Society of Agricultural Scientists-Nepal (SAS-Nepal) was elected as its executive board member responsible for publications management for 1996–1999 periods. During 2008–09, he served in the board of directors of the Saskatchewan Epidemiology Association (SEA) and chaired its Website Development Committee. He was elected as the vice president of Saskatchewan Public Health Association (SPHA), Regina, Saskatchewan in Canada, for 2011. In 2012 he chaired the Surveillance and Innovation Working Group (SIWG) of the Canadian Alliance for Regional Risk Factor Surveillance (CARRFS), a national network of public health professionals who are interested in chronic disease risk factor surveillance at the regional and local level in Canada.

Russell Dominic Peters (born on September 29, 1970, in Toronto, Ontario)[is a Canadian comedian and actor. He has set records for sales and attendance at a comedian's performance, in 2007 the first comedian to sell out Toronto's Air Canada Centre, in 2009 a sales record in London, in 2010 attracting the largest audience in Australia for a stand-up comedy show. Peters began performing in Toronto in 1989. His popularity extends to several countries, as he has since also performed in the United Kingdom, USA, Australia, New Zealand, Ireland, Afghanistan, Sweden, South Africa, India, Caribbean countries, Philippines, Vietnam, China, Sri Lanka, Singapore, UAE, Bahrain, Jordan, Denmark, Norway, Lebanon, Oman, the Netherlands, and Malaysia. In 1992 Peters met comedian Geogre Carlin, one of his biggest influences, who advised him to get on stage whenever and wherever possible. He said he "took that advice to heart, and I think that's the reason I am where I am now." In 2007, fifteen years later, he hosted one of Carlin's last shows before his death the following year.

Peters attributes a performance he did on the Canadian TV comedy show *Comedy Now!* in 2004, which was uploaded onto YouTube and became viral, as the turning point in his career. While the initial video upload featured his performance in its forty-five-minute entirety, subsequent videos uploaded by other YouTube users were snippets of that performance, chopped into each of the cultural groups he targeted. According to Peters, those snippets made their way to those specified cultural groups and were well received by them.[16] The video and its viral nature were referenced by Peters on the DVD performance of his show *Outsourced*, when he entered and jokingly addressed the audience with "Look at you, you filthy downloaders!"

In 2007 Peters was the first comedian to sell out Toronto's Air Canada Centre with more than sixteen thousand tickets sold in two days for the single show. He ended up selling over thirty thousand tickets nationally over the two-day sales period. He broke a UK comedy sales record at London's O2 Arena when he sold over sixteen thousand tickets to his show in 2009. His show in Sydney, Australia, on May 15, 2010, had an audience of 13,880, making it the largest stand-up comedy show in Australian history. Peters's performances on May 5–6, 2012, in Singapore also set attendance records for a single stand-up comedian at the Singapore Indoor Stadium. He hosted the Canada Day Comedy Festival 2006. Peters participated in a USO tour of Iraq, Afghanistan, Germany, Africa, and Greenland in November 2007 with Wilmer Valderrama and Mayra Veronica. Peters also currently produces and stars on the radio station series *Monsoon House*, on CBS Radia One. Peters was the host of the 2008 Juno Awards televised ceremonies in Calgary on April 6, 2008, for which he won a Gemini Award for Best Performance or Host in a Variety Program or Series. The 2008 awards broadcast received the second-highest ratings ever for the program.

On September 28, 2013, Peters was awarded the 2013 Trailblazer award by SAMMA—the Association of South Asians in Media, Marketing, and Entertainment, for his contributions to the world of comedy. He is among the first South Asians to enter the field and has become one of the most successful comedians in the industry.

Peters has appeared in many films. He acted in the Punjabi Canadian *Breakaway* (2011), alongside Camilla Belle, Anupam Kher, and Vinay Virmani. That year he also acted in Duncan Jones's *Source Code* (2011) as

Max, an amateur comedian with a bad attitude; and as Pervius in *National Lampoon's 301: The Legend of Awesomest Maximus* (2011).

He appeared in *Senor Skip Day* (2008), which starred Larry Miller, Tara Reid, and Gary Lundy. That year he was also in *The Take* (2008) as Dr. Sharma. Earlier he had cameo roles in *Boozecan* (1994) as Snake's friend, *Tiger Claws III* (2000) as Detective Elliott, *My Baby's Daddy (*2004) as the obstetrician, and *Quarter Life Crisis* (2006) as Dilip Kumar. Peters has guest starred on the TV series, *Mr. D*, as the school superintendent. In 2011 he starred in a TV Christmas special, *A Russell Peters Christmas*, which aired in Canada. Guests included Michael Buble, Pamela Anderson, and Jon Lovitz, among others. It had the highest number of viewers of any CTV Canadian holiday special.

Emmanuel Noveen Malhotra is a Canadian professional ice hockey centre and alternate captain of the Carolina Hurricanes of the National Hockey League (NHL). He previously played in the NHL for the Vancouver Canucks, San Jose Sharks, Columbus Blur Jackets, Dallas Stars, and New York Rangers. Malhotra is known as a two-way forward and for his faceoff proficiency.

Malhotra was drafted in the first round as the seventh overall pick of the 1998 NHL Entry Draft by the New York Rangers. He joined the NHL after a two-year career in the Ontario Hockey League (OHL) with the Guelph Storm with whom he served as captain in his final year. Winning a J. Ross Robertson championship and subsequently appearing in the 1998 Memorial Cup with the Storm, Malhotra also earned a Bobby Smith Trophy, George Parsons Trophy, and Memorial Cup All-Star honours as a junior.

He played with the Rangers from 1998 to 2002. During this time, he was assigned on numerous occasions to the team's AHL affiliate, the Hartford WolfPack with whom he won a Calder Cup championship in 2000. At the 2001–02 trade deadlines, he was dealt to the Stars and spent parts of three seasons with the club. Beginning in 2003–04, Malhotra began to see increased offensive production, marked by his acquisition off waivers by the Blue Jackets. After four seasons in Columbus, he signed a one-year contract with the Sharks in September 2009. He recorded a career high in goals with San Jose before joining the Canucks on a three-year deal. In his first season with Vancouver, Malhotra suffered a major injury to his left eye, requiring several surgeries. Despite having lost a significant amount of his vision, he returned the same year to compete in the 2011 Stanley Cup Finals. He struggled to play with the injury until Canucks management placed him on the injured reserve for the remainder of the 2012–13 in February 2013.

Internationally, Malhotra has represented Canada in two Under 18 World Junior Championships and one World Championship. Serving as team captain at the 2000, Malhotra led Canada to a bronze medal.

Malhotra was born (May 18, 1980) and raised in Mississauga, Ontario. His father, Shadi, was born in Lahore, Pakistan, and worked as a research chemist for Xerox. He holds over 110 patents and is now retired. His mother, Lise, is a French Canadian and was a stay-at-home mom. His parents both hold doctorate degrees from the University of Lavel in Quebec City—his father's in polymer chemistry, and his mother's in biochemistry. Due to his mother's French background, he spoke both French and English at home. Malhotra has three siblings, two brothers and a sister.

14

Annex 4: Canada's Best Diversity Employers[172]

Alberta-Pacific Forest Industries
Boyle, Alberta alpac.ca
- recruits from, offers apprenticeships to, and partners with local aboriginals
- provides mandatory aboriginal awareness training to all employees

Assiniboine Credit Union
Winnipeg
assiniboine.mb.ca
- meets or exceeds local averages in representation of aboriginal, minority, and disabled workers
- is an employer where 50 percent of its executive management team are women

Bell Aliant Regional Communications
Halifax
aliant.ca
- promotes the personal career development of women employees through community involvement and networking
- recently launched a diversity section on its company intranet site
- includes a diversity module in its leadership development training program

Blake, Cassel and Grayson LLP
across Canada
blakes.com
- established a Diversity Champion award to recognize employees who have promoted diversity within Blakes or the legal profession
- established an equity and diversity committee
- has a dedicated budget to fund its diversity projects and programs

Boeing Canada Technology
Winnipeg division
boeing.com
- has an employment equity and diversity team that meets biweekly to discuss diversity initiatives
- offers BlackBerrys to deaf employees

Canada Mortgage and Housing Corporation
Ottawa
cmhc-schl.gc.ca/en
- provides mentoring and skills development to individuals with Down syndrome
- integrates diversity accountability into the performance measurement process for managers
- advertises job openings in ethnic newspapers

Canada Post
across Canada
canadapost.ca
- distributes job advertisements to Equitek Employment Equity Solutions to find job candidates who are hard to reach through traditional recruitment strategies
- regularly assesses whether diversity and equity goals are being met
- recently updated its recruitment policies to include sections on how to reach a more diverse labour market

Canadian Pacific Railway
Calgary
cpr.ca
- created forum to develop recruitment initiatives for women engineers
- manages diversity and employment equity advisory panels in offices across Canada

- hosts a variety of information sessions on topics such as aboriginal spirituality, Islam, Judaism, Buddhism, and learning disabilities

Catholic Children's Aid Society of Toronto
Toronto
ccas.toronto.on.ca
- all employees undergo mandatory training sessions on race relations
- helps other children's aid societies develop diversity programs
- nearly a third of its management-level employees are visible minorities

Corus Entertainment
Toronto
corusent.com
- targets and develops women and visible minorities for managerial positions in radio programming
- manages nationwide employment equity committees who advise the company on diversity and equity issues and gather feedback from employees
- recently launched a new recruitment and selection program that includes a diversity-in-the-workplace training module

Ernst & Young
Toronto
ey.com/ca
- its partners mentor and coach minority managers
- measures workplace inclusiveness through employee diversity census
- holds regular leadership training conferences for visible minority and women employees

Hewlett-Packard (Canada)
Mississauga
hp.com/canada
- provides training in diversity in the workplace, managing diversity in the workplace and diversity workshops
- offers resources programs for disabled, LGBT (lesbian, gay, bisexual, and transgender) and women employees
- hosts "safe space" sessions to discuss LGBT workplace issues

HSBC Bank Canada
Vancouver
hsbc.ca
- maintains a central, corporate budget dedicated to workplace accommodation
- provides training to senior employees on how to develop talented employees from diverse groups
- recognizes employees through a diversity peer recognition award

Information Services Corporation of Saskatchewan
Regina
isc.ca
- formed diversity and equity working group
- forwards job postings to aboriginal schools and organizations
- encourages more job applications from members of equity groups through targeted recruitment

Intuit Canada
Edmonton
intuit.ca
- established LGBT network to provide support and professional development opportunities
- established a women's network to provide peer mentoring and skills development

KPMG
across Canada
kpmg.ca
- diversity advisory board meets quarterly to help direct company's diversity, inclusion and equity strategy
- vows to increase women and minority employees by 10 percent over five years
- introduced a director of diversity role

L'Oréal Canada
Montreal
loreal.ca
- provides diversity training programs to all employees
- has a global diversity director

McGill University
Montreal
mcgill.ca
- actively recruits aboriginal and disabled employees
- offers training on how to integrate deaf employees into the workplace
- provides equity and diversity in the workplace training for supervisors

Nexen
Calgary
nexeninc.com
- recruits aboriginal students through recruitment fairs and aboriginal student associations
- provides two-day aboriginal awareness training sessions for employees

Ontario Public Service
Toronto
gov.on.ca
- manages a pilot program where deputy ministers mentor minority, disabled, aboriginal, LGBT, or Francophone employees
- hosts an internship program for disabled individuals
- provides special training for managers on how to accommodate employees with disabilities

Pfizer Canada
Kirkland, Quebec
Pfizer.ca
- has a vice president of diversity and inclusion
- provides a well-developed diversity training program to employees
- offers paid language training classes for employees in English or French

Procter & Gamble
Toronto
pgcanada.ca
- all employees must complete diversity training
- hosts employee networks for Asian, French, LGBT, black, and Latino groups
- created a diversity leadership assessment tool that allows employees to assess how well their managers create diverse and inclusive work environments

Royal Bank of Canada
across Canada
rbc.com
- actively recruits disabled and aboriginal employees
- diversity mentoring program matches employees with a senior-level mentor
- has a diversity leadership council that meets quarterly

Saskatchewan Government Insurance
Regina
sgi.sk.ca
- sets annual diversity goals and measures managers' success through monthly reports
- established aboriginal peer-to-peer advisory network
- more than half of the participants in their summer student program were members of equity groups last year

SaskPower
Regina
saskpower.com
- new diversity strategy includes a company-wide awareness campaign
- hosts workshops on disability and aboriginal awareness
- advertises job openings in ethnic publications, aboriginal radio and television stations, and multicultural radio stations

Scotiabank Group
across Canada
scotiabank.com
- interview and selection process for managers and recruiters includes diversity component
- has a website and networking series for female employees
- works with employment services to recruit employees from diversity groups, especially disabled employees

Statistics Canada
Ottawa
statcan.gc.ca
- manages recruitment, retention, and internship programs for aboriginal employees and jobseekers
- has a subcommittee on disability issues

- established targeted recruitment and retention programs for members of designated groups

Telus Corporation
Vancouver
telus.com
- network for women employees offers leadership and career development opportunities
- special training program helps women further develop leadership skills
- created a diversity steering committee and working council to develop and implement diversity-related HR programs

Toronto Police Service
Toronto
torontopolice.on.ca
- established recruiting coalition of employees from Asian, black, Somali, Jewish, and LGBT groups
- hosts women-only prep sessions, where women interested in policing receive training and mentoring from female officers
- established a diversity management unit to oversee its diversity policy, procedures, and programs

University Health Network
Toronto
uhn.on.ca
- provides customized diversity training
- manages an internal diversity website
- its diversity councils raise awareness and act as a resource

University of British Columbia
Vancouver
ubc.ca
- equipment accommodation fund helps meet the needs of disabled faculty and staff
- manages an ongoing Positive Space campaign for LGBT employees
- requires managers and supervisors to attend a one-day training program in bias-free interviewing

University of Toronto
Toronto
utoronto.ca
- LGBT human resources committee provides training to other staff
- manages equity offices for initiatives in antiracism, LGBT issues, and the status of women
- host leadership seminars and networking breakfasts for senior-level women employees

Vancity Group
Vancouver
vancity.com
- a leading sponsor of Vancouver's Pride Parade
- launched a recruitment ad campaign to immigrant settlement agencies and ethnic newspapers
- trains its recruiters to recognize how job candidates from other cultures may answer interview questions differently

WorkSafeBC
Vancouver
worksafebc.com
- senior leadership team includes female, minority, aboriginal, and LGBT employees
- provides work placements for disabled college students
- More than half of the employees enrolled in their in-house leadership development program are women.

Xerox Canada Ltd.
Toronto
xerox.ca
- publishes a guide for hiring managers on ensuring a bias-free selection process
- organizes a variety of workshops for hiring managers, including how to create inclusive work environments and gender awareness in the workplace

[Note: Every year the list is revamped. Please see the site: www.canadastop100.com/diversity/ for annual updated list.]

15

Annex 5: Glossary of Terms

Aboriginal People

The term "aboriginal people" refers to the original inhabitants of a country or territory before European contact. In Canada, "aboriginal people" or "indigenous people" is used to collectively refer to different cultural groups—namely, the First Nations, Inuit, Dene, and Metis people of Canada. Each group is very distinct with unique languages, cultural practices, spiritual beliefs, and histories.

Acculturation

Acculturation is a process in which members of one cultural group adopt the beliefs and behaviours of another group. Although acculturation is usually in the direction of a minority group adopting habits and language patterns of the dominant group, acculturation can be reciprocal—that is, the dominant group also adopts patterns typical of the minority group. Assimilation of one cultural group into another may be evidenced by changes in language preference, adoption of common attitudes and values, membership in common social groups and institutions, and loss of separate political or ethnic identification.

The term also refers to a series of psychosocial changes experienced by an individual to become a functioning member of a new culture. The acculturation process also includes a sequence of emotional and psychological changes because of having to adjust to a new or different culture.

Baby boom

A dramatic increase in fertility rates and in the absolute number of births in the United States, Canada, Australia, and New Zealand during the period following World War II (1947–1961).

Bilingualism

Bilingualism means the ability to speak two languages. In Canada the term "bilingualism" usually refers to the ability to speak both English and French, the two official languages of Canada, and to Canadian federal government policies to encourage the use of the two official languages in Canadian society.

Business immigrant

Canada has three classes of business immigrants, each with separate eligibility criteria: investors, entrepreneurs, and self-employed persons. Applications can be made for only one class, even if the applicant fulfils the requirements of the other classes. Once an application is submitted, the class cannot be changed.

Birth rate (or crude birth rate)

The number of live births per one thousand population in a given year; not to be confused with the growth rate.

Canadian Experience Class

The Canadian Experience Class is a Canadian immigration program intended for foreign students and foreign workers who have already lived in Canada for some time (perhaps with a work permit or a study permit) and thus have gained Canadian experience. The Canadian government believes that these people will be more successful than other applicants at adapting to life in Canada and becoming economically established, since they are most likely proficient in English and/or French and most likely have work experience in Canada.

Cultural assimilation

Cultural assimilation (often called merely *assimilation*) is a process of integration whereby members of an ethnocultural community (such as immigrants or ethnic minorities) "absorbed" into another, generally larger, community. This implies the loss of the characteristics of the absorbed group, such as language, customs, ethnicity, and self-identity. It can be assumed that the power of the majority will be too much for any minority or immigrant group to resist, and therefore, the group will assimilate into the majority.

Chinese Head Tax and Exclusion Act

When the Canadian Pacific Railway was finished and cheap labour in large numbers was no longer needed, there was a backlash from union workers and some politicians against the Chinese. After Royal Commission on Chinese Immigration, the Canadian federal government passed the *Chinese Immigration Act* in 1885, putting a head tax of fifty dollars on Chinese immigrants in the hopes of discouraging them from entering Canada. In 1900 the head tax was increased to one hundred dollars. In 1903 the head tax went up to $500, which was about two years' pay. The Canadian federal government collected about $23 million from the Chinese head tax. In 1923 Canada passed the *Chinese Exclusion Act*, which in effect stopped Chinese immigration to Canada for nearly a quarter of a century. July 1, 1923, the day the Canadian *Chinese Exclusion Act* came into effect, is known as "humiliation day." The Chinese population in Canada went from 46,500 in 1931 to about 32,500 in 1951.

Canadian Charter of Rights and Freedoms

The Canadian Charter of Rights and Freedoms (also known as the Charter of Rights and Freedoms, or simply the Charter; French: *La Charte canadienne des droits et libertés*) is a bill of rights entrenched in the

Constitution of Canada. It forms the first part of the *Constitution Act* 1982. The Charter guarantees certain political rights to Canadian citizens and civil rights of everyone in Canada from the policies and actions of all areas and levels of government. It is designed to unify Canadians around a set of principles that embody those rights. The Charter was signed into law by Queen Elizabeth II of Canada on April 17, 1982.

Diversity

A term used to encompass all the various differences among people—including race, religion, gender, sexual orientation, disability, socioeconomic status, etc.—and commonly used in the United States and increasingly in Canada to describe workplace programs aimed at reducing discrimination promoting equality of opportunity and outcome for all groups. Concern has been expressed by antiracism and race relations practitioners that diversity programs may water down efforts to combat racism in all its forms.

Dominant group

It is the most powerful and privileged group in a particular society. The dominant group in Canada is white, Christian, male, and English speaking, perceiving themselves to be superior to and more privileged than aboriginal people, black people, and other people of colour or people of minority religious or linguistic groups.

Designated groups

The *Federal Employment Equity Act* refers to four groups that are underrepresented in the public sector. These groups include persons with disabilities, First Nations people, members of visible minorities, and women.

Discrimination

Discrimination is behaviour that excludes individuals or treats them unfairly because they are members of specific groups. According to the Ontario Human Rights Code, individuals cannot be discriminated against in services and facilities based on their race, sex, sexual orientation, transgender status, same sex partner status, colour, ancestry, place of origin, ethnic origin, marital status, age, disability, citizenship, family status, or religion. There are two types of discrimination—direct (intentional) and systemic.

Diaspora

The word can also refer to the movement of the population from its original homeland. The term "diaspora" is derived from the Greek words "dia," which means "through"; and "kpeiro," which means "to scatter." Literally "diaspora" means scattering or dispersion. It was originally used for the dispersion of Jews after their exile from Babylon in the sixth century BC, and later to refer to all the Jewish people scattered in exile outside Palestine. Today it has come to describe any group of people who are dispersed or scattered away from their home country with a distinct collective memory and a myth of return. Over the past two centuries, India has achieved world's most diverse and complex migration histories, forming the Modern Indian Diaspora. Spread across all 6 continents and 125 countries, it is estimated to number around thirty million.

Emigration

The process of leaving one's home or country in order to settle in another home, place, or country, for personal, economic, political, religious, or social reasons.

Economic immigrant

Permanent residents selected for their skills and ability to contribute to Canada's economy. The economic immigrant category includes workers, business immigrants, provincial or territorial nominees, live-in caregivers, and Canadian Experience Class.

Entrepreneurs

Economic immigrants in the business immigrant category who are selected on the condition that they managed and controlled a percentage of equity of a qualifying business for at least two years in the period beginning five years before they apply, and that they have a legally obtained net worth of at least CAN$400,000. They must own and manage a qualifying business in Canada for at least one year in the three years following arrival in Canada.

Ethnocultural group

An ethnocultural group is made up of people who share a particular cultural heritage or background. Every person living in Canada belongs to an ethnic group. There are a variety of ethnocultural groups among people of African, Asian, European, and indigenous North, Central, and South American backgrounds in Canada. Some Canadians may experience discrimination because of ethnocultural affiliation (ethnicity, religion, nationality, language).The term "ethnicity" often refers to a consciousness of shared or common origin, common beliefs and values, and a common sense of survival. Many definitions of ethnicity are marked by reference to shared ancestry, territory or land, language, religion, kinship groups, and cultural practises. Ethnicity is a socially constructed concept, not a biological category.

The terms "ethnicity" and ethnic" are often used to label or categorise individuals or groups and are often imposed by others. This can result in an intended or unintended differentiation between those who are considered to be "ethnic" and those who are considered not be "ethnic." This can inadvertently normalise people from some groups and position everyone else as "other." Therefore these terms should always be used with caution.

Employment equity

Achieve equality in the workplace so that no person shall be denied employment opportunities or benefits for reasons unrelated to ability and, in the fulfillment of that goal, to correct the conditions of disadvantage in employment experienced by *women, aboriginal people, persons with disabilities, and members of visible minorities* by giving effect to the principle that employment equity means more than treating persons in the same way but also requires special measures and the accommodation of differences.

Federal skilled workers

An immigration class where skilled workers are selected as permanent residents based on their education, work experience, knowledge of English and/or French, and other criteria that have been shown to help them become economically established in Canada.

Foreign credential recognition

The process of assessing and/or evaluating credentials obtained abroad in terms of Canadian equivalencies. Organizations that assess foreign credentials include credential assessment agencies, educational institutions, and regulatory bodies.

Foreign worker

A foreign national who has been authorised to enter and remain in Canada on a temporary basis as a worker. This category excludes foreign students and people who have been issued employment authorisations for humanitarian reasons. Every foreign worker must have an employment authorisation, but may also have other types of permits or authorisations.

Integration

Generally, it can describe the bringing together of different cultures to create a cohesive dynamic culture. Unlike assimilation whereby the dominant culture is adopted, integration involves the creation of a new culture based on aspects of each contributing culture.

Immigration and Refugee Protection Act

Canada's new Immigration and Refugee Protection Act replaces the Immigration Act, which was approved in 1976 and has been amended more than thirty times. The new act modernizes Canada's immigration policy. It provides Canada with the tools to attract workers with flexible skills, and it speeds up family reunification. The act is tough on those who pose a threat to Canadian security, while maintaining Canada's humanitarian tradition of providing safe haven to people in need of protection.

Immigrant and migrant

The terms "immigrant" and "migrant" are often used interchangeably; however, they have subtle differences. An immigrant is a person and their family members that move into a country, other than where they were born, to live; whereas, a migrant is a person and their family members that move from their country of birth to live in another country.

Marginalization

Marginalization is the social process by which a person or a group of people are made marginal or become relegated to the fringe or edge of society usually on the basis of minority identity such as culture, race, religion, sexual orientation, and disability. It occurs when people is pushed to the edge of a society as an effect of discrimination, making the person stand out and look different from everybody else. They consequently feel alone and left out from the rest of society.

Multiculturalism

Commonly used to refer to the fact that the different ethnic and cultural groups are free to maintain and practice their culture while residing in Canada. In Canada, the Multiculturalism Act (Bill C-93) states that the government "recognizes the diversity of Canadians as regards to race, national or ethnic origin, colour and religion as a fundamental characteristics of Canadian society and is committed to a policy of multiculturalism designed to preserve and enhance the multicultural heritage of Canadians while working to achieve the equality of all Canadians in the economic, social, cultural and political life of Canada."

Melting pot

Term usually used to refer to the American monocultural society in which there is a conscious attempt to assimilate diverse people into a homogeneous culture, rather than to integrate as equals in the society while maintaining various cultural or ethnic identities.

National Occupational Classification (NOC)

The National Occupational Classification is a list of all the occupations in the Canadian labour market. It describes each job according to skill type and level. The NOC is used to collect and organize job statistics and to provide labour market information. It is also used as a basis for certain immigration requirements.

Permanent residency

Permanent residency is a legal status that enables someone to live in Canada for an indefinite period. Permanent residency does not give someone Canadian citizenship, and thus the permanent resident does not have the right to join the military or vote in a federal election, but the permanent resident benefits from all the other rights of a Canadian citizen.

Provincial Nominee Program (PNP)

Canadian immigration applications can be made via Provincial Nomination Program (PNP), which enables provinces to choose applicants who they feel will contribute to the economy of their province. The selection criteria are similar to that of the federal skilled workers, but may have some province-specific aspects that differ from the federal criteria.

Population increase

The total population increase resulting from the interaction of births, deaths, and migration in a population in a given period of time.

Population projection

Computation of future changes in population numbers, given certain assumptions about future trends in the rates of fertility, mortality, and migration. Demographers often issue low, medium, and high projections of the same population based on different assumptions of how these rates will change in the future.

Persons with disabilities

Refers to persons who identify themselves as experiencing difficulties in carrying out the activities of daily living or experience disadvantage in employment, and who may require some accommodation because of a long-term or recurring physical or developmental condition.

Race

Refers to a group of people of common ancestry; distinguished from others by physical characteristics such as colour of skin, shape of eyes, hair texture, or facial features. (This definition refers to the common usage of the term "race" when dealing with human rights matters. It does not reflect the current scientific debate about the validity of phenotypic descriptions of individuals and groups of individuals.) The term is also used to designate social categories into which societies divide people according to such characteristics. Race is often confused with ethnicity. Various types of broad-based groups (e.g., racial, ethnic, religious, and regional) are rarely mutually exclusive, and the degree of discrimination against any one or more varies from place to place, and over time.

Replacement-level fertility

It is defined as the level of fertility at which a couple has only enough children to replace themselves, or in other words, two children per couple.

Racism and racial discrimination

Canada has a legacy of racism—particularly towards aboriginal persons, but to other groups as well including African, Chinese, Japanese, South Asian, Jewish, and Muslim Canadians—a legacy that profoundly permeates our systems and structures to this day, affecting the lives of not only racialized persons but also all people in Canada. The Ontario Human

Rights Commission describes communities facing racism as "racialized." This is because society artificially constructs the idea of "race" based on geographic, historical, political, economic, social, and cultural factors, as well as physical traits that have no justification for notions of racial superiority or racial prejudice.

Racism is a broader experience and practice than racial discrimination. It is an ideology that either directly or indirectly asserts that one group is inherently superior to others. Racism can be openly displayed in racial jokes and slurs or hate crimes, but can also be more deeply rooted in attitudes, values, and stereotypical beliefs. In some cases, these are unconsciously held and have evolved over time, becoming embedded in systems and institutions, and also associated with the dominant group's power and privilege.

Racial discrimination is a legally prohibited expression of racism. It is any action based on a person's race, intentional or not, that imposes burdens on a person or group and not on others, or that withholds or limits access to benefits available to other members of society in areas covered by the *Code*. Race only needs to be one factor in a situation for racial discrimination to have occurred.

Refugee protection claimant

Refugee claimant is a person who arrives in Canada and seeks Canada's protection. If such a person receives a final determination that he or she has been determined to be a protected person, he or she may then apply for permanent residence.

Skilled worker

Immigrants selected for their skills, which will ensure their success in a fast-changing labour market and benefit the Canadian economy. The regulations stress education, English or French language abilities, and work experience involving certain skills, rather than specific occupations.

Social welfare system

It is a system whereby the state undertakes to protect the health and well-being of its citizens, especially those in financial or social need. The objectives of Canada's welfare system are to achieve a just society, to reach a more even distribution of wealth, to provide direct services (health, education, etc.) and cash transfers (pensions, unemployment benefits, etc.), and to construct a progressive tax system.

Systemic discrimination

The institutionalization of discrimination through policies and practices, which may appear neutral on the surface but have an exclusionary impact on particular groups, such that various minority groups are discriminated against, intentionally or unintentionally. This occurs in institutions and organizations where the policies, practices, and procedures (e.g., employment systems—job requirements, hiring practices, promotion procedures, etc.) exclude and/or act as barriers to racialized groups. Systemic discrimination also is the result of some government laws and regulations.

Universal Declaration of Human Rights

The Universal Declaration of Human Rights (UDHR) is a declaration adopted by the United Nations General Assembly (December 10, 1948, at Palais de Chaillot, Paris). The declaration arose directly from the experience of the Second World War and represents the first global expression of rights to which all human beings are inherently entitled. It consists of thirty articles, which have been elaborated in subsequent international treaties, regional human rights instruments, national constitutions, and laws. The International Bill of Human Rights consists of the Universal Declaration of Human Rights, the International Covenant on Economic, Social and Cultural Rights, and the International Covenant on Civil and Political Rights and its two optional protocols. In 1966 the General Assembly adopted the two detailed covenants, which complete the International Bill of Human Rights; and in 1976, after the covenants had been ratified by a sufficient number of individual nations, the bill took on the force of international law.

Visible minority

Term used to describe nondominant groups who are not white. Although it is a legal term widely used in human rights legislation and various policies, currently the term "racialized minority" or "people of colour" is preferred by people labelled by others to be "visible minorities."

Temporary foreign worker

A temporary foreign worker is a foreign national who has permission to enter and work in Canada temporarily.

Total fertility rate (TFR)

Total fertility rate (or sometimes called simply fertility rate) of a population is the average number of children that would be born to a woman over her lifetime if (1) she were to experience the exact current age-specific fertility rates (ASFRs) through her lifetime, and (2) she were to survive from birth through the end of her reproductive life. It is calculated by summing the single-year age-specific rates at a given time.

Work permit

It is the authorization that allows a non-Canadian citizen or a nonpermanent resident to work in Canada. Some temporary jobs in Canada may not require a work permit—for example, news reporters, public speakers, performing artists, and foreign government officials.

16

Annex 6: Recommended Reading

1. **"The Distinctiveness of Canadian Immigration Experience."** Jeffrey G. Reitz. *Patterns of Prejudice,* Vol. 46, No. 5, 2912

Main theme: Canada's experience about immigration is positive and mass immigration has popular support. Canadian immigration policy model (skill-based selection, multiculturalism, integration, and provincial autonomy) deserves international attention. However, Canada's success with immigration is only a partly related to its policies. Skill-based immigrant selection may be the most important feature of the Canadian model, and the effectiveness of this policy is contingent on border context, which in the case of Canada is facilitated by geographical isolation. Canada's symbolic commitment to multiculturalism emphasizes the social integration of immigrants, and this goal is also served by social services supporting settlement and language learning. The most distinctive feature of the Canadian approach to immigration may be the belief that immigration represents an opportunity to build the economy and develop the country. This belief represents a resource helping the country address problems confronting immigration. The belief in mass immigration as a positive resource and development opportunity underlies much of the positive discourse on immigration in Canada.

2. **"Race, Religion, and Social Integration of New Immigrant minorities in Canada."** Jeffrey G. Reitz, Rupa Banerjee, Mai Phan, and Jordan Thompson. *University of Toronto,* March 2009.

Main theme: The social integration of Canada's new religious minorities is determined more by their racial minority status than by religious affiliation or degree of religiosity. Muslims, Sikhs, Buddhists, and Hindus were found to be slower to integrate socially, mainly because they are mostly racial minorities. Degree of religiosity affects social integration in the same ways as ethnic community attachments in general; positively for some for some dimensions and negatively for others. Patterns are similar all over Canada.

3. **"The Role of Culture in Intergenerational Value Discrepancies Regarding Intergroup Dating."** Ayse K. Uskal, Richard N.Lalinde, and Sheila Konanur. *Journal of Cross-Cultural Psychology*, 2011, 42: 1165.

Main theme: Examines cultural and generational differences in views on intergroup dating relationships among members of younger and older generation South asian and European Canadians and the role of mainstream and heritage cultural identities in shaping these views. In response to a scenario describing an intergroup dating conflict between a young adult and his or her parents, as well as on self-report measures of attitudes towards intergroup dating, South Asian Canadians and members of the older generation exhibited less favourable views on intergroup dating compared to European Canadians and members of the younger generation. Moreover, Canadian identity was consistently associated with more favourable views on intergroup dating, and this relationship was stronger for the South Asians.

4. **"Generation Flux: Understanding the seismic shifts that are shaking Canada's youth."** Prepared for *Community Foundations of Canada* by Dominique O'Rourke, Accolade Communications, October 2012.

Main theme: Predictable trajectory that guided the lives of the current generation's parents is gone. Canada's youths are growing up in an era of complexity and uncertainty that has delayed, or even destroyed, the landmarks that once signalled a transition from one phase of life to another. (On October 3, 2012, CFC hosted its first Vital Youth Dialogue in Ottwa, reporting on national youth issues to engaging youth in a creative, forward-thinking conversation.)

5. **"Living at the Crossroads of Cultural Worlds: The Experience of Normative Conflicts by Second Generation Immigrant Youths."** Bejamin Giguere, Richard Lalonde, and Evelina Lou. *Social and Personality Psychology Compass*, 4/1 (2010).

Main theme: Although there is tremendous diversity among second-generation youths, they often share the common experience of being bicultural by holding both heritage and mainstream cultural identities.

Given that cultures generally promote similar expectations for youth, holding two cultural identities is not necessarily problematic. Even when cultural expectations do differ, these individuals can typically switch between cultural identity (e.g., South Asian at home; mainstream Canadian at school) as a strategy to avoid conflict. For some issues, however, switching between identities will not resolve the conflict because fulfilling the normative expectations associated with one identity is not at the expense of the other (e. g., choosing a romantic partner that is either from the heritage culture or from mainstream culture).

6. **"South Asian Canadian Young Men and Women's Interest Development in Science: Perception of Contextual Influences."** Priya S. Mani. *Canadian Journal of Family and Youth*, 3(1), 2011.

Main theme: Examined the contextual and cultural influences on interest development in science for South Asian young adults. Issues related to socialization with respect to self-efficacy and outcome expectations of engaging in the sciences are consistent with existing formulations on South Asian families. Family (parents and siblings) supports the development of interest in science, and implications for counselling practice are discussed.

7. **"Transnational Belonging among Second Generation Youth: Identity in a Globalized World."** Kara Somerville. *Journal of Social Sciences*, Special Volume No. 10, 2008.

Main theme: The significance of the transitional social field in the construction of second-generation youth's identities is demonstrated at three levels: (1) at the level of emotions—they feel Indian yet also Canadian; (2) at the level of appearance—they express their transitional belonging through fashion styles and clothing; and (3) at the level of allegiance—they feel a sense of loyalty to India at the same time that they feel a sense of loyalty to Canada. The implication is that the second generation negotiates identities within a social space that includes flows from their parents' country of origin and country of settlement.

8. **"Identity and Social Integration: Girls from a Minority Ethno-Cultural Group in Canada."** Ratna Ghosh. *McGill Journal of Education*, Vol. 35, No 3, Fall 2000.

Main theme: Identity is an important factor in integration into society. Integration is not only a personal and individual process but also a dialectical one. It involves contradiction and/or conflicts in individual self-construction (identity). It also implies construction and reconstruction of social relationships related to an individual's experiences defined by their location in terms of gender, race, culture, and class. This process is what has been called "a process of becoming and being." Canadian girls of South Asian origin strive hard to live up to their parents' expectations, and yet they do not possess culture in a form identical to their parents. They are creating a "hybrid identity" in a new context using part of the cultural capital from their parents and creating a "space" for themselves in Canadian society.

9. **"Welcome to Canada, Now what? Unlocking the potential of immigrants for business growth and innovation."** *White Paper Summary of Deloitte's 2911 Dialogue on Diversity.* November 2011.

Main theme: It is time to put the theory of diversity into action: more proactive steps must be taken to quickly enable skilled foreign-born workers to contribute to Canada's economy and achieve their own dreams. Various provinces offer programs through community organizations and employers across Canada. The dialogue on diversity study conducted by Deloitte serves to highlight opportunity and programs in this critically important area. One important message: "The Canadian system has to change because we are quite small globally and traditional industries are evaporating. What's that next generation of innovation going to look like—how does diversity fit into that?"

10. **"Challenges of the Visible Minority Families: Cultural Sensitivity to the Rescue."** Adenike Yesufu. *Canadian Journal of Family and Youth* 5 (1), 2013

Main Theme: Outline many barriers faced by visIble minority families in their effort to integrate into Canadian society and solution of the problem. On the premise that education is transformational, programs like global education, multicultural education, intercultural education, antiracist education, and diversity education have been instituted in Canadian schools. Unfortunately, these programs have serious problems and have been severely criticized in their implementation and by their supporters. They all have different focuses and agendas that do not strike at the core of the problem. The problems of the visible minority families were persistent, and the frustrations of the younger generation of visible minorities continue to be bewildering.

11. **"Violence in the Lives of Muslim Girls and Women in Canada."** Krista Melanie Riley. *Symposium,* September 2011. London, Ontario.

Main theme: The paper attempted to look at some of the sources of violence in the lives of Muslims girls and women in Canada taking into account violence based on race, gender, religion, class, disability, sexual orientation, immigration status, and other issues. Author tried to identify some of the main sites of violence that Muslim girls and women face including families, ethnocultural communities, the wider Canadian society, schools, the health-care system, the immigration system, and the workforce. Strategies that girls and women can take to combat and overcome violence were addressed.

12. **"The Role of Migrant Labour Supply in the Canadian Labour Market."** Stan Kustec. Research and Evaluation, *Citizenship and Immigration Canada (CIC)*; June 2012.

Main theme: How will the Canadian labour market evolve over the coming decade, and what will be the role of the immigration program in the challenging demographic, social, and economic condition Canada is facing? What is the contribution of immigration programs within the framework of the overall Canadian labour market? It is thought that Canadian immigration programs alone cannot address the major challenges faced by the Canadian labour market. However, immigration can be an effective tool for dealing with the shortages in critical occupations and regions through the admission of both permanent immigrants of various skill set and temporary workers.

13. **"Immigration and the Canadian Welfare State 2011."** Herbert Grubel and Patrick Grady. *Studies in Immigration and Refugee Policy*, May 2011.

Main theme: An estimate of the fiscal burden created by recent immigration into Canada and proposes reforms to existing immigration selection policies to eliminate the burden. Authors presented a proposal for immigration reform aimed at eliminating fiscal burden imposed on Canadians through current policies. The principle for reform as suggested is that the number and composition of immigrants should be determined largely by market forces within a framework set and managed by the government of Canada. Under the proposal, the overall immigration levels could increase, decrease, or remain unchanged, but would most likely decline significantly.

14. **"Life on the Reef in the Canadian Ocean: The New Second Generation in Canada."** Stuart Sykes. *Policy Research Institute, Government of Canada*, 2008.

Main theme: A framework to review what is known about how the second generation is currently integrating into society, with an emphasis on the children of immigrants from non-European source countries. Discussed challenges that the second generation faces in defining the process of personal adaptation and broader social integration—a process called "acculturation."

15. **"Preparing for life: Gender, Religiosity and Education Amongst Second Generation Hindus in Canada"** Cathy Holtmann and Nancy Nason-Clark. *Religion and Gender*, Vol. 2, No. 1 (2012).

Main theme: Examined the role that Hinduism and gender play in the process of identity construction in visible minority groups. Second-generation adults were raised in families where tradition Hindu religious and cultural practices were valued by immigrants as they creatively adjusted to Canadian society. Parents tried to actively involve their children in their way of life but largely unable to assist them in articulating the meaning of Hindu rituals and beliefs.

16. **"The housing preferences and location choices of second generation South Asians living in ethnic enclaves."** Virpal Kataure and Margaret Wlton-Roberts. *South Asian Diaspora*, 2012, 1-20, First Article. Routledge Taylor and Francis Group.

Main theme: Explain the housing preferences and location choices of second-generation South Asians residing in Brampton's ethnic enclaves, a suburban city on the periphery of Toronto. Research draws on the home-leaving process and integrates the theoretical perspectives of ethnic enclaves and the life cycle. The life cycle perspective has proven to be a powerful explanatory tool during the household-formation phase, but does not appear to be valuable during the independent-living stage, since ethnic enclave residency seems to persist. The importance of familial ties in the South Asian culture, the growth of ethnic enclave, traditional ideas of socioeconomic success, and life cycle values during family-formation shape preferences for second-generation South Asian Canadians.

17. **"Canada's Colour Coded Labour Market: The gap fort racialized workers."** Sheila Block and Grace-Edward Galabuzi.-, 2011. *Wellesley Institute. Canadian Centre for Policy Alternatives.*

Main theme: Compared work and income trends among racialized and nonracialized Canadians during the heyday of the economic boom. The study revealed that the pay gap between racialized and nonracialized Canadians was large even in the best economic times. The income gap stems from disparities in the distribution of good-paying and more secure jobs. Racialized Canadians had higher levels of labour market participation, yet they continued to experience higher levels of unemployment and earned less income than nonracialized Canadians.

18. "The visible minority earnings gap across generations of Canadians." Mikal Skuterud, 2010. *Canadian Journal of Economics,* Vol.43. No.3.

Main theme: This paper argues that failing to account for the Canadian ancestry of visible minorities overestimates discrimination if immigrant assimilation is an intergenerational process. Using the 2001 and 2006 Canadian censuses, weekly earnings, conditional on a rich set of worker, and job characteristics were compared with immigrant second- and third- and higher generation Canadian men. The results revealed a tendency for earnings to increase across subsequent generations of visible minority. Though the pattern was strongest between the first and second generations, for black men, it was also evident between the Canadians born with and without a Canadian-born parent. Despite this progress, for most visible minority groups, earnings gaps were identified even among third- and higher generation Canadians.

19. "An Opportunity to Lead: South Asian Philanthropy in Canada." Archana Sridhar, 2011. *The Philanthropist,* Volume 24.

Main theme: Based on the work of the South Asian Philanthropy Project, this article described the philanthropic practices of the South Asian diaspora, outlining some themes and challenges. What emerges is how little we actually know about the South Asian diaspora in Canada in terms of its philanthropy. While themes are emerging about South Asian philanthropy, no single gift or donor yet stands out, and no overarching community vision or commitment has yet emerged.

20. "Canadian Multiculturalism." Micheal Dewing, 2009. *Parliamentary Information and Research Service, Library of Parliament.*

Main theme: Multiculturalism at the policy level was structured around the management of diversity through formal initiatives in the federal, provincial, and municipal levels. Finally, it was the process by which racial and ethnic minorities compete to obtain support from central authorities for the achievement of certain goals and aspirations. This study focused on an analysis of Canadian multiculturalism both as a demographic and as public policy.

21. "Bedtime Stories: Canadian Multiculturalism and Children's Literature." Louise Saldanha. Available at http://www.ucalgary.ca/uofc/eduweb/eng1392/louise.htm.

Main theme: This paper seeks to "show and tell" how even those children's books that potentially trouble multicultural clichés of pluralism in Canada are overlaid and "read" within naturalized codes of racial hegemony. As both feminism and poststructuralist critiques emphasize, readers inhabit multiple and contradictory social positions from which they make sense of their worlds. Nonetheless, it is crucial to examine how official multiculturalism, as a national Canadian ideology, permeates reading practices wherein textual representations of race and ethnicity are managed through Eurocentric normative ideals. Thus, the commonsense understanding of Canada as a national space where "we are all same inside" and therefore as "equal and as Canadian as the white kid down the street" orchestrates normative interpretive paradigms through which the category of otherness, is established.

22. **"How are the Children of Visible Minority Immigrants Doing in the Canadian Labour Market?"** Patrick Grady, 2011. *Global Economics Working Paper 2011-1.*

Main theme: This paper examined the performance of the children of immigrants (second-generation immigrants) to Canada. As the composition of immigration inflows has shifted after 1980 from the traditional European source countries to the third world, the analysis focused on the labour market performance of second-generation visible minority immigrants of whom here were about four hundred thousand aged fifteen and over who reported employment income in the 2006 census.

23. **"Reflecting Changing face of Canada: Employment Equity in the Federal Public Service."** The Honourable Janis G. Johnson and The Honourable Mobina S. B. Jaffer; June 2010. *Standing Senate Committee on Human Rights.*

Main theme: In this report, the Standing Senate Committee on Human Rights charts the progress that has been made by the federal government in meeting the key objective of the Employment Equity Act: achieving representation rates in the federal public service for *women, aboriginal people, persons with disabilities,* and *visible minorities* (the four groups classified as designated groups under the act), which are at least equivalent to their workforce availability numbers. The committee last reported on this issue in February 2007 with the release of its report, "Employment Equity in the Federal Public Service—Not There Yet."

24. "Literature Review: Integration Outcomes." Citizenship and Immigration Canada. Dr. Livianna S. Tossutti. *Welcome Community Initiative.*

Main theme: Review research on the factors shaping the economic and social integration outcomes of permanent immigrants to Canada. The impact of source country and immigration class are of principal interest, but the effects of explanatory variables such as education, gender, age, and language ability are also addressed. The research findings are drawn from English and French language books, articles, and reports published by academic, government, and nongovernmental sources between 2001 and 2011.

25. "This is a man's problem: Strategies for working with South Asian male perpetrators of intimate partner violence." Gary Thandi with Bethan Lloyd. Centre for Prevention and Reduction of Violence, Office of Applied Research, Justice Institute of British Columbia. 2011.

Main theme: Presents the perspective of seventeen frontline practitioners who (together) have more than two hundred years of direct experience working with South Asian male perpetrators of intimate partner violence of their families. All the research participants (psychologists, program managers and counsellors, police and probation officers) are members of South Asian communities. They emphasize that men are responsible for the violence they perpetrate. No one excuses them—their choice to perpetrate violence has resulted in significant physical, emotional, and psychological harm not only to their families but also to their children, their extended family, and their communities.

17

End Notes

1. Introduction

1. Banting K. Courchene; and Seidle L. "Belonging?—Diversity, Recognition and Shared Citizenship in Canada." Institute for Research on Public Policy (IRPP), 2007.
2. Immigration from Wikipedia
3. Immigration from Wikipedia—encyclopedia (en.wikipedia.org/wiki/Immigration)
4. Massey S. Gouglas et al. 1993 :Theories of International Migration: A Review and Appraisal
5. Massey S. Gouglas et al. 1993 :Theories of International Migration: A Review and Appraisal
6. Massey S. Gouglas et al. 1993 :Theories of International Migration: A Review and Appraisal
7. Massey S. Gouglas et al. 1993 :Theories of International Migration: A Review and Appraisal
8. Includes India, Pakistan, Bangladesh, Sri Lanka, Nepal

2. Canadian Immigration and Immigrants

9. (www://heritage.nf.ca/exploration/engfrench.html)
10. (www://heritage.nf.ca/exploration/engfrench.html).
11. (Http: //www.sabresocials.com/kevin/ss11/ss11history/IMMIG.pdf.).

12. Cited from http://www.mapleafweb.com/features/immigration-policy-canada-history-adminitration
13. www.mapleleafweb.com/features/immigration-policy-canada-history-administration
14. (http://www.mapleleafweb.com/features/immigration-policy-canada-history-administration.
15. www.mapleleafweb.com/features/immigration-policy-canada-history-administration
16. (http://www.mapleleafweb.com/features/immigration-policy-canada-history-administration.
17. www.mapleleafweb.com/features/immigration-policy-canada-history-administration
18. (http://www.mapleleafweb.com/features/immigration-policy-canada-history-administration.
19. Under the *Canada-Quebec Accord on Immigration,* Quebec establishes its own immigration requirements and selects immigrants who will adapt well to living in Quebec.
20. http://www.cicnews.com/2013/01/review-immigration-2012-part-2-012217.html
21. http://maytree.com/blog/2013/02/top-10-canadian-immigration-stories-of-2012
22. http://www.cicnews.com/2012/04/summary-canadian-immigration
23. http://ccrweb.ca/en/refugee-reform.
24. http://maytree.com/blog/2013/02/top-10-canadian-immigration-stories-of-2012
25. http://www.cicnews.com/2012/04/summary-canadian-immigration
26. http://maytree.com/blog/2013/02/top-10-canadian-immigration-stories-of-2012
27. http://maytree.com/blog/2013/02/top-10-canadian-immigration-stories-of-2012
28. A member of a visible minority in Canada may be defined as someone (other than aboriginal person) who is nonwhite in colour/race, regardless of place of birth. For example, black, Chinese, Filipino, Japanese, Korean, South Asian, Southeast Asian, nonwhite East Asian, North American, or Arab, nonwhite Latin American, persons of mixed origin (with one parent in one of the visible minority group in this list), or other visible minority group.
29. Cited from a) Employment Equity in the Federal Public Service—Not There Yet. Preliminary findings of the Stading Senate Committee on Human Rights. February 2007. Available at www.senate-senat.ca/rights-droits.asp; b) Reflecting the Changing face of Canada: Employment

Equity in the Federal Public Service. Standing Senate Committee on Human Rights; June 2010. Available on the Parliamentary Internet: www.perl.gc.ca.

30 See Embracing Change in the Federal Public Service; Task Force in the Participation of Visible Minorities in the Federal Public Service, 2000. Available at http://www.visiblepresence.com

31 See Standing Senate Committee on Human Rights report: "Reflecting the Changing Face of Canada: Employment Equity in the Federal Public service", June 2010

32 (http://www.pipsc.ca/portal/page/portal/website/news/magazine/winter13/8).

33 See Canadian Multiculturalism by Micheal Dewing, 2009

34 (http://www.statcan.gc.ca/daily-quotidien/110817/dq).

35 There are legitimate concerns regarding the quality of data from 2011 NHS which replaced the 2006 Census, yet these are the only data we have since the Labour Force Survey does not ask questions regarding racial status.

36 (http://sgnews.ca/2013/06/27/minorities-face-higher-unemployment-rates/)

37 (http://m.theglobeandmail.com/incoming/visible-minorities-face-hidden-discrimination)

38 (http://senatordonaldoliver.ca/index.php?option=com_content&task=view&id).

39 (http://www.canadaupdates.com/content/visible-minorities-still-struggling-their-fair-share).

40 (http://www.darpanmagazine.com/2011/03/canadian-born-visible-minorities-earn-less/).

41 See for detail—"Summary Report for the Engagement Sessions for a Racism-Free Workplace" (Focus Groups, Workshops and Partnerships) by John Samuel Associates Inc.; March 2006.

42 Human Resources and Social development Canada, Foreign Credentials Recognition, http://www.hrsdc.gc.ca/en/workplaceskills/publications/for/brochures.html.

43 Government of Canada, *Going to Canada*: http://www.goingtocanada.gc.ca

44 See the Foreign Credentials Referral Office website at http://www.credentials.gc.ca

45 *Fair Access to Regulated Professionals Act, 2006*; S.O. 2006, c. 31

46 Government of Ontario, *Office of the Fairness Commission*, http://www.fairnesscommission.ca/

47 Government of Ontario, Ontario Immigration, *Global Experience Ontario*, http://www.ontarioimmigration.ca/english/geo.asp

4. South Asian Immigrants

48 (http://www.etfo.ca/AdvocacyandAction/SocialJusticeandEquality/)
49 (http://www.hrea.org/index.php?doc_id).
50 http://www.cic.gc.ca/english/department/media/statements).
51 (http://cupe.ca/racism/march-21-international-day-elimination).
52 (http://www.bnaibrith.ca/statement-on-the-international-day-for-the-elimination-of-racial-discrimination

54 There is no country called East India; East India term is used to distinguish Indians from the West Indians and Native Canadian Indians.
55 Myanmar (previously known as Burma) may be considered part of either South Asia or South East Asia. However, it is more often classified as the South Asian country. This map is cited from "South Asian Concern" at http://www.southasianconcern.org/south_asians/
56 Cited from http://vancouverhistory.ca/archives_komagatumaru.htm; and http://kabia freeservers.com/komagatumaru.html
57 The region British India know as South Asia includes not only India but also includes Bangladesh, Pakistan, Sri Lanka, Nepal, and Myanmar
58 Cited from http://kabia.freeserves.com/komagatumaru.html
59 Cited from *Komagata Maru* incidence—Wikipedia
60 http://www.britannica.com/EBchecked/topic/
61 http://www.britannica.com/EBchecked/topic/
62 Cited from 21st February—International Mother Language Day at www.tombraiderforums.com
63 (http://www.suhaag.com/living/reconfiguring-the-joint-family/)
64 (http://www.suhaag.com/living/reconfiguring-the-joint-family/)
65 (http://www.suhaag.com/living/reconfiguring-the-joint-family/)
66 (http://www.suhaag.com/living/reconfiguring-the-joint-family/)
67 Cited from various sources through Google search
68 (http://en.wikipedia.org/wiki/South_Asian_Heritage_Month).
69 (http://ofl.ca/index.php/southasian-2-13/).

6. Experience and Challenges face the South Asian Immigrants

70 See http://www.saglobalaffairs.com/features/423-faith-and-marriage.html
71 See http://www.saglobalaffairs.com/features/423-faith-and-marriage.html
72 http://canadianimmigrant.ca/featured/soma-choudhury-breaks-lawyer-stereotypes

73. http://www.indianentertainment.info/2012/03/23/deesha.html
74. http://www.sagennext.com/2012/06/14/sunny-uppal-puts
75. http://www.sagennext.com/category/interviews/
76. http://canadianimmigrant.ca/immigrant-stories/afgan-writer-and-community-leader
77. http://canadianimmigrant.ca/immigrant-stories/pakistani-born-journalist-natasha-fatah-
78. http://canindia.com/2012/06/deepalis-research-saves-human-lives/
79. http://www.thatllneverwork.ca/ent_gupta.php
80. http://www.thestar.com/business/small_business/people/2011/10/20/do_immigrants_make
81. http://www.sagennext.com/category/interview
82. http://www.sagennext.com/category/interview
83. http://thenext36.ca/content/reza-satchu
84. http://www.sagennext.com/2013/01/16/when-new-immigrants-succeed-all-of-canada-wins/
85. http://canadianimmigrant.ca/featured/indian-immigrant-and-obstetrician-delivers-saskatchewans-littlest-newcomers
86. http://canadianimmigrant.ca/work-and-education/succeeding-as-an-internationally-trained-physician
87. http://canadianimmigrant.ca/immigrant-stories/bangladesh-born-ashish-paul-voted-as-reginas-favourite-doctor
88. http://www.sagennext.com/category/interview
89. http://canadianimmigrant.ca/immigrant-stories/afgan-born-doctors-canadian-dream-fulfilled
90. http://www.oyetimes.com/views/columns/4360-know-roots-hopes-a-struggles-of-
91. http://www.sagennext.com/2011/07/11/9183/
92. http://www.sagennext.com/2012/12/12/19/im-only-attracted-to-positive-things/
93. http://canindia.com/2012/09/what-can-su-south-asians-and-canadians-learn-from-each-other
94. http://canadianimmigrant.ca/immigrant-stories/no-mountain-too-high-for-amputee-sudarshan-gautam
95. http://canadianimmigrant.ca/featured/former-canadian-idol-finalist-devila-mathur-becomes-successful-radio-jockey
96. http://www.safennext.com/2011/03/25/south-asian-community-issues-and-what-it-must-do/
97. (www.maytree.com/speeches/five-reasons-canada-leads-the-world-on-immigration.htme).

98 (www.theglobeandmail.com/news/national/time-to-lead/why-canada-needs-a-flood-of-immigrants
99 (www.theglobeandmail.com/news/national/time-to-lead/why-canada-needs-a-flood-of-immigrants
100 (www.theglobeandmail.com/news/national/time-to-lead/why-canada-needs-a-flood-of-immigrants
101 (www.theglobeandmail.com/news/national/time-to-lead/why-canada-needs-a-flood-of-immigrants
102 (www.theglobeandmail.com/news/national/time-to-lead/why-canada-needs-a-flood-of-immigrants)
103 (www.theglobeandmail.com/news/national/time-to-lead/why-canada-needs-a-flood-of-immigrants
104 (www.theglobeandmail.com/news/national/time-to-lead/why-canada-needs-a-flood-of-immigrants
105 (http://maytree.com/speeches/five-reasons-canada-leads-the-world-on-immigration.html).
106 (http://www.canadianimmigrationreform.blogspot.ca/2012/12/canadas-population-surpasses)
107 (http://www.canadianimmigrationreform.blogspot.ca/2012/12/canadas-population-surpasses)
108 (http://www.canadianimmigrationreform.blogspot.ca/2012/12/canadas-population-surpasses)
109 (http://www.canadianimmigrationreform.blogspot.ca/2012/12/canadas-population-surpasses).
110 (http://canadianimmigrant.ca/immigrate/new-policies-could-the-demographics/).
111 (http://canadianimmigrant.ca/immigrate/new-policies-could-the-demographics/).
112 (http://www.visaplace.com/blog-immigration-law/canadian-immigration-lawyer/).
113 (http://huffingtonpost.ca/2012/12/19/generation-y-canada-immigration).
114 (http://canadianimmigrant.ca/work-and-education/trending-jobs-for-canadian-immigrants).
115 (www.thestar.com/news/investigations/immigration/article/)
116 (www.theepochtimes.com/n2/canada/public-service-minorities-proportional-representation)
117 (http://canadianimmigrant.ca/family/raising-a-canadian-immigrant-children-develop-different).
118 (http://www.amirazzekry.com/home/2013/02/01/acculturation-how-individuals-and...).

119 (http://www.canada.com/Canada+Ethnic+communities+mark+150th+focusing+Canadian.)
120 (http://www.indolink.com/Living/America/).
121 http://www.indolink.com/Living/America/a66.php).
122 (http://www.southasianobserver.com/ediorialopd_news.php?)
123 See: The Skilled South Asian Diaspora and its Role in Source Economies" by Rupa Chanda. (http://southasiandiaspora.org/the-skilled-south-asian-diaspora-and-its-role-in-source-economies)
124 See "Others in Their own Land—Second Generation South Asian Canadian Women, Racism, and the Persistence of Colonial Discourse", by Angela Aujla. *Canadian Women Studies.* Vol 20, No. 2.
125 See "Six Major Characteristics of Second Generation Youth in Toronto, Winnipeg, and Calgary." Yvonne H, Lori W, and Mehrunnisa A. Cited in "Canadian Diversity—The Experiences of Second Generation Canadians." Vol. 6:2 Spring, 2008.
126 See "Perceived Discrimination by Children of Immigrant Parents: Responses and Resiliency." N. Arthur; A. Chaves; D. Este; J. Frideres; and N. Hrycak. Cited in "Canadian Diversity—The Experiences of Second Generation Canadians." Vol. 6:2 Spring, 2008.
127 See "Immigrant Entrepreneurs—creating wealth for Canadian communities." (http://maytree.com/blog/2012/05/immigrant-entrepreneurs-creating-wealth-for-canadian.)
128 http://canindia.com/2012/04/south-asian-singles-want-to-mingle/
129 http://canindia.com/2012/06/deepalis-research-saves-human-loves/
130 http://www.sagennext.com/2012/01/20/making-community-work-a-passion-munira-ravji/
131 http://www.sagennext.com/2011/07/11/9183
132 http://www.sagennext.com/2012/01/20/sandy-sidhu-making-an-exciting-future-in-hollywood
133 http://www.sagennext.com/2012/12/12/cultural-divide-still-exists-here/
134 http://www.sagennext.com/2012/12/19/im-only-attracted-to-positive-things/
135 http://www.sagennext.com/2013/01/09/my-art-reflects-life-of-a-south-asian-women/
136 http://www.sagennext.com/2012/06/14/sunny-uppal-puts-%E2%80%/9Ccanadian-values-
137 http://www.sagennext.com/category/interview/
138 http://www.sagennext.com/category/interview/
139 http://canindia.com/2012/09/what-can-su-south-asians-and-canadians-learn-from-each-other

140. http://www.sagennext.com/2013/04/03/hip-hop-voice-of-social-change-deejay-ra/
141. http://www.sagennext.com/2013/01/16/when-new-immigrants-succeed-all-of-canada-wins/
142. http://www.sagennext.com/2013/04/17/undeterred-by-challenges-bahi-krishnakhanthan/
143. http://www.sagennext.com/category/interview
144. http://www.sagennext.com/category/interview
145. http://www.canindia.com/2014/04/mina-khraria-looking-to-lead-by-example/
146. http://www.sagennext.com/category/interview
147. http://www.sagennext.com/category/interview
148. http://www.sagennext.com/2011/03/25/south-asian-community-issues-and-what-it-must-do/
149. http://www.canindia.com/2013/02/77750/#sthash.dfkKuTBf.dpuf

Discussion

150. (http://www.darpanmagazine.com/2010/03/south-asian-marriage-2/).
151. (http://www.worldweddingtradition.com/).
152. (http://en.wikipedia.org/wiki/Wedding_customs_by_country)
153. (http://en.wikipedia.org/wiki/Wedding_customs_by_country)
154. (http://www.abcarticledirectory.com)
155. (http://hinduism.about.com/od/matroniam1/a/bengaliwedding.htm)
156. (http://www.shaaditimes.com/wedding/indian-wedding/srilankan-wedding)
157. (http://volunteersummernepal.org/get-married-in-nepal).
158. The Sherpas in Nepal are best known for living at high altitudes and for facilitating mountaineering and trekking expeditions, who moved to Nepal from Tibet about five hundred years ago. They are the smallest ethnic group of the overall population of Nepal. They were responsible for the construction and maintenance of the beautiful monasteries found in this region of Nepal. Sherpas are warm people, whose Buddhist religion dictates the need to care for other living creatures. They typically take this requirement extremely seriously, and as such, many Westerners claim that their generosity may sometimes cause them to feel uncomfortable. If you are ever in this position, however, during your stay in Nepal, then be sure to reciprocate the favours that they have shown you.
159. (http://www.kwintessential.co.uk/articles/nepal/Weddings-and-Marriage-in-Nepal/)

160 (http://www.thisismyanmar.com/mynmars/b-wedding.htm).
161 "The Fertility and Marriage Patterns of Australia's Ethnic Groups." Price, C. A (1982). Canberra: Department of Demography, ANU:100
162 http://en.wikipedia.org/wiki/Interracial_marriage
163 http://www.openthemagazine.com/article/international/mixed-marriages-and-a-referral
164 http://www.openthemagazine.com/article/international/mixed-marriages-and-a-referral
165 http:/blogs.theprovince.com/2013/10/21/portraits-og-mixed-race-couples/
166 http:/blogs.theprovince.com/2013/10/21/portraits-og-mixed-race-couples/
167 http:/blogs.theprovince.com/2013/10/21/portraits-og-mixed-race-couples/
168 http:/blogs.theprovince.com/2013/10/21/portraits-og-mixed-race-couples/
169 http:/blogs.theprovince.com/2013/10/21/portraits-og-mixed-race-couples/
170 http:/blogs.theprovince.com/2013/10/21/portraits-og-mixed-race-couples/
171 www.en.wikipedia.org/wiki/List_of_Canadians_of_Asian_ancestry and www.en.wikipedia.org/wiki/South_Asian_Canadian
172 http://canadaianimmigration.ca/work-and-education/canada/best-diversity-employers

Index

A

aboriginal people (ABO), 33, 56, 61–63, 65–66, 74, 82, 187, 204, 215, 360, 363, 365, 380
acculturation, 108, 121, 124, 144, 163–64, 166–67, 181, 188, 211–13, 223, 225, 360, 378
age groups, 68, 96, 106–7, 202
arranged marriages, 130, 182–84, 199, 209, 244, 254, 304, 313, 318
artists, 99–100, 216
arts, 98–99, 117, 128, 137, 222, 259
Asia, 26, 29, 33, 38, 46, 57, 67, 88–89, 323, 347
Asian immigrants, 34, 44
  first-generation South, 25, 225
Asian parents in Canada, 207
Asian workers in Canada, 117
assimilation, cultural, 362
authority, parental, 101, 108
"Avish Sood: Looking at Marketing and Sports," 284

B

baby boom, 39, 67, 173, 191, 361

backgrounds, 74, 98, 100, 113, 142, 147, 149, 159, 162, 168, 170, 173, 179–80, 182–83, 186, 188, 365
  ethnic, 43, 84, 128, 178, 186
  religious, 130, 145, 174–75, 180–83, 185, 187
Bangladesh, 84–85, 96–98, 101–5, 116–17, 130, 162–63, 308–10, 382, 385
Bangladeshi, 84, 101, 104–6, 162, 208, 212, 309
behaviours, 108, 120–22, 157, 179, 189, 206, 305, 360, 363
beliefs, 119, 121, 155, 163, 167, 181, 184, 187, 211, 304–5, 360, 373, 378
  religious, 129, 147, 153, 159, 210, 304
Bengali, 84, 99, 102, 105–6, 149, 152, 309, 316
Berry, J. W., 101, 119
bilingualism, 55, 361
Bill C-31, *49*
Bill C-43, *51*
boat people, 36
Bokhari, Tahmena, 324
bridges, cultural, 151, 219, 225

British Columbia (BC), 14, 76, 86, 88–89, 92, 101, 110–11, 113–14, 216, 253, 334–35, 341, 344, 346, 348
Buddhism, 101, 129, 310–11, 314–15, 337, 354
business immigrant, 38, 361, 364

C

Calcutta, India, 90–91
Canada
  economy, 38, 70, 117, 219, 364, 376
  labour market, 39, 45, 68, 197
  population, 31, 39, 52–53, 192, 195
Canadian-born visible minorities, 69–70
Canadian Charter of Rights and Freedoms, 47, 66, 362
Canadian Experience Class (CEC), 47–48, 50, 76, 200, 361, 364
Canadian Immigration, 3, 13, 15, 31, 33–38, 40–41, 44, 46–47, 51–52, 110, 139, 192, 361, 368, 373, 377, 382
Canadian labour market, 67, 69, 71, 368, 377, 380
Canadian mainstream society, 124, 199, 224
Canadian media, 77–79, 222
Canadian multiculturalism, 65, 70, 72, 201, 225, 379, 384
Canadian Multiculturalism Act, 201, 209
Canadianness, 125, 128, 136, 158, 170, 213
Canadian norms, 123, 126, 139, 145
Canadian Pacific Railway (CPR), 34, 42, 216, 353, 362
Chinese Head Tax, 42–43, 215–16, 362

Chow, Olivia, 199
cultural backgrounds, 24, 55, 143, 155, 161, 168, 174, 181–83, 210, 315
"Cultural Divide Still Exist Here," 254
cultural heritage, 100, 123, 152, 167, 185, 201, 213
cultural identities, 101, 125, 129, 153, 162, 165, 169, 210, 212–13, 316, 374–75
cultural norms, 120, 122, 124–26, 132, 145, 155, 157–58, 162, 164, 166–67, 222
cultural values, 29, 31, 101, 107, 119, 145, 152, 176, 181–82, 207
cultures, 13, 24, 55, 64, 67, 84, 92, 99, 101, 107–8, 115, 117, 119–20, 123, 126, 128, 130, 132, 141, 143–45, 151, 153–54, 156–57, 159–73, 176–78, 181–82, 184–88, 205–9, 212–15, 217–18, 222, 224–26, 306, 316–17, 324, 341, 359, 361, 366–67, 374–76
  dominant, 80, 119, 162, 205, 210–12, 223, 366

D

designated groups, 56, 61, 187, 358, 363, 380
Dhaka, Bangladesh, 102, 104–5
Dhalla, Ruby, 92, 111–12
diaspora, 85–86, 96, 196, 216, 316, 333, 336, 338, 347, 364, 378–79, 388
Dimant, Frank, 83, 215
discrimination, 43, 62, 68, 82, 101, 125–26, 146, 150, 161, 187, 225, 363, 365
  labour market, 32, 136, 144, 149–50

racial, 32, 35, 44, 67–69, 81–83, 214, 369–70
systemic, 24–25, 69, 148, 187, 213, 371
diversity, 3, 13, 16, 25, 39, 45, 55, 59, 64–69, 71, 74, 78–80, 84, 100–102, 105, 118, 126, 128, 140, 149, 168–69, 172–74, 178, 200–201, 205, 210, 212–14, 216, 219, 221–22, 306, 316, 324, 334–35, 352–59, 363, 367, 374, 376, 379, 382, 388
cultural, 55, 65–66, 102, 105, 128, 140, 201
dominant group, 32, 164, 175, 216, 360, 363, 370
Dominion Land Act, 42
dual or segmented labour market theory, 27–28

E

economic growth, 39, 43–44, 52–53, 192, 219
economic immigrant, 48, 193–94, 199, 364
EE groups, 63–64
Ekushey February, 105–6
"Embracing Change," 61, 205, 384
emigration, 26, 364
employment, 35, 60, 68, 72, 74, 78, 82, 145–47, 151, 170, 207, 219, 365, 369, 383
employment equity (EE), 60, 62–64, 69, 149, 170, 353, 365, 380, 383–84
"Encouraging Women to Become Resilient and Resourceful," 267
entrepreneurial-class immigrants, 38, 322

ethnic groups, 23, 30, 43, 60, 121, 131–32, 145, 147, 200, 209, 214, 313, 333, 365, 390
ethnic identity, 65, 72, 120, 129, 176, 200, 205–6, 225, 368
ethnicity, 32, 39, 42, 72, 85, 128–29, 146, 178, 201, 205, 209, 215, 221, 225, 313, 315, 362, 365, 369, 380
ethnic minorities, 16, 23–24, 65, 73–74, 77, 79–80, 114, 132, 136, 143, 187, 189, 223–24, 226, 315, 319, 362, 379
ethnocultural group, 164, 167, 198, 365

F

federal public service, 60–64, 204–5, 380, 383–84
Federal Skilled Worker Program (FSWP), 49
federal skilled workers, 198, 368
Fellegi, Ivan, 63
fertility rate, 53, 67, 361, 372
Foreign credential recognition, 75, 366
foreign credentials, 68, 74–75, 124, 366, 384
Foreign Credentials Referral Office (FCRO), 75
foreign workers, 39, 50, 75, 199, 361, 366
temporary, 47–48, 50, 82, 200, 372

G

Gandhi, Mahatma, 90, 120
Gaye Holud. *See* turmeric ceremony
generation gap, 124, 200
globalization, 29, 31, 163

Grady, Patrick, 71, 377, 380
green paper, 45
Grewal, Nina, 111–12
groups
  designated, 56, 61, 187, 358, 363, 380
  dominant, 32, 164, 175, 216, 360, 363
  ethnocultural, 164, 167, 198, 365

H

head tax, 34, 42–43, 92, 215–16, 362
heritage, 84, 106, 115–17, 119, 127, 132, 150, 159, 162–67, 170, 181, 187–88, 206, 209, 222, 225, 309–11, 374, 385
heritage culture, 107, 119, 121–22, 127, 144, 157, 159, 161, 164, 166–67, 169, 173, 188, 205, 213, 223, 375
hijab, 150, 170, 179, 211, 342
"Hip-Hop: Voice of Social Change: Deejay Ra," 273
Human Resources and Skills Development Canada (HRSDC), 50, 74–75

I

identity, 13, 107, 121, 123–26, 129, 136, 144, 158, 160, 162, 164, 166–67, 169, 172, 174, 181, 188, 200–201, 210, 212–14, 218, 224, 375
  consolidated bicultural, 120
  ethnocultural, 223, 225
  national, 200, 222–23
  religious, 129, 168, 210–11
identity conflicts, 121, 127

immigrant parents, 24, 69, 122, 125, 151, 153, 156, 160, 181, 206–7, 388
immigrant population, 38–40, 58, 63, 172, 198, 219
immigrants, 3, 23–26, 28–31, 33–35, 37–42, 44–58, 64–72, 74–76, 84–86, 91–94, 96, 101–2, 106–8, 110, 113, 116, 118–20, 122, 124–25, 127, 129, 135–40, 143–45, 147–50, 153, 157, 159, 169–79, 182, 189, 191–200, 202–5, 209, 211–12, 214–17, 221, 223–26, 276, 302, 316, 322, 324, 361–62, 364, 367, 370, 373, 376–83, 385–86
  new, 45, 52–53, 56, 67, 69–70, 74–75, 118, 135, 137, 139, 148, 170, 198–99, 202, 209, 216, 224, 373
  recent, 41, 56, 65, 69, 71, 75, 169, 193
  skilled, 53, 74, 192, 194
immigrant workers, 41
Immigration Act, 36, 42, 44–46, 91, 366
Immigration and Refugee Protection Act, 46, 366
immigration levels, 191–93, 377
immigration policy, 31, 34, 38, 41–45, 55, 194, 198, 202
immigration system, 47, 49, 194, 377
inclusion, 64–66, 132, 136, 142, 144, 151, 169–71, 173–74, 189, 219–20, 223, 355–56
indentured labourers, 84, 86
India, 5, 31, 57, 84–91, 96–99, 101, 104, 111, 114, 116–17, 130, 173, 196, 199, 216, 302–3, 315–16, 318, 320, 322, 326–28, 331, 334,

336, 338–39, 341, 343–45, 348, 364, 375, 382, 385
Indian Arrival and Heritage Month, 115–16
Indian culture, 306–7
Indian dance, 100, 151
Indian music, 99, 336
Indians, 34, 71–72, 86, 100–101, 115–16, 126, 161, 177, 201, 208, 212, 317–18, 375, 385
Indian subcontinent, 37, 84, 98–99, 101, 115–16, 159
Indo Trinidad Canadian Association (ITCA), 115
integration, 24, 119–20, 132, 136, 143, 170, 189, 195, 209, 211–14, 216, 219, 223–25, 303, 315, 317, 362, 366, 373–75, 378, 381
intermarriages, 130–32, 189, 208–9, 222–23, 225, 315–18
International Day for the Elimination of Racial Discrimination, 81–83
International Mother Language Day, 102–6, 385
interracial marriage, 182, 209, 317
Islam, 80, 129, 159, 210–11, 316, 327, 329–30, 340, 342, 354

J

Jaffer, Mobina, 111–14
job market, 24, 35, 72–73, 96, 125, 144, 147, 149–50, 170, 172, 187, 197, 224–25

K

Kelly, Maureen, 224
Khan, Wajid Ali, 332

"Knowledge of Law Essential for Combating Human Rights Violations," 265
Komagata Maru, 87–93, 216, 335, 385

L

labour market, 25, 27, 39–41, 47, 52, 67, 69, 71–72, 75–76, 93, 124–25, 146, 192, 194–95, 200, 207
Locher, Uli, 226

M

"Making an Exciting Future in Hollywood," 253
"Making Community Work a Passion," 248
Malhotra, 138, 350–51
mangala, 313–15
marginalization, 119, 210, 212, 223, 225, 367
marriage, 101, 107, 126–27, 129–30, 132, 180–81, 183–87, 189, 217, 225, 304–14, 317–18, 390
  interethnic, 128, 315–16
  interfaith, 131–32, 209
marriage customs, 310
marriage rites, 313
media, 77–78, 80, 116, 126, 178, 184, 211, 324, 338, 343, 349
news, 77–78
melting pot, 171, 200–201, 315, 367
member of Parliament (MP), 59, 92, 111–12, 219, 332
migrants, 25–26, 29–30, 86–87, 367
migration, 23, 25–30, 128, 180, 368–69
"Mina Khtaria: Looking to Lead by Example," 287

minorities, 60, 65, 70, 77, 79–80, 146, 149, 152, 171, 173–74, 176–78, 204, 335, 352, 359, 362–63
minority groups, 62, 66, 152, 360
mixed marriages, 123, 128–29, 131–32, 144, 180–84, 186, 189, 208–9
"MomShift: Providing Real-Life Relatable Success Stories for Postbaby Career, The," 291
mother tongue, 57–58, 102, 105, 107, 149, 151, 159, 164, 185
multiculturalism, 16, 39, 43, 52, 54, 59, 65–66, 70, 72, 82, 92, 132, 136, 150, 165, 172, 179, 191, 199–201, 205, 209, 212–13, 216, 222, 225, 337, 367, 373, 379–80, 384
Multiculturalism Act, 205, 216, 367
multilingual society, 57
music, 98–100, 136, 206, 208, 222, 306, 308, 313–14
Muslims, 78, 87, 101, 111, 131–32, 146, 178, 182, 184–85, 189, 210–11, 306–10, 321, 329, 332, 340, 342–43, 374
"My Art Reflects Life of a South Asian Woman," 259
"My Works Critically Examine My Environment," 282

N

National Council of Visible Minorities (NCVM), 204–5
National Occupational Classification (NOC), 198, 368
neoclassical economics macrotheory, 27
neoclassical economics microtheory, 27

new economics of migration, 27–28

O

Omidvar, Ratna, 66, 194, 224
Ontario Society for Services to Indo-Caribbean Canadians (OSSICC), 115

P

Pakistan, 57, 83–85, 96–98, 101–2, 105, 113, 117, 130, 153, 323–25, 332–33, 340, 342, 351, 382, 385
parent-children communication, 123
parenting stress, 121–22
"Passionate Advocate for Renewable Energy, A," 250
permanent residency, 47, 49–51, 368
permanent residents, 47–48, 51, 200, 364, 366, 368
persons with disabilities (PWD), 42, 61–64, 187, 204, 363, 365, 369, 380
pluralism, 24, 82, 143, 327, 380
population projection, 193, 368
poruwa, 311–12
preferred classes, 44
Protection Canada's Immigration System Act, 49
public service, 60, 62–64, 117, 204, 327, 348
Public Service Commission (PSC), 64

R

race, 30, 35–36, 39, 44, 56, 70, 79, 91, 113, 141, 145–50, 153, 157, 165, 170, 172–77, 179, 186, 189, 192, 195, 200–201, 206, 213–15,

225, 335, 346, 354, 363–64, 367, 369–70, 373, 376–77, 380, 383
racism, 24, 32, 65, 70, 79, 81–83, 124–25, 136–37, 143–45, 147, 171, 175–80, 187, 189, 206, 214–16, 219, 222, 225, 335, 363, 369–70, 384, 388
Ratansi, Yasmin, 111–12, 332
rate, unemployment, 41, 67–68, 70
refugee, 30, 34, 36–38, 40, 44–46, 49–50, 52–53, 66, 80, 91, 113, 150, 193, 318, 341, 366, 370, 377
refugee claimants, 37, 46, 49, 53, 66, 370
refugees, 30, 34, 36–37, 40, 44–46, 48–50, 52–53, 66, 80, 193
religiosity, 100–101, 209, 374, 378
religious affiliations, 100–101, 374
Replacement-level fertility, 369
restrictions, 34, 36, 42, 44, 91, 93, 156, 199
Rode, Ajmer, 335–36

S

Sankar, Uday, 99
Satchu, Reza, 138, 224
second generation, 24–25, 32, 71, 100–101, 118, 143, 148, 150, 169, 213, 218–19, 222, 304, 316, 375, 377, 379
second-generation Canadians, 118, 147, 158, 164, 202–3, 214, 219, 221
second-generation children, 24, 124–25, 129, 143, 160, 174, 200, 213–14, 224
Second generation of South Asian origin, 218
second generation of South Asians, 25, 140
second-generation South Asian adults, 222, 225
second-generation South Asian adults internalize, 127
Second-Generation South Asian Canadians, 118, 126, 378
"Second-Generation South Asian Political Leaders Please," 301
second-generation South Asians, 32, 127, 180, 203, 206, 209, 219–20, 222, 302, 378
second-generation youths, 119, 124–26, 129–30, 135, 151, 155, 157, 159, 170, 187, 206, 214, 220, 223–25, 374
Shaheed Minar, 103
Shariff, Aneesa, 205
Shastri Indo-Canadian Institute, 99
Singh, Gurdit, 88, 90–91
skilled worker program (SWP), 47–48
skilled workers, 28, 47–48, 191, 194, 198, 366, 368, 370
social capital theory, 27, 29
social cohesion, 66, 145, 169–70, 174, 188–89, 315
social inclusion, 64–66, 132, 136, 142, 189, 220, 223
social welfare system, 38, 370
South Asia, 84, 97, 99, 101, 129, 173, 223, 315, 327, 385
South Asian arts, 98, 141
South Asian Association for Regional Cooperation (SAARC), 84
South Asian Canadians, 16, 25, 100, 108, 111, 114, 131, 136, 141–42, 164, 189, 218–19, 221–22, 374

"South Asian Community Issues and What It Must Do," 295
South Asian cultures, 109, 119, 121, 127, 130, 153, 160, 162, 170, 188, 206, 378
South Asian Diaspora, 86, 378
"South Asian Doctor Who Received One of the Highest Canadian Awards for Research," 246
South Asian families, 100, 123–24, 129, 174, 207, 304, 375
South Asian immigrants, 3, 84–85, 110, 135, 202, 244, 385
South Asian population, 32, 84, 94, 96, 222
South Asians, 3, 13, 25, 32, 57, 60, 68, 71, 84–87, 93–102, 106–12, 114–24, 127–32, 135–37, 139–45, 150–53, 156, 164, 167–68, 173, 180, 182, 184–86, 188–89, 199, 201–2, 205–7, 209, 211–12, 217–18, 220–26, 244–45, 253, 302–6, 316–18, 325–26, 337, 344, 369, 374–75, 379, 381, 383, 385
  young, 206–7, 211
South Asians in Canada, 14, 32, 94, 96, 107–8, 115, 225, 244
"South Asian Singles Want to Mingle," 244
stress, 108, 119, 121–22, 211, 304
"Sunny Uppal Puts Canadian Values in Action," 262

T

temporary foreign worker (TFWs), 47–48, 50, 82, 193, 200, 372
temporary residency, 48, 50
theoretical models, 27–29

traditions, 13, 31, 86, 98, 101, 106–8, 117, 132, 151, 157, 160, 167–69, 185, 187, 205, 210, 218, 306, 309, 311, 315–17, 327
turmeric ceremony, 308–9

U

"Undeterred by Challenges," 279

V

values, 16, 73, 107, 109, 119–20, 122, 125, 129, 132, 151–52, 154–57, 159, 163, 169, 173, 181–82, 185–87, 195, 202, 205–8, 211–12, 305, 311, 360, 365, 370
  core, 156, 158, 162, 168, 183, 186
  religious, 168, 181–82
visa, 25, 46, 51
visible minorities, representation of, 61–63, 69
visible minority, 24, 31–32, 55–61, 65, 67–73, 77–79, 84, 94–95, 114, 118–19, 124, 131, 144–51, 157, 163, 167–68, 171–73, 175, 179, 187, 200, 203–5, 212–14, 221, 225, 354, 372, 376, 378–80, 383
  groups, 56–58, 61, 65, 67, 70–71, 77, 150, 205, 214, 378–79, 383
  immigrants, 57, 65, 69, 71, 124, 144, 149, 200, 212, 380
  population, 31, 56, 58, 94, 124
  youths, 68, 72–73, 119, 145, 150, 157, 163, 167–68, 179

W

wages, 27–28, 50
weddings, 306–10, 312–14

"What Can Us South Asians and Canadians Learn from Each Other?," 271
"When New Immigrants Succeed, All of Canada Wins," 276
white Canadians, 68, 70, 78, 80, 88, 93, 125, 128, 132, 136, 145, 147, 155, 159, 165, 172, 180, 193, 195, 201–2, 207, 222–23, 225, 317
white culture, 181, 206, 211, 213, 222
white paper, 44, 376
workers, 26–28, 47, 53, 82, 101, 191, 197, 204, 316, 364, 366, 379
   racialized, 82, 378
   temporary, 76, 192–94, 200, 377
work experience, 49, 68, 72, 194, 362, 366, 370
   in-Canada, 50
workforce, 39, 48, 52, 70, 145, 148, 171, 173, 191–92, 377
workforce availability numbers, 61–62, 380
Working in Canada Tool, 75, 203
work permit, 29, 361, 372
workplace, 52, 60, 68–69, 74, 117, 145–48, 157, 175–79, 217, 354, 356, 359, 365
world system theory, 27

Y

young adults, 101, 127, 129–30, 135, 142, 144, 156, 189, 206, 220, 225, 375
younger generations, 101, 124, 132, 178, 211, 317, 374, 376
youths, 25, 72–74, 95, 120, 141, 143–45, 149, 157–58, 162, 165, 175, 182, 205–6, 210, 217–18, 220, 223, 225, 302, 344, 374–76
   minority, 73, 223
   second-generation immigrant, 180, 210
   second-generation Muslim, 210
   second-generation South Asian, 119–21, 132, 142–43, 189, 203, 210, 225
   white Canadian, 68, 128, 145

Edwards Brothers Malloy
Thorofare, NJ USA
November 3, 2014